Business Statistics for Competitive Advantage w

Cynthia Fraser

Business Statistics for Competitive Advantage with Excel 2019 and JMP

Basics, Model Building, Simulation and Cases

 Springer

Cynthia Fraser
McIntire School of Commerce
University of Virginia
Charlottesville, VA, USA

ISBN 978-3-030-20373-3   ISBN 978-3-030-20374-0   (eBook)
https://doi.org/10.1007/978-3-030-20374-0

This Springer imprint is published by the registered company Springer Nature Switzerland AG
The registered company address is: Gewerbestrasse 11, 6330 Cham, Switzerland

Table of Contents

Preface

Exceptional managers know that they can create competitive advantages by basing decisions on performance response under alternative scenarios. To create these advantages, managers need to understand how to use statistics to provide information on performance response under alternative scenarios. Statistics are created to make better decisions. Statistics are essential and relevant. Statistics must be easily and quickly produced using widely available software, Excel or JMP. Then results must be translated into general business language and illustrated with compelling graphics to make them understandable and usable by decision makers. This book helps students master this process of using statistics to create competitive advantages as decision makers.

Statistics are essential, relevant, easy to produce, easy to understand, valuable, and a powerful source of competitive advantage.

The Examples, Assignments, and Cases Used to Illustrate Statistics for Decision Making Come from Business Problems

McIntire Corporate Sponsors and Partners, such as Hilton, Margaritaville, Alcoa, Rolls-Royce, Procter & Gamble, Dell, and Vastly, and the industries that they do business in, provide many realistic examples. Supporting data files feature data from Annual Reports, the World Bank, and online government sources, such as bea.gov. The book also features a number of examples of global business problems, including those from important emerging markets in China, India, and Chile. Students are excited when statistics are used to study real and important business problems. This makes it easy to see how they will use statistics to create competitive advantages in their internships and careers.

Learning Is Hands on with Excel and Shortcuts

Each type of analysis is introduced with one or more examples. Following is an example of how to create the statistics in Excel or JMP, and what the numbers mean in English. In cases in which Excel does not offer the desired analyses, user friendly JMP is used.

Included in Excel and JMP sections are screenshots which allow students to easily create the desired statistics. Featured are a number of popular Excel shortcuts, which are, themselves, a competitive advantage.

Powerful PivotTables and PivotCharts are introduced early and used throughout the book. Results are illustrated with graphics from Excel.

In each chapter, assignments or cases are included to allow students to practice using statistics for decision making and competitive advantage.

Focus Is on What Statistics Mean to Decision Makers and How to Communicate Results

From the beginning, results are translated into English. In Chapter 7, results are condensed and summarized in PowerPoints and memos, the standards of communication in businesses. Later chapters include example memos for students to use as templates, making communication of statistics for decision making an easy skill to master.

Instructors, give your students the powerful skills that they will use to create competitive advantages as decision makers. Students, be prepared to discover that statistics are a powerful competitive advantage. Your mastery of the essential skills of creating and communicating statistics for improved decision making will enhance your career and make numbers fun.

New in the Fifth Edition

A number of new cases have been added, some focusing on multinationals. Some cases from earlier editions have been updated, as well.

Because Excel does not offer every type of analysis, JMP is introduced to handle analysis where Excel cannot be. JMP is user friendly, popular, and widely available in businesses. Nonetheless, Excel is invaluable for building great models and understanding where the statistics come from.

Acknowledgements

First, Second, Third and Fourth editions of *Business Statistics for Competitive Advantage* were used in the Integrated Core Curriculum at The McIntire School, University of Virginia, and I thank the many bright, motivated and enthusiastic students who provided comments and suggestions.

Cynthia Fraser
Charlottesville, VA

Chapter 1
Statistics for Decision Making and Competitive Advantage

In the increasingly competitive global arena of business in the Twenty First century, the select few business graduates distinguish themselves by enhanced decision making backed by statistics. Statistics are useful when they are applied to improve decision making. No longer is the production of statistics confined to quantitative analysis and market research divisions in firms. Managers in each of the functional areas of business use statistics daily to improve decision making. Excel and other statistical software live in our laptops, providing immediate access to statistical tools which can be used to improve decision making.

1.1 Statistical Competences Translate into Competitive Advantages

The majority of business graduates can create descriptive statistics and use Excel. Fewer have mastered the ability to frame a decision problem so that information needs can be identified and satisfied with statistical analysis. Fewer can build powerful and valid models to identify performance drivers, compare decision alternative scenarios, and forecast future performance. Fewer can translate statistical results into general business English that is easily understood by everyone in a decision making team. Fewer have the ability to illustrate memos with compelling and informative graphics. Each of these competences provides competitive advantage to those few who have mastery. This text will help you to attain these competences and the competitive advantages which they promise.

Most examples in the text are taken from real businesses and concern real decision problems. A number of examples focus on decision making in global markets. By reading about how executives and managers successfully use statistics to increase information and improve decision making in a variety of mini case applications, you will be able to frame a variety of decision problems in your firm, whether small or multi-national. The end-of-chapter assignments will give you practice framing diverse problems, practicing statistical analyses, and translating results into easily understood reports or presentations.

Many examples in the text feature bottom line conclusions. From the statistical results, you read what managers would conclude with those results. These conclusions and implications are written in general business English, rather than statistical jargon, so that anyone on a decision team will understand. Assignments ask you to feature bottom line conclusions and general business English.

Translation of statistical results into general business English is necessary to insure their effective use. If decision makers, our audience for statistical results, don't understand the conclusions and implications from statistical analysis, the information created by analysis will not be used. A chapter is devoted to writing memos that your audience will read and understand, and to effective PowerPoint slide designs for effective presentation of results. Memos and PowerPoints are predominant forms of communication in businesses. Decision making is compressed and information must be distilled, well written and illustrated. Decision makers read memos. Use memos to make the most of your analyses, conclusions and recommendations.

© Springer Nature Switzerland AG 2019

C. Fraser, *Business Statistics for Competitive Advantage with Excel 2019 and JMP*, https://doi.org/10.1007/978-3-030-20374-0_1

In the majority of examples, analysis includes graphics. Seeing data provides an information dimension beyond numbers in tables. To understand well a market or population, you need to see it, and its shape and dispersion. To become a master modeler, you need to be able to see how change in one variable is driving a change in another. Graphics are essential to solid model building and analysis. Graphics are also essential to effective translation of results. Effective memos and PowerPoint slides feature key graphics which help your audience digest and remember results. PivotTables and PivotCharts are featured in Chapters Two and Thirteen. These are routinely used in business to efficiently organize and effectively display data. When you are at home in the language of PivotTables and PivotCharts, you will have a competitive advantage. Practice using PivotTables and PivotCharts to organize financial analyses and market data. Form the habit of looking at data and results whenever you are considering decision alternatives.

1.2 The Path Toward Statistical Competence and Competitive Advantage

This text assumes basic statistical knowledge, and reviews basics quickly. Basics form the foundation for essential model building. Chapters Two and Three present a concentrated introduction to data and their descriptive statistics, samples and inference. Learn how to efficiently describe data and how to infer population characteristics from samples.

Inference from Monte Carlo simulation based on a decision maker's assumptions is introduced in Chapter Four. Model building with simple regression begins in Chapter Five and occupies the focus of much of the remaining chapters. To be competitive, business graduates must have competence in model building and forecasting. A model building mentality, focused on performance drivers and their synergies is a competitive advantage. Practice thinking of decision variables as drivers of performance. Practice thinking that performance is driven by decision variables. Performance will improve if this linkage becomes second-nature.

The approach to model building is steeped in logic and begins with logic and experience. Models must make sense in order to be useful. When you understand how decision variables drive performance under alternate scenarios, you can make better decisions, enhancing performance. Model building is an art that begins with logic.

Model building chapters include nonlinear and logit regression. Nearly all aspects of business performance behave in nonlinear ways. We see diminishing or increasing changes in performance in response to changes in drivers. It is useful to begin model building with the simplifying assumption of constant response, but it is essential to be able to grow beyond simple linear models to realistic models which reflect nonconstant response. Visualize the changing pattern of response when you consider decision alternatives and the ways they drive performance.

1.3 Use Excel for Competitive Advantage

This text features widely available Excel software, including many commonly used shortcuts. Excel is powerful and user friendly. For cases in which Excel does not offer the desired analyses, JMP is featured to supplement. Appendices with screenshots follow each chapter to make software interactions simple. Recreate the chapter examples by following the steps in the Excel sections. This will give you confidence using the software. Then forge ahead and generalize your analyses by working through end of chapter assignments. The more often you use the statistical tools and software, the easier analysis becomes.

1.4 Statistical Competence Is Powerful and Yours

Statistics and their potential to alter decisions and improve performance are important to you. With more and better information from statistical analysis, you will be equipped to make superior decisions and outperform the competition. You will find that the competitive advantages from statistical competence are powerful and yours.

Chapter 2
Describing Your Data

This chapter introduces *descriptive* statistics, center, spread, and distribution shape, which are almost always included with any statistical analysis to characterize a dataset. The particular descriptive statistics used depend on the *scale* that has been used to assign numbers to represent the characteristics of entities being studied. When the distribution of continuous data is bell shaped, we have convenient properties that make description easier. Chapter Two looks at dataset types and their description.

Chapter Two also introduces PivotTables, which provide efficient means to compare segments in terms of averages and counts. PivotCharts enable easy graphic displays of the comparisons.

2.1 Describe Data with Summary Statistics and Histograms

We use numbers to measure aspects of businesses, customers and competitors. These measured aspects are *data*. Data become meaningful when we use statistics to describe patterns within particular *samples* or collections of businesses, customers, competitors, or other entities.

Example 2.1 Nationals' Salaries: Is it a Winning Offer? Suppose that the Nationals want to sign a promising rookie. They expect to offer $1M, and they want to be sure they are neither paying too much nor too little. What would the General Manager need to know to decide whether or not this is the right offer?

He might first look at how much the other Nationals players earn. Their 2017 salaries are in Table 2.1:

Table 2.1 2017 Nats' salaries (in $M)

Name	Salary ($M)	Name	Salary ($M)	Name	Salary ($M)	Name	Salary ($M)
Scherzer	22.1	Wieters	10.5	Drew	3.5	Romero	0.6
Werth	21.6	Rendon	5.8	Lind	2.0	Solis	0.5
Strasburg	16.4	Kelley	5.5	Lobaton	1.6	Glover	0.5
Zimmerman	14.0	Roark	4.3	Helsey	1.4	Difo	0.5
Harper	13.6	Eaton	4.0	Treinen	0.6	Marolejos	0.5
Gonzalez	12.0	Perez	4.0	Taylor	0.6		
Murphy	12.0	Blanton	4.0	Turner	0.6		

The GM can see that the lowest Nats salary, the *minimum*, is $500,000, and the highest salary, the *maximum*, is $22.1M. The difference between the maximum and the minimum is the *range* in salaries, which is $21.6M, in this example. The *median*, or middle, salary is $4.0M. The lower paid half of the team earns between $500,000 and $4.0M, and the higher paid half of the team earns between $4.0M and $22.1M. Thus, the rookie would be in the bottom half.

© Springer Nature Switzerland AG 2019
C. Fraser, *Business Statistics for Competitive Advantage with Excel 2019 and JMP*,
https://doi.org/10.1007/978-3-030-20374-0_2

Often, a *histogram* and a *cumulative distribution plot* are used to visually assess data, as shown in Figures 2.1 and 2.2. A histogram illustrates central tendency, dispersion, and symmetry, three descriptive statistics that reveal the center, spread and shape of the salary distribution.

Below, the width of the histogram bins are set to one standard deviation of $6M. Choosing the mean of $6M as the top value for a bin reveals that about 70% of the players' salaries are within one standard deviation below the mean. And about 10% of the players' salaries are within one standard deviation above the mean. About 20% earn substantially more than the rest.

The histogram further reveals that the data are positively skewed and not symmetric. This is not the familiar bell shaped distribution that we see with Normally distributed data. Skewness, a measure of symmetry, is 1.1, outside approximately normal skewness of -1 to +1. The lack of symmetry is further demonstrated by the difference between the mean of $6.3M and the median of $4.0M. With a symmetric distribution, the mean and median would be identical.

Mean	$	6.3 M
Median	$	4.0 M
Standard Deviation	$	6.8 M
Skewness		1.1
Range	$	21.6 M

Figure 2.1 Histogram of Nats' salaries

The cumulative distribution makes it easy to see the median, or 50th percentile, which is one measure of central tendency. It is also easy to find the *interquartile range*, the range of values that the middle 50% of the datapoints occupy, providing an alternative measure of the data dispersion.

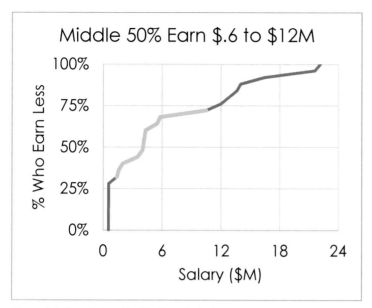

Salary ($M)	
25%	*.6*
median	*4.0*
75%	*12.0*

Figure 2.2 Cumulative distribution of salaries

The cumulative distribution reveals that the *Interquartile Range,* between the 25th percentile and the 75th percentile, is more than $11M. A quarter earns less than $.6M, the 25th percentile. More than 25% earn less than the proposed offer of $1M. The million dollar offer may be too high, since that would exceed the salaries of more than a quarter of the team.

About half earn between $.6 and $12M, and a quarter earns more than $12M, the 75th percentile. Half of the players have salaries below the *median* of $4M and half have salaries above $4M.

2.2 Round Descriptive Statistics

In the example above, statistics in the output from statistical packages are presented with many decimal points of accuracy. The Nationals General Manager in Example 2.1 and will most likely be negotiating in hundred thousands. It would be distracting and unnecessary to report descriptive statistics with significant digits more than two or three. In the **Nationals** example, the average salary would be reported as $6.3M (*not* $6,259,314). It is deceptive to present results with many significant digits, creating an illusion of precision. In addition to being honest, statistics in two or three significant digits are much easier for decision makers to process and remember. If more significant digits don't affect a decision, round to fewer and make your statistics easier to process and remember.

2.3 Share the Story That Your Graphics Illustrate

Use your graphics to support the conclusion you have reached from your analysis. Choose a "bottom line" title that shares with your audience what it is that they should be able to see. Often this title should relate specifically to your reasons for analyzing data. In the executive compensation example, The General Manager was considering a $1M offer. The chart title captures his interest by highlighting this critical value. The "bottom line," that a $1M offer is relatively high, when compared with similar firms, makes the illustrations relevant.

Many have the unfortunate and unimaginative habit of choosing chart titles which name the type of chart. "Histogram of executive salaries" tells the audience little, beyond the obvious realization that they must form their own, independent conclusions from the analysis. Choose a "bottom line" title so that decision makers can take away your conclusion from the analysis. Develop the good habit of titling your graphics to enhance their relevance and interest.

2.4 Data Is Measured with Quantitative or Categorical Scales

If the numbers in a dataset represent amount, or magnitude of an aspect, **and** if differences between adjacent numbers are equivalent, the data are *quantitative* or *continuous.* Data measured in dollars (i.e., revenues, costs, prices and profits) or percents (i.e., market share, rate of return, and exam scores) are continuous. Quantitative numbers can be added, subtracted, divided or multiplied to produce meaningful results.

With quantitative data, report central tendency with the *mean, M:*

$$\mu = \frac{\sum x_i}{N} \quad \text{for describing a } population \text{ and}$$

$$\overline{X} = \frac{\sum x_i}{N} \quad \text{for describing a } sample \text{ from a population,}$$

where x_i are data point values, and N is the number of data points being describing.

The *median* can also be used to assess central tendency, and the *range, variance,* and *standard deviation* can be used to assess dispersion.

The *variance* is the average squared difference between each of the data points and the mean:

$$\sigma^2 = \frac{\sum (x_i - \mu)^2}{N} \quad \text{for a population and}$$

$$s^2 = \frac{\sum (x_i - \overline{X})^2}{(N-1)} \quad \text{for a sample from a population.}$$

The *standard deviation SD,* σ for a population and s for a sample, is the square root of the variance, which gives us a measure of dispersion in the more easily interpreted, original units, rather than squared units.

To assess distribution symmetry, assess its skewness:

$$\text{Skewness} = \frac{n}{(n-1)(n-2)} \sum \left(\frac{x_i - \bar{x}}{s} \right)^3$$

Skewness of zero indicates a symmetric distribution, and skewness between -1 and +1 is evidence of an approximately symmetric distribution.

If numbers in a dataset are arbitrary and used to distinguish categories, the data are *nominal,* or *categorical.* Football jersey numbers and student IDs are nominal. A larger number doesn't mean that a player is better or that a student is older or smarter. Categorical numbers can be tabulated to identify the most popular number, occurring most frequently, the *mode,* to report central tendency. Categorical numbers cannot be added, subtracted, divided or multiplied.

Quantitative measures convey more information, including direction and magnitude, while categorical measures convey less, sometimes direction, and sometimes, merely category membership. *Ordinal* scales are categorical scales used to rank order data, or to convey direction, but not magnitude. With ordinal data, an element (which could be a business, a person, a country) with the most or best is coded as '1', second place as '2', etc. With ordinal numbers, or rankings, data can sorted, but not added, subtracted, divided or multiplied. As with other categorical data, the mode represents the central tendency of ordinal data.

When focus is on membership in a particular category, the *proportion* of sample elements in the category is a continuous measure of central tendency. Proportions are quantitative and can be added, subtracted, divided or multiplied, though they are bounded by zero, below, and by one, above.

2.5 Central Tendency, Dispersion and Skewness Describe Data

The baseball salaries example focused on two measures of *central tendency*: the *mean*, or average, and the *median*, or middle. The example also refers to two measures of *dispersion* or variability: the *range* separating the minimum and maximum and the standard deviation. *Skewness* reflects distribution symmetry. Player salaries are positively skewed and not Normal; SATs are approximately symmetric and Normal; To describe data, statistics to assess central tendency, dispersion, and skewness are needed. The statistics we choose depends on the *scale* which has been used to code the data being analyzed.

2.6 Describe Categorical Variables Graphically

Numbers representing category membership in nominal, or categorical, data are described by tabulating their frequencies. The most popular category is the *mode.* Visually, we show our tabulations with a *Pareto* chart, which orders categories by their popularity.

Example 2.3 Who Is Honest & Ethical? Figure 2.3 shows a column chart of results of a survey of 1,014 adults by Gallup:

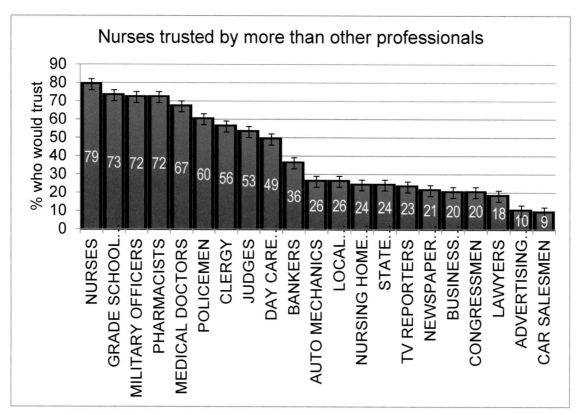

Figure 2.3 Pareto charts of the percents who judge professions honest

More Americans trust and respect nurses (79%, the *modal* response) than people in other professions, including doctors, clergy and teachers. Though a small minority judge business executives (20%) and advertising professionals (10%) as honest and ethical, most do not judge people in those fields to be honest (which highlights the importance of ethical business behaviors in the future).

2.7 PivotTables Inform by Revealing Segment Distribution Differences

Returning to the Nationals salary example, the General Manager doesn't want to lose the promising rookie with an offer that is too low. He seeks more information on salaries earned by rookies in 2017. A PivotTable easily splits the players into those who began playing with the Nationals in 2017, versus those who became Nationals players in earlier years. Splitting into these two segments, we see the salary breakdown in the PivotChart, below:

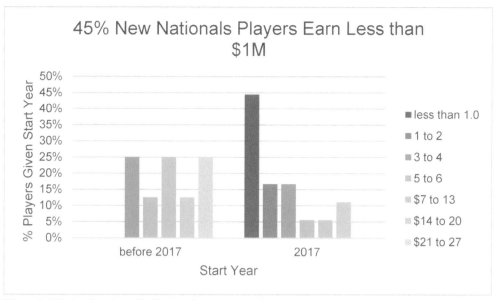

Figure 2.4 Nationals salary distribution for experienced versus new players

While more than 45% of first year Nationals players earn less than $1M, others earn as much as $20M. The proposed $1M offer is not unreasonable.

2.8 Descriptive Statistics Depend on the Data and Rely on Your Packaging

Descriptive statistics, graphics, central tendency and dispersion, depend upon the type of scale used to measure data characteristics (i.e., quantitative or categorical).

Table 2.2 summarizes the descriptive statistics (graph, central tendency, dispersion, shape) used for both types of data:

Table 2.2 Descriptive statistics (central tendency, disperson, graphics) for two types of data

	Quantitative	**Categorical**
Central Tendency	*mean*	*mode*
	median	*proportion*
Dispersion	*range*	
	standard deviation	
Symmetry	*skewness*	
Graphics	*histogram*	*Pareto chart*
	cumulative distribution	*pie chart*
		column chart

If continuous data are Normally distributed, a dataset can be completely described with just the mean and standard deviation. We know from the *Empirical Rule* that 2/3 of the data will lie within one standard deviation of the mean and that 95% of the data will lie within two standard deviations of the mean.

Effective results are those which are remembered and used to improve decision making. Your presentation of results will influence whether or not decision makers remember and use your results. Round statistics to two or three significant digits to make them honest, digestible, and memorable. Title your graphics with the "bottom line," to guide and facilitate decision makers' conclusions.

Control + Shift + Down
        (touch AI)

Excel 2.1 Produce Descriptive Statistics

Best Paid CEOs.   We will describe executive compensation packages by producing descriptive statistics, a histogram and cumulative distribution.

First, freeze the top row of **Excel 2.1 Executive Compensation of Best Paid CEOs** so that column labels are visible when you are at the bottom of the dataset.	From the first cell, **A1** **Alt WFR** (The shortcuts, activated with **Alt** select the vie**W** menu, the **F**reeze panes menu, and then freeze **R**ows.)

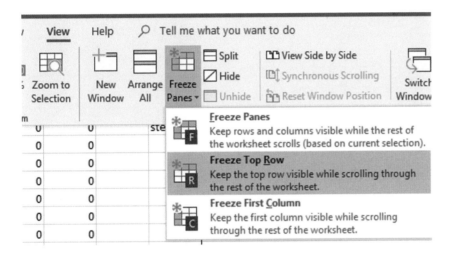

Descriptive statistics.

Turn on the Excel statistics add-in, Analysis ToolPak.	**Alt TI**

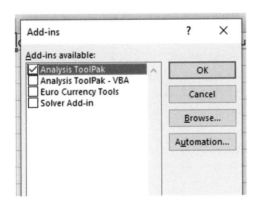

Request Descriptive Statistics of *Compensation.* The number ***n*** varies. Enter what you see in the menu.	42 **Alt AY*n* D** **B1:B201 tab LS** **OK**

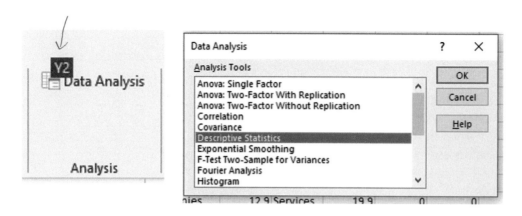

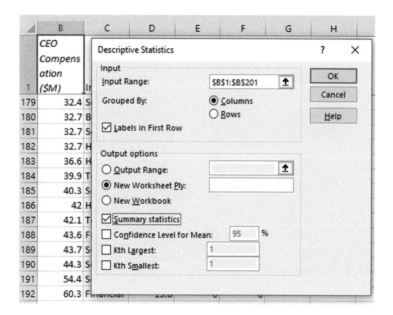

Excel 2.2 Produce a Histogram of the Distribution

Set up Histogram Bins. To make a histogram of *compensation*, Excel needs to know what ranges of values to combine. To take advantage of the *Empirical Rule,* create *bins*, or categories, using differences from the approximate sample mean that are in widths of approximate standard deviations.   In this case, the mean is about 25 and the standard deviation is about 20.

Move back to the data page. | **Cntl+Page Down**

In column G, enter bin values:

Excel uses bin values to set the upper limit for each category. Start with a bin with upper limit equal to 5 (=M-SD), which will include compensation values that are at less than or equal to 5.

This will be the first bin, since subtracting one standard deviation from the mean produces a negative number, and none of the executives earns negative salary dollars.

In each of the cells below this first bin, add one SD of 20 to the cell above, creating bins with upper limits of M + 1SD, M + 2SD and M + 3SD, and so on.

	F	G
1		compensation bins
2	M-SD	5
3	M	25
4	M+SD	45
5	M+2SD	65
6	M+3SD	85
7	M+4SD	105
8	M+5SD	125
9	M+6SD	145
10	M+7SD	165

Request a tabulation. *frequency tabulation*

Alt AY*n* H
B1:B201 tab G1:G10 tab LM

	B	C	D	E	F	G	H
1	CEO Compensation ($M)	Industry	2014 Reve	Female		compensation bins	
10	12.8	Industrial	16.7	0	M+7SD	165	
11	12.9	Healthcar	1.2	0			
12	12.9	Financial	7.5	0			
13	12.9	Consumer	13.2	0			
14	12.9	Services	19.9	0			
15	12.9	Services	100.9	0			
16	13	Financial	0.6	0		7	
17	13	Consumer	17.3	0			
18	13	Consumer	35.2	0		8	
19	13	Healthcar	40.3	0		9	
20	13.1	Basic Mate	12.3	1			

Histogram dialog box:

Input
Input Range: $B$1:$B$201
Bin Range: $G$1:$G$10
☑ Labels

Output options
○ Output Range:
◉ New Worksheet Ply:
○ New Workbook
☐ Pareto (sorted histogram)
☐ Cumulative Percentage
☐ Chart Output

OK Cancel Help

	A	B
1	pensation	Frequency
2	5	0
3	25	159
4	45	30
5	65	3
6	85	4
7	105	1
8	125	1
9	145	1
10	165	1
11	More	0

To produce a histogram showing percents of the sample in each compensation bin, add a column C with *Percents* by dividing column B cells by the sample size, 200.

Convert the proportions to percents	**Cntl+Shift+Down**
From C2	**Alt HP**

	A	B	C	D	E
1	pensation	Frequency	percent of Best Paid CEOs		
2	5	0	0%		
3	25	159	80%		
4	45	30	15%		
5	65	3	2%		
6	85	4	2%		
7	105	1	1%		
8	125	1	1%		
9	145	1	1%		
10	165	1	1%		
11	More	0	0%		

To increase readability of the histogram, change category labels in column A to indicate ranges:

	A	B	C
1	pensation	Frequency	percent of Best Paid CEOs
2	≤5	0	0%
3	6-25	159	80%
4	26-45	30	15%
5	46-65	3	2%
6	66-85	4	2%
7	86-105	1	1%
8	106-125	1	1%
9	126-145	1	1%
10	146-165	1	1%
11	166+	0	0%

manually or type it in?

Produce the histogram by selecting data in columns A and C
From A1 | **Cntl+shift+down**

Hold cntl down and select column C with your mouse.

Request a column chart. | **Alt NC1**

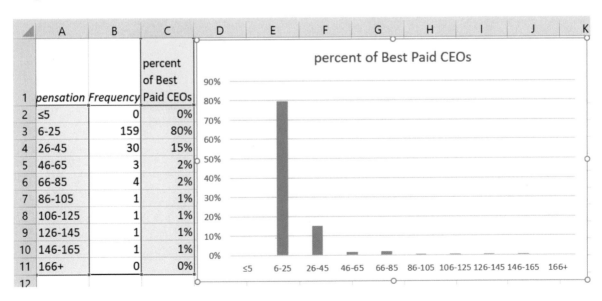

Add a horizontal axis title.	**Alt JCAAH**
Add a vertical axis title.	**Alt JCAAV**

To make better use of the chart space, reformat the vertical axis, setting the maximum to 80%.	**Alt JAE down to Vertical (Value) Axis** **Alt JAM**

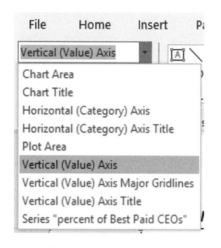 

Replace the chart title with a standalone title:

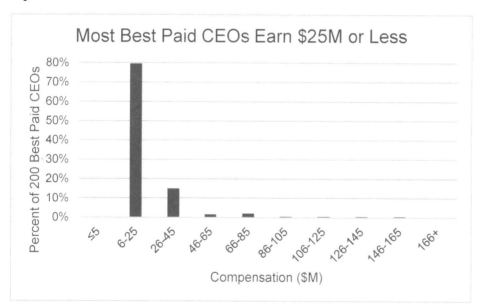

Excel 2.3 Plot a Cumulative Distribution

Return to the data page and request the cumulative distribution of total compensation.

Cntl+Page Dn
Alt AY*n*, R down
B1:B201 tab L

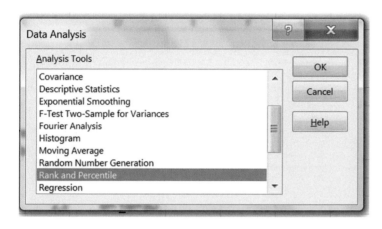

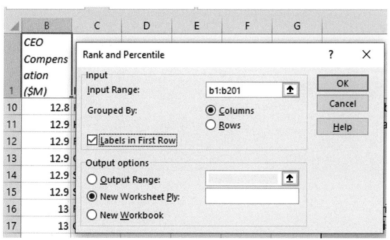

Select the cumulative percent data in column | **Cntl+shift+down**
D and reduce decimals. | **Alt H9**
From D2

Select columns B and D and insert a scatterplot showing the cumulative distribution.
From B1 | **Cntl+shift+down**
                                          | **Hold Cntl down and select column D with**
                                          | **your mouse**
                                          | **Alt ND**

Choose the third scatter option.

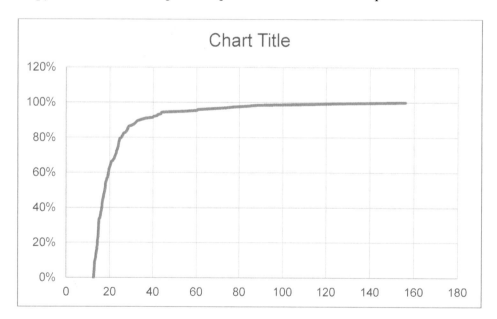

To highlight the *interquartile range* (25% to 75%), select those cells in B, hold **Cntl** down, and select those cells in D, then insert a second scatterplot.
Copy the second scatterplot and paste into the first scatterplot.

Set the maximum vertical axis to 100%, and set the maximum horizontal axis to 160.
Add vertical and horizontal axis labels.
Replace the title with a standalone title describing the middle half.

Excel 2.4 Use a PivotTable to Sort by Industry

Use a PivotTable to sort the 200 best paid CEOs by industry.

Select data and labels in columns B through E. Insert a PivotTable to compare compensation by gender.
From C1,

table range?

Cntl+shift+down
Shift+right
Alt NV Enter

Drag Gender to the Rows.
Drag Compensation to the ∑Values

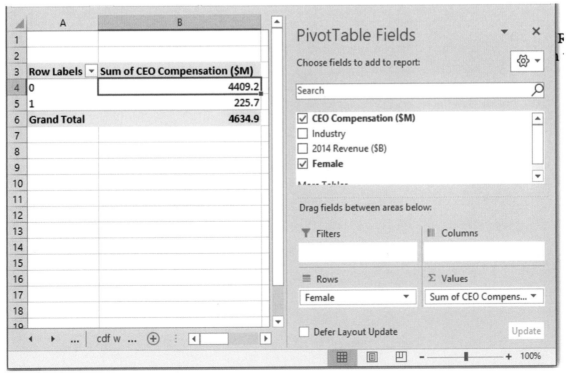

Excel shows the sums of continuous variables in PivotTables.

Convert the sums to averages. | **Alt JTG tab tab** down to Average

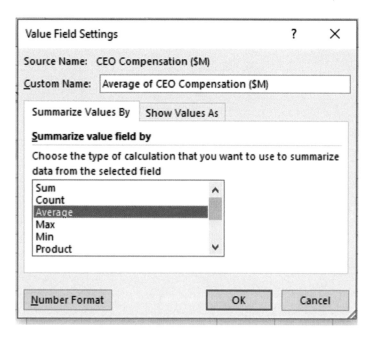

Reduce decimals and replace row label 0 with men, row label 1 with women.

Show compensation by gender in a | **Alt JTC**
PivotChart.

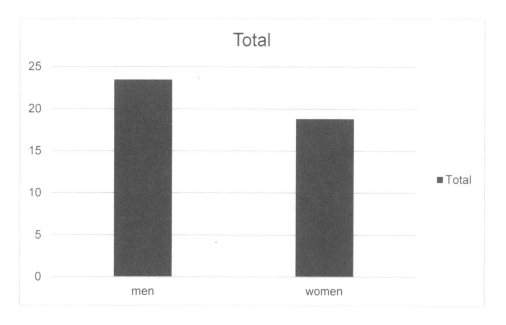

Add a vertical axis label, delete the legend, and replace the title with a standalone title.

Excel Shortcuts Used in Chapter 2

Home menu shortcuts

Insert c**E**lls that were copied or cut	**Alt HIE**
set **F**ont**S**ize	**Alt HFS**
reduce decimals	**Alt H9**
Delete a **C**olumn	**Alt HDC**

Insert menu shortcuts

i**N**sert a **C**olumn chart	**Alt NC1**
i**N**sert a scatterplot	**Alt ND**
i**N**sert a Pi**V**otTable	**Alt NV**

Data menu shortcuts

analyze d**A**ta	**Alt AY***n*
Sort selected d**A**ta	**Alt ASS**

View menu shortcuts

Freeze top **R**ow	**Alt WFR**

Cntl+ to move, select an array, extend formula down an array, or cut selected array

move to the page right	**Cntl+Page Down**
move to bottom of data array	**Cntl+down**
select data below	**cntl+shift+down**
select a column	**cntl+spacebar**
fill down	**cntl+D**
cut selected cells	**cntl+X**

Shift+ to select adjacent cells

select adjacent cells	**shift+down**
	shift+right

Chart or scatterplot design
add a horizontal axis title | **Alt JCAAH**

Chart or scatterplot element selection, formatting
select an axis | **Alt JAE**
format selected chart element | **Alt JAM**

Reformat or graph a PivotTable
  show averages instead of sums | **Alt JTG**
  produce a PivotChart | **Alt JTC**

Other
turn on Add-In | **Alt TI**

Alt activates shortcuts menus, linking keyboard letters to Excel menus. Press **Alt,** then release and press letters linked to the menus you want.

Alt Home:

Home menu leys, from left to right, include:

V	paste	FF	Choose a font	FS	Choose a font size	W	Wrap text	9	Reduce decimals	I	Insert
X	cut	1	Bold	FC	Choose font color					D	Delete
C	copy	2	Italicize								
		3	underline								

Other useful menus activated with **Alt** include:

A	Data	N	Insert	W	View

From a chart or plot, **Alt** provides access to chart menus:

JC	Chart design	JA	Chart format	JT	Reformat PivotTable data or chart

Significant Digits Guidelines

The number of significant digits in a number are those which convey information. Significant digits include:

1) all nonzero numbers
2) zeros between nonzero numbers, and
3) trailing zeros.

Zeros acting as placeholders aren't counted.

The number 2,061 has four significant digits, while the number 2,610 has three, since the zero is merely a placeholder. The number 0.0920 has three significant digits, "9," "2," and the final, trailing "0." The first two zeros are placeholders that aren't counted.

In rare cases, it is not clear whether zero is a placeholder or a significant digit. The number 40,000 could represent the range 39,500 to 40,499. In that case, the number of significant digits is one, and the zeros are placeholders. Alternatively, 40,000 could represent the range 39,995 to 40,004. In this latter case, the number of significant digits is four, since the zeros convey meaning. When in doubt, a number could be written in scientific notation, which is unambiguous. For one significant digit, 40,000 becomes $4 \times E^4$. For four significant digits, 40,000 becomes $4.000 \times E^4$.

Don't

Lab 2-1 Description: Compensation of Best Paid CEOs

I. Best Paid CEOs in the U.S.

The New York Times recently published the compensation packages of the 200 best compensated CEOs of publicly traded firms in the U.S. These data are in **Lab 2 Compensation of Best Paid CEOs**.

A. Describe the compensation of the best paid U.S. CEOs.

1. The distribution of the best paid U.S. CEOs is __✓_ positively OR ___ negatively skewed.

    Is U.S. CEO compensation approximately Normal? ___ Y _✓_ N   (-1,1) would be normal

2. Make the histogram of compensation for top paid U.S. CEOs.

    Average compensation of best paid U.S. CEOs is _23_ $M.   (mean)

3. Plot the cumulative distribution of U.S. CEO compensation, adding reference markers at the 25th and 75th percentiles.

    50% of the best paid U.S. CEOs earn _17.8_ $M or less.   17.6

    The middle 50% of the best paid U.S. CEOs earn between _14._ $M and _23_ $M.

B. Distribution of 200 best paid U.S. CEOs by Industry

Make a PivotTable of percents to see in which industries the best paid U.S. CEOs work.

1. The best paid U.S. CEOs work in eight different industries, though more than half work in three of those eight industries: _HC_ , _Serv_, or _Fin_ .

2. Illustrate with a PivotChart:

C. Average Compensation of 200 best paid U.S. CEOs by Industry

Make a PivotTable of average compensation by industry.

1. CEOs in _Services_ , _Tech_, and _____ industries earn more than the average of 200 best paid U.S. CEOs.

2. Illustrate with a PivotChart.

II. Best Paid CEOs in Asia

Data revealing the 25 best paid CEOs in Asia are also in **Lab 2 Compensation of Best Paid CEOs.**

A. Describe compensation of best paid CEOs in Asia

1. The distribution of the best paid CEOs in Asia is ___ positively OR ___ negatively skewed.

2. Is CEO compensation in Asia approximately Normal? ___ Y _✓_ N

3. Make the histogram of compensation for top paid CEOs in Asia.

    Average compensation of best paid CEOs in Asia is _12.5_ $M.

4. Plot the cumulative distribution of Asian CEO compensation, adding reference markers at the 25th and 75th percentiles.

    50% of the best paid CEOs in Asia earn _10.1_ $M or less.

    50% of the 25 best paid CEOs in Asia earn between _8.5_ $M and _13.6_ $M.

B. Distribution of best paid CEOs in Asia by Country

Make a PivotTable of counts to see in which countries the best paid CEOs in Asia work.

1. The best paid CEOs in Asia work in five countries, though more than a third work in: _Hong Kong_ .

2. Illustrate with a PivotChart: ✓

C. Average Compensation of CEOs in Asia by Economic Development

Make a PivotTable of averages of CEO compensation by economic development.

1. The best paid CEOs in Asia earn more in _✓_ BRIC OR ___ developed economy/ economies.

2. Illustrate with a PivotChart: ✓

Assignment 2-1 Shortcut Challenge

Complete the steps in Lab 2 (find descriptive statistics, make a histogram, plot the cdf, make a PivotTable, make a PivotChart, and record your first attempt time. If your time is more than five

minutes, repeat twice, and then record your best time out of three; _____

Case 2-1 Where Are the Billionaires?

68 countries in the World are home to the World's 1,845 billionaires. Data are in **billionaires.xlsx.**

A. Describe the population of countries which are home to billionaires

1. The distribution of the World's billionaires is ✓ positively OR ___ negatively skewed.

   Is the distribution of World's Billionaires in a country approximately Normal? ___ yes ✓ no

2. The average number of billionaires in a country is _27_.

   50% of the countries are home to _6_, the median, or fewer billionaires.

3. Create a histogram of the distribution of percent of billionaires in a country across the 68 countries. Create four histogram bins with upper boundaries set to: the mean (rounded to the nearest tens), and the mean plus one, two, and three standard deviations (rounded to the nearest tens). Add axes labels and a standalone chart title.

4. Plot the cumulative distribution of billionaires per country. Plot the cumulative distribution of billionaires per country that are within the interquartile range (25% to 75%), copy and paste onto the first cdf..

   The middle 50% of countries are home to _4_ to _24_ billionaires..

B. Billionaires by Global Region

1. Use a PivotTable of sums of billionaires in a country to find the percent of billionaires by global region and produce a PivotChart to illustrate your results. Add axes labels and a standalone chart title.

2. The vast majority, _90_%, of the World's 1,845 billionaires reside in one of three global regions: _NA_ , _Asia_ and _Europe_

C. Billionaires by level of economic development

1. Use a PivotTable of sums of billionaires to find the distribution of percent of billionaires by country level of development and produce a PivotChart to illustrate your results. Add axes labels and a standalone chart title.

2. While _51_ % of the World's 1,845 billionaires reside in one of 26 developed countries, _25_ % live in a BRIC (Brazil, Russia, India or China) country.

Chapter 3
Hypothesis Tests and Confidence Intervals to Infer Population Characteristics and Differences

Samples are collected and analyzed to efficiently estimate population characteristics. Chapter Three explores the practice of *inference*: how *hypotheses* about what may be true in the population are tested and how population parameters are estimated with *confidence intervals*. Included in this chapter are tests of hypotheses and confidence intervals for

   (i)   a population mean difference from a single sample of matched pairs,
  (ii)   the difference between means of two populations, or segments from two independent samples, and
 (iii)   a population proportion from a single sample.

Inference relies on the properties of Normally distributed sample means. Those properties of Normal distributions are explored first, below.

3.1 Continuous Data Are Sometimes Normal

Continuous variables are often *Normally distributed*, and their histograms resemble symmetric, bell shaped curves, with the majority of data points clustered around the mean. Most elements are "average" with values near the mean; fewer elements are unusual and far from the mean.

Skewness reflects lack of symmetry. Normally distributed data have skewness of zero, and approximately Normal data have skewness between -1 and +1.

If continuous data are Normally distributed, we need only the mean and standard deviation to describe this data and description is simplified.

Example 3.1 Normal SAT Scores. Standardized tests, such as SAT, capitalize on Normality. Math and verbal SATs are both specifically constructed to produce Normally distributed scores with *mean* M = 500 and *standard deviation* SD = 100 over the population of students (Figure 3.1):

© Springer Nature Switzerland AG 2019
C. Fraser, *Business Statistics for Competitive Advantage with Excel 2019 and JMP*,
https://doi.org/10.1007/978-3-030-20374-0_3

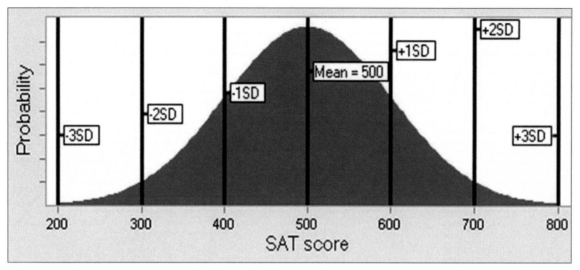

Figure 3.1 Normally distributed SAT scores

3.2 The Empirical Rule Simplifies Description

Normally distributed data have a very useful property described by the *Empirical Rule:*
- 2/3 of the data lie within one standard deviation of the mean
- 95% of the data lie within two standard deviations of the mean

If data are Normally distributed, data can described with just two statistics: the mean and the standard deviation.

Returning to SAT scores, if we know that the average score is 500 and the standard deviation is 100, we also know that

- 2/3 of SAT scores will fall within 100 points of the mean of 500, or between 400 and 600,
- 95% of SAT scores will fall within 200 points of the mean of 500, or between 300 and 700.

3.3 Assess the Difference Between Alternate Scenarios or Pairs

Sometimes management is concerned with the comparison of means from a single sample taken under varying conditions---at different times or in different scenarios---or comparison of sample pairs, like the difference between an employee's opinion and the opinion of the employee's supervisor.

- Financial management might be interested in comparing the reactions of a sample of investors to "socially desirable" stock portfolios, excluding stocks of firms that manufacture or market fossil fuels, weapons, tobacco, or alcohol, versus alternate portfolios which promise similar returns at similar risk levels, but which are not "socially desirable."
- Marketing management might be interested in comparing taste ratings of sodas which contain varying levels of red coloring---do redder sodas taste better to customers?

- Management might be interested in comparing satisfaction ratings following a change which allows employees to work at home.

These examples compare *repeated samples*, where participants have provided multiple responses that can be compared.

- Financial management might also be interested in comparing the risk preferences of husbands and wives.
- Marketing management might want to compare children and parents' preferences for red sodas.
- Management might also be interested in comparing the satisfaction ratings of those employees with their supervisors' satisfaction ratings.

In these examples, interest is in the mean difference from *matched pairs*.

In either case of repeated or matched samples, a *t test* can be used to determine whether or not the difference is non-zero.

Example 3.2 Are "Socially Desirable" Portfolios Undesirable? An investment consulting firm's management believes that they have difficulty selling "socially desirable" portfolios because potential investors assume those funds are inferior investments. Socially Desirable funds exclude stocks of firms which manufacture or market fossil fuels, weapons, tobacco or alcohol. There may be a perceived sacrifice associated with socially desirable investment which causes investors to avoid portfolios labeled "socially desirable." The null hypothesis is:

H_0: Investors rate "socially desirable" portfolios at least as attractive as equally risky, conventional portfolios promising equivalent returns:

$$\mu_{Conventional\text{-}Socially\ Desirable} \leq 0.$$

If investors do not penalize "socially desirable" funds, the null hypothesis cannot be rejected. The alternative hypothesis is:

H_1: Investors rate "socially desirable" portfolios as less attractive than other equally risky portfolios promising equivalent returns:

$$\mu_{Conventional\text{-}Socially\ Desirable} > 0.$$

Note that the alternate hypothesis describes the suspected mean difference. The null hypothesis describes the mean difference if suspicions are not supported.

Thirty-three investors were asked to evaluate two stock portfolios on a scale of attractiveness (-3 = "Not At All Appealing" to 3="Very Appealing"). The two portfolios promised equivalent returns and were equally risky. One contained only "socially desirable" stocks, while the other included stocks from companies which sell tobacco, alcohol and arms. These are shown in Table 3.1.

Table 3.1 Paired ratings of other & socially desirable portfolios

appeal of conventional portfolio	appeal of socially desirable portfolio	difference	appeal of conventional portfolio	appeal of socially desirable portfolio	difference
-3	1	-4	2	-1	3
-3	2	-5	2	-1	3
-3	3	-6	2	-2	4
-3	3	-6	2	2	0
0	-1	1	2	1	1
0	1	-1	2	2	0
1	-3	4	2	2	0
1	-3	4	2	3	-1
1	-1	2	3	-3	6
1	-1	2	3	-3	6
1	-1	2	3	-3	6
1	1	0	3	-1	4
1	1	0	3	-1	4
1	2	-1	3	-3	6
2	-3	5	3	3	0
2	-3	5	3	3	0
2	-2	4			

From a random sample of 33 investors' ratings of conventional and Socially Desirable portfolios of equivalent risk and return, the average difference is 1.5 points on a 7-point scale of attractiveness.

$$\overline{X}_{dif} = -1.5$$

The sample mean and the distribution of sample differences are shown in Figure 3.2:

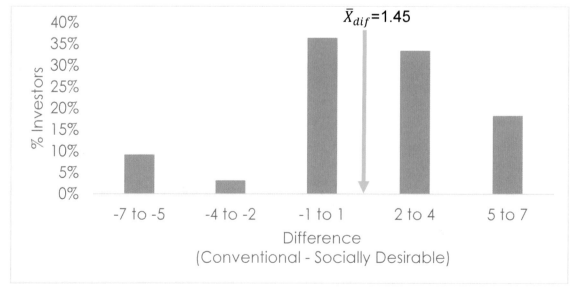

Figure 3.2 Distribution of sample differences.

3.4 Sample Means Are Random Variables

The descriptive statistics from each sample of a population are unique.   If many random samples of a given size were drawn from a population, the means from those samples will be similar and their distribution would be Normal and centered at the population mean. No matter what the population distribution is, sample means from that population will be distributed Normal.

Sample statistics are used to determine whether or not the population mean difference between two alternatives is likely to be less than or equal to zero, using the sample mean as the estimate. The distribution of mean differences of many "large" ($N \geq 30$) random samples is Normal and centered on the unknown population mean difference:

On average, across all random samples of the same size N, the spread in the distribution of sample mean differences around the population mean difference is described by the standard error of sample mean differences:

$$\sigma_{\bar{X}_{dif}} = \sigma_{dif} / \sqrt{N}$$

where σ_{dif} is the standard deviation of differences in the population, and N is the sample size. The standard error is larger when there is more variation in the population and when the sample size is smaller.

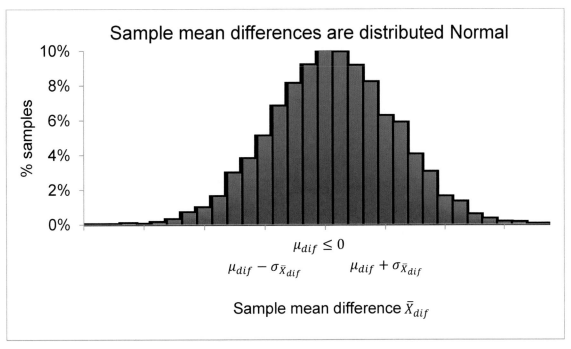

Figure 3.3 Distribution of sample mean differences under the null hypothesis

From the Empirical Rule, we would expect 2/3 of sample mean differences to fall within one standard error of the population mean difference:

$$\mu_{dif} - \sigma_{\bar{X}_{dif}} \le \bar{X}_{dif} \le \mu_{dif} + \sigma_{\bar{X}_{dif}}$$

and we expect 95% of the sample mean differences to fall within two standard errors of the population mean difference:

$$\mu_{dif} - 2 \times \sigma_{\bar{X}_{dif}} \le \bar{X}_{dif} \le \mu_{dif} + 2 \times \sigma_{\bar{X}_{dif}}$$

Nearly all of sample means can be expected to fall within three standard errors of the mean.

Since the population difference standard deviation is almost never known, but estimated from a sample, the standard error is also estimated from the sample difference standard deviation s_{dif}:

$$s_{\bar{X}_{dif}} = s_{dif}/\sqrt{N}$$

When the standard deviation is estimated from a sample (which is nearly always), the distribution of standardized sample mean differences $\bar{X}_{dif}/s_{\bar{X}_{dif}}$ is distributed as *Student t*, which is approximately Normal.

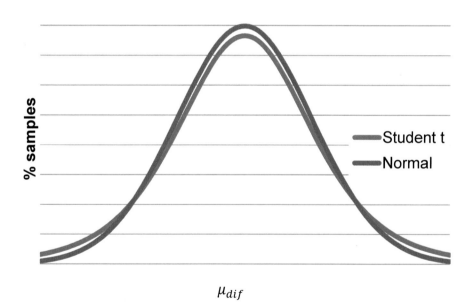

Figure 3.4 Distribution of standardized sample mean differences

Student t has slightly fatter tails than Normal, since we are estimating the standard deviation. How much fatter the tails are depend on the sample size. *Student t* is a family of distributions indexed by sample size. There is more difference from Normal if a sample size is small. For sample sizes of about thirty or more, there is little difference between Student t and Normal. An estimate of the standard deviation from the sample is close to the true population value if the sample size meets or exceeds thirty.

With this sample of 33, the standard error of the mean difference is .59.

$$s_{\overline{X}_{dif}} = \frac{s_{dif}}{\sqrt{N}} = \frac{3.4}{\sqrt{33}} = .59$$

The average difference in attractiveness between the Conventional and the Socially Desirable portfolio is 2.5 standard errors:

$$t_{32} = \frac{\overline{X}_{dif}}{s_{\overline{X}_{dif}}} = \frac{1.45}{.59} = 2.46$$

The *p value* for $t_{32} = 2.46$, for a sample size of 33, is .009. Were the Socially Desirable portfolio at least as attractive as the Conventional portfolio with equivalent risk and return, it would be unusual to observe such a large sample mean difference in ratings. Based on sample evidence, shown in Figure 3.5, we reject the null hypothesis and conclude that a "socially desirable" label reduces portfolio attractiveness.

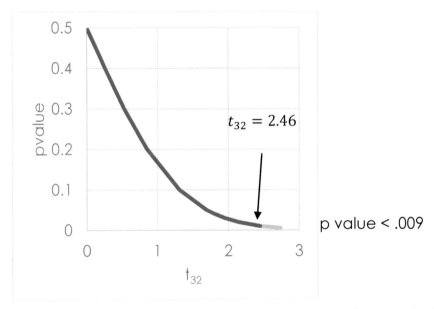

Figure 3.5 *t test* of differences between paired ratings of socially desirable & conventional portfolios

Before statistical software became popular and statistical calculations were done by hand, it was standard practice to conduct a *one tail t test* by finding the *critical t* value for a given sample size which cut off 5% of the t distribution right tail. *Critical t* values were published in the appendices of texts, indexed by sample size. Comparing a sample *t* statistic with the *critical t* enabled a yes-no test of the null hypothesis. If the sample *t* exceeded the *critical t*, the null hypothesis was rejected.

From the portfolio difference example, for a sample of 33, the *critical t* value for 32 *df* (= N-1 = 33-1 = 32) is 1.70. Figure 3.6 illustrates *p values* returned by Excel for *t* values with a sample size of 33, or *df* of 32.

The wide availability of statistical software allows easy determination of the *p value*, providing a more informative estimate of the chance that the sample mean would be observed if the null hypothesis were true. Consequently, it has become standard practice to compare the sample *p value* to the *critical p value* of .05 to test the null hypothesis.

Whether you choose to compare the sample *p value* with the *critical p value* or, alternatively, the sample *t* to the *critical t value* for a given sample size will lead to the same conclusion. Both comparisons are correct choices.

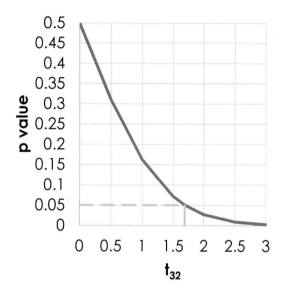

Student's t Distribution *critical t*	
Df	Critical t (α = .05)
32	1.69

Figure 3.6 *p values* returned by Excel for *t* statistics from a sample of 30

3.5 Confidence Intervals Estimate the Population Mean

Rearranging the formula for a *t test*, the sample mean difference, standard error and the critical Student t value for the sample size of 32 and the desired level of confidence, 95%, can be used to estimate the range that is likely to contain the true population mean difference:

$$\bar{X}_{dif} - t_{\alpha/2,N-1} \times s_{\bar{X}_{dif}} < \mu_{dif} < \bar{X}_{dif} + t_{\alpha/2,N-1} \times s_{\bar{X}_{dif}}$$

where α is the chance that a sample is drawn from one of the sample distribution tails, and $t_{\alpha/2, (N-1)}$ is the *critical Student t* value for a chosen level of certainty $(1-\alpha)$ and sample size N.

The *confidence level* $(1-\alpha)$ allows us to specify the level of certainty that an interval will contain the population mean. Generally, decision makers desire a 95% level of confidence $(\alpha=.05)$, insuring that in 95 out of 100 samples, the interval would contain the population mean. The *critical Student t* value for 95% confidence with a sample of thirty three $(N=33)$ is $t_{\alpha/2, (N-1)=32}$ = 2.04. In 95% of random samples of thirty drawn, we expect the sample means to be no further than 2.04 standard errors from the population mean.

The 95% confidence interval for the difference is:

$$\overline{X}_{dif} \pm t_{.025,32} \times s_{\overline{X}_{dif}}$$

$$1.45 +/- 2.04 \,(.59)$$

$$1.45 +/- 1.20$$

OR .25 to 2.66 on the 6 point scale:

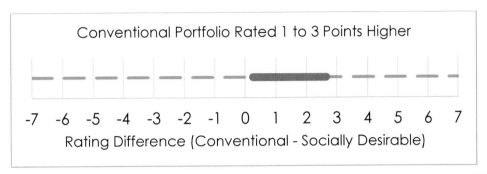

Figure 3.7 Confidence interval for the difference between conventional and socially desirable portfolios.

The investment consultants would conclude:
A "socially desirable" label reduces investors' judged attractiveness ratings.   Investors downgrade the attractiveness of "socially desirable" portfolios by about 1 to 3 points on a -7 to +7 scale, relative to equivalent, but conventional, portfolios.

3.6 Determine Whether Two Segments Differ with Student t

Example 3.3 SmartScribe: Is Income a Useful Base for Segmentation? SmartScribe, manufacturers of a brand of smart pens, would like to identify the demographic segment with the highest demand for its new concept. Smart pens record presentation notes onto a file that can be downloaded. Since the new pens were being sold at a relatively high price, Adopters might have higher incomes. To test this hypothesis, customers at an office supply retail store were sorted into SmartScribe purchasers, which management refers to as The Adopters, and other Nonadopter customers. Random samples from these two segments were drawn and offered a store coupon in exchange for completion of a short survey, which included a measure of annual household income. Fifty six SmartScribe pen Adopters and forty one Nonadopters completed the survey.

The null hypothesis states the conclusion that the average annual household income of Adopters is not greater than that of Nonadopters.

H_0:   Average annual household income of Adopters is equal to or less than that of Nonadopters of the new pen.

$$\mu_{Adopters} \leq \mu_{Nonadopters}$$

OR

$$\mu_{Adopters} - \mu_{Nonadopters} \leq 0.$$

Alternatively:

H_1: Average annual household incomes of Adopters exceeds that of Nonadopters of the new pen:

$$\mu_{Adopters} > \mu_{Nonadopters}$$

OR

$$\mu_{Adopters} - \mu_{Nonadopters} > 0.$$

If there is no difference in incomes between the two segment samples, or if Adopters earn lower incomes, the null hypothesis cannot be rejected based on the sample evidence.

Average income in the sample of Nonadopters was \$35K, and \$80K in the sample of Adopters. A test of the significance of the difference between the two segments' average annual household incomes is based on the difference between the two sample means.

SmartScribe needs to determine whether or not this difference in average incomes,

$$\overline{X}_{Adopters} - \overline{X}_{Nonadopters} = \$80K - \$35K = \$45K$$

is large enough to be significant.

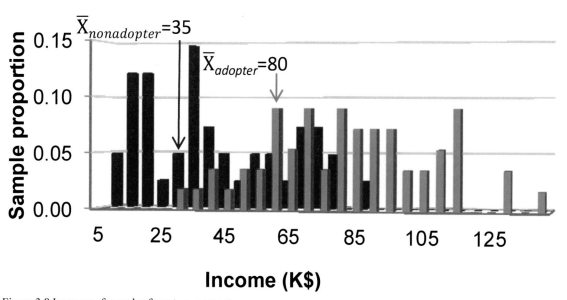

Figure 3.8 Incomes of samples from two segments.

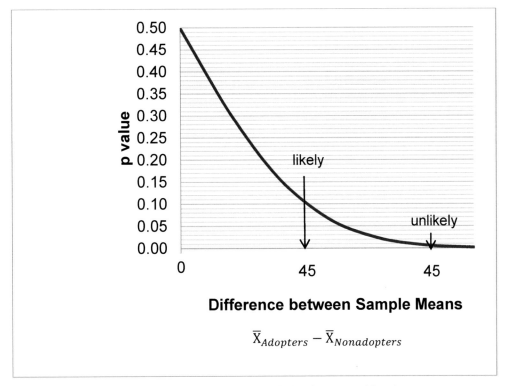

Figure 3.9 The null hypothesis Adopters earn less or equivalent incomes to Nonadopters.

Whether the difference between two sample means is large enough to be significant depends on the amount of dispersion in the two populations, in this case $\sigma_{Adopters}$ and $\sigma_{Nonadopters}$, and the two sample sizes, $n_{Adopters}$ and $n_{Nonadopters}$ in this case. The standard error of the difference between two sample means, from the sample standard deviations, $s_{Adopters}$ and $s_{Nonadopters}$ and the two sample sizes is:

$$s_{\overline{X}_{Adopters} - \overline{X}_{Nonadopters}} = \sqrt{\left(\frac{s_{Adopters}}{\sqrt{n_{Adopters}}}\right)^2 + \left(\frac{s_{Nonadopters}}{\sqrt{n_{Nonadopters}}}\right)^2}$$

$$= \sqrt{s_{\overline{X}_{Adopters}}^2 + s_{\overline{X}_{Nonadopters}}^2}$$

The standard error of average difference in annual household income (in thousands) is the square root of the two sample standard errors squared, equal to $4.9K in this case:

$$s_{\overline{X}_{Adopters} - \overline{X}_{Nonadopters}} = \sqrt{\left(\frac{25}{\sqrt{56}}\right)^2 + \left(\frac{23}{\sqrt{41}}\right)^2}$$

$$= \sqrt{(3.3)^2 + (3.6)^2}$$

$$= \sqrt{11.2 + 12.9}$$

$$= \sqrt{24.1}$$

$$= 4.9(\$K)$$

This estimate for the standard error of the difference between segment means assumes that the two segment standard deviations may differ. Since it is not usually known whether or not the segment standard deviations are equivalent, this is a conservative assumption.

The number of standard errors of difference between sample means is measured with Student t.

$$t_{90} = \left(\overline{X}_{Adopters} - \overline{X}_{Nonadopters}\right)/s_{\overline{X}_{Adopters}-\overline{X}_{Nonadopters}}$$

$$= \$45K / \$4.9K$$

$$= 9.2$$

When the two samples have unique standard deviations, the degrees of freedom for a two segment t test depend on the standard errors of both samples:

$$df = \frac{(s_{\overline{X}_{Adopters}}^2 + s_{\overline{X}_{Nonadopters}}^2)^2}{s_{\overline{X}_{Adopters}}^4/(N_{Adopters}-1)+s_{\overline{X}_{Nonadopters}}^4/(N_{Nonadopters}-1)}$$

$$= \frac{(3.3^2+3.6^2)^2}{(3.3^4/(56-1)+3.6^4/(41-1)}$$

$$= 89.5$$

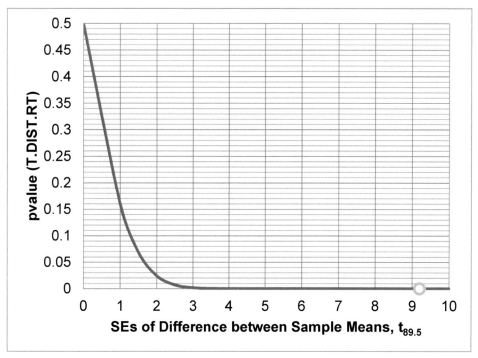

Figure 3.10 *t* test of difference between segment means

The *p value* for this *t* with 89.5 degrees of freedom is less than .0001.

From the *t test* of difference between segment incomes, shown in Figure 3.10, SmartScribe management could conclude:

"In segment samples of 56 Adopters and 41 Nonadopters, the corresponding average segment sample incomes are $80K and $35K, a difference of $45K, more than 9 standard errors. Were there no difference in segment mean incomes in the population, it would be unusual to observe this difference in segment average incomes. Based on sample evidence, we conclude that average incomes of Adopters cannot be less than or equal to the average incomes of Nonadopters. Income is a useful basis for segmentation."

3.7 Estimate the Extent of Difference Between Two Segments

To construct confidence intervals for the difference in means of two segments, we assume that either (i) both segments' characteristics are bell-shaped (distributed approximately Normal) and we've randomly sampled both segments, or (ii) "large" random samples from both segments have been collected.

From the sample data, SmartScribe managers estimated the average annual household income difference (in thousands) between Adopters and Nonadopters:

$$\overline{X}_{Adopters} - \overline{X}_{Nonadopters} = \$80K - \$35K = \$45K$$

The 95% confidence interval around the difference in annual household incomes between Adopters and Nonadopters is made by adding and subtracting the *margin of error*.

The *margin of error* is equal to the two tail *critical t*, with degrees of freedom corresponding to the two sample sizes and α equal to .05 (for 95% confidence), times the standard error for the difference between sample means:

$$me = t_{df,\alpha} \times s_{\overline{X}_{Adopters} - \overline{X}_{Nonadopters}} = 1.99 \times \$4.9K = \$9.7K$$

The difference between means of the two samples would be no further than $9.7K from the difference between means in the two segments.

The 95% confidence interval for the difference between means is $35K to $55K:

$$\left(\overline{X}_{Adopters} - \overline{X}_{Nonadopters}\right) - t_{df,\alpha} \times s_{\overline{X}_{Adopters} - \overline{X}_{Nonadopters}}$$

$$< \mu_{Adopters} - \mu_{Nonadopters}$$

$$< \left(\overline{X}_{Adopters} - \overline{X}_{Nonadopters}\right) + t_{df,\alpha} \times s_{\overline{X}_{Adopters} - \overline{X}_{Nonadopters}}$$

$$\$45K - 2.99 \times \$4.9K < \mu_{Adopters} - \mu_{Nonadopters} < \$45K + 2.99 \times \$4.9K$$

$$\$45K - \$9.7K < \mu_{Adopters} - \mu_{Nonadopters} < \$45K + \$9.7K$$

$$\$35K < \mu_{Adopters} - \mu_{Nonadopters} < \$55K$$

Management will conclude that annual household income can be used to differentiate the two market segments, and that Adopters are wealthier than Nonadopters.

In samples of 56 Adopters and 41 Nonadopters, the corresponding average difference in income between segment samples is $45K, and the margin of error of the difference is $9.7K. Relative to Nonadopters, we estimate that Adopters earn $35K to $55K more on average, annually.

3.8 Estimate a Population Proportion from a Sample Proportion

Example 3.4 Climate Change Views. Under the Trump administration, there is some disagreement among policy makers regarding the cause of climate change. In April 2018, CBS News conducted a poll of 1,004 adults nationwide to assess popular sentiment about the causes of climate change:

Table 3.2 Sample approval proportions by poll

"Which statement comes closest to your view about global warming? Global warming is caused mostly by human activity such as burning fossil fuels. Global warming is caused mostly by natural patterns in the earth's environment. OR, Global warming does not exist."				
	Mostly human activity %	Mostly natural patterns %	It does not exist %	Caused by both (vol.) %	Don't know what causes it/Unsure %
4/11-15/18	54	24	13	5	4

If numerous random samples are taken, sample proportions P will be approximately Normally distributed around the unknown population proportion π, as long as this true proportion is not close to either zero or one.

The standard deviation of the sample proportions P, the *standard error of the sample proportion,* measures dispersion of samples of size N from the population proportion π:

$$\sigma_\pi = \sqrt{\pi \times (1 - \pi)/N}$$

which is estimated with the sample proportion P:

$$s_P = \sqrt{P \times (1 - P)/N}$$

Focusing on the proportion that attribute global warming to "mostly human activity," "mostly natural patterns," or "it does not exist," the standard errors, margins of error and 95% confidence intervals for the population proportions are:

Table 3.3 Confidence interval of proportions by poll, N=1004

Poll i	Sample Proportion, P_i	Standard Error, s_{P_i} (N=30)	Margin of Error for 95% Confidence, $Z \times s_{P_i} = 1.96 \times s_{P_i}$	Interval containing the Population Proportion with 95% confidence $P_i \pm Z \times s_{P_i}$
Mostly human	.54	.016	.031	.51 to .57
Mostly natural	.24	.013	.026	.21 to 27
Doesn't exist	.13	.011	.021	.11 to .15

From these results, CBS News can report that the majority view global warming as caused by human activity.

3.9 Conditions for Assuming Approximate Normality

It is appropriate to use the Normal distribution to approximate the distribution of possible sample proportions if sample size is "large" ($N \geq 30$), and both $N \times P \geq 5$ and $N \times (1\text{-}P) \geq 5$. When the true population proportion is very close to either zero or one, we cannot reasonably assume that the distribution of sample proportions is Normal. A rule of thumb suggests that $P \times N$ and $(1\text{-}P) \times N$ ought to be at least five in order to use Normal inferences about proportions. For a sample of 1,000, the sample proportion P would need to be between .01 and .99.

3.10 Conservative Confidence Intervals for a Proportion

Polling organizations report the sample proportion and margin of error, rather than a confidence interval. For example, "54% view human actions as the major cause of climate change.. (The margin of error from this poll is 3 percentage points.)" A 95% level of confidence is the industry standard. Because the true proportion and its standard deviation are unknown, and because pollsters stake their reputations on valid results, a *conservative* approach, which assumes a true proportion of .5, is used. This conservative approach

$$s_P = \sqrt{.5 \times (1 - .5)/N}$$

yields the largest possible standard error for a given sample size and makes the margin of error ($Z \times s_P$) a simple function of the square root of the sample size N.

With this conservative approach and a sample of $N = 1,004$, the poll results are shown in Table 3.4. Notice that the confidence interval for "mostly human" is virtually unchanged with the conservative margin of error, since that sample proportion is near 50%. The confidence interval for "doesn't exist" changes the most, since that sample proportion is furthest from 50%.

Table 3.4 Conservative confidence intervals for approval proportions, $N=1004$

	Sample Proportion, P	*Conservative Margin of Error for 95% Confidence,* $Z \times s_P = 1.96 \times s_P$	*Conservative 95% Confidence Interval* $P - Z \times s_P \leq \pi \leq P + Z \times s_P$	
Mostly human	.54	.031	.51	.57
Mostly natural	.24	.031	.21	.27
Doesn't exist	.13	.031	.10	.16

CBS News could report:

"Fifty four percent of American adults agree that human actions are the primary cause of global warming. Poll results have a margin of error of 3.1 percentage points. The majority of Americans believe human actions are responsible for global warming."

Other appropriate applications for confidence intervals to estimate population proportions or shares include:

- Proportion who prefer a new formulation to an old one in a taste test
- Share of retailers who offer a brand
- Market share of a product in a specified market
- Proportion of employees who call in sick when they're well
- Proportion of new hires who will perform exceptionally well on the job

3.11 Inference from Sample to Population

Managers use sample statistics to infer population characteristics, knowing that inference from a sample is efficient and reliable. Because sample standard errors are approximately *Normally* distributed, we can use the Empirical Rule to build confidence intervals to estimate population means and to test hypotheses about population means with *t tests*. We can determine whether a population mean is likely to equal, be less than, or exceed a target value, and we can estimate the range which is likely to include a population mean.

Our certainty that a population mean will fall within a sample based confidence interval depends on the amount of population variation and on the sample size. To double precision, sample size must be quadrupled, because the margin of error is inversely proportional to the square root of sample size.

Differences are important to managers, since differences drive decision making. If customers differ, segments are targeted in varying degrees. If employee satisfaction differs between alternate work environments, the workplace may be altered. Inference about differences between two populations is similar, and relies on differences between two independent samples. A *t test* can be used to determine whether there is a likely difference between two population means, and with a confidence interval, we can estimate the likely size of difference.

Confidence intervals and hypothesis tests are consistent and complementary, but are used to make different decisions. If a decision maker needs to make a qualitative Yes/No decision, a hypothesis test is used. If a decision maker instead requires a quantitative estimate, such as level of demand, confidence intervals are used. Hypothesis tests tell us whether demand exceeds a critical level or whether segments differ. Confidence intervals quantify demand or magnitude of differences between segments.

Sample statistics are used to estimate population statistics because it is often neither possible nor feasible to identify and measure the entire population. The time and expense involved in identifying and measuring all population elements is prohibitive. To survey the bottled water consumption of each faculty member, student, and staff member on campus would take many hours. An estimate of demand is inferred from a random, representative sample which includes faculty, students, and staff. Though sample estimates will not be exactly the same as population statistics because of sampling error, samples are amazingly efficient if properly drawn and representative of the population.

Excel 3.1 Test the Mean Difference in Between Alternate Pairs with a Paired t Test

Difference between Conventional and Socially Desirable Portfolio Ratings. Test the hypothesis that the average difference between ratings of a Conventional portfolio and ratings of a Socially Desirable portfolio is greater than zero.

Open **3 SD Portfolio.**

Use the function **T.TEST**(*array1, array2, tails, type*) to calculate a paired *t test*. For *array1*, enter the *conventional portfolio ratings*. For *array2*, enter the *socially desirable portfolio ratings*. For *tails*, enter **1** for a *one tail* test, and for *type*, enter **1** to specify a paired *t test*.

In B35,	p value
In C35	,=**T.TEST(A2:A34,B2:B34,1,1)**

DEVSQ	▾	⋮	✕	✓	*fx*	=T.TEST(A2:A34,B2:B34,1,1)

◢	A	B	C	D	E
1	conventional rating	socially desirable rating	conventional minus socially desirable difference	differenc e	
33	-3	3	-6		
34	-3	3	-6		
35		p value	=T.TEST(A2:A34,B2:B34,1,1)		

Excel 3.2 Construct a Confidence Interval for the Difference Between Pairs

To estimate the population difference in investors' ratings of Socially Desirable and Conventional portfolios from sample data, construct a confidence interval of the average rating difference.

Find the mean and standard deviation of the difference and the margin of error of the difference (labelled *Confidence*, in row 16 of descriptives).

Order Descriptives, including Confidence	**Alt AYn B** select + OK
Level for Mean	**C1:C34 tab LSO**

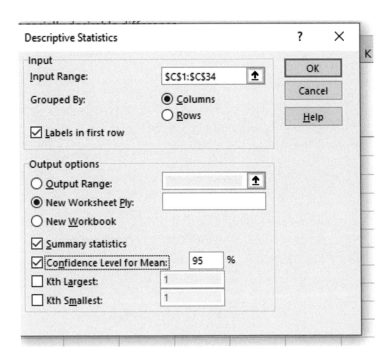

Subtract and add the margin of error (in B16) from the mean difference to find the 95% confidence interval bounds for the difference.

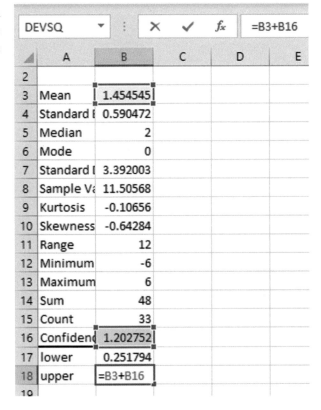

Illustrate the difference, within the range of possible differences, -6 to +6 with scatterplots (which will be a line). To get Excel to plot the 95% confidence interval bounds as a line, add an arbitrary number, such as 1 in cells C17:C18. Select the four cells and insert a scatterplot:

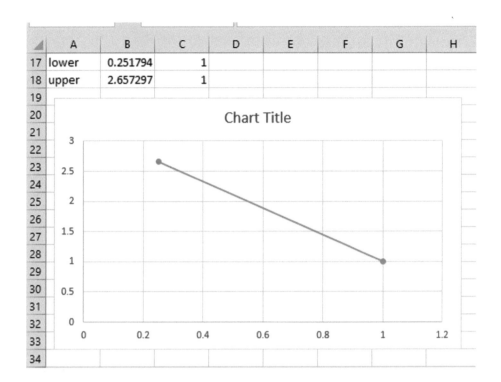

This is not the line we want. When we ask Excel to plot two points, often the axes are reversed.

Switch rows and columns   **Alt JCW**

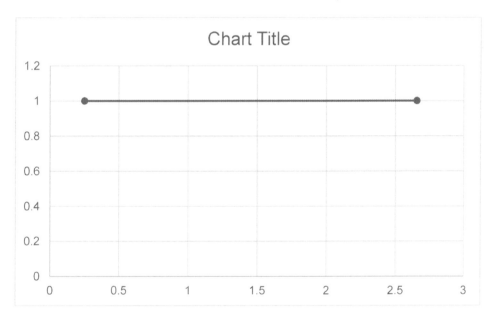

Below the 95% confidence intervals, input the potential lower and upper interval bounds, -6 and +6. Again add the arbitrary number for the y axis, create the scatterplot, switching rows and columns. Then copy the first scatterplot and paste into the second.

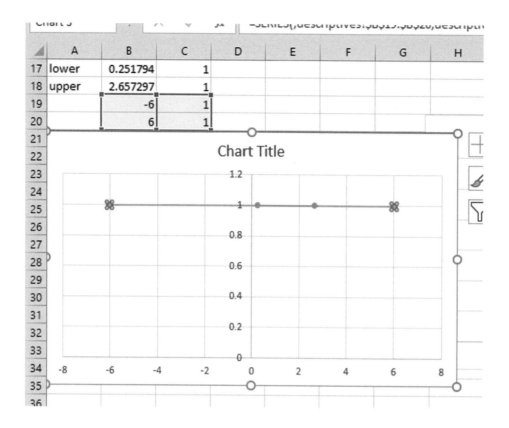

To remove the vertical axis and gridlines (which adds no value), reformat the axis with major axis units of 2. Delete the axis.

Add a horizontal axis label and replace the title with a standalone title.

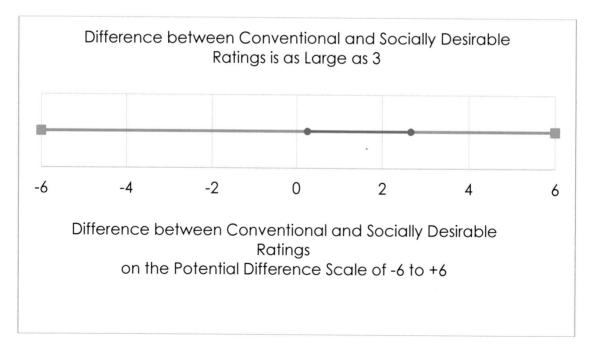

Excel 3.3 Test the Difference Between Two Segment Means with a Two Sample t Test

Moneyball. Compare Phillies' salaries with salaries of players for the other teams in the National League East. Data are in **3 Phillies.**

Use the Excel function **T.TEST(***array1,array2,tails,type***)** to find the *p value* from a *t test* of the difference between average salaries of the two segments. For *array1*, enter the sample *NLE* values. For *array2*, enter the sample *Phillies* values. For *tails*, enter **1** for a *one tail* test, and for *type*, enter **3** to signal a two sample *t test* which allows the standard deviations to differ between segments.

| In C55, | | p value |
| In D55, | | **=T.TEST(J2:J218,D2:D54,1,3)** |

	C	D	E	F	G	H	I	J
1	POS	salary ($M)	years	season	NLE team	NAME	POS	salary ($M)
53	OF	$1.80	5	2017	Braves	Julio Teheran	P	$3.47
54	P	$27.50	5	2016	Braves	Julio Teheran	P	$6.47
55	pvalue	=T.TEST(			Braves	Brandon Phillips	2B	$13.97
56		J2:J218, D2:D54,1,			Braves	Freddie Freeman	1B	$12.36
57		3)			Braves	Freddie Freeman	1B	$20.86

Excel 3.4 Construct a Confidence Interval for the Difference Between Two Segments

Estimate the difference between the *NLE* and *Phillies* mean salaries.

1.0

Use descriptives to find the segment sample means, standard deviations, and standard errors.

	A	B	C	D	E
1	NLE	salary ($M)	Phillies	salary ($M)	
2					
3	Mean	4.299674	Mean	3.037271	
4	Standard E	0.342845	Standard E	0.683036	
5	Median	1.5625	Median	0.552	
6	Mode	0.535	Mode	0.5075	
7	Standard D	5.633511	Standard D	4.972574	
8	Sample Va	31.73645	Sample Va	24.7265	
9	Kurtosis	3.338078	Kurtosis	11.46029	
10	Skewness	1.918578	Skewness	3.079428	
11	Range	26.9925	Range	26.9925	
12	Minimum	0.5075	Minimum	0.5075	
13	Maximum	27.5	Maximum	27.5	
14	Sum	1160.912	Sum	160.9754	
15	Count	270	Count	53	
16	Confidence	0.675	Confidence	1.370611	

Find the difference between segment means and the standard error of the difference from the segment sample standard errors.

In A17,	Difference
In A18,	se
In B17,	**=B3-D3**
In B18,	**=SQRT(B8/B15+D8.D15)**

| DEVSQ | ▼ | ⋮ | ✕ | ✓ | f_x | =SQRT(B8/B15+D8/D15) |

	A	B	C	D	E
1	NLE	salary ($M)	Phillies		salary ($M)
2					
3	Mean	4.608003	Mean	3.037271	
4	Standard I	0.390465	Standard I	0.683036	
5	Median	2	Median	0.552	
6	Mode	0.535	Mode	0.5075	
7	Standard I	5.751905	Standard I	4.972574	
8	Sample VI	33.08441	Sample VI	24.7265	
9	Kurtosis	2.459606	Kurtosis	11.46029	
10	Skewness	1.74343	Skewness	3.079428	
11	Range	26.82055	Range	26.9925	
12	Minimum	0.5075	Minimum	0.5075	
13	Maximum	27.32805	Maximum	27.5	
14	Sum	999.9367	Sum	160.9754	
15	Count	217	Count	53	
16	Confidenc	0.769609	Confidenc	1.370611	
17	Difference				
18	SE	=SQRT(B8/B15+D8/D15)			

Find the degrees of freedom required for the critical t. First, find the numerator from the segment sample variances and sample sizes.

In E8, $\quad=(B8/B15+D8/D15)^{\wedge}2$

DEVSQ			✕	✓	f_x	=(B8/B15)^2/(B15-1)+(D8/D15)^2/(D15-1)

◢	A	B	C	D	E	F
1	NLE	salary ($M)	Phillies	salary ($M)		
2						
3	Mean	4.608003	Mean	3.037271		
4	Standard I	0.390465	Standard I	0.683036		
5	Median	2	Median	0.552		
6	Mode	0.535	Mode	0.5075		
7	Standard I	5.751905	Standard I	4.972574		
8	Sample VI	33.08441	Sample VI	24.7265		
9	Kurtosis	2.459606	Kurtosis	11.46029	=(B8/B15)^2/(B15-1)+(D8/D15)^2/(D15-1)	
10	Skewness	1.74343	Skewness	3.079428		
11	Range	26.82055	Range	26.9925		
12	Minimum	0.5075	Minimum	0.5075		
13	Maximum	27.32805	Maximum	27.5		
14	Sum	999.9367	Sum	160.9754		
15	Count	217	Count	53		
16	Confidenc	0.769609	Confidenc	1.370611		
17	Difference	1.570733				

Next, find the denominator from the segment sample variances and sample sizes.

In E9, $\quad=((B8/B15)^{\wedge}2)/(B15\text{-}1)+(D8/D15)^{\wedge}2/(D15\text{-}1)$

DEVSQ			✕	✓	f_x	=(B8/B15+D8/D15)^2

◢	A	B	C	D	E
1	NLE	salary ($M)	Phillies	salary ($M)	
2					
3	Mean	4.608003	Mean	3.037271	
4	Standard I	0.390465	Standard I	0.683036	
5	Median	2	Median	0.552	
6	Mode	0.535	Mode	0.5075	
7	Standard I	5.751905	Standard I	4.972574	
8	Sample VI	33.08441	Sample VI	24.7265	=(B8/B15+D8/D15)^2
9	Kurtosis	2.459606	Kurtosis	11.46029	
10	Skewness	1.74343	Skewness	3.079428	
11	Range	26.82055	Range	26.9925	
12	Minimum	0.5075	Minimum	0.5075	
13	Maximum	27.32805	Maximum	27.5	
14	Sum	999.9367	Sum	160.9754	
15	Count	217	Count	53	
16	Confidenc	0.769609	Confidenc	1.370611	

In E10, find degrees of freedom of 89.2 by dividing the numerator by the denominator.
    Find the critical t with 89.2 degrees of freedom.

In B19, | **=T.INV.2T(.05,E10)**

DEVSQ	▼	⋮	✕ ✓ *fx*	=T.INV.2T(0.05,E10)

◢	A	B	C	D	E
1	NLE	salary ($M)	Phillies	salary ($M)	
2					
3	Mean	4.608003	Mean	3.037271	
4	Standard I	0.390465	Standard I	0.683036	
5	Median	2	Median	0.552	
6	Mode	0.535	Mode	0.5075	
7	Standard I	5.751905	Standard I	4.972574	
8	Sample V	33.08441	Sample V	24.7265	0.3831615
9	Kurtosis	2.459606	Kurtosis	11.46029	0.0042933
10	Skewness	1.74343	Skewness	3.079428	89.245668
11	Range	26.82055	Range	26.9925	
12	Minimum	0.5075	Minimum	0.5075	
13	Maximum	27.32805	Maximum	27.5	
14	Sum	999.9367	Sum	160.9754	
15	Count	217	Count	53	
16	Confidenc	0.769609	Confidenc	1.370611	
17	Difference	1.570732			
18	SE				
19	critical t	=T.INV.2T(0.05,E10)			
20					

Find the margin of error, 1.56, by multiplying the critical t times the pooled SE.
Subtract and add the margin of error to the difference to find the lower and upper 95%
confidence intervals, .0074 to 3.1 ($M).

    To illustrate, create a scatterplot (which will be a line), following the steps in Excel 3.2.
(There is no reference line, in this case, since the difference between means is not bounded.)

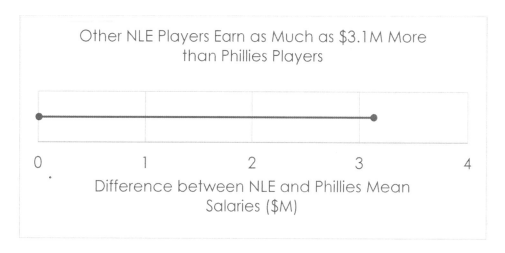

Labels (handwritten, top right)
- Summary Stats
- confidence level for mean

in AA (handwritten)

Lab 3-1 Inference

Socially Desirable Portfolio Perceptions

if does not include 0 in lower & upper bound it is significant (handwritten)

An investment advisory is considering promoting *socially desirable* portfolios which exclude stocks of firms related to guns, cigarettes, alcohol, and fossil fuels. To learn whether or not investors value socially desirable stocks below conventional stocks, an experiment was conducted. 33 investors rated the attractiveness of two portfolios which offered equivalent rates of return at equivalent levels of risk. Data are in SD Portfolio.xlsx. *paired*

1. State the hypothesis to be tested: *Ho Soc Des ≥ Conventional*
   H₁ SD < Conventional

2. Test the mean difference between ratings of the two portfolios and report your conclusions and p value: *The mean ratings for SD is Statistically significantly (p = .0097) lower than conventional*

3. Construct a *95% confidence interval* of the mean difference in portfolio ratings and interpret your results for management. *Difference between soc Dec and Conventional can be as little as .25 to as large as 2.66.*

4. Illustrate the 95% confidence interval with a scatterplot (which will be a line), against the line showing the range of differences possibilities, -7 to +7.

Moneyball

In 2017, the Phillies finished last in the National League East division. Phillies players are convinced that players for other NLE teams are being paid more. The Phillies General Manager has asked you to compare Phillies' salaries with salaries of players for the other teams in the National League East. Data are in **Lab 3 Phillies.**

1. What is the hypothesis to be tested? *Ho = Phillies Salaries ≥ Others in NLE*
   H₁ = Phillies Salaries < Others in NLE

2. Test the mean difference between team salary means and report your conclusions and p value: *Diff $1.57M   Stat Sig Diff (p = .025)*

3. The General Manager can conclude that, relative to the Phillies, other NLE players are paid

   _✓_ More ___ the same ___ Less.

Value of a Phillies Uniform. If you conclude that other NLE players earn higher salaries, estimate the average difference at a 95% level of confidence.

1. With 95% confidence other players for the NLE earn an average salary that is *$74.45K* _____ to

   3.13M more than players for the Phillies.

   ↑ *confidence intervals*

2. What other differences between the Phillies and other NLE teams may explain the difference in mean salaries? Phil: Distribution (large peak)

Global Warming Views

In April 2018, CBS News polled 1,004 adults nationwide to collect views about global warming.

	Mostly human activity %	Mostly natural patterns %	It does not exist %	Caused by both (vol.) %	Don't know what causes it/Unsure %
4/11-15/18	54	24	13	5	4

"Which statement comes closest to your view about global warming? Global warming is caused mostly by human activity such as burning fossil fuels. Global warming is caused mostly by natural patterns in the earth's environment. OR, Global warming does not exist."

1. With 95% confidence, what is the conservative margin of error?

2. With 95% confidence what percent of adults view global warming as a "Caused mostly by human activity such as burning fossil fuels?" _____ to _____

Assignment 3-1 McLattes

McDonalds recently sponsored a blind taste test of lattes from Starbucks and their own McCafes. A sample of thirty Starbucks customers tasted both lattes from unmarked cups and provided ratings on a -3 (=worst latte I've ever tasted) to +3 (=best latte I've ever tasted) scale. McDonalds managers were confident that their lattes would be rated equivalently to Starbucks lattes. These data are in **Assignment 3 Latte.**

1. State the hypotheses to be tested:

$H_0 = MCD \neq StarB$

$H_1 = MCD = StarB$

2. Test the hypotheses and report your results to management, including the p value:

The null of no difference cannot be rejected (p = .099 > alpha .05)

3. Illustrate the 95% confidence interval for the population difference between Starbucks and McCafe ratings with a scatterplot (which will be a line), against the line showing the range of differences possibilities, -6 to +6.

No sig dif between the two lattes. the two being equivalent in taste is plausable

Assignment 3-2 Inference: Dell Smartphone Plans

Managers at Dell are considering a joint venture with a Chinese firm to launch a new, competitively priced smartphone.

I. Estimate the percent of smartphone owners who will replace with Dell

In a concept test of 1000 smartphone owners, 20% indicated that they would probably or definitely replace their smartphone with the new Dell concept in the next quarter. Norms from past research suggest that 80% of those who indicate intent to replace actually will.

1. Expected Dell smartphone share = 80% × sample intent proportion: ___160___

2. Conservative confidence interval for Dell smartphone share: _159_ to _161_   ME = 1.161

II. Distinguish Likely Dell Smartphone Adopters

Those who indicated that they were likely to switch to the Dell smartphone may be more price conscious than other smartphone owners. In the concept test, participants were asked to rate the importance of several smartphone attributes, including price. These data are in **Lab 3 Inference Dell smartphone.**

1. Do Likely Adopters rate price higher in importance than Unlikely Adopters?

   $H_0: LA \leq others$
   $H_1: LA > others$

   a. State the null and alternative hypotheses:

   b. State your conclusion, including the statistic that you relied upon to form your conclusion and its p value.

   We performed a one-tail t-test assuming unequal variance to determine if price attributed

   p < .001

   we rejected the null that price is less than or equally important. price is more important to LA doctors

2. Illustrate approximate 95% confidence interval for the difference between Likely and Unlikely Adopters' average price importances with a scatterplot (which will be a line). Add a "stand alone" title and label axes.

Assignment 3-3 The Hilton Difference

There are more than one hundred branded hotels in Washington, DC, owned or managed by Hilton or competitors. The hotel industry in Washington, DC is representative of the hotel industry in cities throughout the U.S. Differences in quality and price distinguish the hotels. Hilton would like to claim that its hotel guest ratings provide evidence of higher average quality lodging than competing hotels and that Hilton's average *starting room price* is equivalent to competitors' average *starting room price*. The dataset **Hilton DC** contains *Stars* and *Guest rating,* measures of quality, and *starting room price* for Hilton hotels and for competitors' hotels.

1. Find guest rating and price averages for Hilton and other hotels:

	Average Guest rating	Average Starting room price
Hilton	4.703	$207.1
Other	4.246	$177.46

2. Regarding average guest ratings: H_{0B} = $price_H$ = $Price_o$

   a. State the null and alternative hypotheses:
   b. State your conclusion and statistical evidence, including p value:

3. What is the 95% confidence interval for the difference between Hilton's average guest rating and other hotels' average guest rating?

4. Illustrate the 95% confidence interval for the difference between means with a scatterplot (which will be a line), including a reference line of possible values from -5 to +5.

5. What claim can Hilton make regarding their average guest rating, relative to the competition's average guest rating? there is correlation

6. Regarding average starting room prices:

   a. State the null and alternative hypotheses: yes there ise correlation
   b. State your conclusion and statistical evidence, including the p value:

7. What claim can Hilton make regarding average starting room price relative to competitors?
There is high competition

One manager is concerned that Hilton's average star rating may be lower than competitors' average star rating.

8. Find star rating averages for Hilton and other hotels:

	Hilton	Other hotels
Average star rating	3.2	3.45

9. Regarding average star ratings:

   a. State the null and alternative hypotheses:
   b. State your conclusion and statistical evidence, including p value:

Assignment 3-4 U.S. Actions to Address Climate Change  Data Missing

In March 2018, Quinnipiac polled 1,291 registered voters nationwide to gauge opinion on U.S. actions to address climate change.

"Do you think the United States is doing enough to address climate change, doing too much, or do you think more needs to be done to address climate change?"			
	Doing enough %	Doing too much %	More needs to be done %	Unsure/ No answer %
3/16-20/18	22	10	63	5

1. What is the conservative margin of error?

2. With 95% confidence, what percent of registered voters believe that the U.S. "needs to do more" to address climate change? _____ to _____

Case 3-1 Polaski Vodka: Can a Polish Vodka Stand Up to the Russians?

Seagrams management decided to enter the premium vodka market with a Polish vodka, suspecting that it would be difficult to compete with Stolichnaya, a Russian vodka and the leading premium brand. The product formulation and the package/brand impact on perceived taste were explored with experiments to decide whether the new brand was ready to launch.

I. **The taste.** First, Seagrams managers asked, "Could consumers distinguish between Stolichnaya and Seagrams' Polish vodka in a *blind* taste test, where the impact of packaging and brand name were absent?"

Consultants designed an experiment to test the null and alternative hypotheses:

H_0: The taste rating of Seagram's Polish vodka is at least as high as the taste rating of Stolichnaya. The average difference between taste ratings of Stolichnaya and Seagrams' Polish vodka does not exceed zero:

$$\mu_{Stolichnaya-Polish} \leq 0$$

H_1: The taste rating of Seagram's Polish vodka is lower than the taste rating of Stolichnaya. The average difference between taste ratings of Stolichnaya and Seagram's Polish vodka is positive:

$$\mu_{Stolichnaya-Polish} > 0$$

In this first experiment, each participant tasted two unidentified vodka samples and rated the taste of each on a ten-point scale. Between tastes, participants cleansed palates with water. Experimenters flipped a coin to determine which product would be served first: if heads, Seagrams' polish vodka was poured first; if tails, Stolichnaya was poured first. Both samples were poured from plain, clear beakers. The only difference between the two samples was the actual vodka.

These experimental data in **Case 3-3 Polaski Taste** are repeated measures. From each participant, we have two measures whose difference is the difference in taste between the Russian and Polish vodkas.

1. Test the difference between taste ratings of the two vodkas and report your conclusions and p value: cannot reject null of no difference (p=.4597)
2. Construct a *95% confidence interval* of the difference in taste ratings, illustrate with a scatterplot (which will be a line), and interpret your results for management.

II. **The brand & package.** Seagrams management proceeded to test the packaging and name, Polaski. The null hypothesis was:

H_0: The taste rating of Polaski vodka poured from a Polaski bottle is at least as   high as the taste rating of Polaski vodka poured from a Stolichnaya bottle. The mean difference between taste ratings of Polaski vodka poured from a Stolichnaya bottle and Polaski vodka poured from the Seagrams bottle bearing the Polaski brand name does not exceed zero.

$$\mu_{Stolichnaya-Polish} \leq 0$$

Alternatively, if the leading brand name and distinctive bottle of the Russian vodka affected taste perceptions, the following could be true:

H_1: The mean difference between taste ratings of Polaski vodka poured from Stolichnaya bottle and Polaski vodka poured from the Seagrams bottle bearing the Polaski brand name is positive.

$$\mu_{Stolichnaya-Polish} > 0$$

 In this second experiment, Polaski samples were presented to participants twice, once poured from a Stolichnaya bottle, and once poured from the Seagrams bottle, bearing the Polaski name. Any minute differences in the actual products were controlled for by using Polaski vodka in both samples. Differences in taste ratings would be attributable to the difference in packaging and brand name.

Thirty new participants again tasted two vodka samples, cleansing their palates with water between tastes. As before, a coin toss decided which bottle the first sample would be poured from: Stolichnaya if heads, Polaski if tails. Each participant rated the taste of the two samples on a ten-point scale.

These data are in **Case 3-3 Polaski Package.**

1. Test the difference in ratings due to packaging, and report your conclusions and p value:
2. Construct a *95% confidence interval* of the difference in ratings due to the packaging, illustrate with a scatterplot (which will be a line), and interpret your results for management.

Chapter 4
Simulation to Infer Future Performance Levels Given Assumptions

Decision makers deal with uncertainty when considering future scenarios. Performance levels depend on multiple influences with uncertain future values. To estimate future performance, managers make assumptions about likely future scenarios and uncertain future values of performance components. To evaluate decision alternatives, the *"best"* and *"worst" case* outcomes are compared. *Monte Carlo simulation* can be used to simulate random samples using decision makers' assumptions about performance driver values, and those random samples can then be combined to produce a distribution of likely future outcomes. Inferences from a simulated distribution of outcomes, given assumptions, can then be made to inform decision making and to adjust assumptions.

4.1 Specify Assumptions Concerning Future Performance Drivers

Example 4.1 A team of young entrepreneurs hatched the idea to offer customized bottled water on campuses. Vending units would offer customers a choice of flavors, essential oils and alkaline drops to produce desired customized water. The **Thirsty** Team partners were concerned that they might either pass up a profitable opportunity or invest in an unprofitable business. From survey research they had determined the average bottles of water demanded per customer per week, which seemed promising. However, they realized that success of the business depended on several other factors, each with uncertain values in the future. An estimate of potential revenues from the first year of operation was desired.

Potential customers, bottles per customer, and revenues, shown in green, below, were outcomes that depended on uncertain factors: the market growth rate, access (restricted or not) to those potential customers, share of customers that the new business could capture, and bottles demanded per customer, shown with blue fill, below. Price would be determined from the access outcome, and weeks in which units were stocked, shown in gold, below, were assumed known. Thus, if the Team were unusually fortunate, the market growth rate would be "best," access would be unrestricted, share of customers would be "best," and bottles demanded per customer would be "best." Alternatively, if the Team were unusually unfortunate, the market growth rate would be "worst," access would be restricted, share of customers would be "worst," and bottles demanded per customer would be "worst."

© Springer Nature Switzerland AG 2019
C. Fraser, *Business Statistics for Competitive Advantage with Excel 2019 and JMP*,
https://doi.org/10.1007/978-3-030-20374-0_4

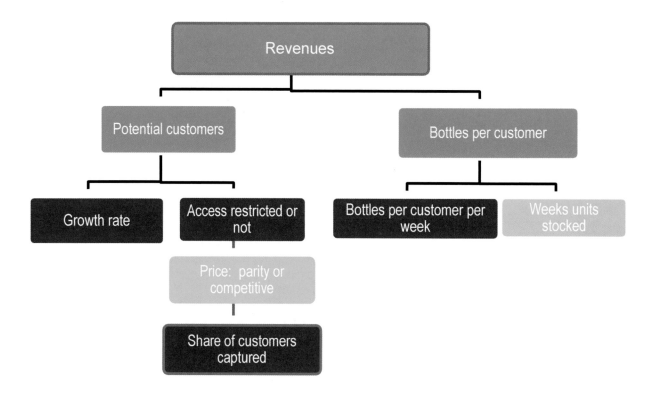

Spreadsheet.   The Team created a spreadsheet linking each of the uncertain revenue influences to annual revenues, given their assumptions about the potential market.

Assumptions concerning possible outcomes for uncertain influences were highlighted in blue, with three scenarios considered: the two extremes, "worst case" and "best case", and the expected, "best guess."   The chance of an uncertain driver level worse than "the worst" or better than "the best" was assumed to be about 5%, making the interval from worst case to best case a 95% confidence interval. Outcomes resulting from uncertain drivers were highlighted in green.

Potential customers in year 1.   Potential customers include faculty, staff, and students on campus, currently 34.1K.

University admissions had been growing between 3 and 4% in recent years, so future growth between 2.5 and 4.5% is anticipated with 95% confidence.   Hiring of faculty and staff is expected to grow at similar rates to accommodate the student population.

The potential market in the first year of business is:

Potential customers (K) = Potential customers last year (K) × *(100% + annual growth%)*

$$= 34.1K × (100\% + annual\ growth\%)$$
$$= 34.1K × 102.5\% = 35.0K \text{ in the worst case,}$$
$$= 34.1K × 104.5\% = 35.6K \text{ in the best case,}$$
$$= 34.1K × 103.5\% = 35.3K \text{ in the expected case.}$$

Table 4.1 Spreadsheet for Bottled Water Revenue

| | | Assumptions | | |
| | | 95% confidence interval | | |
		worst	expected	best
(1)	Potential Customers Last Year (K)	34.1	34.1	34.1
(2)	Annual Growth %	2.5%	3.5%	4.5%
(3)	Potential Customers in Year 1 (K) = (1) × (100% + (2))	35.0	35.3	35.6
(4)	P(Unrestricted Access)	0%	67%	100%
(5)	% Customers w Access = (4) × 100% + (1 - (4)) × 80%	80%	93%	100%
(6)	Customers Accessed (K) = (3) × (5)	28.0	33.0	35.6
(7)	Price per Bottle ($) given Access = $1.5 - (4) × $.25	$1.50	$1.33	$1.25
(8)	Share captured at parity price	10%	15%	20%
(9)	Share captured at competitive price	20%	35%	50%
(10)	Share captured given price = (100%-(4)) × (8) + (4) × (9)	10%	28%	50%
(11)	Customers captured (K) = (6) × (10)	2.8	9.4	17.8
(12)	Bottles sold per customer per week	8	10	12
(13)	Bottles sold per week (K) = (11) × (12)	22.4	93.6	213.8
(14)	Weeks in business	38	38	38
(15)	Bottles sold in year 1 (M) = (13) × (14)/1000	.85	3.6	8.1
(16)	Revenues in Year One ($M) = (7) × (13)	$1.28	$ 4.74	$ 10.2

Access. If the new business is successful in gaining approval to place units in residence and dining halls, 100% of the potential market would have access. Without this approval, restricted access for vending units would reach about 80% of the potential market.

Customers accessed (K) = %Accessed × Potential customers (K)

The Team assumed that chance of unrestricted access, *P(Unrestricted Access)*, was about 67%:

% customers accessed = 67% × 100% + (100% – 67%) × 80% = 93% in the expected case.

Price. Bottled water on campus sells for $1.50 from vending units and in campus eateries. If access is unrestricted, the Team assumes that the volume of business to be great enough to enable volume discounts on plastic bottles and natural flavorings. In this case, a lower price of $1.25 could be charged, which would be assumed to stimulate trial and repeat sales.

Share. With restricted access and a parity price, the Team assumes that the business could capture at least 10% of the market, and possibly as much as 20%. With unrestricted access and the lower price, they assume that at least 20% of the market would be captured, and that 50% share would be possible.

% Customers captured = Share captured × % Customers with access

From their market research, the Team estimates that the average number of bottles of water demanded per customer per week falls within the range of 8 to 12, with 95% confidence, and an average of 10 bottles per customer per week is expected.

Given this level of demand per customer, weekly sales would be

Bottles sold per week (K) = Bottles per customer per week × Customers captured (K)

The Team assumes that the business will operate during the 38 weeks in which classes are in session. Therefore, volume in the first year, in millions (M), would be:

Bottles sold (M) = 38 × Bottles sold per week (K)/ 1000

At those potential volumes, with the two alternative prices, revenue in the first year would be:

Potential revenue ($M) = Price × Bottles sold (M),

4.2 Compare Best and Worst Case Performance Outcomes

Best versus Worst. In the very unfortunate case, all revenue drivers would take on the worst case outcomes (slower growth, restricted access, parity price at $1.50, low 10% share, and low demand per customer per week of 8 bottles) and revenue would be just $1.3M in the first year, making the investment unattractive.

Unfortunate worst case revenues ($M) = 34.1(K) customers
$$\times \,(100\% + 2.5\%) \text{ market growth}$$
$$\times \,80\% \,accessed \;\times\, 10\% \,share$$
$$\times \,\$1.50 \,per \,bottle$$
$$\times \,8 \,bottles \,per \,customer \,per \,week$$
$$\times \,38 \text{ weeks}/1000 = \$1.3M$$

However, in the very fortunate case that all revenue drivers show "best" outcomes (fast market growth, unrestricted access of 100%, competitive price at $1.25, 50% share, high demand of 12 bottles per customer per week), revenue would be $10.2M, making the investment extremely attractive.

Unfortunate worst case revenues ($M) = 34.1(K) customers
$\times$ (100%+4.5%) market growth
$\times$ 100% *accessed* $\times$ 50% *share*
$\times$ $1.25 *per bottle*
$\times$ 12 *bottles per customer per week*
$\times$ 38 weeks/1000 = $10.2M

These extreme outcomes differ widely. How likely are these two extremes?

Based on the Team's assumptions, the chance of the unfortunate worst case outcome is equal to the joint probability assumed for the four uncertain influences.

The chance that annual market growth would be as low as 2.5%, *P(annual growth $\leq$ 2.5%)*, the low end of the 95% confidence interval, is 2.5%.

The chance that share would be as low as 10%, *P(Share $\leq$ 10%)*, the low end of the 95% confidence interval, is 2.5%.

The chance that demand would be as low as 8 bottles per customer per week, *P(demand $\leq$ 8)*, the low end of the 95% confidence interval, is 2.5%.

Therefore, considering the chance of each of these unfortunate outcomes, the chance the revenue could be as low as $1.3M, or lower, is:

P(the worst case outcomes) = *P(annual growth $\leq$ 2.5%)* $\times$ *P(access restricted)*
$\times$ *P(Share $\leq$ 10%)*
$\times$ *P(Demand $\leq$ 8 bottles per customer per week)*
= *.025$\times$ .33 $\times$ .025 $\times$ .025 = 5.2E-06 = .00052%*

Or one in 190,000 (=1/5.2E-06),

The unfortunate worst case is extremely unlikely. The Team could be 95% certain that, given their assumptions, the worst case would not occur.

Based on the Team's assumptions, the chance that the best case outcome would occur is equal to the joint probability of four fortunate circumstances:

The chance that annual market growth would be as high as 4.5%, *P(annual growth $\geq$ 4.5%)*, the high end of the 95% confidence interval, is 2.5%.

The chance that share would be as high as 50%, *P(Share $\geq$ 50%)*, the high end of the 95% confidence interval, is 2.5%.

The chance that demand would be as high as 12 bottles per customer per week, *P(demand $\geq$ 12)*, the high end of the 95% confidence interval, is 2.5%.

Therefore, considering the chance of each of these fortunate outcomes, the chance the revenue could be as high as $10.2M is:

P(best case outcomes) = *P(annual growth $\geq$ 4.5%)* $\times$ *P(access unrestricted)*
$\times$ *P(Share $\geq$ 50%)*
$\times$ *P(Demand $\geq$ 12 bottles per customer per week)*
= *.025*.667*.025*.025 = 1.0E-05 = .0010%7*

Or one in 100,000 (=1/1.0E-05).

The extremely fortunate best case is extremely unlikely, as well. The Team could be 95% certain that the best case outcome would also not occur.

Both the worst case and the best case outcomes were clearly not likely enough to warrant consideration. What range of revenues actually was likely?

To quantify the risks and produce a range of likely revenues that could actually occur, the Team decided to use Monte Carlo simulation. They could then incorporate the uncertainty, given their assumptions, into their forecast. Results would show the distribution of possible outcomes and their likelihoods under the Team's assumptions, and they would be able to determine a 95% confidence interval for possible outcomes.

4.3 Spread and Shape Assumptions Influence Possible Outcomes

Spread and Shape Assumptions. The Team updated their revenue spreadsheet, specifying the spread and shape for each of the uncertain influences in Table 4.2:

Table 4.2 Updated **Spreadsheet for Bottled Water Revenue**

			Assumptions		
		expected	SD = 95% CI /4 or range	Distribution
(1)	Potential Customers Last Year (K)	34.1		
(2)	Annual Growth %	3.5%	2.5% to 4.5%	Normal
(3)	Potential Customers in Year 1 (K) = (1) × (100% + (2))	35.3		
(4)	P(Unrestricted Access)	67%		binomial
(5)	% Customers w Access = (4) × 100% + (1 - (4)) × 80%	93%		
(6)	Customers Accessed (K) = (3) × (5)	33.0		
(7)	Price per Bottle ($) given Access = $1.5 - (4) × $.25	$ 1.33		
(8)	Share captured at parity price	15%	2.5%	Normal
(9)	Share captured at competitive price	35%	7.5%	Normal
(10)	Share captured given price = (100%-(4)) × (8) + (4) × (9)	28%		
(11)	Customers captured (K) = (6) × (10)	9.4		
(12)	Bottles sold per customer per week	10	1	Normal
(13)	Bottles sold per week (K)= (11) × (12)	93.6		
(14)	Weeks in business	38		
(15)	Bottles sold in year 1 (M) = (13) × (14)/1000	3.6		
(16)	Revenues in Year One ($M) = (7) × (15)	$ 4.7		

4.4 Monte Carlo Simulation of the Distribution of Performance Outcomes

The distribution of performance outcomes, *revenues in year 1*, in the **Thirsty** case, depends on the distributions of performance influences. With assumptions for center, spread, and shape of each influence now specified in their spreadsheet, the Team drew simulated samples for each. Formulas in their spreadsheet then combined the simulated samples to produce the distribution of possible revenues in year 1.

Growth possibilities. The Team assumed a normal distribution for growth in the next year within the range of likely possibility, 2.5 to 4.5%. A random sample of 1000 simulated possible growth values was drawn.

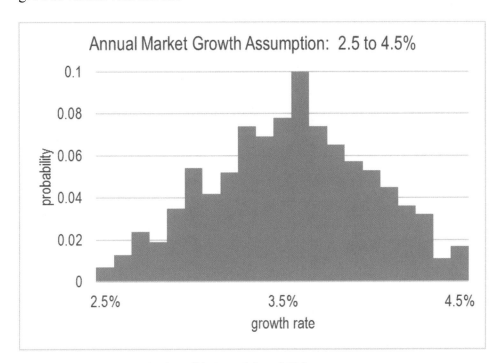

Figure 4.1 Simulated Sample of Possible Annual Growth Values.

With the assumption of a Normal distribution of potential growth rates, the distribution of possible values for potential customers would be Normal.

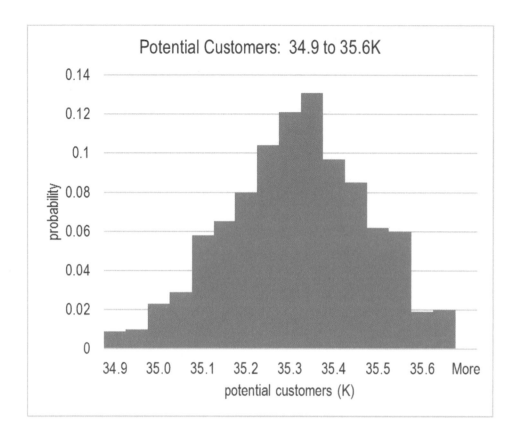

Figure 4.2 Simulated sample of possible potential customers.

Access. A random sample of 1,000 possible access outcomes was drawn, with the probability for a favorable unrestricted outcome set at 67%. With the random sample of access outcomes, possible outcomes for customers accessed is bimodal. The 95% confidence interval is 28 to 36K.

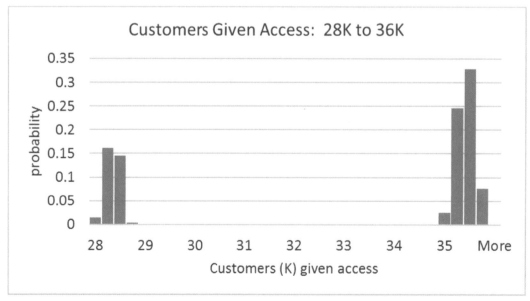

Figure 4.3 Simulated sample of customers accessed.

Share. With restricted access, the parity price of $1.50 would be charged. With unrestricted access, the competitive price of $1.25 could be charged, which the Team assumes would yield a higher share of customers captured. A random sample of 1000 possible shares at each price was drawn, and the share corresponding to the each randomly selected *access* outcome and price was chosen, yielding the bimodal distribution with 95% confidence interval 11% to 50%.

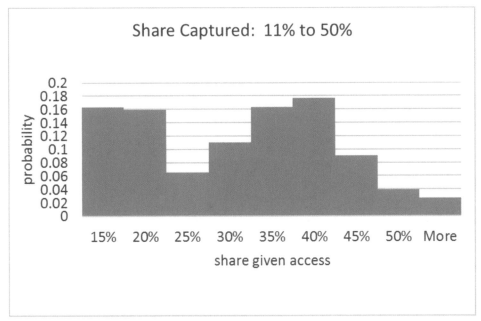

Figure 4.4 Simulated distribution of possible shares.

Combining the random sample of *customers accessed* with the random sample of possible *shares of customers*, given access outcome and price, yields the random sample of *customers captured* with 95% confidence interval 4K to 18K.

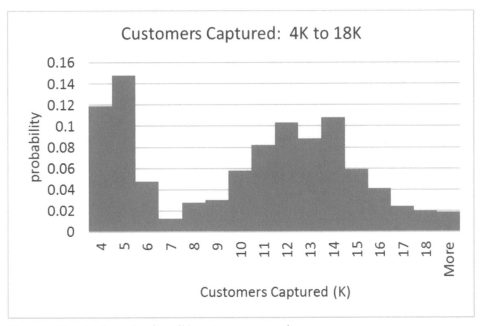

Figure 4.5 Simulated sample of possible customers captured.

Demand per customer. A random sample of 1000 Normally distributed *bottles per customer per week* was drawn, producing a 95% confidence interval 8.1 to 11.9 bottles per customer per week:

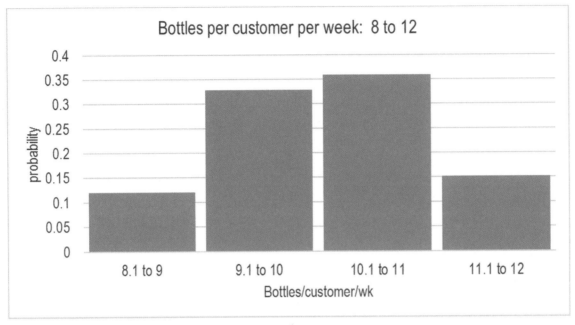

Figure 4.6 Simulated sample of bottles per customer per week.

Bottles sold in year 1. Combining the random sample of *customers captured* with the random sample of *bottles per customer per week* and 38 weeks in the operating year provides the distribution of possible volumes in *bottles sold* in year 1 with 95% confidence interval 1 to 7M.

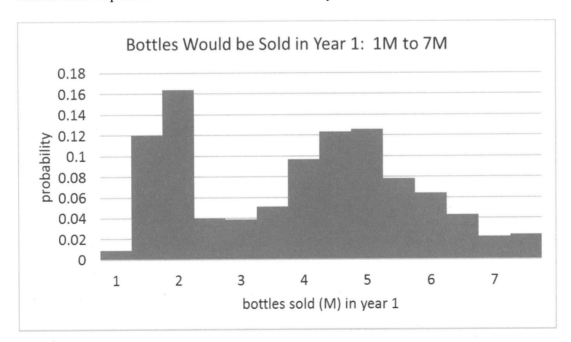

Figure 4.7 Simulated sample of bottles sold in year 1.

Revenues in year 1. Combining the random sample of *bottles sold in year 1* with the sample of prices, given *access* outcomes, the Team could see the distribution of possible *revenues in year 1,* with 95% confidence interval $1.7M to $8.6M.

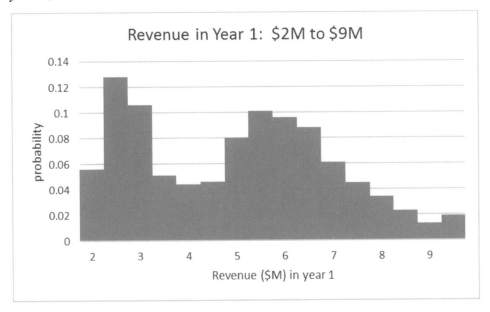

Figure 4.8 Simulated sample of revenues in year 1.

This range in likely *revenues*, $6.9M (= $8.6M - $1.7M) is narrower and, therefore, more informative, than the comparison of the extremely unlikely best and worst case outcomes, whose wider range was $8.9M (= $10.2M - $1.3M).

If their assumptions were correct, the Team could expect business of at least $1.7M. Expected revenues in year 1 are $4.7M, given the Team's assumptions, and the median of possible revenues is $4.9M, given assumptions: There was a 50% chance that the business would produce revenues of at least $4.9M in year 1.

4.5 When Results Are Unbelievable or Too Uncertain, Adjust Assumptions

The range in potential revenues was too large. Their assumptions regarding share of customers captured included wide ranges of possibilities.

To fine-tune, they conducted a concept test. One hundred randomly selected faculty, staff and students were asked how likely they would be to try the custom water at $1.25 per bottle. A second sample of one hundred were asked their intent to try at $1.50 per bottle. 56% reacting to the lower price intend to try, and even more, 62%, of those who heard the higher price intend to try. The higher price signaled quality and enhanced potential share. The Team agreed to price at $1.50, regardless of access.

From market research, it was known that concept test results are biased high. Not everyone who intends to try actually will. Therefore, the Team shrank the 62% potential share to 80%, or 50%. The conservative standard error for a proportion of a sample of one hundred, 5%, would be used to draw a new sample of likely share of customers captured.

After a conversation with the Director of Student Life, the students were assured that access would be unrestricted. The updated spreadsheet is shown in Table 4.3:

Table 4.3 Updated **Spreadsheet for Bottled Water Revenue** given new assumptions

		Assumptions		
		expected	SD = 95% CI /4	Distribution
(1)	Potential Customers Last Year (K)	34.1		
(2)	Annual Growth %	3.5%	2.5% to 4.5%	Normal
(3)	Potential Customers in Year 1 (K) = (1) × (100% + (2))	35.3		
(4)	P(Unrestricted Access)	100%		
(5)	% Customers w Access = (4) × 100% + (1 - (4)) × 80%	100%		
(6)	Customers Accessed (K) = (3) × (5)	35.3		
(7)	Price per Bottle ($)	$ 1.50		
(8)	Share captured	50%	5%	Normal
(9)	Customers captured (K) = (6) × (8)	17.6		
(10)	Bottles sold per customer per week	10	1	Normal
(11)	Bottles sold per week (K)= (9) × (10)	176		
(12)	Weeks in business	38		
(13)	Bottles sold in year 1 (M) = (11) × (12)/1000	6.7		
(14)	Revenues in Year One ($M) = (7) × (13)	$ 10.0		

The Team decided that a five year revenue forecast would be needed in later profit projections. Each year, the market would grow, growing potential revenues. With the adjusted assumptions reflecting more certainty, a revised Monte Carlo analysis was conducted to produce 95% confidence intervals for revenues in Years 1-5, shown in Figure 4.9. The median revenue in year 5, given assumptions is $11.5M. There was a fifty percent chance that revenues would exceed $11.5M, given assumptions. The range of possibilities is now much narrower at $6.6M (=$14.9-$8.3). Comfortable with their adjusted assumptions, and buoyed by this enticing level of potential revenues, the Team decided to proceed to estimate costs and potential profits.

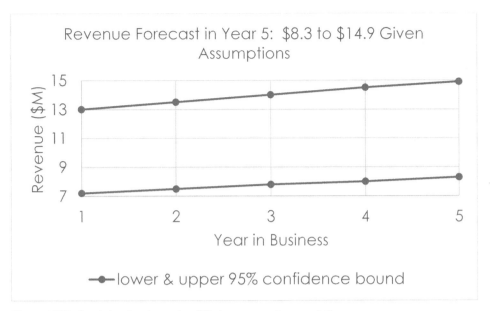

Figure 4.9 Updated simulated sample of likely revenues in years 1-5

4.6 Monte Carlo Simulation Reveals Possible Outcomes Given Assumptions

Decisions concerning investments or allocation of resources depend on inference of likely future performance outcomes. Those performance outcomes hinge on the values that multiple uncertain influences will take on in the future. Monte Carlo simulation offers a view of the possibilities, given the assumptions we make about each of those uncertain influences.

It is naïve and misleading to focus on the all outcomes "best" or "worst" case scenarios. Multiple influences are always at play. The chance that all influences will take on the least favorable value, producing the "worst" case outcome is virtually zero. The chance that all influences will assume the most favorable value is also virtually zero. While these two extreme outcomes provide a range of possibility, it is an exaggerated range. Attractive decision alternatives may appear to be unattractive in a "worst" case. Unattractive decision alternatives may similarly appear to be attractive in a "best" case. It is much more productive and realistic to link performance drivers together in a spreadsheet, specify assumptions about the center, spread, and shape of each influence, then simulate a distribution of likely outcomes for each. Together, these reflections of our assumptions enable us to see the results of those influences on a distribution of future performance outcomes, with corresponding descriptive statistics. With a 95% confidence interval for outcomes, based on assumptions, decision makers are much more likely to choose favorable investments or resource allocations and to avoid unfavorable outcomes.

Monte Carlo simulation is a powerful means to generate data when actual data is not available. . . either because it has not yet occurred, or because it is unaccessible. Simulation offers the additional advantage of allowing us to see how our multiple assumptions will together combine to produce possible outcomes. Decision making hinges on assumptions, and simulation provides a reflection of those assumptions.

Excel 4.1 Set Up a Spreadsheet to Link Simulated Performance Components

Use Team 8's revised assumptions to link revenue influences together in a spreadsheet.

Potential customers. Potential customers are the product of the existing market, 34.1K faculty, staff and students on campus, and the annual growth rate, which has been 3 to 4% in recent years.

Team 8 assumes that growth in the next year could be slightly lower or higher than in recent years, 2.5 to 4.5%.

Generate five random sample of 1000 possible market growth values in years 1 through 5 using Excel's Random Number Generation, specifying a Normal distribution with mean .035 and standard deviation .005 (which, by the Empirical Rule is equal to one quarter of the assumed 95% range of possibilities, .025 to .045). Ask for output in B2.

**Alt AY*n* R OK
5 tab 1000 tab N tab .035 tab .005 tab tab
O tab B2 OK**

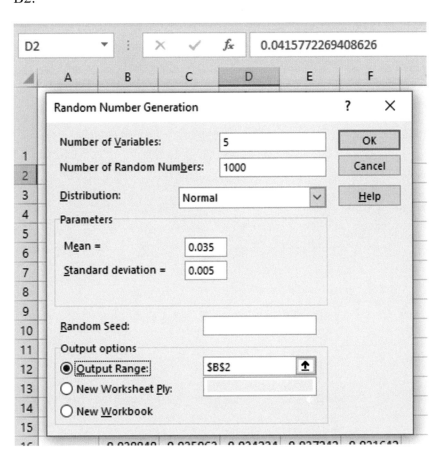

Add labels *market growth 2.5 to 4.5% yr 1* in B1 and in C1:F1 for years 2 through 5.

Make five random samples of *customers* in years 1 through 5 from existing customers, 34.1K, and each of the simulated market growth rates. (Your numbers will differ from those shown here since samples are random.)

Add labels *customers* in years 1 through 5 in columns G:K.

In G2,	**=34.1*(1+B2)**
In H2,	**=(1+C2)*G2**
In H2	**Shift+right right right**
	Cntl+R
In G2	**Cntl+Shift+right**
	Double click the lower right corner to fill in new columns

G2		▾	:	✕	✓	*fx*	=34.1*(1+B2)			

	B	C	D	E	F	G	H	I	J	K
1	market growth 2.5 to 4.5% yr 1	market growth 2.5 to 4.5% yr 2	market growth 2.5 to 4.5% yr 3	market growth 2.5 to 4.5% yr 4	market growth 2.5 to 4.5% yr 5	customers in year 1 (K)	customers in year 2 (K)	customers in year 3 (K)	customers in year 4 (K)	customers in year 5 (K)
2	0.030853	0.03125	0.041577	0.035446	0.033785	35.15209	36.25059	37.75779	39.09617	40.41702
3	0.038338	0.037661	0.04084	0.038073	0.025682	35.40732	36.74079	38.24128	39.69724	40.71674
4	0.027721	0.027916	0.032228	0.036466	0.032756	35.04529	36.02362	37.18459	38.54058	39.80303
5	0.042138	0.026873	0.027931	0.038489	0.043367	35.53692	36.49189	37.51115	38.95491	40.64428

Insert a new column L, with label *Access,* and generate a random sample of *access* outcomes using Excel Random Number Generation. Set the distribution to binomial and the p value to .67, with number of trails at 1. Direct output to L2.	**Alt AY*n* R OK** **1 tab 1000 tab B B tab 1 tab .67 tab tab O tab L2 OK**

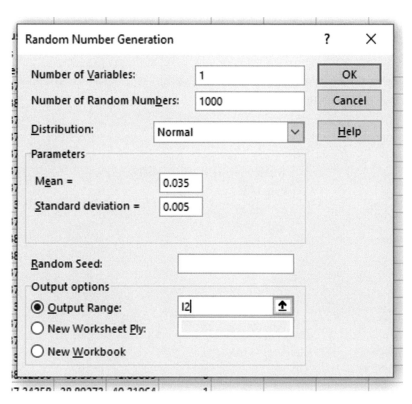

If access is restricted, dorms would be off limits, and the Team assumes that only 80% of potential customers could be reached. Find the sample of *customers (K) with access* in years 1 through 5 from the product of access and customers. Add labels in columns M:Q.

In M2, locking the column reference to L with Fn 4 Fn 4 Fn 4, In M2,	**=(.8+.2*$L2)*G2** **Shift+right right right right** **Cntl+R** Click the lower right corner to fill in the column

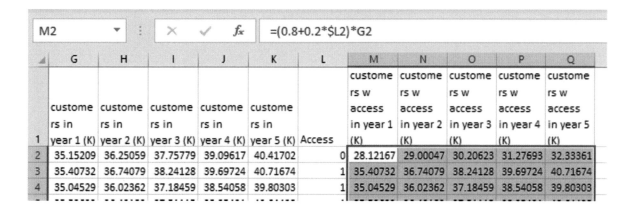

The concept test led to revision of share captured to 50%. The conservative standard error for a proportion of the concept test sample of one hundred is 5% (=.5/sqrt(N)),

Generate a sample of 1000 Normally distributed *shares* in column R, with mean .5 and standard deviation .05.

Insert new columns S:W, *customers captured* in years one through five with values for *customers given access* and *share given access* in R.

In S2,locking the column reference with Fn 4 Fn 4 Fn 4	=M2*$R2
From S2,	**Shift+right right right right** **Cntl+R** Double click lower right corner to fill columns

M25	▼	⋮	×	✓	*fx*	=(0.8+0.2*$L25)*G25				

	M	N	O	P	Q	R	S	T	U	V	W
	custome rs w access in year 1 (K)	custome rs w access in year 2 (K)	custome rs w access in year 3 (K)	custome rs w access in year 4 (K)	custome rs w access in year 5 (K)	share	Custome rs captured year 1 (K)	Custome rs captured year 2 (K)	Custome rs captured year 3 (K)	Custome rs captured year 4 (K)	Custome rs captured year 5 (K)
2	28.12167	29.00047	30.20623	31.27693	32.33361	0.51273	14.41882	14.8694	15.48763	16.03661	16.5784
3	35.40732	36.74079	38.24128	39.69724	40.71674	0.467383	16.54876	17.172	17.87331	18.5538	19.0303
4	ᴬᴱ ᴼᴬᴱᴿᴬ	ᴬᴱ ᴼᴿᴿᴬᴿᴬ	ᴬᴿ ᴬᴼᴬᴱᴿ	ᴿᴬ ᴱᴬᴼᴱᴬ	ᴬᴼ ᴬᴬᴬᴬᴬ	ᴬ ᴬᴱᴼᴬᴬ	ᴬᴱ ᴬᴬᴼᴬᴿ	ᴬᴱ ᴼᴼᴼᴬᴬ	ᴬᴿ ᴬᴿ	ᴬᴼ ᴼᴼᴼᴬᴬ	ᴬᴼ ᴿᴼᴿᴼ

Demand per customer. From earlier market research, the Team believes that average bottles demanded per customer per week falls within the range 8 to 12, with 95% confidence. The Team assumes that demand is Normally distributed, with standard deviation equal to one quarter of the 95% confidence interval:
SD = (12-8)/4 = 1. Generate a sample of 1000 Normally distributed levels for *bottles per customer per week* in column X with mean 10 and standard deviation 1.

Insert new columns Y:AC *revenues ($M)* in years one through five, from the *price ($)* of $1.50, *customers captured, bottles per customer per week*, and the assumed 38 weeks per year. Divide by 1000 to produce *revenues* in million dollars.

In Y2, locking the column reference to X with Fn 4 Fn 4 Fn 4	=1.5*$X2*S2*38/1000
In Y2	**Shift+right right right right** **Cntl+R** Double click lower right corner to down fill

	Y2		▼	:	× ✓	f_x		=1.5*$X2*S2*38/1000			

▲	S	T	U	V	W	X	Y	Z	AA	AB	AC
1	Customers captured year 1 (K)	Customers captured year 2 (K)	Customers captured year 3 (K)	Customers captured year 4 (K)	Customers captured year 5 (K)	bottles per customer per week	revenues year 1 ($M)	revenues year 2 ($M)	revenues year 3 ($M)	revenues year 4 ($M)	revenues year 5 ($M)
2	14.4188	14.8694	15.4876	16.0366	16.5784	11.117	9.13677	9.4223	9.81405	10.1619	10.5052
3	16.5488	17.172	17.8733	18.5538	19.0303	12.6201	11.9043	12.3527	12.8571	13.3466	13.6894
4	16.4461	16.9052	17.45	18.0863	18.6788	9.88111	9.26281	9.52139	9.82825	10.1866	10.5203
5	16.4001	16.8408	17.3112	17.9775	18.7571	11.3348	10.5958	10.8805	11.1844	11.6149	12.1186

Find the *95% prediction interval bounds* for revenues in years one through five in rows 1003 and 1004.

In Y1003,	**=PERCENTILE(Y2:Y1001,.025**
In Y 1004,	**=PERCENTILE(Y2:Y1001,.975)**
In Y1003,	**Shift+right right right right**
	Cntl+R

To plot the five year forecast, add year number in row 1002.

	Y1003		▼	:	× ✓	f_x	=PERCENTILE(Y1:Y1001,0.025)		

▲	X	Y	Z	AA	AB	AC	AD
1	bottles per customer per week	revenues year 1 ($M)	revenues year 2 ($M)	revenues year 3 ($M)	revenues year 4 ($M)	revenues year 5 ($M)	
1000	12.553	13.3982	13.9622	14.5138	15.085	15.6296	
1001	10.3536	11.3511	11.7884	12.2009	12.6569	13.0409	
1002	year	1	2	3	4	5	
1003	lower 95%	6.35667	6.56769	6.83517	7.06144	7.26637	
1004	upper 95%	12.3837	12.8428	13.276	13.7437	14.2432	
1005							

To illustrate the forecast, select the years and prediction interval bounds, with labels, and insert a scatterplot with **Alt ND.**

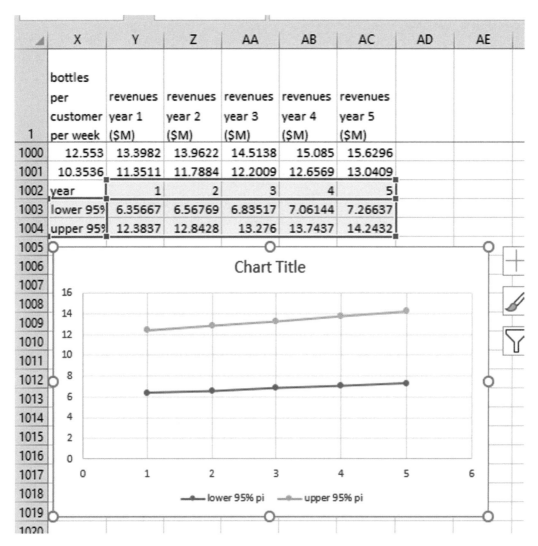

	X	Y	Z	AA	AB	AC	AD	AE
1	bottles per customer per week	revenues year 1 ($M)	revenues year 2 ($M)	revenues year 3 ($M)	revenues year 4 ($M)	revenues year 5 ($M)		
1000	12.553	13.3982	13.9622	14.5138	15.085	15.6296		
1001	10.3536	11.3511	11.7884	12.2009	12.6569	13.0409		
1002	year	1	2	3	4	5		
1003	lower 95%	6.35667	6.56769	6.83517	7.06144	7.26637		
1004	upper 95%	12.3837	12.8428	13.276	13.7437	14.2432		

Add axes labels, adjust the axes to make good use of white space, change the color of one of the prediction interval bounds to match the other, and replace the title with a standalone title.

Lab 4-1 Inference: Bottled Water Revenues

After conducting Monte Carlo analysis, the Thirsty Team elected to adjust their assumption to produce a narrower, more informative range of potential revenues. They also decided that a five year revenue forecast would enhance later profit forecasts. Going forward, their assumptions are:

The potential market, now 34.1K, will grow 2.5% to 4.5% annually in the next five years.
There is a 100% chance of unrestricted access.
Share of customers captured will be 40% to 60%.
Customers consume 8 to 12 bottles per week.
The vending units will be stocked 38 weeks in a year.
Bottles will be priced at $1.50.

Conduct a Monte Carlo simulation to find the 95% confidence interval for revenues in years 1-5..

(1) Projected market. Generate five random samples of 1,000 possible market growth rates in years 1-5. From those possible growth rates, find the number of customers in the market in years 1-5.

(2) Projected customers captured. Generate a random sample of 1,000 possible shares of customers. From possible shares and customers (1), find the number of customers captured in years 1-5.

(3) Projected bottles sold. Generate a random sample of 1,000 possible weekly consumption values (bottles). From possible consumption levels and customers captured (2), find bottles sold in years 1-5.

(5) Projected revenues. From projected bottles sold (3), find projected revenues in years 1-5. Plot the 95% confidence intervals for projected revenue by year:,

Case 4-1 Inference: Dell Android Smartphone Plans.

Managers at Dell are considering a joint venture with a Chinese firm to launch a new Android platform smartphone.

As of the first quarter in 2017, Samsung and Apple control 38% of the market, though 39% of the market remains to be captured by a major vendor. The third, fourth and fifth place vendors each control six to ten percent of the market

	shipments (M)		2017Q1 growth over		market share	
	2017Q1	2016Q1	2016Q1		2017Q1	2016Q1
Samsung	80.2	79.3		1%	23%	24%
Apple	50.6	51.3		-1%	15%	15%
Huawei	34.4	28.0		23%	10%	8%
OPPO	25.8	19.6		31%	8%	6%
Vivo	18.9	14.7		29%	6%	4%
Others	134.3	140.2		-4%	39%	42%
Total	344.3	333.0		3%		

Dell managers agree that 6% is a reasonable estimate of the new smartphone's potential share in 2022, though share could be as low as 4% or as high as 8%.

Possible 2022Q1 Dell shares. Use Excel to create a sample of 1000 possible Dell smartphone shares from a Normal distribution with mean equal to management's best guess of 6%.

To choose a standard deviation for your simulation, estimate the standard deviation of Dell smartphone share by dividing the likely range by 4, following the Empirical Rule. Managers want to estimate potential shipments of Dell smartphones in 2022Q1 with 95% confidence, given assumptions. Shipments of Dell smartphones would be driven by world smartphone shipments, annual growth in world shipments, and Dell smartphone share.

Possible annual market growth rates. Management assumes that annual growth will average 4% in each of the next five years, though annual growth could be as low as 3%, and possibly as high as 5%.

Use Excel to draw a random sample of 1000 Normally distributed growth rates for 2018Q1, 2019Q1, 2020Q1, 2021Q1 and 2022Q1.

Possible 2022Q1 world shipments. Find the 2022Q1 possible world smartphone shipments from 2017Q1 world smartphone shipments and the samples of simulated annual growth rates in 2018Q1 through 2022Q1.

1. Illustrate your assumptions regarding total world shipments in Q1 with a scatterplot of total world shipments, Q1, for years 2016-2022, showing upper and lower 95% prediction interval bounds for 2022.

2. The 95% confidence interval for total world shipments in 2022Q1: ____ to ____

3. **Possible 2022Q1 Dell smartphone shipments.** Use your samples of simulated Dell smartphone share and 2022Q1 World smartphone shipments to find the distribution of possible Dell smartphone shipments in 2022Q1.

   The 95% confidence interval for Dell smartphone shipments in 2022Q1: ___ to ___

4. Several conservative managers worry that Dell smartphone share could be 4% or less and annual growth in world shipments of smartphones could stagnate at 3% or less, producing a forecast of Dell smartphone shipments of 14M or fewer.

   What is the chance that this unfortunate "worst case" could occur? _____

Case 4-2 Can Whole Foods Hold On?

Organic food and nonfood sales were $43B in 2015, and had grown to **$47B** in 2016, annual growth of 8.4%. *Analysts forecast annual growth rates between 5 and 9% for years 2017 through 2020.*

In 2016, WFM added 25 new stores. WFM 2016 revenue grew to $15.7B from 456 stores, with average sales per store falling by 4.6%. *Managers assume that average sales per store would continue to fall by 4 to 6% annually in years 2017 through 2020.*

WFM share of organic food and nonfood sales in a given year depends on organic food and nonfood sales, the number of WFM stores, and average sales per WFM store:

WFM share$_t$ = WFM stores$_t$ × sales per WFM store$_t$ / organic food and nonfood sales$_t$

In 2020, organic food and nonfood sales will depend on the annual organic food and nonfood growth rates:

$$Organic\ food\ and\ nonfood\ sales_{2020} = (1 + organic\ food\ and\ nonfood\ growth\ rate_{2017})$$
$$\times (1 + organic\ food\ and\ nonfood\ growth\ rate_{2018})$$
$$\times (1 + organic\ food\ and\ nonfood\ growth\ rate_{2019})$$
$$\times (1 + organic\ food\ and\ nonfood\ growth\ rate_{2020})$$
$$\times organic\ food\ and\ nonfood\ sales_{2016}$$

2018 WFM stores depend on the annual WFM growth in number of stores, 6 to 10% in recent years, but with growth slowing more recently. WFM expects to continue aggressively adding stores, with an expected growth rate of 4 to 6% per year.

$$WFM\ stores_{2020} = (1 + WFM\ nstore\ growth\ rate_{2017}) \times (1 + WFM\ nstore\ growth\ rate_{2018})$$
$$\times (1 + WFM\ nstore\ growth\ rate_{2019}) \times (1 + WFM\ nstore\ growth\ rate_{2020})$$
$$\times WFM\ stores_{2016}$$

2020 Sales per WFM store depend on annual growth in average store sales, -4 to -6% considered possible:

$$Sales\ per\ WFM\ store_{2020} = (1 + same\ store\ sales\ growth_{2017})$$
$$\times (1 + same\ store\ sales\ growth_{2018})$$
$$\times (1 + same\ store\ sales\ growth_{2019})$$
$$\times (1 + same\ store\ sales\ growth_{2020})$$
$$\times sales\ per\ WFM\ store_{2016}$$

Historical data are in **4 WFM.xlsx**.

In 2016, WFM held 33% share of the organic food and nonfood market, down from 35% in 2015. Can WFM hold on?

Forecast WFM's market share of the organic food sales market in 2020.

A. Illustrate your assumptions:

1. Present a scatterplot of *organic food sales* in years 2015, 2016 and 2020, showing your upper and lower 95% prediction interval for 2020.

2. Present scatterplots of *number of WFM stores, sales per WFM store* and *WFM sales,* for years 2012 through 2020, showing your upper and lower 95% prediction interval for 2020.

B. Your forecasts of WFM share, given assumptions

1. Your 2020 forecast of WFM share, with 95% confidence: _____ to _____

2. Present a scatterplot of *WFM share* in years 2015-2020, showing your upper and lower 95% prediction interval for 2020.

C. Likelihood of an unfortunate outcome

A conservative manager forecasts that, in the "worst case," *WFM share_{2020}* could be 22% or lower. Based on your assumptions, how likely is such an unfortunate outcome?

Chapter 5
Simple Regression

Regression analysis is a powerful tool for quantifying the influence of a continuous, *independent, driver* x on a continuous *dependent, performance* variable y. Often we are interested in both explaining how an independent decision variable x drives a dependent performance variable y and also in predicting performance y to compare the impact of alternate decision variable x values. X is also called a *predictor,* since from x we can predict y. Regression allows us to do both: quantify the nature and extent of influence of a performance driver x and predict performance or response y from knowledge of the driver x.

With regression analysis, we can statistically address these questions:

- Is variation in a dependent, performance, response variable y influenced by variation in an independent variable x?

If x is a driver of y, with regression, we can answer these questions:

- What percent of variation in performance y can be accounted for with variation in driver x?
- If driver x changes by one unit, what range of response can we expect in performance y?
- At a specified level of the driver x, what range of performance levels y are expected?

Regression analysis is used with cross sectional data, to explain differences, or variation within a population, and to identify drivers, and with time series data, to explain changes in a population over time, identify drivers and/or to forecast future values. In this chapter, simple regression based on stable, linear trend is introduced, as the means to make long range forecasts with time series data.

In some circumstances, managers want to estimate the *trend*, or stable level of growth in performance, in order to produce a longer term forecast. Regression allows estimation of trend, using the time period as the independent variable. Forecasting based on trend is *naïve,* because the focus is not on understanding why performance varies across time periods, but only on forecasting what future performance would look like if future performance resembled past performance.

Forecasting based on trend is quick and easy and provides a view of the future, under the status quo. In chapter 11, multiple regression models with cross sectional data will be introduced for cases in which explanation of variation and identification of drivers is desired. In chapter 12, more sophisticated forecasting, which includes explanation of variation across time periods, will be introduced. In addition to the introduction of simple regression, this chapter also includes exploration of the link between correlation and simple linear regression, since the two are closely related.

© Springer Nature Switzerland AG 2019
C. Fraser, *Business Statistics for Competitive Advantage with Excel 2019 and JMP,*
https://doi.org/10.1007/978-3-030-20374-0_5

5.1 The Simple Linear Regression Equation Describes the Line Relating an Independent Variable to Performance

Regression produces an equation for the line which best relates changes or differences in a continuous, dependent performance variable y to changes or differences in a continuous, independent driver x. This line comes closest, in terms of squared distances, of each of the points in a scatterplot of y and x:

$$\hat{y} = b_0 + b_1 \times x$$

Where $\hat{y}$ is the expected value of the dependent performance, or response, variable,
       called "*y hat*",
    x is the value of an independent variable, decision variable, or driver,
    b_0 is the *intercept* estimate, which is the expected value of y when x is zero,

    b_1 is the estimated *slope* of the regression line, which indicates the expected

       change in performance $\hat{y}$ in response to a unit change from the driver's
       average $\bar{x}$

In the context of a naïve model based on stable, linear trend, x is a measure of time, such as quarter, q, or year, t. The slope, b_1, estimates average change per time period. A simple regression model to estimate trend and to forecast is written with a subscript to identify time periods:

$$\hat{y}_t = b_0 + b_1 \times t$$

Example 5.1 Concha y Toro. Concha y Toro vineyards, a Chilean global multinational, is the largest producer of wines in Latin America. The firm produces and exports wine to 135 markets in Europe, North, Central and South American, Asia, and Africa. Concha y Toro has been successful in developing wine varieties that appeal to the unique tastes of the various global segments.

    In 2010, the Board of Directors was reviewing performance. While the firm's wines had earned multiple distinctions, export revenues had grown only 8% in the past year, which was a startling slow down, relative to revenue growth as high 45% in earlier years. The Board needed a forecast of export revenues. The modeling team elected to estimate the trends in volume in the three largest export regions, Europe, the U.S, and Asia.

5.2 Hide the Two Most Recent Datapoints to Validate a Time Series Model

In most cases, before a time series model is used to forecast future performance, it is validated:

- the two most recent observations are hidden while the model is built,
- the model equation is used to forecast performance in those two most recent periods,

- model prediction intervals are compared with actual performance values in those two most recent periods, and if the prediction intervals contain actual performance values, this is evidence that the model has *predictive validity* and can be reliably used to forecast unknown performance in future periods.

The process for naïve time series models based on trend is shown in Figure 5.1.

In the U.S. market, volume had grown consistently, as Figure 5.2 illustrates. While volume growth elsewhere was celebrated, there was concern that growth in the U.S. had fallen short of that desired. Wine consumption in the U.S. was growing faster than in other global regions, presenting an opportunity that could not be ignored.

In order to inform future discussions, regressions were used to estimate the annual trends in sales volume for the three major export regions. Trends were estimated with the following model:

$$sales\ \hat{volume}(ML)_{i,t} = b_{0_i}(ML) + b_{1_i}(\frac{ML}{t}) \times t$$

where i is the i'th global region, and t is the year.

The slope estimates, b_{1_i} will provide estimates of average annual changes in sales volume.

The null and alternate hypotheses which the modelling team wanted to test are:

H_0: Average annual growth in export volume β_1 is less than or equal to zero.
H_1: Average annual growth in export volume β_1 is greater than zero.

Regression results, shown in Table 5.1, suggest that sales volume in the U.S. is increasing annually, since the slope estimate (coefficient for year t) is positive at .118 ML per year.

Model Building Process
Trend from Time Series

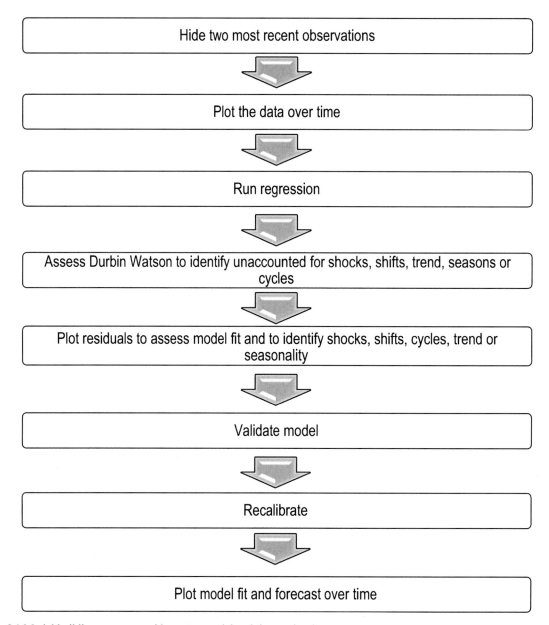

Figure 5.1 Model building processes with a naïve model and time series data

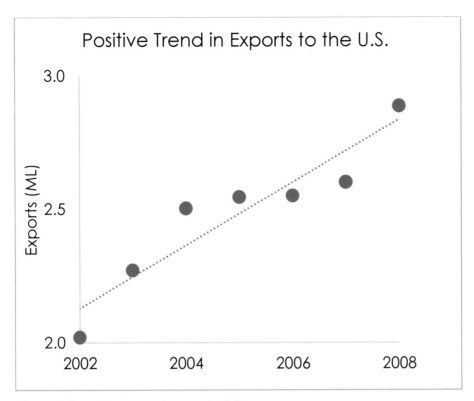

Figure 5.2 Growth in export volumes to the U.S.

Table 5.1 Regression of U.S. export volume by year

Regression Statistics: U.S. sales (ML)					
R Square	.88				
Standard Error	.104				
Observations	7				

ANOVA					
	df	SS	MS	F	Significance F
Regression	1	.391	.391	36.1	.0018
Residual	5	.054	.011		
Total	6	.445			

	Coefficients	Standard Error	t Stat	p value	Lower 95%	Upper 95%
Intercept	-230	39	-5.9	.0019	-336	-133
t	.12	.02	6.0	.0018	.068	.169

The average annual increase in export volume to the U.S. is .12(ML) per year. Expected annual exports to the U.S. $\hat{y}$ increase at a constant rate of .12ML per year.

Because variation in revenues y seems to be related linearly to variation in year t, the linear regression line is a good summary of the data:

$$\hat{exports}(ML)_t = -230(ML) + .12(ML/t) \times t$$

5.3 Test and Infer the Slope

Because the true trend, or average annual change β_1 in exports y is unknown, this *slope*, or *coefficient*, is estimated from a sample. This estimate b_1 and its sample standard error s_{b_1} are also used to test the hypothesis that the trend drives variation in y:

H_0: The regression slope is less than or equal to zero: $\beta_1 \leq 0$.

Alternatively,

H_1: The regression slope is greater than zero: $\beta_1 > 0$

Managers know that the trend is exports is positive. In many instances, including this example, from experience or logic, we know the likely direction of influence. In those instances, the alternate hypothesis requires a *one tail* test. This one sided alternate hypothesis describes an upward slope. A similar alternate hypothesis could be used when logic or experience suggests a downward slope.

Sample slopes b_1 are Normally distributed around the population slope β_1, which is less than or equal to zero, under the null hypothesis. Whether the sample slope is consistent with the null hypothesis depends on its distance from zero and dispersion of the sample slope distribution. Figure 5.3 illustrates two possibilities. The sample slope to the left is "close" to the hypothetical population slope of zero. The sample slope on the right is "far" from the hypothetical population slope, providing evidence that the population slope is unlikely to be zero.

To judge whether a sample slope is close or far from zero, the *standard error of the slope* is needed. The slope standard error depends on unexplained variation unrelated to trend, the sample size N, and population dispersion, and is equal to .020 ML per year for the trend in U.S. export volume:

$$s_{b_1} = \sqrt{\frac{\sum(y - \hat{y})^2 / (N-2)}{\sum(X - \bar{X})^2}} = .020$$

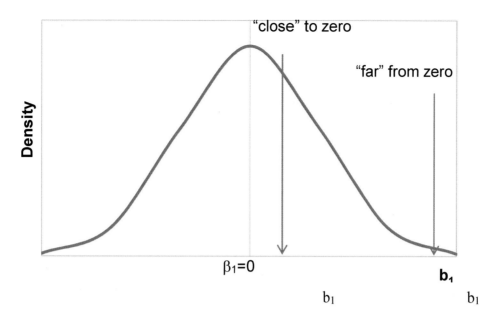

Figure 5.3 *Distribution of sample slope under the null hypothesis*

To form a conclusion about the significance of the slope, calculate the number of standard errors which separate the slope estimate b_1 from zero.

$$t_{N-2} = b_1/s_{b_1} = .12 / .020 = 6.0$$

The slope estimate is six standard errors greater than zero.

From both experience and logic, managers had a good idea that the trend in U.S. export volume had been positive, so a *one tail* test is appropriate, corresponding to the alternate hypothesis is that the slope is positive. Figure 5.4 illustrates *p values* for *t* statistics for a sample of 7 years. A *t* value of 6.0 is far from zero, with corresponding *p value* .0092.

There is a very small chance that we would observe the sample data were the trend not positive. From our sample evidence, we reject the null hypothesis of a flat or negative slope and conclude that the trend is positive.

Excel does these calculations. The slope and intercept estimates are labeled *Coefficients* in Excel, shown in Table 5.1, on the left. To the right of the coefficient estimates are their standard errors, *t* statistics, and *p values*, as well as 95% confidence intervals for the population intercept and slope.

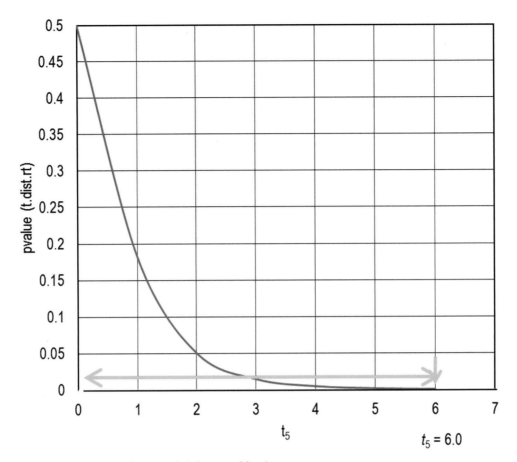

Figure 5.4 *p values for a one tail t test with 5 degrees of freedom*

Excel assumes that we have no prior information concerning the direction of driver influence, and so Excel provides a *two tail p value.* Divide the Excel *p value* by 2 to find the *one tail p value.*

There is a 95% chance that the true population slope will fall within $t_{.05,(N-2)}$ standard errors of the slope estimate:

$$b_1 - t_{.05,50} \times s_{b_1} < \beta_1 < b_1 + t_{.05,50} \times s_{b_1}$$

$$.12 - 2.57 \times .020 < \beta_1 < .12 + 2.57 \times .020$$

$$.068 < \beta_1 < .169$$

The expected annual increase in U.S. export volume is .068 (ML) to .169 (ML).

5.4 The Regression Standard Error Reflects Model Precision

Using the regression formula, we can predict the expected volume $\hat{y}$ for in a given year t.
The differences between expected and actual revenue are the *residuals* or error*s*. Residuals from these four years are shown in Table 5.2 and Figure 5.5.

Table 5.2 Residuals from the regression line

year	Actual exports(ML)	Expected exports (ML)	Residual (ML)
T	y	$\hat{y}$	$e = y - \hat{y}$
2005	2.55	2.48	.063
2006	2.55	2.60	-.061
2007	2.60	2.72	-.118
2008	2.89	2.84	.050

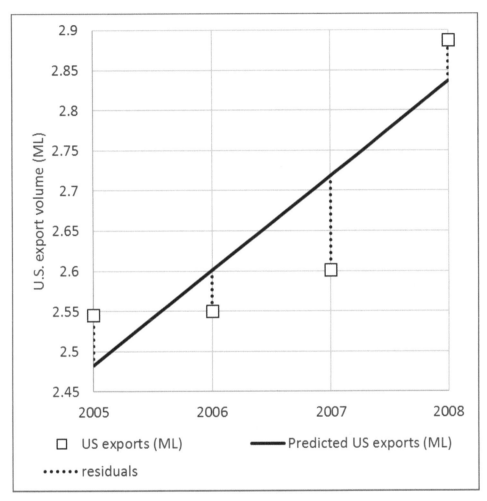

Figure 5.5 Four residuals from the regression line

The *Sum of Squared Errors* in a regression,

$$SSE = \sum e_i^2 = \sum (y_i - \hat{y})^2 = \sum (y_i - b_0 - b_1 \times X_i)^2$$

$$= .054$$

is the portion of total variation in the dependent variable, *SST*, which remains unexplained after accounting for the impact of variation in *X*. In this case, *SSE* is .054. The *Least Squares* regression line is the line with the smallest SSE of all possible lines relating *x* to *y*.

The regression *standard error,* equal to the square root of *Mean Square Error,* reflects the precision of the regression equation.

$$s_{\hat{y}} = \sqrt{SSE/(N-2)} = \sqrt{MSE}$$

In the Concha y Toro U.S. export volume regression, the standard error is .104(ML):

$$s_{\hat{y}} = \sqrt{.054/5} \qquad = \sqrt{.011} \qquad = .104(ML)$$

To find prediction intervals for a particular value of *x,* in this case, a particular year *t,* the regression standard error must be modified. The prediction intervals near the mean of *x,* of the mean year *t,* in this case will be narrower and more certain than prediction intervals farther from the mean $\bar{x}$ or $\bar{t}$. equal to 2005, in this case. This adjustment uses T, the total number of observations in the validation model (without the two most recent years), 7, in this case:

$$se_t = se_{regression} \times \sqrt{1 + \frac{1}{T} + \frac{(t-\tilde{t})^2/(T-1)}{\Sigma(t-\tilde{t})^2}}$$

$$= .104(ML) \times \sqrt{1 + \frac{1}{7} + \frac{(t-2005)^2/(7-1)}{28}}$$

$$= .104(ML) \times \sqrt{1.143 + \frac{(t-2005)^2/6}{28}}$$

The forecast *margin of error* is approximately twice the standard error:

$$me_t = t_{.05,residual\ df} \times s_{\hat{y}_t}$$

where the residual degrees of freedom are N – 2, or T-2 in this case, for a regression model with one driver (and the intercept).

The margin of error in the Concha y Toro U.S. export volume regression is:

$$me_t = 2.57 \times s_{\hat{y}_t}$$

We expect forecasts to be no further from actual performance than the margin of error 95% of the time.

5.5 Prediction Intervals Enable Validation

95% prediction intervals

$$\hat{y} \pm me_t$$

for U.S. export volumes by year are shown in Table 5.3 and Figure 5.6. Note that though data from 2009 and 2010 were not used to fit the model, the 95% prediction intervals correctly forecast actual exports in 2009 and 2010. We have evidence that the model has predictive validity.

Table 5.3 Individual 95% prediction intervals

Year	expected exports (ML)	standard error	margin of error me	95% prediction interval	
t	$\hat{y}$	$s_{\hat{y}_t}$	$t_{.05,5} \times s_{\hat{y}}$	$\hat{y} \pm me$	
2008	2.84	.13	.294	2.51	3.16
2009	2.95	.12	.300	2.60	3.31
2010	3.07	.11	.307	2.69	3.45

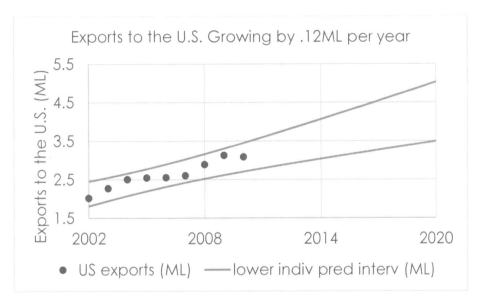

Figure 5.6 95% prediction intervals for annual U.S. export volume.

5.6 *Rsquare* Summarizes Strength of the Hypothesized Linear Relationship and *F* Tests Its Significance

ANOVA, an acronym for *Analysis of Variance*, focuses on explained and unexplained variation. The difference, SST - SSE, called the *Regression Sum of Squares, SSR*, or *Model Sum of Squares*, is the portion of total variation in y influenced by variation in x.

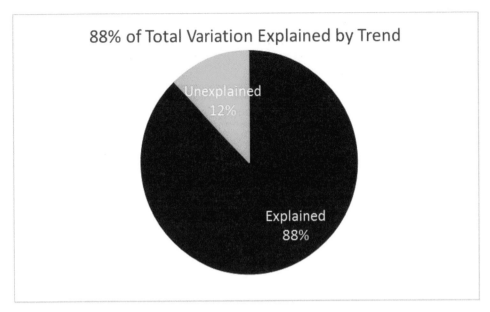

Figure 5.7 ANOVA showing explained variation, SSR, and unexplained variation, SSE

RSquare is the ratio of explained to total variation:

$$RSquare = SSR/SST$$

RSquare reflects the power of the driver *x* in explaining variation in performance *y*. At the extremes, *RSquare* is zero, if no variation is explained, and one, if all of the variation is explained. In the Concha y Toro example of U.S. export volume, *RSquare* is .88, or 88%.

$$RSquare = .391 / .445 = .88$$

Trend in U.S. export volume accounts for 88% of the variation. Other factors account for the remaining 12%.

A test of the null hypothesis that the independent variable does not influence the dependent variable in the population is equivalent to a test that RSquare is equal to zero, and no variation in the dependent variable is explained by variation in the independent variable:

H_0: Trend *t* does not drive variation in *y*, *U.S. export volume,*

OR H_0: *RSquare* = 0

Versus

H_1: Trend *t* does drive variation in *y*, U.S. export volume,

OR H_1: *RSquare* > 0

Adding independent variables to a model adds explanatory power. Explained variation, *SSR*, is divided by the number of independent variables for the hypothesis test on variation explained per independent variable. Unexplained variation, *SSE*, is divided by the sample size, less the number of variables in the model (including the intercept), for the relevant comparison of variation explained per independent variable, *MSR*, to unexplained variation for a model of given size and sample size, *MSE*. This ratio of mean squares is distributed as an *F*, and the particular *F* distribution is indexed by model size and sample size. The numerator degrees of freedom is the number of predictors and the denominator degrees of freedom is the sample size, less the number of variables in the model (including the intercept).

$$F_{regression\ df, residual\ df} = \frac{SSR/regression\ df}{SSE/residual\ df} = \frac{MSR}{MSE}$$

The *F* statistic can also be determined with *RSquare*:

$$F_{regression\ df, residual\ df} = \frac{RSquare/regression\ df}{(1 - RSquare)/residual\ df}$$

In Concha y Toro U.S. exports volumes, a relatively large proportion of variation is explained by just one driver, the year *t*, making the *F* statistic relatively large:

$$F_{1,50} = \frac{.391/1}{.054/5} \qquad = \frac{.391}{.011} = 36.1$$

OR

$$= \frac{.878/1}{(1-.878)/5} \qquad = \frac{.878}{.024} = 36.1$$

F distributions are skewed with minimum value of zero. *p values* for *F* statistics with 1 and 5 degrees of freedom are shown in Figure 5.8. In the Concha y Toro U.S. export volume regression, the $F_{1,5}$ equal to 36.1 has a *p value* < .0018, providing evidence that the sample data would not be likely to be observed if *RSquare* were zero.

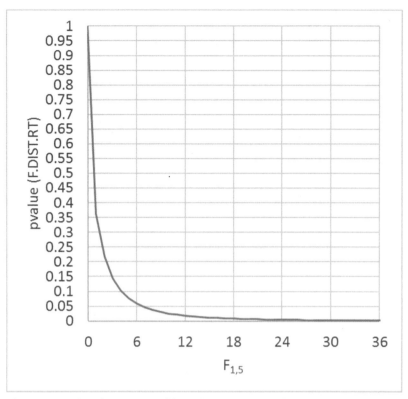

Figure 5.8 *p values* from *F* tests with one independent variable and sample size 5.

In Excel, regression model fit and ANOVA statistics appear in two tables. *RSquare* and the *standard error* appear in SUMMARY OUTPUT, which is followed by the ANOVA table with Regression, Residual, and Total *SS* (*SSR, SSE,* and *SST*), Regression and Residual MS (*MSR* and *MSE*), *F*, and *significance F* (*p value* for the *F* test). The SUMMARY OUTPUT and ANOVA tables from Excel for the Concha y Toro regression are shown in Table 5.4.

Table 5.4 Model summary of fit and ANOVA table

SUMMARY OUTPUT					
Regression Statistics					
RSquare	.88				
Standard Error	.104				
Observations	7				
ANOVA	*df*	*SS*	*MS*	*F*	*Significance F*
Regression	1	.391	.391	36.1	.0018
Residual	5	.054	.011		
Total	6	.445			

5.7 Assess Residuals to Learn Whether Assumptions Are Met

The Durbin Watson (*DW*) statistic incorporates serial correlation between residuals across adjacent time periods which allows assessment of the presence of unaccounted for trend, cycles, shifts or shocks in the residuals. If there is an unaccounted for trend, cycle, shift or shock, higher residuals are likely to be followed by similar higher residuals, and lower residuals are likely to be followed by similar lower residuals. In such a case, the residuals are not randomly distributed, but, instead, exhibit pattern.

In the Concha y Toro model, the trend accounts for much of the variation in export volumes to the U.S., however some unexplained variation remains.

DW indicates *positive autocorrelation,* the serial correlation of residuals over time, which signals that a shift, shock or cycle has been ignored. The Durbin Watson statistic compares the sum of squared differences between pairs of adjacent residuals with the sum of squared residuals:

$$DW = \frac{\sum_2^N (e_q - e_{q-1})^2}{\sum_1^N e_q^2}.$$

If all of the trend, shifts, shocks and cycles in the data have been accounted for *DW* will be "high." Exactly how high depends on the length of time series, which is the number of observations used in the regression, and the number of independent variables, including the intercept. *DW* critical values are available online at stanford.edu/~clint/bench/dwcrit.htm, found by googling "Durbin Watson critical values." (In this online table, sample size is indexed by *T*, and the number of independent variables, plus intercept, is indexed by *K*.)

There are two relevant critical values, a lower value and an upper value, dL and dU.

As Figure 5.9 illustrates, there are four possible outcomes of the Durbin Watson test:

> DW below the lower critical value, dL, indicates presence of positive autocorrelation from unaccounted for trend, cycle, shift or shock which we would then attempt to identify and incorporate into the model.

> DW between dL and dU is the gray area, indicative of possible autocorrelation and possible presence of unaccounted for trend, cycle or shift or shock. When DW is in the gray area, we look for pattern in the residuals due to unaccounted for trend, cycle, shift or shock, knowing that there is a reasonable chance that pattern may not be identified.

> DW above the upper critical value, dU, and less than two, indicates lack of positive autocorrelation and freedom from unaccounted for trend, cycle, shift or shock, which is the goal.

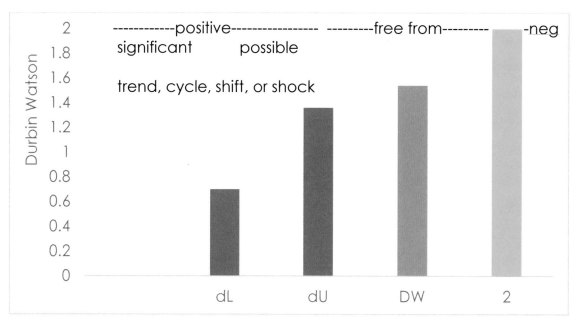

Figure 5.9 Durbin Watson critical values

DW above 2 suggests presence of negative autocorrelation due to unaccounted for seasonality, sometimes found in quarterly data.

Figure 5.10 illustrates critical values for several sample and model sizes: Notice that the gray area, dL to dU, shrinks as sample size increases, but expands as the number of predictors increases.

The Concha y Toro model, with one driver, plus intercept, and a sample size of 7, has *DW* critical values of *dL*=.70 and *dU*=1.36 The model *DW* statistic is 1.51, leading to the conclusion that the residuals are free of positive autocorrelation. The residuals are pattern free, and no important shifts, shocks or cycles have been ignored.

A plot of the residuals by time period, Figure 5.11, with gridlines set to the regression standard error, suggests that all are within two standard errors, and that fit is equally good in earlier and later years. There is some indication, however, that exports are cyclical.

Linear regression assumes that the residuals are *Normally* distributed. The distribution of residuals has skewness of 0.00, confirming that residuals are symmetric.

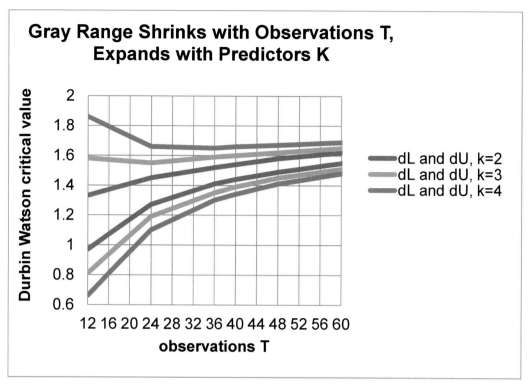

Figure 5.10 Durbin Watson critical values by sample size T and predictors k

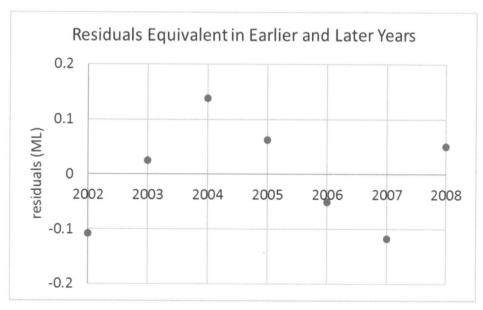

Figure 5.11 Residuals by year

5.8 Recalibrate to Update a Valid Model

The modelling team has created a valid model that correctly predicts the two most recent datapoints. Next, the model will be recalibrated to update coefficient estimates by including those two datapoints. Those two most recent points are likely to resemble future export volumes more than earlier data.

The recalibrated model shows a slightly stronger trend:

$$\hat{exports}(ML)_t = -250(ML) + .13(ML/t) \times t$$

To illustrate both the model fit to past data and the forecast, the data are plotted with the lower and upper 95% prediction intervals, shown in Figure 5.12.

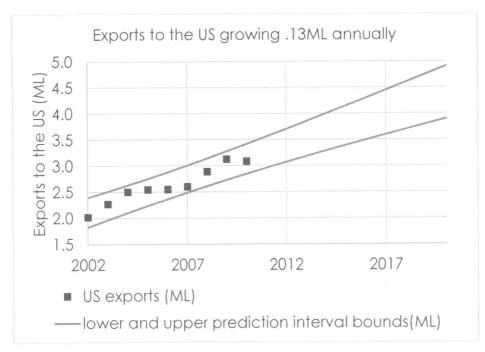

Figure 5.12 Fit and forecast of exports to the U.S.

Not all models are valid. It is not uncommon for a shift, such as an acquisition, entry into new markets, entry of exit of competitors, or a shock, such as global recession or hurricane, to have occurred in the two most recent time periods. Without those two most recent time periods, a regression model would ignore recent driver changes and may not successfully forecast those two most recent periods. Should such a model, lacking predictive validity be recalibrated? Given the choice of information from a model lacking predictive validity or no information, the model, though without proven predictive validity, is still valuable and provides the best information available. Results from such a model would be presented with the caveat that the model ought to be updated in the near future, since recent changes are expected to influence future performance.

From the regression analysis, the modelling team could

- conclude that the trend in U.S. exports is positive,
- estimate the trend, and
- predict export volumes in future years.

In the presentation of results to management, the team could conclude:

"Sample evidence suggests that the trend in U.S. export volume is positive.

The positive trend accounts for 93% of the variation in annual export volume to the U.S. within the series of nine previous years.

Each year a volume increase of 96K to 159K liters can be expected.

The forecast for 2020 U.S. export volume is 3.9M to 4.9M liters."

5.9 Present Regression Results in Concise Format

The regression equation is presented in a standard format, with the dependent variable on the left, RSquare below the equation, and significance levels of the model and parameter estimates indicated with superscripts:

$$\hat{y} = b_0^a + b_1^a \times X$$
$$RSquare = \underline{\quad}^a$$
$$^a Significant\ at\ \underline{\quad},$$

where the variable names and units are specified.

Significance is reported at two levels, .05 and .01.
p values greater than .01, but less than or equal to .05 are reported as significant at .05.
p values less than or equal to .01 are reported as significant at .01:

Table 5.5 Significance levels from p values.

	Reported as Significant at
$.01 < p\ value \leq .05$	.05
$p\ value \leq .01$	.01

The Concha y Toro regression equation is:

$$\widehat{exports}(ML)_t = -253^a(ML) + .127^a(ML/t) \times t$$
$$RSquare:\ .93^a$$
$$^a Significant\ at\ .0001$$

For the general business audience, the verbal description with graphical illustration conveys all of the important information. The three additional lines, the equation, RSquare, and significance level, provide the information that statistically savvy readers will want in order to assess how well the model fits and which parameter estimates are significant.

5.10 Assumptions We Make When We Use Linear Regression

Often a group of independent variables together jointly influence a dependent variable. If we attempt to explain or predict a dependent variable with an independent variable, but omit a third (or fourth) important influence, results will be misleading. If just one from the group is included in a regression, it may seem to be responsible for the joint impact of the group. It will seem that the independent variable chosen is more important than it actually is. Chapters 11 and 12 introduce diagnosis of *multicollinearity,* the situation in which predictors are correlated and jointly influence a dependent variable.

Linear regression assumes that the dependent variable, which is often a performance variable, is related linearly to the independent variable, often a decision variable. In reality, few relationships are linear. More often, performance increases or decreases in response to increases in a decision variable or time period, but at a diminishing rate. In these cases, linear regression doesn't fit the data perfectly. Extrapolation beyond the range of values within a sample can be risky if we assume constant response when response is actually diminishing or increasing. Though often not perfect reflections of reality, linear relationships can be useful approximations. In Chapters 9 and 10, we will explore simple remedies to improve linear models of nonlinear relationships by simply rescaling to square roots, logarithms or squares.

5.11 Correlation Reflects Linear Association

A correlation coefficient ρ_{xy} is a simple measure of the strength of the linear relationship between two continuous variables, x and y. The sample estimate of the population correlation coefficient ρ_{xy} is calculated by summing the product of differences from the sample means $\bar{x}$ and $\bar{y}$, standardized by the standard deviations s_x and s_y:

$$r_{xy} = \frac{1}{(N-1)} \sum \frac{(x_i - \bar{x})}{s_x} \frac{(y_i - \bar{y})}{s_y},$$

where x_i is the value of x for the i'th sample element, and

$\quad\quad y_i$ is the value of y for the i'th sample element.

When x and y move together, they are positively correlated. When they move in opposite directions, they are negatively correlated.

Table 5.6 contains years t and U.S. export volumes y from a sample of nine years:

Table 5.6 Year and U.S. export volumes

Year	U.S. Export Volume (ML)
T	Y
2002	2.02
2003	2.27
2004	2.50
2005	2.55
2006	2.55
2007	2.60
2008	2.89
2009	3.31
2010	3.08

A scatterplot in Figure 5.13 reveals that export volumes are higher in later years.

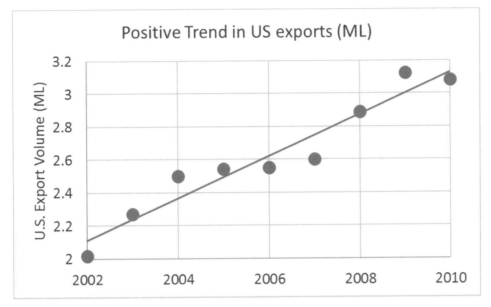

Figure 5.13 Positive trend in U.S. Export Volume

Differences from the sample means and their products are shown in Table 5.7.

Table 5.7 Differences from sample means and crossproducts

x_i	Year $\overline{X}$	$x_i - \overline{X}$	Export volume y_i	$\overline{Y}$	$y_i - \overline{Y}$	$(x_i - \overline{X}) \times (y_i - \overline{Y})$
2002	2006	-4	2.02	2.62	-0.60	2.40
2003	2006	-3	2.27	2.62	-0.35	1.05
2004	2006	-2	2.50	2.62	-0.12	0.24
2005	2006	-1	2.55	2.62	-0.08	0.08
2006	2006	0	2.55	2.62	-0.07	0.00
2007	2006	1	2.60	2.62	-0.02	-0.02
2008	2006	2	2.89	2.62	0.27	0.53
2009	2006	3	3.13	2.62	0.50	1.51
2010	2006	4	3.08	2.62	0.46	1.85

The sample standard deviations are $s_x = 2.74$ years and $s_y = .362$(ML).

The correlation coefficient is:

$$r_{xy} = \frac{1}{(9-1)}\left[\frac{2.40 + 1.05 + .24 + .08 + .00 - .02 + .53 + 1.51 + 1.85}{(2.74)(.362)}\right]$$

$$= \frac{1}{8}\left[\frac{7.64}{.991}\right]$$

$$= .964$$

A correlation coefficient can be as large in absolute value as 1.00, if two variables were perfectly correlated. All of the points in the scatterplot lie on the regression line in that case. RSquare, which is the squared correlation in a simple regression, would be 1.00, whether the correlation coefficient were -1.00 or +1.00.

In the Concha y Toro example above, *RSquare* is

$$RSquare = r_{xy}^2 = .964^2 = .929$$

In some cases, x and y are not related *linearly*, though they *are* strongly related. There are situations, for example, where more is better up to a point and improves performance, then, *saturation* occurs and, beyond this point, response deteriorates.

- Without enough advertising, customers will be not aware of a new product. Spending more increases awareness and improves performance. Beyond some saturation point, customers grow weary of the advertising, decide that the company must be desperate to advertise so much, and switch to another brand, reducing performance.

- A factory with too few employees x to man all of the assembly positions would benefit from hiring. Adding employees increases productivity y up to a point. Beyond some point, too many employees would crowd the facility and interfere with each other, reducing performance.

5.12 Correlation Coefficients Are Key Components of Regression Slopes

Correlation coefficients are closely related to regression slopes. From the correlation between x and y, as well as their sample standard deviations s_x and s_y, the regression slope estimate can be calculated:

$$b_1 = r_{xy} \frac{s_y}{s_x}$$

Similarly, from the regression slope estimate and sample standard deviations s_x and s_{xy}, the correlation coefficient can be calculated:

$$r_{xy} = b_1 \frac{s_x}{s_y}$$

The *t* test of hypothesis that a slope is zero

$$H_0: \beta_1 = 0$$

Versus

$$H_1: \beta_1 \neq 0$$

is equivalent to the t test used to test the hypothesis that a correlation is zero:

$$H_0: \; \rho_{xy} = 0$$

Versus

$$H_1: \; \rho_{xy} \neq 0:$$

$$t_{N-2} = \frac{b_1}{s_{b_1}} = \sqrt{N-2}\,\frac{r_{xy}}{\sqrt{1 - r_{xy}^2}}$$

.

In the Concha y Toro example, with the correlation coefficient, $r_{t,exports} = .963$, and the sample standard errors, $s_t = 2.74$ and $s_{exports} = .362$, the regression slope estimate can be calculated,

$$b_{titles} = .963\,\frac{.362}{2.74} = .13$$

as well as the t value to test the hypothesis that the slope is less than or equal to zero or, equivalently, that the correlation is less than or equal to zero:

$$t_7 = \sqrt{7} \times \frac{.963}{\sqrt{(1 - .963)}} = 9.57$$

with $p\ value < .01$.

Based on sample evidence, there is little chance that exports to the U.S. and trend are uncorrelated or negatively correlated.

5.13 Correlation Complements Regression

The correlation coefficient summarizes direction and strength of linear association between two continuous variables. Because it is a standardized measure, taking on values between -1 and +1, it is readily interpretable. Unlike regression analysis, it is not necessary to designate a dependent and an independent variable to summarize association with correlation analysis. Later, in the context of multiple regression analysis, the correlations between independent variables will be an important focus in our diagnosis of multicollinearity, introduced in Chapters 11 and 12.

Correlation analysis should be supplemented with visual inspection of data. It would be possible to overlook strong, nonlinear associations with small correlations. Inspection of a scatterplot will reveal whether or not association between two variables is linear.

Correlation is closely related to simple linear regression analysis:

- The squared correlation coefficient is *RSquare*, our measure of percent of variation in a dependent variable accounted for by an independent variable.

- The regression slope estimate is a product of the correlation coefficient and the ratio of the sample standard deviation of the dependent variable to sample standard deviation of the independent variable.
  - o Slope estimates from simple linear regression are unstandardized correlation coefficients.
  - o Correlation coefficients are standardized simple linear regression slope estimates.

5.14 Linear Regression Is Doubly Useful

Linear regression handles two modeling jobs, quantification of a driver's influence and forecasting. Regression models quantify the direction and nature of influence of a driver on a response or performance variable. Regression models also enable forecasts and to compare decision alternatives. In this chapter, focus was on naïve models of trend, which provide long range forecasts, but without explanation. In Chapter 11, regression models to identify drivers with cross sectional data are introduced, and in Chapter 12, regression models to both identify drivers and to forecast short term with time series data are introduced.

Excel 5.1 Build a Simple Linear Regression Model

Impact of Trend on Concha y Toro Export Volume to the U.S. Use regression analysis to explore the linear influence of trend on *U.S. export volume* differences across a time series sample of nine years.

Open **Excel 5.1 Concha y Toro US exports.**

Use shortcuts to run regression. Be sure to exclude the two most recent datapoints from 2009 and 2010, so that you can later validate your model.

Alt AY3, R, down, down
B1:b8 tab a1:a8 tab LR

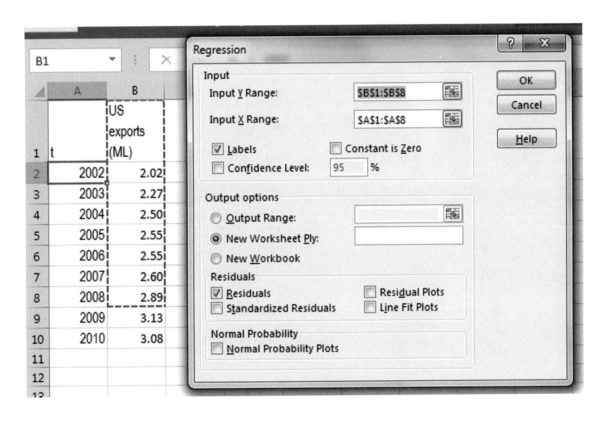

	A	B	C	D	E	F	G
1	SUMMARY OUTPUT						
2							
3	*Regression Statistics*						
4	Multiple F	0.937184					
5	R Square	0.878315					
6	Adjusted I	0.853978					
7	Standard I	0.104047					
8	Observati	7					
9							
10	ANOVA						
11		*df*	*SS*	*MS*	*F*	*gnificance F*	
12	Regressio	1	0.390695	0.390695	36.08958	0.001836	
13	Residual	5	0.054128	0.010826			
14	Total	6	0.444823				
15							
16		*Coefficient*	*andard Err*	*t Stat*	*P-value*	*Lower 95%*	*Upper 95%*
17	Intercept	-234.357	39.42424	-5.94449	0.001924	-335.7	-133.014
18	t	0.118124	0.019663	6.007461	0.001836	0.067579	0.16867
19							
20							
21							
22	RESIDUAL OUTPUT						
23							
24	*bservation*	*d US expo*	*Residuals*				
25	1	2.12806	-0.1076				
26	2	2.246184	0.024816				

Excel 5.2 Assess Residuals

Assess the residuals by finding the Durbin Watson statistic to test presence of positive autocorrelation, unaccounted for trend, shifts, shocks or cycles.

In D24,
DW
In D25,
=sumxmy2(c25:c30,c26:c31)/sumsq(c25:c31)

DW
Formula

D25   fx   =SUMXMY2(C25:C30,C26:C31)/SUMSQ(C25:C31)

	A	B	C	D	E	F	G	H
22	RESIDUAL OUTPUT							
23								
24	Observation	US expo	Residuals	DW				
25	1	2.12806	-0.1076	1.507755				
26	2	2.246184	0.024816					
27	3	2.364309	0.13815					
28	4	2.482433	0.062567					
29	5	2.600557	-0.05056					
30	6	2.718682	-0.11768					
31	7	2.836806	0.050304					

Compare DW with the lower and upper critical values on the Stanford website, T=7, K=2:

http://web.stanford.edu/~clint/bench/dw05a.htm

Page ▾   Safety ▾   Tools ▾

See Blackboard

Critical Values for the Durbin-Watson Test:

T=6 to 100, K=2 to 21 (K <= T-4)

K includes intercept

T	K	dL	dU
6.	2.	0.61018	1.40015
7.	2.	0.69955	1.35635

To assess Normality of the residuals, find the residual skew.

In C32,
=skew(c25:c31)

C32   fx   =SKEW(C25:C31)

	A	B	C	D	E
22	RESIDUAL OUTPUT				
23					
24	Observation	US expo	Residuals	DW	
25	1	2.12806	-0.1076	1.507755	
26	2	2.246184	0.024816		
27	3	2.364309	0.13815		
28	4	2.482433	0.062567		
29	5	2.600557	-0.05056		
30	6	2.718682	-0.11768		
31	7	2.836806	0.050304		
32			0.0053		

Excel 5.3 Construct Prediction Intervals to Validate

Copy the data and paste next to residuals, and then use the regression equation with the coefficients (always in B17 and B18) to find predicted exports. (Use **f4,** function 4, to lock cell references so that your equation will use the coefficients to make predicted values in each row.)

Cntl+Page down
In A1,
Cntl+shift+down
Shift+right
Cntl+C
Cntl+Page up
In E24,
Cntl+V
In G24,
Predicted exports (ML)
In G25,
=b17 f4 +f18 f4 *e24
In G25,
Double click the lower right corner to down fill

G25		▾	⋮	✕	✓	f_x	=$B$17+$B$18*E25	
⊿	A	B	C	D	E	F	G	
16		Coefficients	andard Err	t Stat	P-value	Lower 95%	Upper 95%	
17	Intercept	-234.357	39.42424	-5.94449	0.001924	-335.7	-133.014	
18	t	0.118124	0.019663	6.007461	0.001836	0.067579	0.16867	
19								
20								
21								
22	RESIDUAL OUTPUT							
23								
24	Observation	d US expo	Residuals	DW	t	US exports (ML)	predicted exports (ML)	
25	1	2.12806	-0.1076	1.507755	2002	2.02	2.12806	
26	2	2.246184	0.024816		2003	2.27	2.246184	
27	3	2.364309	0.13815		2004	2.50	2.364309	
28	4	2.482433	0.062567		2005	2.55	2.482433	
29	5	2.600557	-0.05056		2006	2.55	2.600557	
30	6	2.718682	-0.11768		2007	2.60	2.718682	
31	7	2.836806	0.050304		2008	2.89	2.836806	
32			0.0053		2009	3.13	2.954931	
33					2010	3.08	3.073055	
34					2011		3.19118	
35					2012		3.309304	

Adjust the regression standard error to enable creation of individual prediction interval bounds.

e44

In F44, find the mean year used in the regression,

e45

In F45, find the squared deviations from the mean year,

Find the standard error adjustment for each year.

In K25,

=**average(F25:F31)**
=**DEVSQ(F25:F31)**

=**SQRT(1+1/\$B\$8+(F25–\$F\$44)^2/\$F\$45)**
Click the lower right corner to downfill.

DEVSQ		▼	:	✕	✓	*fx*	=SQRT(1+1/$B$8+(F25-$F$44)^2/$F$45)			
▲	F	G	H	I	J	K	L	M	N
24	t	US exports (ML)	intercept (ML)	trend pw (ML)	predicte d (ML)	sqrt(1+1/ T+(t- tbar)^2/s sx)			
25	2002	2.02	-234.36	236.49	2.13	=SQRT(1+1/$B$8+(F25-$F$44)^2/$F$45)			
26	2003	2.27	-234.36	236.60	2.25	1.13			

Adjust the regression standard error for each year.

In L25,

=**K25*\$B\$7**

DEVSQ		▼	:	✕	✓	*fx*	=K25*$B$7	
▲	F	G	H	I	J	K	L
24	t	US exports (ML)	intercept (ML)	trend pw (ML)	predicte d (ML)	sqrt(1+1/ T+(t- tbar)^2/s sx)	set=K*$b $7
25	2002	2.02	-234.36	236.49	2.13	1.21	=K25*$B$7
26	2003	2.27	-234.36	236.60	2.25	1.13	0.12

Click the lower right corner to downfill.

Find the critical t value from the critical t for residual degrees of freedom (always in B13).

In C7,

=**T.INV.2T(.05,B13)**

DEVSQ	▼	⋮	×	✓	*fx*	=T.INV.2T(0.05,B13)

◢	A	B	C	D	E	F
1	SUMMARY OUTPUT					
2						
3	*Regression Statistics*					
4	Multiple F	0.937184				
5	R Square	0.878315				
6	Adjusted I	0.853978	critical t			
7	Standard E	0.104047	=T.INV.2T(0.05,B13)			

Find the margin of error for each year, multiplying the critical t times the adjusted standard error.

In M25, locking the cell reference to C7   =$C$7*L25
with Fn 4

DEVSQ	▼	⋮	×	✓	*fx*	=L25*$C$7

◢	F	G	H	I	J	K	L	M
24	t	US exports (ML)	intercept (ML)	trend pw (ML)	predicte d (ML)	sqrt(1+1/ T+(t- tbar)^2/s sx)	set=K*$b $7	met
25	2002	2.02	-234.36	236.49	2.13	1.21	0.13	=L25*$C$7
26	2003	2.27	-234.36	236.60	2.25	1.13	0.12	0.303271

Click the lower right corner to downfill.

To test the predictive validity of the model, find the *lower 95%* and *upper 95%* prediction interval bounds for each year by adding and subtracting the margin of error to and from *predicted revenues.*

DEVSQ	▼	⋮	×	✓	*fx*	=J25-M25

◢	J	K	L	M	N	O
24	predicted (ML)	sqrt(1+1/ T+(t- tbar)^2/(T- 1)/sqrt(de vsq))	set=(M)* b7	met=criti cal t*set	lower indiv pred interv (ML)	upper indiv pred interv (ML)
25	2.13	1.194291	0.124262	0.319425	=J25-M25	2.45
26	2.25	1.12642	0.117201	0.301275	1.94	2.55

Downfill.

Compare actual exports for 2009 and ~~20010~~ 2010, in F32 and F33, with 95% prediction interval bounds.

N32 f_x =J32-M32

	F	G	H	I	J	K	L	M	N	O
24	t	US exports (ML)	intercept (ML)	trend pw (ML)	predicte d (ML)	sqrt(1+1/ T+(t- tbar)^2/s sx)	set=K*$b $7	met	lower indiv pred interval bound(ML)	upper indiv pred interval bound(ML)
25	2002	2.02	-234.36	236.49	2.13	1.21	0.13	0.323647	1.80	2.45
26	2003	2.27	-234.36	236.60	2.25	1.13	0.12	0.303271	1.94	2.55
27	2004	2.50	-234.36	236.72	2.36	1.09	0.11	0.29036	2.07	2.65
28	2005	2.55	-234.36	236.84	2.48	1.07	0.11	0.285927	2.20	2.77
29	2006	2.55	-234.36	236.96	2.60	1.09	0.11	0.29036	2.31	2.89
30	2007	2.60	-234.36	237.08	2.72	1.13	0.12	0.303271	2.42	3.02
31	2008	2.89	-234.36	237.19	2.84	1.21	0.13	0.323647	2.51	3.16
32	2009	3.13	-234.36	237.31	2.95	1.31	0.14	0.350188	2.60	3.31
33	2010	3.08	-234.36	237.43	3.07	1.43	0.15	0.381608	2.69	3.45
34	2011		234.36	237.55	3.18	1.55	0.16		2.77	3.61

Excel 5.4 Recalibrate and Present Fit and Forecast in a Scatterplot

Recalibrate to update your fit and forecast. Run regression again, this time including the two most recent datapoints.

	A	B	C	D	E	F	G
1	SUMMARY OUTPUT						
2							
3	*Regression Statistics*						
4	Multiple F	0.963858					
5	R Square	0.929023					
6	Adjusted I	0.918883	critical t				
7	Standard I	0.103082	2.364624				
8	Observati	9					
9							
10	ANOVA						
11		*df*	*SS*	*MS*	*F*	*gnificance F*	
12	Regressio	1	0.973579	0.973579	91.62281	2.85E-05	
13	Residual	7	0.074382	0.010626			
14	Total	8	1.04796				
15							
16		*Coefficients*	*andard Err*	*t Stat*	*P-value*	*Lower 95%*	*Upper 95%ov*
17	Intercept	-252.909	26.69558	-9.4738	3.05E-05	-316.034	-189.784
18	t	0.127383	0.013308	9.571981	2.85E-05	0.095914	0.158851

Update your fit and forecast by reusing formulas for predicted exports, the standard error adjustment, critical t, margins of error, and the lower and upper 95% individual prediction interval bounds from the first regression.

Select year *t* and *U.S. exports*, hold **Cntl** down, and, with your mousse, select the *lower and upper prediction interval* cells and request a scatterplot of the fit and forecast.

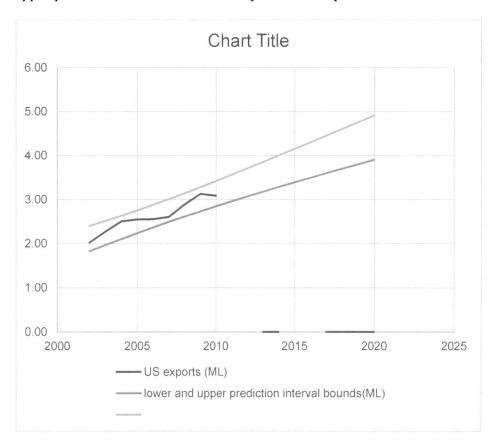

Change the actual exports from a line to markers.

Select the Series U.S. Exports.   **Alt JAE down to Series U.S. Exports**
Format the series.   **Alt JAM**

Choose No Line, click Marker, Marker Options, Built In.

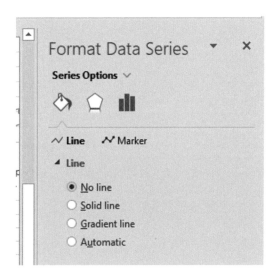

Change the color of one of the prediction interval lines to match the other.
Alt JAE down to Series lower 95% prediction interval bound
Alt JASO
Use arrow keys to choose color,

Add a vertical axis title and chart title. Adjust the axes to make better use of white space.

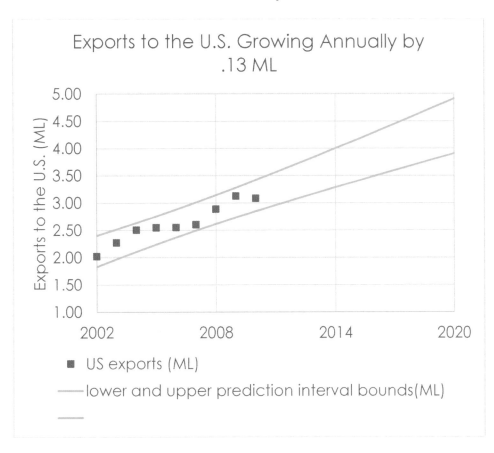

Lab 5-1 Forecast 2020 Concha y Toro Exports to the U.S.

1. What is the expected trend in exports to the U.S.? $b_1 =$ __10__ ML/year

2. Can H_0: $\beta_1 \leq 0$ be rejected based on sample evidence? __✓Y __ N

3. Can H_0: $RSquare = 0$ be rejected based on sample evidence? __ Y __✓N

Plot the residuals.

4. Do you see unaccounted for __4 cycle __8 shift ____ shock or ____ no pattern?

5. Are there residuals more than two standard errors from zero?

6. Are residuals in recent years noticeably larger?

7. DW: ____ with dL: ____ dU: ____

8. Are residuals free from unaccounted for trend, cycle, shift or shock? __ Y __ N

9. Is your model valid for forecasting?

Recalibrate your model.

10. How powerful is your model of trend in exports to the U.S.? RSquare: __x^2__

11. How precise are your forecasts of exports to the U.S. in 2020?   Margin of error:

    __39____ (ML)

12. Present your final equation for trend in exports to the U.S.:

$$ex\hat{p}orts(ML)_t = b_0(ML) + b_1\left(\frac{ML}{year}\right) \times t$$

13. What is your forecast for exports to the U.S. in 2020? __1__ to __8__ ML

14. Plot your fit and forecast and paste below. Label the vertical axis, adjust axes to reduce unnecessary white space, remove unwelcome zeros, and add a standalone title. Set all text to font size 12. Recolor on of the confidence interval bounds to match the other and change actual exports from a line to markers.

Assignment 5-1 Forecast Concha y Toro Exports to Europe and Asia

With forecasts for the U.S. export market segment executives are convinced that forecasts for the remaining major export segments would provide invaluable information. Build forecasts for export segments in Asia and Europe.

   The time series of annual export volumes to Asia and Europe are in **Concha y Toro exports.**

Asia

1. Can H_0: $\beta_1 \leq 0$ be rejected based on sample evidence? __Y __ N

2. What is the 95% confidence interval for the trend in exports to Asia?

    23 ≤ β_1 ≤ 21 ML/year

3. Can H_0: $RSquare = 0$ be rejected based on sample evidence? __Y __ N

Plot the residuals.

4. Do you see unaccounted for _4_ cycle _8_ shift _9_ shock or ___ no pattern?

5. Are there residuals more than two standard errors from zero?

6. Are residuals in recent years noticeably larger?

7. DW: _11_ with dL: _3.50_ dU: 1.46_5_

8. Are residuals free from unaccounted for trend, cycle, shift or shock? __Y __N

9. Is your model valid for forecasting? _Y __N

Recalibrate your model.

10. How powerful is your model of trend in exports to Asia? RSquare: _62_

11. How precise are your forecasts of exports to Asia in 2020? Margin of error: _7_ (ML)

12. Present your final equation for trend in exports to Asia:

$$ex\hat{p}orts(ML)_t = b_0(ML) + b_1 \left(\frac{ML}{year}\right) \times t$$

13. What is your forecast for exports to Asia. in 2020? _7ol_ to _2.07_ ML

14. Plot your fit and forecast and paste below. Label the vertical axis, adjust axes to reduce unnecessary white space, remove unwelcome zeros, and add a standalone title. Set all text to font size 12. Recolor on of the confidence interval bounds to match the other and change actual exports from a line to markers.

Europe

1. Can H_0: $\beta_1 \leq 0$ be rejected based on sample evidence? __✓ Y   __ N

2. What is the 95% confidence interval for the trend in exports to Europe?

   __1__ $\leq \beta_1 \leq$ _8_ ML/year

3. Can H_0: $RSquare = 0$ be rejected based on sample evidence? __ Y __ N

Plot the residuals.

4. Do you see unaccounted for___ cycle ✓ shift ___ shock or ___ no pattern?

5. Are there residuals more than two standard errors from zero?

6. Are residuals in recent years noticeably larger?

7. DW: _14_   with dL: ___ dU: ___

8. Are residuals free from unaccounted for trend, cycle, shift or shock? __ Y __ N

9. Is your model valid for forecasting? ✓ Y __ N

Recalibrate your model.

10. How powerful is your model of trend in exports to Europe? RSquare: _69_

11. How precise are your forecasts of exports to Europe in 2020? Margin of error:

    __47__ (ML)

12. Present your final equation for trend in exports to Europe:

$$exp\hat{o}rts(ML)_t = b_0(ML) + b_1\left(\frac{ML}{year}\right) \times t$$

13. What is your forecast for exports to Europe. in 2020? _3_ to _7_ ML

14. Plot your fit and forecast and paste below. Label the vertical axis, adjust axes to reduce unnecessary white space, remove unwelcome zeros, and add a standalone title. Set all text to font size 12. Recolor on of the confidence interval bounds to match the other and change actual exports from a line to markers.

Comparing Export Segments

Below are the shares of 2010 exports by segment. Create a pie chart of expected 2020 exports by segment and paste below.

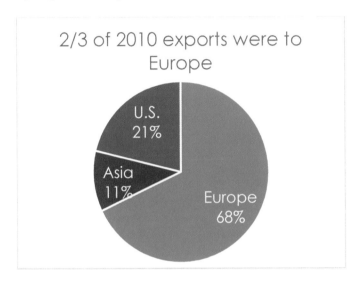

1. Which segment will be the largest export market in 2020? _Europe_

2. Which segment is growing fastest? _U.S_

Chapter 6
Finance Application: Portfolio Analysis with a Market Index as a Leading Indicator in Simple Linear Regression

Simple linear regression of stock rates of return with a Market index provides an estimate of *beta*, a measure of risk, which is central to finance investment theory.

Investors are interested in both the mean and the variability in stock price growth rates. Preferred stocks have higher expected growth---expected *rates of return*---shown by larger percentage price increases over time. Preferred stocks also show predictable growth---low variation---which makes them less risky to own. A portfolio of stocks is assembled to diversify risk, and estimates of portfolio *beta* can be used to estimate risk.

6.1 Rates of Return Reflect Expected Growth of Stock Prices

Example 6.1 Amazon and Tesla Figure 6.1 contains plots of share prices of two well-known companies, Amazon and Tesla, over a 60 month period, December 2013 to November 2018.

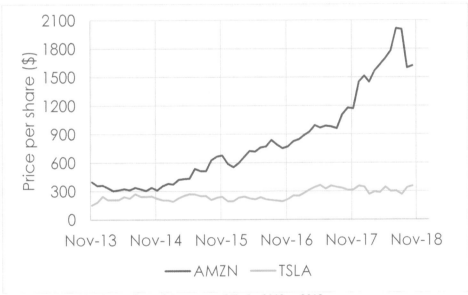

Figure 6.1 Monthly share prices of Amazon and Tesla, 2013 to 2018.

It is important to note that although prices in some months are statistical outliers, those unusual months are not excluded. A potential investor would be misled were unusually high or low prices ignored. Extreme values are expected and included, since they influence conclusions about the appeal of each potential investment. The larger the number of unusual months, the greater the dispersion in a stock price, and the riskier the investment.

To find the growth rate in each of the stock investments, calculate the monthly percent change in price, or *rate of return, RR*:

© Springer Nature Switzerland AG 2019

C. Fraser, *Business Statistics for Competitive Advantage with Excel 2019 and JMP*,

https://doi.org/10.1007/978-3-030-20374-0_6

$$RR_{stock,t} = \frac{(price_{stock,t} - price_{stock,t-1})}{price_{stock,t-1}}$$

where t is month.

Investors seek stocks with higher average rates of return and lower standard deviations. They would prefer to invest in stocks that exhibit higher expected, average growth and less volatility or risk. The standard deviation in the rate of return captures risk. If a stock price shows little variability, it is a less risky investment.

Figure 6.2 illustrates monthly rates of return in Amazon and Tesla stocks and a Market index, the S&P 500, over the five year period:

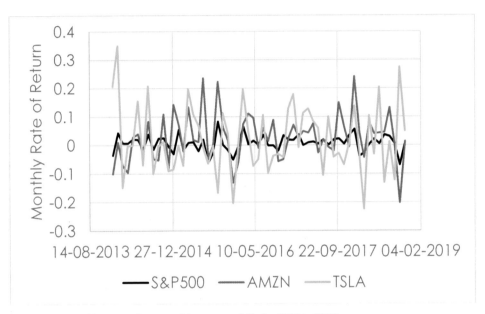

Figure 6.2 Monthly rates of return of Amazon and Tesla, 2013 to 2018

Table 6.1 Monthly Rates of Return of Amazon and Tesla Stock, 2013 to 2018.

Monthly Rate of Return			
	Amazon AMZN	Tesla TSLA	S&P 500
M	2.7%	2.1%	0.7%
SD	8%	12%	3%
Minimum	-20%	-22%	-7%
Maximum	24%	35%	8%

From Table 6.1, notice that mean monthly rates of return of both stocks exceed the Market mean monthly rate of return, though both stocks' rates of return are more volatile, with a standard deviations greater than the Market standard deviation.

6.2 Investors Trade Off Risk and Return

Investors seek stocks which offer higher expected rates of return, *RR,* and lower risk. Relative to a Market index, such as the S&P 500, which is a composite of 500 individual stocks, many individual stocks offer higher expected returns, but at greater risk. Market indices are weighted averages of individual stocks. Like other weighted averages, a Market index has an expected rate of return in the middle of the expected returns of the individual stocks making up the index. An investor attempts to choose stocks with higher than average expected returns and lower risk.

6.3 Beta Measures Risk

A Market index reflects the state of the economy. When a time series of an individual stock's rates of return is regressed against a Market index, the simple linear regression slope β indicates the expected percent change in a stock's rate of return in response to a percent change in the Market rate of return. β is estimated with b using a sample of stock prices:

$$\hat{RR}_{stock,t} = a + b \times RR_{Market,t}$$

Where $RR_{stocki,t}$ is the estimated rate of return of a stock i in month t, and

$RR_{Market,t}$ is the rate of return of a Market index in month t.

In this specific case, the simple linear regression slope estimate b is called *beta.* Beta captures Market specific risk. If, in response to a percent change in the Market rate of return, the expected change in a stock's rate of return b is greater than one, the stock is more volatile, and exaggerates Market movements. A one percent increase in the Market value is associated with an expected change in the stock's price of more than one percent change. Conversely, if the expected change in a stock's rate of return b is less than one, the stock dampens Market fluctuations and is less risky. A one percent change in the Market's value is associated with an expected change in the stock's price of less than one percent. Beta reflects the amount of risk a stock contributes to a portfolio.

Recall from Chapter 5 that the sample correlation coefficient between two variables r_{xy} is closely related to the simple regression slope estimate b:

$$b = r_{x,y} \times \frac{s_y}{s_x}$$

In a model of an individual stock's rate of return against a Market index, the estimate of beta b is directly related to the sample correlation between the individual stock's rate of return and the Market rate of return:

$$\hat{beta}_{stock_i} = b_{stock_i} = r_{stock_i,Market} \times \frac{s_{stock_i}}{s_{Market}}$$

The estimate of beta is a direct function of the sample correlation between an individual stock's rate of return and the Market rate of return, as well as Market sample variance.

Stocks with rates of return that are more strongly correlated with the Market rate of return and those with larger standard deviations have larger betas.

Notice in Figure 6.2 that both stocks tend to move with the Market, though Amazon tends to more closely follow the Market moves. And when both stocks move with the Market, Amazon moves more, and Tesla moves less.

It would not be surprising to find that Amazon stock is riskier than Tesla stock, since the relatively expensive luxury cars are probably less sensitive to Market fluctuations

Table 6.2 contains sample correlation coefficients, standard deviations, and betas for both of the stocks using five years of monthly data.

Table 6.2 Correlations, Standard Deviations, Covariances and Betas for 2013 to 2018

	correlation with the Market		SD	beta
	$r_{stock,Market}$		SD	b_{stock}
SP500 RR			2.9%	
Amazon RR	.58		8.4%	1.67[a,c]
Tesla RR	.14		12.0%	.57

[a]Significant at .01.
[b]Significant at .05
[b]Significantly greater than 1.0 at a 95% confidence level.

Correlations between each of the stocks' returns and the Market are positive, indicating that they do move with the Market.

Amazon returns are more strongly correlated with the Market index returns than Tesla returns. Because Amazon rates of return are more strongly correlated with the Market, Amazon stock has a larger beta than Tesla stock.

Betas b_{stocki} are shown in the last column of Table 6.3. A percent increase in the Market produces more than one percent expected increase in the Amazon stock price.

Beta estimates are shown in Table 6.3 and Figure 6.3.

Table 6.3 Estimates of betas

AMZN

Regression Statistics					
R Square	0.333				
Standard Error	0.069				
Observations	59				

ANOVA	df	SS	MS	F	Significance F
Regression	1	0.137	0.137	28.4	1.72E-06
Residual	57	0.275	0.005		
Total	58	0.412			

	Coefficients	Standard Error	t Stat	P-value	Lower 95%	Upper 95%
Intercept	0.016	0.009	1.7	0.099918	0.00	0.03
S&P500	1.674	0.314	5.3	1.72E-06	1.05	2.30

TSLA

Regression Statistics					
R Square	0.019				
Standard Error	0.120				
Observations	59				

ANOVA	df	SS	MS	F	Significance F
Regression	1	0.016	0.016	1.13	0.293
Residual	57	0.815	0.014		
Total	58	0.831			

	Coefficients	Standard Error	t Stat	P-value	Lower 95%	Upper 95%
Intercept	0.017	0.016	1.08	0.28	-0.015	0.049
S&P500	0.574	0.540	1.06	0.29	-0.508	1.656

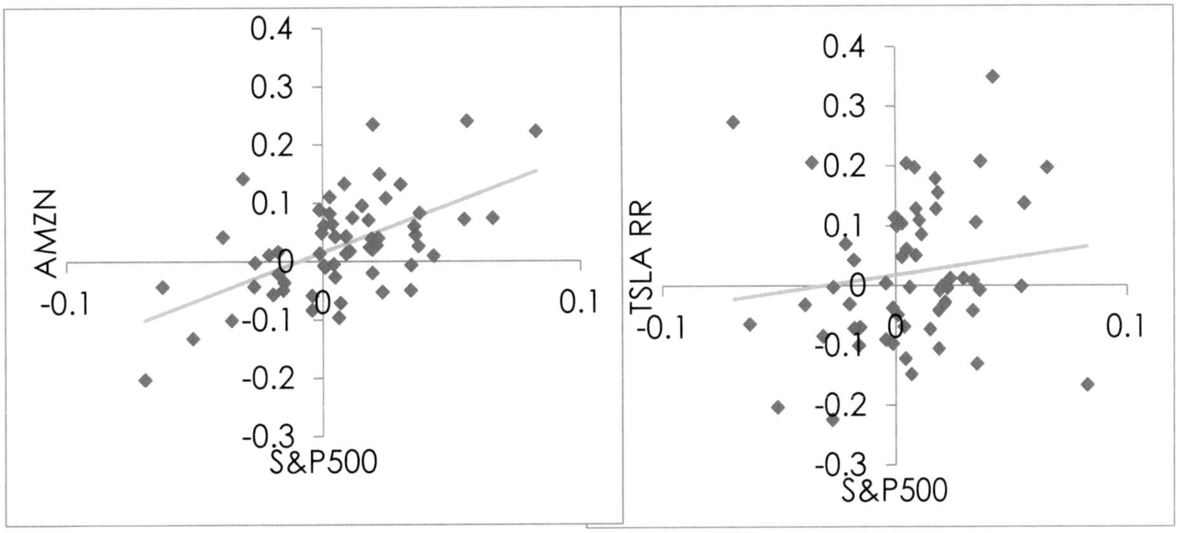

$$\hat{R}R_{AMZN_t} = .016 + 1.7^a \times S\&P500_t$$
$$RSquare: .33^a$$

$$\hat{R}R_{TSLA_t} = .017 + .57 \times S\&P500_t$$
$$RSquare: .019$$

[a]Significant at .01

Figure 6.3 Response of Amazon and Tesla stocks to The Market

Relative to Tesla, Amazon rates of return have a higher correlation with The Market, a component of specific risk, producing the larger beta.

Comparing betas, a potential investor would conclude:

"Tesla stock, with an estimated beta equivalent to zero ($b_{Wal-Mart}$ = .57), is a low risk investment. With a percent increase in the Market rate of return, we expect to see an average increase of .57% in Tesla's rate of return.

Amazon stock, with an estimated beta greater than one (b_{Apple}= 1.7) is riskier than Tesla and exaggerates Market movement. With a percent increase in the Market rate of return, we expect to see an average increase of about 170%, in Apple's rate of return. "

6.4 A Portfolio Expected Return, Risk and Beta Are Weighted Averages of Individual Stocks

An investor is really interested in the expected return and risk of her portfolio of stocks. These are weighted averages of the expected returns and betas of the individual stocks in a portfolio:

$$E(RR_P) = \sum_i w_i \times E(RR_i)$$

$$b_P = \sum_i w_i \times b_i$$

Where $E(RR_P)$ is the expected portfolio rate of return,
$\qquad$ w_i is the percent of investment in the i'th stock,
$\qquad$ $E(RR_i)$ is the expected rate of return of the i'th stock,
$\qquad$ b_P is the portfolio beta estimate,
$\qquad$ b_i is the beta estimate of the ith stock,

Example 6.2 Three Alternate Portfolios. An Investment Manager has been asked to suggest a portfolio of two stocks from three being considered by a client: Amazon, Apple and Tesla.

$\qquad$ To confidently advise her client, the Investment Manager compared three portfolios of two equally weighted stocks from the three requested options. Individual stock weights in each portfolio equal one half. Table 6.4 contains the expected portfolio rates of return and betas for the three possible combinations:

Table 6.4 Expected portfolio returns and beta estimates

Portfolio	Expected Portfolio Return		Portfolio Beta Estimate	
	$\sum E(RR_i)/2$	$E(RR_P)$	$\sum b_i/2$	b_P
Amazon+Tesla	(2.7% + 2.1%)/2	2.4%	(1.67 +.57)/2	1.12
Amazon+Apple	(2.7% + 1.7%)/2	2.2%	(1.67 + 1.21)/2	1.44
Tesla+Apple	(2.1% +1.7%)/2	1.9%	(.57 + 1.21)/2	0.89

$\qquad$ Alternatively, she could find expected portfolio returns and betas with software, and this would be the practical way to compare more than a few portfolios. Figure 6.4 shows expected (mean) rates of return and regression beta estimates for the three portfolios from Excel:

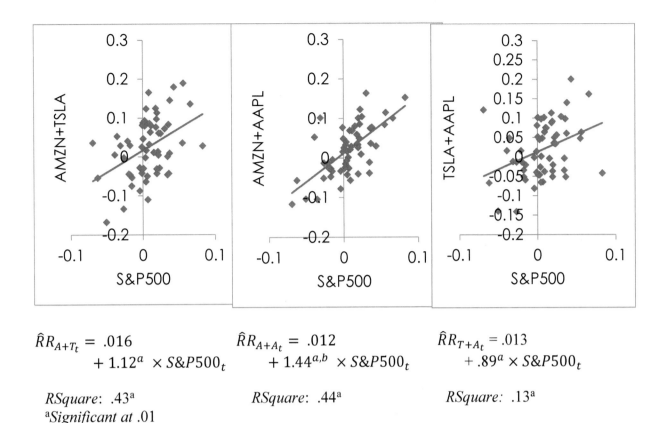

$$\hat{R}R_{A+T_t} = .016$$
$$\quad + 1.12^a \times S\&P500_t$$

$$\hat{R}R_{A+A_t} = .012$$
$$\quad + 1.44^{a,b} \times S\&P500_t$$

$$\hat{R}R_{T+A_t} = .013$$
$$\quad + .89^a \times S\&P500_t$$

RSquare: .43[a]   *RSquare*: .44[a]   *RSquare*: .13[a]

[a]*Significant at* .01
[b]*Significantly greater than* 1.

Figure 6.4 Beta estimates of three alternate portfolios

6.5 Better Portfolios Define the Efficient Frontier

In the comparison of alternative portfolios, the Investment Manager wanted to identify alternatives which promised greater expected return without greater risk---or, alternatively, those which reduced risk without reducing return. Better portfolios, which promise the highest return for a given level of risk, define the *Efficient Frontier*. To see the Efficient Frontier, she made a scatterplot of portfolio expected rates of return by portfolio risk. Those relatively efficient portfolios lie in the upper left.

Figure 6.5 Relatively Efficient Portfolios Offer Greater Expected Return and Lower Risk

Comparing portfolios in Figure 6.5, the Investment Manager found that the Amazon+Tesla portfolio outperforms the Market, offering higher expected rates of return at lower levels of risk, though both Tesla portfolios outperform the Amazon+Apple combination.

$$RR_{TSLA+AAPL} = 1.9\% < RR_{AMZN+AAPL} = 2.2\% < RR_{AMZN+TSLA} = 2.4\%$$

$$b_{TSLA+AAPL} = .89 < b_{AMZN+TSLA} = 1.12 < b_{AMZN+AAPL} = 1.44$$

The better choice would depend on the prospective investor's risk preference. The Tesla+Apple combination is less risky than the Amazon+Tesla combination, but offers a lower return.

The Investment Manager presented results of her analysis with recommendations in this memo to her client:

MEMO

Re: Recommended Portfolio Is Diversified
To: Rich N. Vest
From: Christine Kasper, Investment Advisor, Stellar Investments

The portfolios combining Tesla with Apple or Amazon stocks are expected to outperform the combination of Amazon with Apple.

Alternate portfolios were compared

Portfolios containing two from the candidate set of three stocks, Amazon, Apple, and Tesla have been compared to assess their expected returns and risk levels. Assessments were based on five years of monthly prices, December 2013 through November 2018, and movement relative to the S&P500 Market Index during this period.

Tesla Combinations Dominate

Expected monthly rates of return range from 1.9 to 2.4%. Amazon+Tesla portfolio outperforms the Market, and both Tesla combinations are preferred to Amazon+Apple.

In response to a 1% change in the S&P500, the Amazon+Apple combination is expected to move more, 1.4%, exaggerating Market movement. This is a risky choice.

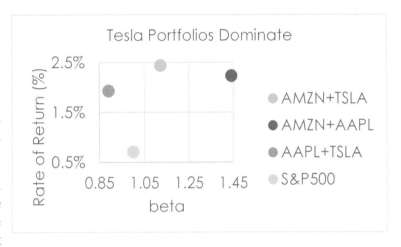

Choose Tesla+Apple for lower risk, Tesla+Amazon for higher expected return

The choice of Tesla+Apple promises a positive expected return, as well as the lowest risk. Amazon+Tesla promises the highest expected return, but with added risk.

A larger number of stocks are suggested

You may wish to consider a portfolio with a larger number of stocks to increase your diversification and reduce your risk.

6.6 Portfolio Risk Depends on Correlations with the Market and Stock Variability

Both the expected rate of return of a portfolio and its risk, measured by its beta, depend on the expected rates of return and betas of the individual stocks in the portfolio. Individual stock betas are direct functions of

- the correlation between a stock's rate of return and the Market index rate of return, and
- the standard deviation of a stock's rate of return

Beta for a stock or a portfolio is estimated by regressing the stock or portfolio monthly rates of return against monthly Market rates of return. The resulting simple linear regression slopes are estimates of the stock or portfolio beta.

Excel 6.1 Estimate Portfolio Expected Rate of Return and Risk

Three Portfolios with Amazon, Apple and Tesla. Monthly rates of return for each of the three stocks and the S&P500 index of the Market are in **8 Three Portfolios.**.

Monthly portfolio returns formula. Insert new columns , F, G and H, for each of the three portfolios containing equally weighted pairs of the three stocks, which will be the average of rates of return of each of pair of stocks in a portfolio. In row 1, enter labels to identify the combinations, AAPL+AMZN, AAPL+TSLA, AMZN+TSLA. In the second row of each new column enter a formula for the average of two stocks. Select the three new cells and down fill the three new columns.

In F2,	**=average(C2,D2)**
In G2,	**=average(C2,E2)**
In H2,	**=average(D2,E2)**
In F2,	**Cntl+shift+right**
	Double click the lower right corner to fill down columns

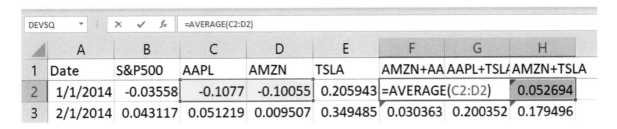

Expected monthly rates of return. Find the expected monthly return for the three portfolios in the first row following the data, row 62.

In F62,	**Alt MUA**
In F62,	**Shift+right right**
	Cntl+R

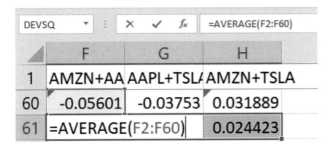

Estimate betas from simple regression. To find the Market specific risk, *beta,* find the simple regression slope of each portfolio rate of return (the Y range) with *S&P500 (*the X range).

	A	B	C	D	E	F	G
1	SUMMARY OUTPUT						
2							
3	*Regression Statistics*						
4	Multiple F	0.661708					
5	R Square	0.437858					
6	Adjusted I	0.427996					
7	Standard E	0.047871					
8	Observati	59					
9							
10	ANOVA						
11		*df*	*SS*	*MS*	*F*	*gnificance F*	
12	Regressio	1	0.101744	0.101744	44.39788	1.16E-08	
13	Residual	57	0.130623	0.002292			
14	Total	58	0.232366				
15							
16		*Coefficients*	*andard Err*	*t Stat*	*P-value*	*Lower 95%*	*Upper 95%c*
17	Intercept	0.012109	0.006418	1.886665	0.064303	-0.00074	0.024961
18	S&P500	1.441874	0.216395	6.663173	1.16E-08	1.008552	1.875197

Excel 6.2 Plot Return by Risk to Identify Dominant Portfolios and the Efficient Frontier

To compare the expected rates of return and estimated risk of the three portfolios, create a summary of the portfolio betas and expected returns below the data, and then plot the portfolio rates of return against their betas (one portfolio at a time) to identify the Efficient Frontier.

Copy row 1 containing portfolio labels and paste into row 62. Below the expected rates of return, use the Excel slope function to produce the portfolio betas.

In row 1,	**Shift+spacebar**
	Cntl+C
	Cntl+down
In row 61	**Shift+spacebar**
	Alt HIE
In F62,	**=slope(f2:f61,b2 Fn4 Fn4 Fn4 :b61 Fn4 Fn4 Fn4)**
In F62,	**Shift+right right**
	Cntl+R

(Pressing **Fn4** three times locks the row reference, so that the slope function will use the S&P500 returns in column B to find betas for portfolios in columns F, G and H.)

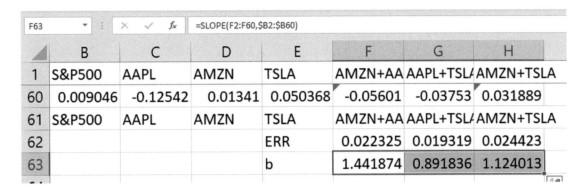

	B	C	D	E	F	G	H
					=SLOPE(F2:F60,$B2:$B60)		
1	S&P500	AAPL	AMZN	TSLA	AMZN+AA	AAPL+TSL/	AMZN+TSLA
60	0.009046	-0.12542	0.01341	0.050368	-0.05601	-0.03753	0.031889
61	S&P500	AAPL	AMZN	TSLA	AMZN+AA	AAPL+TSL/	AMZN+TSLA
62				ERR	0.022325	0.019319	0.024423
63				b	1.441874	0.891836	1.124013

Use the Excel average function to add the expected rate of return for the S&P500 and enter 1 for the S&P500 beta.

In E63,   **=average(e2:e61)**
In E64,   1

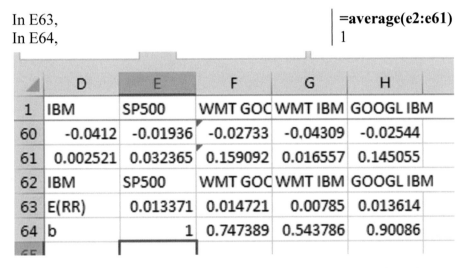

	D	E	F	G	H
1	IBM	SP500	WMT GOC	WMT IBM	GOOGL IBM
60	-0.0412	-0.01936	-0.02733	-0.04309	-0.02544
61	0.002521	0.032365	0.159092	0.016557	0.145055
62	IBM	SP500	WMT GOC	WMT IBM	GOOGL IBM
63	E(RR)	0.013371	0.014721	0.00785	0.013614
64	b	1	0.747389	0.543786	0.90086

Select the S&P500 label, expected rate of return and beta in column E and request a scatterplot of the point.

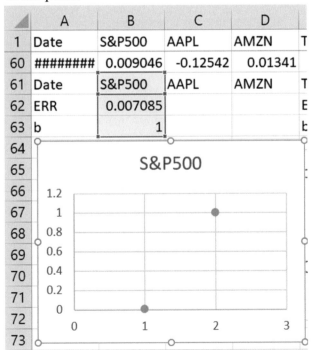

	A	B	C	D	
1	Date	S&P500	AAPL	AMZN	T
60	########	0.009046	-0.12542	0.01341	
61	Date	S&P500	AAPL	AMZN	T
62	ERR	0.007085			E
63	b	1			b

When we are plotting a single point, Excel will read both *b* and the *E(RR)* as a single series, plotting two points. To correct this, edit the series,

Alt JCE Tab Tab Tab Enter B63 Tab
Change 63 to 62
OK

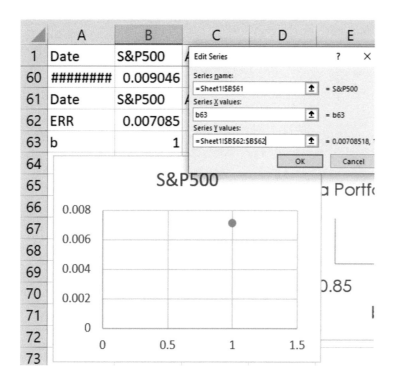

Add each of the three portfolios as separate series, inputting the portfolio label in row 61 for name, beta in row 63 for X and the expected rate of return in row 62 for Y.

| **Alt JCE Tab Tab Tab A**

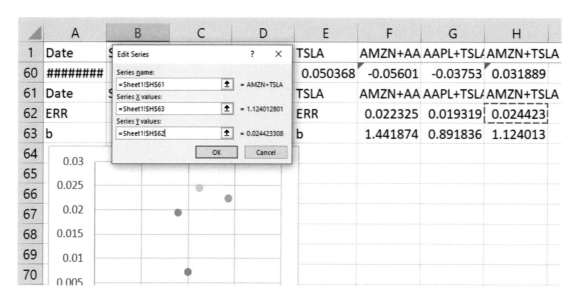

Select the expected rates of return and convert to percentages with

Add chart and axes titles, adjust axes and set font size.

Add the legend.

Alt HP.
Alt JCAL

Lab 6-1 Portfolio Risk and Return

6 stocks contains a five year times series of monthly prices for 36 stocks and the S&P500 Market index for months July 2010 through July 2015. Stocks include ten "blue chips," as well as several others that have been in recent news.

Find the *rate of return* for each of the stocks.
Find the *beta* for each of the stocks.

Use logic to choose two stocks to combine in an equally weighted portfolio.

1. The expected rate of return of my portfolio:

Use regression to find the 95% confidence interval for beta of your portfolio

2. The Market specific risk, beta, of my portfolio: _____ to _____

3. My portfolio ____dampens,   ____mirrors,   ____exaggerates Market swings.

Create an alternative portfolio with two other stocks.
Find the expected rate of return expected *beta*.

4. Plot *E(RR)* by *b* for the S&P500 and your portfolios to see the *Efficient Frontier*, then compare the two portfolios:

    Portfolio_____ dominates Portfolio_____   OR   ___neither dominates the other

Assignment 6-1 Portfolio Risk and Return

Your client, a novice investor, was excited about investing in Nike and would like to invest 50% in Nike and 50% in a second stock. He is considering a Blue Chip, GE, an up and coming U.S. stock, Amazon, a Chinese stock, Haier, a European stock, Nestle, and a South American stock, Newmont. Stock rates of return are in Nike portfolio.xlsx.

1. Of the five possible choices to combine with Nike, which would you advise against?

   ___ GE   ___ Amazon   ___ Haier   ___ Nestle   ___ Newmont

2. Your client is not risk averse and prefers a portfolio that mirrors or exaggerates Market swings (i.e., beta equal to or greater than one). Which stock(s) do you recommend to combine with Nike?

   ___ GE   ___ Amazon   ___ Haier   ___ Nestle   ___ Newmont

Chapter 7
Indicator Variables

In this chapter, 0-*1 indicator* or "*dummy*" variables are used to incorporate segment differences, shocks, or structural shifts into regression models. With cross sectional data, indicators can be used to incorporate the unique responses of particular groups or segments. With time series data, indicators can be used to account for external shocks or structural shifts. Indicators also offer one option to account for seasonality or cyclicality in time series.

Model variable selection begins with the choice of potential drivers from logic and experience. The addition of indicators in the variable selection process is considered in this chapter.

7.1 Indicators Modify the Intercept to Account for Segment Differences

To compare two segments, a 0-1 indicator can be added to a model. One segment becomes the baseline, and the indicator represents the amount of difference from the base segment to the second segment. Indicators are like switches that turn on or off adjustments to a model intercept.

Example 7.1 Electric Fuel Economy. Sakura Motors would like to compete with Tesla, developing a luxury electric car with excellent fuel economy. Tesla models are heavier than other electric cars, which appeals to some conventional car owners. What was the impact on fuel economy of weight, for electric, hybrid, and conventional cars? Managers were sure that weight was a driver of fuel economy. Accounting for weight, what average improvement in gas mileage do electric cars achieve?

A sample of 31 conventional, hybrid, and electric cars, drawn from cars that achieved at least 20 mpg, was used to build a model of fuel economy. The sample included Japanese, Korean, German and U.S. models, whose weights ranged from 2100 to 5400 pounds. (Tesla's electric model X was the heaviest in the sample.)

In addition to the weight driver, an *electric* indicator and a *hybrid* indicator were added. For the baseline, conventional cars, those indicators were set to zero. For electric cars, the *electric* indicator was turned on (set to one). For hybrid cars, the *hybrid* indicator was turned on.

Regression results are shown in Table 7.1.

© Springer Nature Switzerland AG 2019
C. Fraser, *Business Statistics for Competitive Advantage with Excel 2019 and JMP*,
https://doi.org/10.1007/978-3-030-20374-0_7

Table 7.1 Regression of mpg by weight and fuel type.

Regression Statistics						
R Square	0.89					
Standard Error	11					
Observations	31					

ANOVA	df	SS	MS	F	Significance F	
Regression	3	28658	9553	75	3E-13	
Residual	27	3419	127			
Total	30	32077				

	Coefficients	Standard Error	t Stat	P-value	Lower 95%	Upper 95%
Intercept	63	10.4	6.1	2E-06	42	84
electric	76	6.3	12.1	2E-12	63	89
hybrid	63	5.6	11.2	1E-11	51	74
weight	-0.011	0.0035	-3.3	0.003	-0.019	-0.004

The model revealed the significant impact of weight on fuel economy, as well as fuel economy differences between conventional, hybrid, and electric cars:

$$\hat{MPG} = b_0(mpg) + b_2(mpg) \times hybrid + b_3(mpg) \times electric$$

$$+ b_4\left(\frac{mpg}{lbs}\right) \times weight(lbs)$$

$$= 63(mpg) + 63(mpg) \times hybrid + 76(mpg) \times electric$$

$$- .011\left(\frac{mpg}{lbs}\right) \times weight(lbs)$$

For conventional cars, where the *electric* and *hybrid* indicators are turned off (set to 0), the intercept is 63 (*mpg*):

$$\hat{MPG} = 63(mpg) + 63(mpg) \times 0 + 76(mpg) \times 0 - .011\left(\frac{mpg}{lbs}\right) \times weight(lbs)$$

$$= 63(mpg) - .011\left(\frac{mpg}{lbs}\right) \times weight(lbs)$$

Before the penalizing impact of weight is included, conventional cars, the *baseline* segment, achieve 63 mpg, on average.

For hybrid cars in the sample, the *hybrid* indicator is 1, which adjusts the intercept for hybrid cars to 126 (mpg) by adding 63 (mpg) to the baseline 63 (mpg):

$$M\hat{P}G = 63(mpg) + 63(mpg) \times 1 + 76(mpg) \times 0 - .011 \left(\frac{mpg}{lbs}\right) \times weight(lbs)$$

$$= 126(mpg) - .011 \left(\frac{mpg}{lbs}\right) \times weight(lbs)$$

For electric cars in the sample, the *electric* indicator is 1, which adjusts the intercept for electric cars to 139 (mpg) by adding 76 (mpg) to the baseline 63 (mpg):

$$M\hat{P}G = 63(mpg) + 63(mpg) \times 0 + 76(mpg) \times 1 - .011 \left(\frac{mpg}{lbs}\right) \times weight(lbs)$$

$$= 139(mpg) - .011 \left(\frac{mpg}{lbs}\right) \times weight(lbs)$$

Relative to conventional cars of equivalent weight, hybrid cars achieve 63 miles per gallon more, and electric cars achieve 76 more miles per gallon, on average.

The regression lines for the three car segments are parallel, with the same slope for weight, but with unique intercepts, as shown in Figure 7.1:

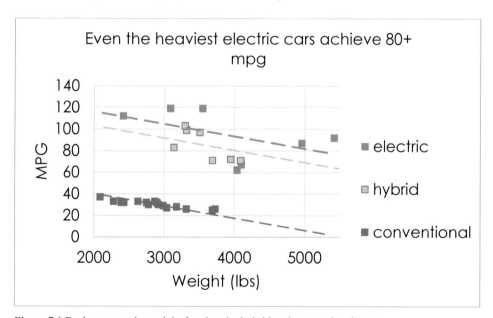

Figure 7.1 Fuel economy by weight for electric, hybrid and conventional cars.

Sakura managers concluded that a heavy, luxury electric could be designed which would offer much improved fuel economy relative to heavy, conventional, luxury cars. While weight significantly reduces fuel economy, the fuel economy benefit of electric more than compensates for added weight. Drivers who desire a large, luxury car may be persuaded to switch from conventional cars, without sacrificing size or luxury.

7.2 Indicators Modify the Intercept to Account for Shifts or Shocks

Example 7.2 Mattel Revenues. Mattel revenues had recovered from the negative impact of the global recession. Management credits much of this resilience to the acquisition of Radica late in '06. Radica added electronic games aimed at the preadolescent market.

Management needs a long range forecast of revenues through 2020. They also seek an estimate of the annual impact of the Radica acquisition.

First, the two most recent datapoints were hidden to enable later validation. Then, a plot of revenues by year was made, which is shown in Figure 7.2. The revenue boost from the acquisition was apparent in 2006-2007, as was the impact of recession in 2009 and 2010 (and possibly 2008).

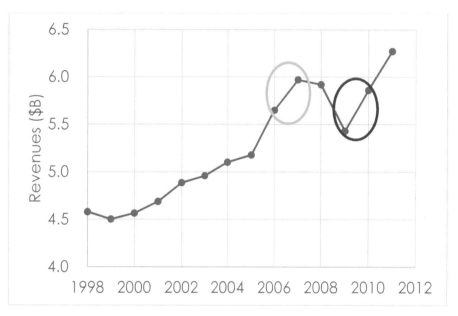

Figure 7.2 Trend in Mattel revenues.

Next, the one driver model of trend was built. Results are shown in Table 7.2 There was a significant positive trend, which explained much of the year to year variation.

Durbin Watson was 1.48, exceeding the upper critical value of 1.35. Residuals were free of unaccounted for shifts, shocks and cycles. However, managers believe that both the acquisition and the recession had impacts. Next the residuals were plotted to identify unaccounted for variation. This plot is shown in Figure 7.3. The residual in 2009 was two standard errors below zero, and the 2010 residual was also negative. The recession had not been accounted for. The residual in 2007 was two standard errors greater than zero, and the 2006 residual was also positive. The acquisition had not been accounted for.

An indicator of the recession was added, equal to one in 2009 and 2010, zero in other years, and a second regression was run. Results are shown in Table 7.3. The recession had a significant, negative impact on revenues.

Table 7.2 One driver trend model regression.

Regression Statistics					
R Square	0.884				
Standard Error	0.211				
Observations	14				

ANOVA	df	SS	MS	F	Significance F
Regression	1	4.073	4.073	91.3	6E-07
Residual	12	0.535	0.045		
Total	13	4.608			

	Coefficients	Standard Error	t Stat	P-value	Lower 95%	Upper 95%
Intercept	-263.0	28.1	-9.4	7.2E-07	-324.1	-201.8
Year	0.134	0.014	9.6	5.8E-07	0.103	0.164

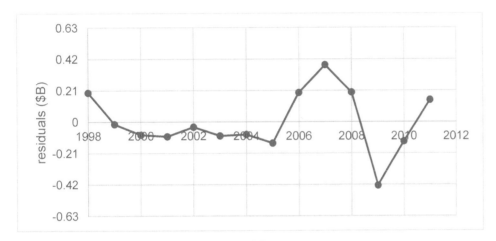

Figure 7.3 Residuals from the one driver model.

Durbin Watson was 1.36, between the lower and upper critical values, .91 and 1.55, suggesting possible autocorrelation. The residual plot is shown in Figure 7.4. The 2007 residual is the largest, and the 2006 residual is also positive. The acquisition has not yet been accounted or.

An acquisition indicator was added to the model, set to one in 2006 through the end of the series, zero elsewhere, and a third regression was run. Results are shown in Table 7.4. All three drivers, trend, recession and acquisition are significant, and in the expected direction.

Table 7.3 Regression with trend and recession indicator.

Regression Statistics						
R Square	0.937					
Standard Error	0.163					
Observations	14					
ANOVA	df	SS	MS	F	Significance F	
Regression	2	4.316	2.158	81.4	2.56E-07	
Residual	11	0.292	0.027			
Total	13	4.608				
	Coefficients	Standard Error	t Stat	P-value	Lower 95%	Upper 95%
Intercept	-301.4	25.1	-12.0	1.15E-07	-356.6	-246.2
Year	0.15	0.01	12.2	9.64E-08	0.125	0.181
recession	-0.44	0.14	-3.0	0.011452	-0.754	-0.120

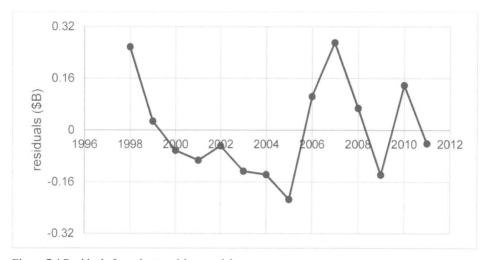

Figure 7.4 Residuals from the two driver model.

Durbin Watson is 2.44, well above the upper critical value of 1.78, suggesting that all trend, shocks, shifts, and cycles have been accounted for. The residual plot is shown in Figure 7.5.

With a powerful model with significant coefficients in the correct directions and pattern free residuals, the next step is to test the model's validity for forecasting.

The prediction interval bounds for individual years require the adjusted regression standard error, which excel does not provide. Consequently, the prediction interval for the mean will be used. This is a tougher test of validity, since the adjusted regression standard error is wider, making the margin of error for individual years also wider. Prediction intervals are shown in Table 7.5 for the two most recent, hidden years. The model accurately forecasts those two most recent years, providing evidence of predictive validity. For comparison, individual prediction intervals from JMP software are also shown in Table 7.5. (JMP is available at a special academic discount from onthehub.com.) With evidence of validity, the model was recalibrated, adding the two most recent observations. Results are shown in Table 7.6.

Table 7.4 Regression with recession and acquisition.

Regression Statistics					
R Square	0.988				
Standard Error	0.106				
Observations	14				

ANOVA	Df	SS	MS	F	Significance F
Regression	3	4.496	1.499	134.0	2.26E-08
Residual	10	0.112	0.011		
Total	13	4.608			

	Coefficients	Standard Error	t Stat	P-value	Lower 95%	Upper 95%
Intercept	-209.3	28.2	-7.4	2.23E-05	-272.0	-146.5
year	0.107	0.014	7.6	1.83E-05	0.076	0.138
recession	-0.468	0.094	-5.0	0.000554	-0.677	-0.259
acquisition	0.449	0.112	4.0	0.002476	0.200	0.699

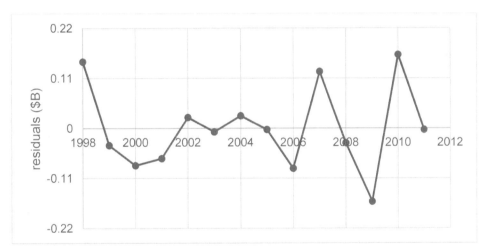

Figure 7.5 Residuals from the three driver model.

Table 7.5 Regression with recession and acquisition.

		mean prediction interval		individual prediction interval from JMP	
year	Revenues ($B)	lower	upper	Lower	upper
2012	6.42	6.14	6.62	6.18	6.79
2013	6.48	6.25	6.72	6.27	6.92

Table 7.6 Recalibrated regression with recession and acquisition.

Regression Statistics					
R Square	0.984				
Standard Error	0.097				
Observations	16				
ANOVA	df	SS	MS	F	Significance F
Regression	3	6.998	2.333	247.2	4.74E-11
Residual	12	0.113	0.009		
Total	15	7.111			

	Coefficients	Standard Error	t Stat	P-value	Lower 95%	Upper 95%
Intercept	-211.0	21.2	-9.9	3.79E-07	-257.2	-164.8
year	0.108	0.011	10.2	2.97E-07	0.085	0.131
recession	-0.473	0.079	-6.0	6.52E-05	-0.646	-0.301
acquisition	0.448	0.100	4.5	0.000738	0.231	0.665

The impact of the global recession, -470($M) is slightly larger than the impact of the acquisition, 450 ($M). The fit and forecast are shown in Figure 7.6. Both the prediction intervals for the mean and for individual years (from JMP) are shown.

7.3 Indicators Enhance Both Cross Sectional and Time Series Regression Models

The examples of a cross sectional model including segment differences and a time series model incorporating a shift (acquisition) and a shock (recession), demonstrate the value of adding indicators to models. Sakura electric learned that though weight reduced fuel efficiency, the electric segment was significantly more fuel efficient, even for the heaviest cars. Mattel management was able to quantify the impact of the Radica acquisition and the damaging impact of the global recession to obtain a long range forecast.

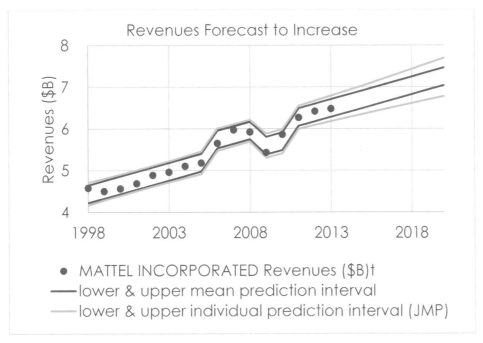

Figure 7.6 Fit and forecast..

Excel 7.1 Build a Regression Model to Compare Segments Using Indicators

Sakura electric.xls contains data from 31 car models on weight and miles per gallon. The sample includes three car segments, gasoline, hybrid, and electric. To quantify the differences between the three segments' fuel economy, also accounting for the impact of weight, add two columns for indicators of hybrid and electric.

From column D, insert two new columns:	Shift+right
Label column D *hybrid* and column E *electric*.	Alt HIC
Set *hybrid* cell values to 1 if a car is a hybrid, 0, otherwise, and set *electric* cars to 1 if a car is electric, 0, otherwise.	
In D2:	=IF(C2="hybrid",1,0)
In E2:	=IF(C2="electric",1,0)
In D2:	Shift+right
Double click the black square in the lower left to downfill both columns.	

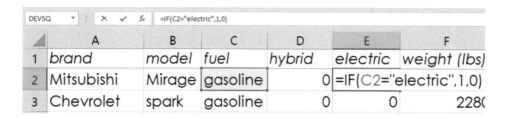

	Run regression of mpg with hybrid, electric and weight.	Alt AY_ R down down Enter G1:G32 Tab D1:F32 Tab L R Enter

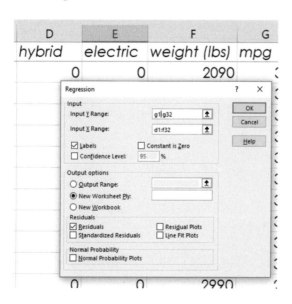

	A	B	C	D	E	F	G
1	SUMMARY OUTPUT						
2							
3	*Regression Statistics*						
4	Multiple F	0.945209					
5	R Square	0.89342					
6	Adjusted I	0.881578					
7	Standard E	11.2526					
8	Observati	31					
9							
10	ANOVA						
11		*df*	*SS*	*MS*	*F*	*gnificance F*	
12	Regressio	3	28658.2	9552.734	75.44351	3.02E-13	
13	Residual	27	3418.767	126.621			
14	Total	30	32076.97				
15							
16		*Coefficients*	*andard Err*	*t Stat*	*P-value*	*Lower 95%*	*Upper 95*
17	Intercept	63.04508	10.40097	6.061461	1.8E-06	41.70405	84.3861
18	hybrid	62.7679	5.596297	11.21597	1.15E-11	51.28525	74.2505
19	electric	75.8222	6.256297	12.11934	1.98E-12	62.98534	88.6590
20	weight (lb	-0.01139	0.003483	-3.26904	0.002942	-0.01854	-0.0042
21							
22							
23							
24	RESIDUAL OUTPUT						
25							
26	*bservatio*	*redicted m*	*Residuals*				
27	1	39.24492	-2.24492				

Excel 7.2 Plot Segment Predictions

Sakura electric.xls contains data from 31 car models on weight and miles per gallon. The sample includes three car segments, gasoline, hybrid, and electric. To quantify the differences between the three segments' fuel economy, also accounting for the impact of weight, add two columns for indicators of hybrid and electric.

To see the regression lines for each of the car segments, make a plot. First, copy the data from the data sheet and paste next to the residuals. Move the predicted values so they are next to actual mpg.

From B26:   Cntl+Shift+down
                                       Cntl+X
In K26:   Alt HIE:
Now, create a scatterplot for each of the
three car segments. Select weight, mpg, and
predicted mpg for gasoline powered cars.
From H25:   Shift+right right
                                       Shift+down (to row 43)
Request a scatterplot: Alt N D

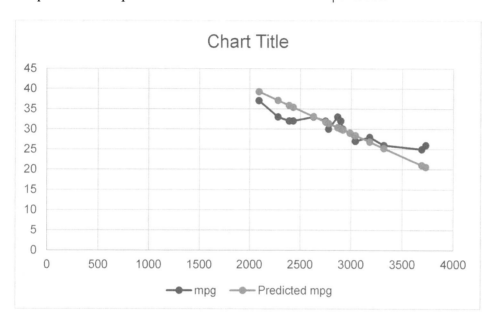

Next, select weight, mpg and predicted mpg   Shift+right right
for hybrid cars.   Shift+down (to row 50)
From H44:   Alt ND

Request a scatterplot:

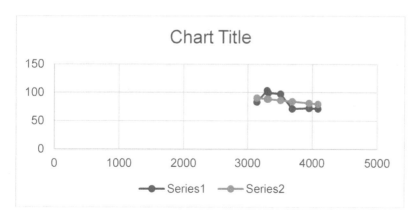

Copy the hybrid scatterplot.   Cntl+C
Paste onto the gasoline scatterplot.   Cntl+V

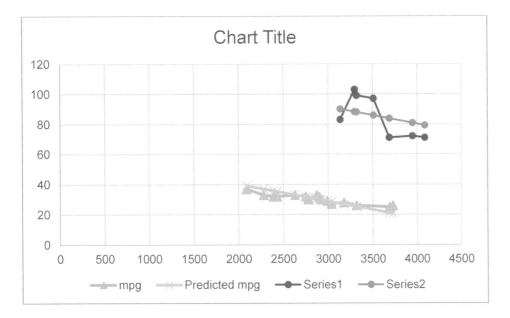

Third, create a scatterplot of the electric car segment, copy and paste onto the gasoline scatterplot:

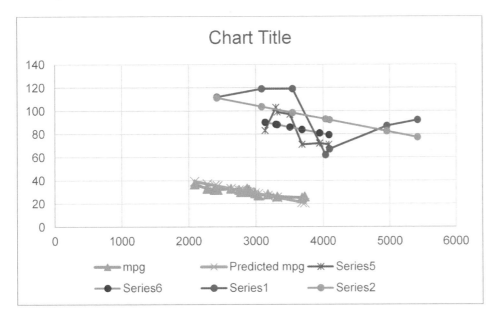

Now, to clean up the graph remove the lines from actual mpg and remove markers from predicted mpg.
Click on the electric mpg series and format data series.

Click the paint can.
Click No Line.

| Alt JAM

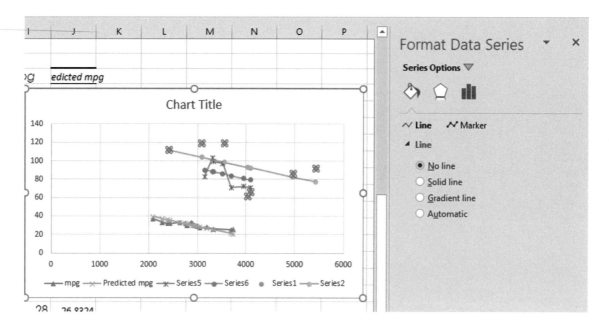

Change the marker fill and border to an electric color, such as gold.
Click marker, then fill and then choose fill color
Click border and then choose border color:

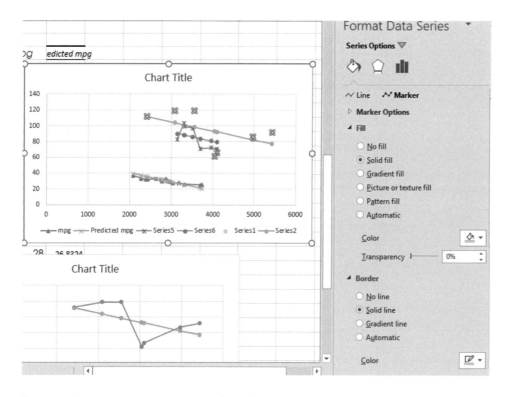

Repeat those steps to remove lines from hybrid and gasoline series and to recolor those.

Now remove markers from the predicted electric series.
Click on the predicted electric series, in the Format Data Series menu, click on markers, choose no markers.

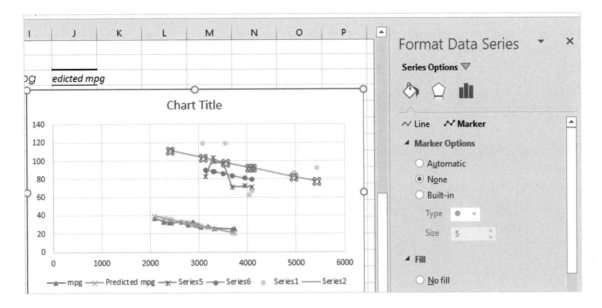

Click on Line and change color to match markers.

Repeat these steps to remove markers from predicted hybrid and gasoline series and to recolor to match markers:

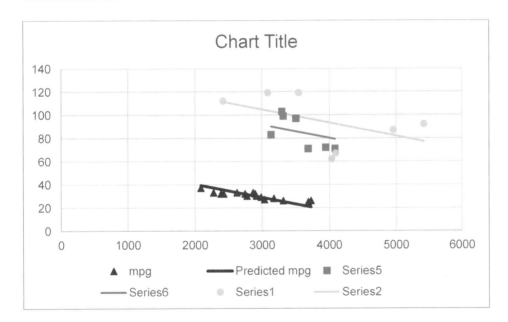

Drag the legend to the right of the plot and resize. The legend needs to identify the car segment predictions.

In the graph, open Select Data Source in the | Alt JCE
Design menu:

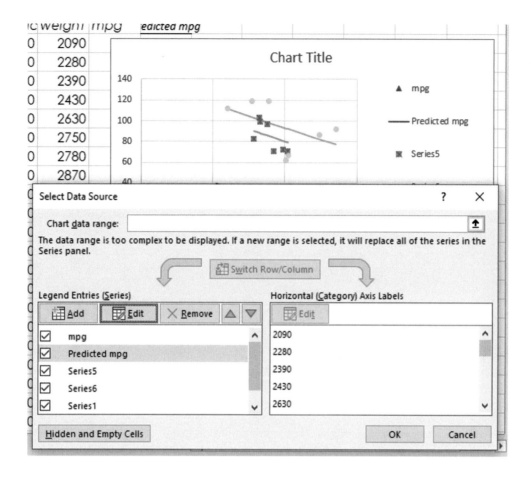

Select Predicted mpg and Edit and then replace the Series name with gasoline:

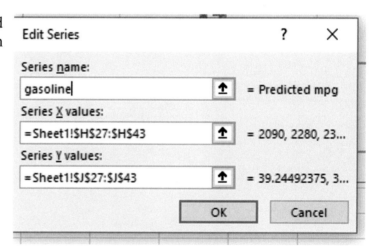

Similarly, replace Series 6 with hybrid and Series 2 with electric.

Reorder the series to correspond to the height in the plot, moving gasoline down and electric up with the blue arrows in the Select Data menu:

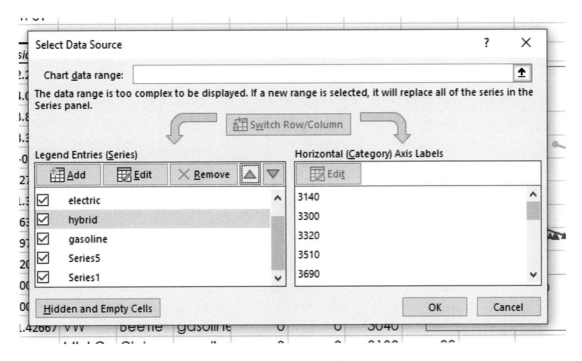

Click on marker items in the legend and | Cntl+1
delete.

To make good use of white space, adjust the
axes.

Click on the vertical axis.

Change the minimum to 20.

Click on the horizontal axis.

Change the minimum to 2000.

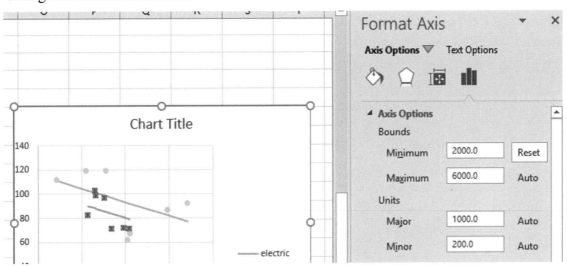

Add a vertical axis label: | Alt JCAAV
Type in miles per gallon | Alt JCAAH
Add a horizontal axis label:
Type in weight (lbs)

Replace the Chart Title with a standalone title:

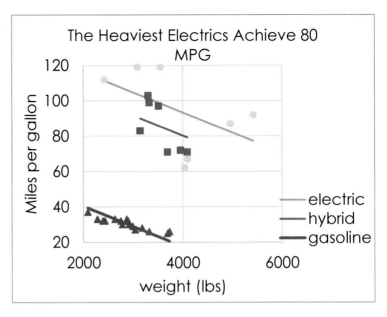

JMP 7 Run Multiple Regression and Find Individual Prediction Intervals

JMP is introduced to complement Excel. Building models in Excel enables deeper understanding of the layers of impact in a time series regression. However, Excel does not provide individual prediction intervals, which can be created in JMP.

Copy the data in the Mattel excel file to paste into JMP. Open JMP and choose File, New Data table:

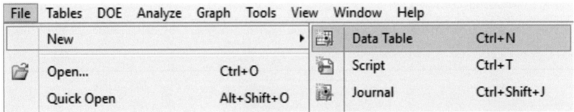

Choose Edit, Paste with Column names:

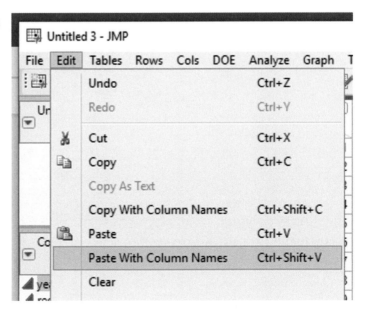

For the validation model, hide and exclude the two most recent observations and future years: Select the rows to be hidden, right click, Hide and Exclude:

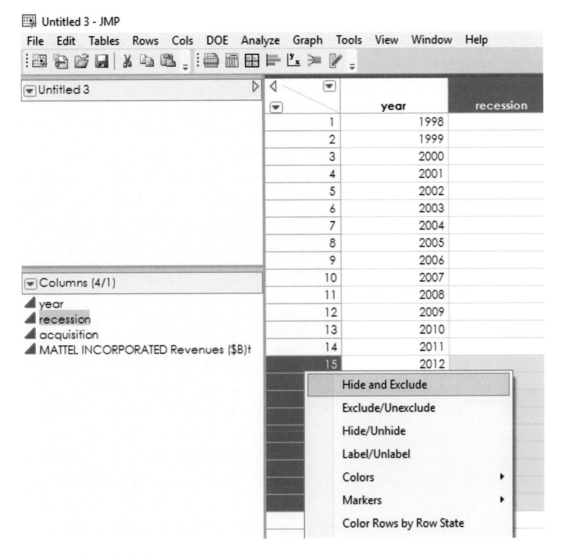

Choose View, JMP Starter:

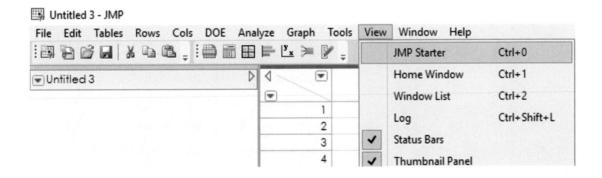

In JMP Starter, choose Fit Model, Fit Model:

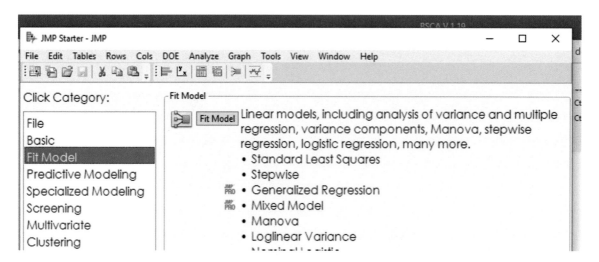

In Fit Model, choose Mattel revenues, then Y:

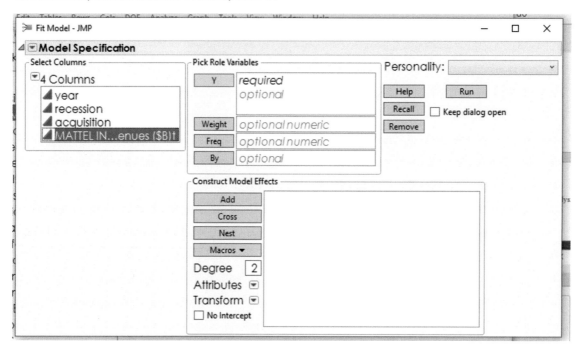

Choose the independent driver variables, year, recession and acquisition, then click Add:

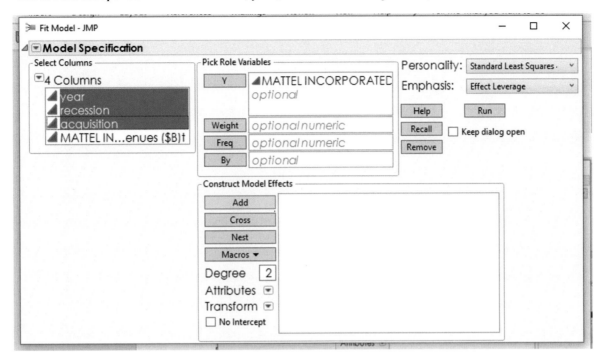

Set Emphasis to Minimal Report:

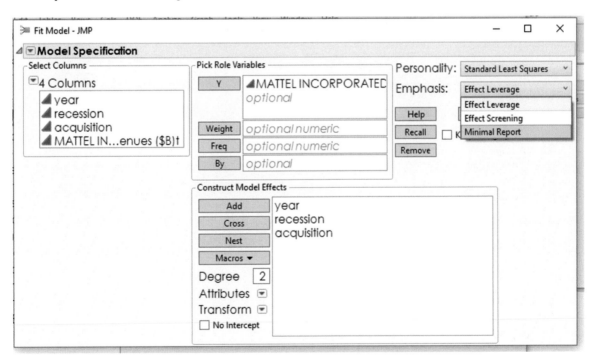

Click Run:

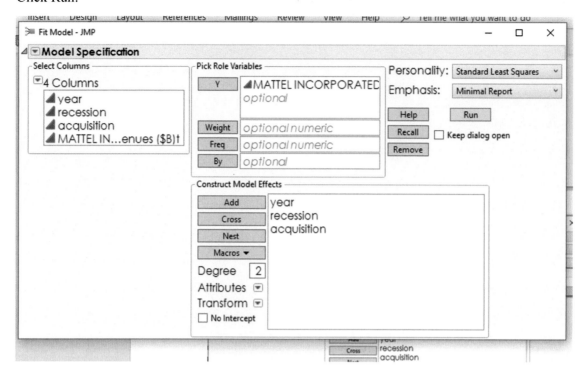

In the Response sheet containing regression results, click the red triangle, Save Columns, Indiv Confidence Limit Formula:

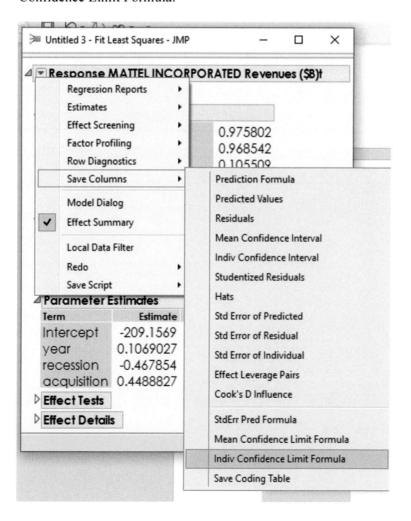

This will add the prediction interval columns to the data, which you can copy and paste into Excel:

	year	recession	acquisition	MATTEL INCORPORATED Revenues ($B)t	Lower 95% Indiv MATTEL INCORPORATED Revenues ($B)t	Upper 95% Indiv MATTEL INCORPORATED Revenues ($B)t
1	1998	0	0	4.58	4.1622729632	4.7069084527
2	1999	0	0	4.5	4.2801736767	4.802813049
3	2000	0	0	4.57	4.3946730825	4.9021189529
4	2001	0	0	4.69	4.5054607199	5.0051366253
5	2002	0	0	4.89	4.6123633747	5.1120392801
6	2003	0	0	4.96	4.7153810471	5.2228269175
7	2004	0	0	5.1	4.814686951	5.3373263233
8	2005	0	0	5.18	4.9105915473	5.4552270368
9	2006	0	1	5.65	5.4685181073	6.0088712733
10	2007	0	1	5.97	5.5809071524	6.1102875379
11	2008	0	1	5.92	5.6896640521	6.2153359479
12	2009	1	1	5.43	5.3032019659	5.8798953793
13	2010	1	1	5.86	5.4101046207	5.9867980341
14	2011	0	1	6.27	5.9941269743	6.5522889549
15	2012	0	1	6.42	6.0890207063	6.6712005326
16	2013	0	1	6.48	6.1811754069	6.7928511418
17	2014	0	1	•	6.2709661033	6.9148657551

After validating, right click on the hidden rows and choose Hide and Exclude to unhide for the recalibration model.

Lab 7-1 Harley-Davidson Revenues

Harley-Davidson is a multinational corporation headquartered in the U.S. which manufactures and sells motorcycles. Revenues in the early 2000s were increasing, but shifted downward in 2009 through 2014. Revenues had increased each year from 2010, though 2014 revenues were still below mid 2000s levels. Management needs a long range forecast of revenues through 2020.

In 2002, to appeal to new, younger motorcycle riders, H-D began selling the Buell Blast, a lighter, lower cost, fuel efficient, single cylinder motorcycle with a number of plastic parts. The expectation had been that Blast owners would trade up to the more expensive Harleys. However, Blast owners weren't trading up. Convinced that the Blast was cannibalizing sales of the more expensive H-D bikes, production of the Blast ceased in 2009.

Data are in **Harley.xlsx**.

Hide the two more recent datapoints, and then plot revenues and describe what you see: ___

increasing trend ___ decreasing trend ___ cycle ___ shift or shock

One Driver Model

1. Is trend (the year) significant? Is trend positive, as hypothesized?

2. Assopess residuals: DW: ___ dL: ___ dU: ___

   Residuals ___ contain ___ possibly contain ___ are free from positive autocorrelation.

3. Plot residuals and describe what you see: ___ increasing trend ___ decreasing trend ___ cycle ___ shift or shock

Two Driver Model

4. Are both drivers significant? Are coefficients of the correct sign?

5. Assess residuals: DW: ___ dL: ___ dU: ___

   Residuals ___ contain ___ possible contain ___ are free from positive autocorrelation.

6. Plot residuals and describe what you see: ___ increasing trend ___ decreasing trend ___ cycle ___ shift or shock

Three Driver Model

7. Are all drivers significant?   Are coefficients of the correct sign?

8. Assess residuals: DW: ___ dL: ____ dU: ____ Residuals ___ contain ___ possible contain ___ are free from positive autocorrelation.

9. Plot residuals and describe what you see: ___ increasing trend ___ decreasing trend ___ cycle ___ shift or shock

Test the validity of your model for forecasting

Use prediction intervals for the mean, rather than individual years, since the regression standard error adjustment is not available in excel for regressions with more than one independent variable.

10. Do the prediction intervals contain the two most recent datapoints?

Recalibrate and Present your Model

11. Plot your fit and forecast:

12. Present your model equation using this template:

$$Re\hat{v}enue(uy)_t = b_0(uy) + b_1(uy) \times I_{1t} + b_2(uy) \times I_{2t} + b_3\left(\frac{uy}{t}\right) \times t$$

13. How much annual revenue has been lost after the Blast was discontinued?

14. How much average annual revenue was lost during the recession?

CASE 7-1 Moneyball II. The Phillies General Manager is concerned that his players earn less than players for the closest two NLE competitors, the Mets and the Nationals. Are Phillies being paid too little? Are their lower salaries due to fewer years of experience with the Team?

From a sample drawn from the 2016 and 2017 rosters, build a model to quantify the impact of years of tenure and team. Add an indicator for team, *Phillies*, setting it to one for Phillies, zero for Nationals or Mets, making the Nationals and Mets the baseline teams. Data are in Phillies Salaries.

1. What hypothesis are you testing regarding the coefficients for *Phillies* and tenure?

2. Can the two null hypotheses regarding the coefficients for *Phillies* and tenure be rejected? Include their p values in your response.

3. How powerful is your model in explaining differences in player salaries?

4. Can the null hypothesis that RSquare is zero be rejected? Include the p value in your response.

5. Based on evidence from your regression, the *Phillies* earn how much less than the Mets/Nationals? _____

6. Present the simplified regression equations for *Phillies* and for Mets/Nationals:

7. Show your regression fit in a scatterplot of predicted and actual salaries for *Phillies* and Mets/Nationals:

Chapter 8
Presenting Statistical Analysis Results to Management

While it is important to be able to conduct the correct statistical analyses, it is equally important that results of analyses are packaged into easily understood PowerPoint presentations and Memos which translate those results to management and decision makers.

Results are often presented with a PowerPoint slide deck or Memo to management. In this chapter, guidelines for clear and compelling presentations are offered.

8.1 Use PowerPoints to Present Statistical Results for Competitive Advantage

PowerPoint presentations are a powerful tool that can greatly enhance your presentation of the results of your analysis. They are your powerful sidekick. Tonto to your Lone Ranger. PowerPoints help your audience member key points and statistics and make available graphics to illustrate and enhance the story you are telling.

The key to effective use of PowerPoints for presenting your results for competitive advantage is to be sure that they are not competing with you. PowerPoints with too much text draw audience attention away from you. Cliff Atkinson, in his 2008 book, beyond bullet points, (Microsoft Press) explains clearly how audience members process information during PowerPoint presentations and why you should move beyond bullet points in the design of your PowerPoints. Much of the material that follows reflects Mr. Atkinson's wisdom, and his book is a recommended investment.

Audience Brains are Designed to Process and Remember Information

Our brains are ingeniously designed to filter and process large amounts of information, selecting the most relevant to be stored in long term memory. Only a small portion of incoming information gains admission into working memory, and only some portion of information processing in working memory survives and is stored in long term memory.

© Springer Nature Switzerland AG 2019
C. Fraser, *Business Statistics for Competitive Advantage with Excel 2019 and JMP*,
https://doi.org/10.1007/978-3-030-20374-0_8

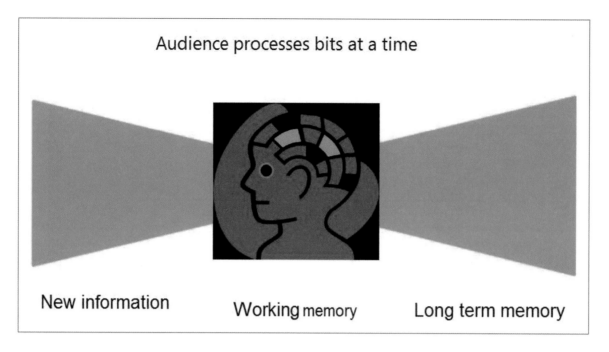

Figure 8.1 Information processing in a given moment

The goal is to help your audience filter information, direct their attention to your key results and interpretation, so that your message will be remembered.

Limit Text to a Single Complete Sentence per Slide

Since brains process only a few select bits of information in a given moment, increase the chance that the key points in your presentation become those select elements. If your slides are loaded with text, the critical point has a small chance of being processed in working memory.

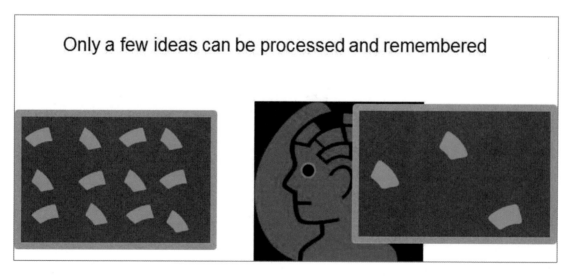

Figure 8.2 Limited processing in working memory

Work to design your slides so that each slide presents a single idea. Use only one complete sentence per slide.

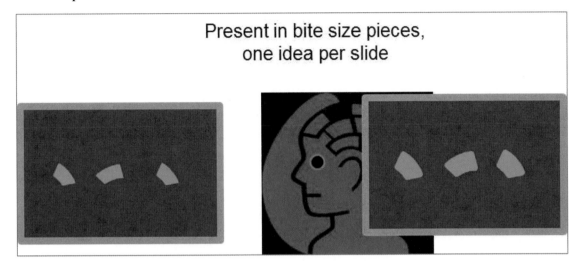

Figure 8.3 Present one idea at a time

Pause to Avoid Competing with Your Slides

Brains process a single channel at a time. Attention is directed toward either visuals or audio in any given moment.

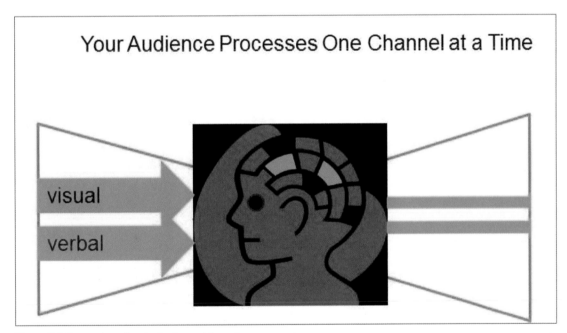

Figure 8.4 Processing of a single channel in a given moment

Your PowerPoints should complement the story that you are delivering. Your PowerPoints should not compete with you for attention. You are the star in the focus of attention. Your PowerPoints should play a supporting role. Pause to allow time for the audience to process that single idea, and then elaborate and explain. This will avoid competition between your slides and you.

Illustrate Results with Graphs Instead of Tables

Tables are effective elements in reports which convey a lot of information for readers to refer to and ponder. Tables are not processed in seconds, which is the time available to process each of your PowerPoint slides.

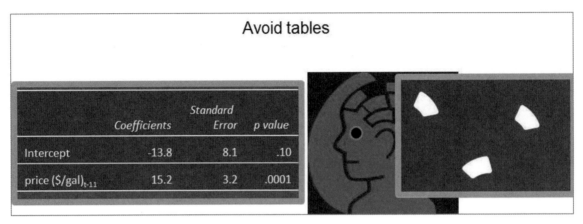

Figure 8.5 Information overload from tables

Synthesize the results in your tables into graphs. Graphs organize your results and illustrate key takeaways. Well-designed graphs can be processed in seconds, allowing audience attention to flow from a slide back to you, the speaker and, ideally, the focus of attention.

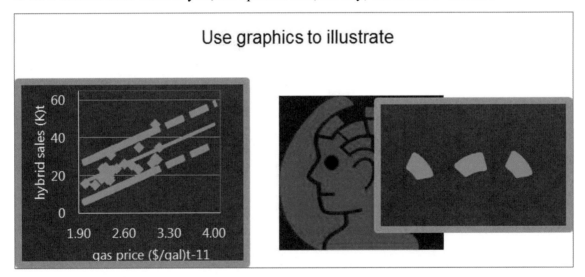

Figure 8.6 Effective presentation of results with graphs

An effective slide contains a single complete sentence, the *headline,* and a graph to illustrate.

Start PowerPoint Design in Slide Sorter

Insure that your PowerPoints are organized effectively. Build your deck by beginning in Slide Sorter view. Choose the main points that you want the audience to remember.

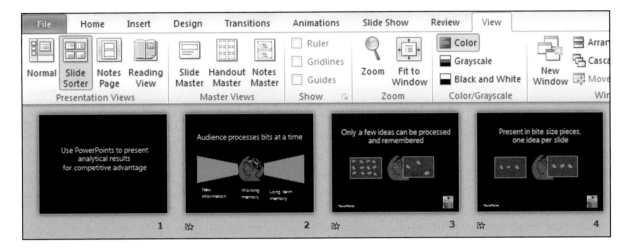

Figure 8.7 Slide sorter view

Next, add slides with supporting information the main point slides.

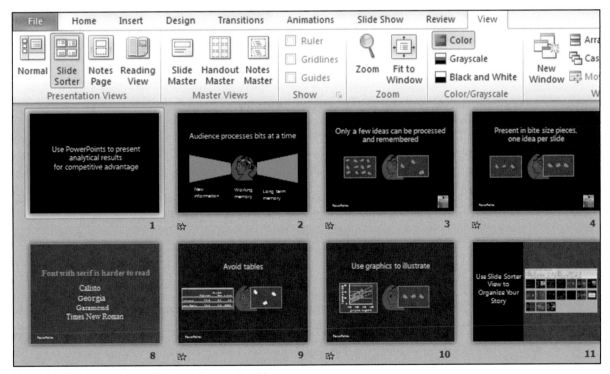

Figure 8.8 Slide sorter view of main and supporting ideas

Put Supporting Text in Slide Notes

Presenters sometimes worry that they will forget the story. For insurance, they include all of the text to be delivered in their slides. You can guess the consequence. Audience members attempt to read and process all of the text in the slides. To do this, they must ignore the presenter. In the few seconds that a slide appears, there is much too little time to read and process all of the text. As a result, the audience processes only remnants of the story. Audience members are frustrated, because at the end of the presentation, they have incomplete information that doesn't make sense.

In addition to supporting your presentation, your PowerPoints deliver an impression. Slides filled with text deliver the impression that the presenter lacks confidence. When audience members fail to process slides laden with text and tables, the natural conclusion is that the speaker is ineffective. "She spoke for fifteen minutes, but I can't remember what she said. Made no sense."

Audience members can reach a second, unfortunate conclusion in cases where a presenter has simply converted report pages into slides. Slides converted from reports are crammed with text and tables, and too often look like report pages, with white backgrounds, black text. This sort of unimaginative PowerPoint deck delivers the impression that the speaker is lazy.

In contrast, slides with a single, complete sentence headline and graph deliver the impression that the presenter is confident. After easily processing the slides and then focusing on explanation and elaboration delivered by the presenter, audience members understand and remember the story.

If you present a single idea in each slide, you will remember what you want to say to explain the idea and add elaboration. The audience will focus on your presentation, since you will provide the missing links.

You can have the best of both worlds. You can include your explanation and elaboration of the main points in the slide Notes. The Notes are not seen during your presentation, but they are available later. Provide handouts at the end of your presentation from the Notes view of your slides.

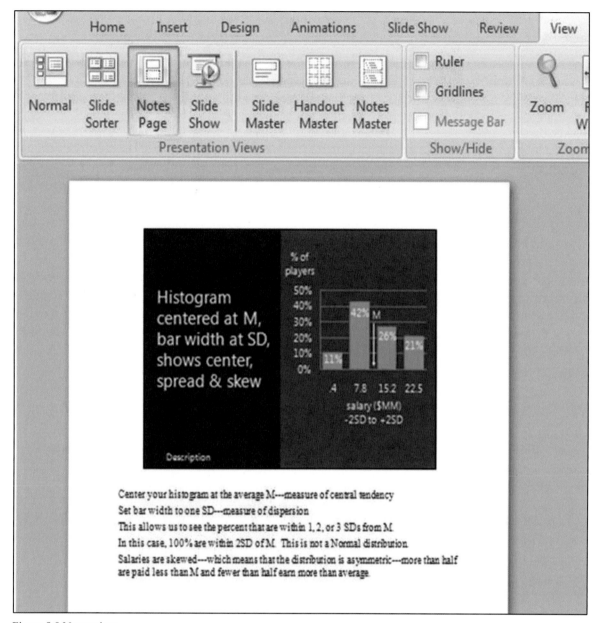

Figure 8.9 Notes view

Choose a Slide Design that Reduces Distraction

Design your slides so that elements are minimally distracting. You want the audience to be able to quickly and easily see the idea in each slide and then focus on you for explanation and elaboration.

Use a Font that can be Easily Read

Use *at least 24 pt* font so that audience members can easily read your headline, numbers, and labels. If you include numbers in your graphs, in the axes or as data labels, they must be easily read. (Be sure to round your numbers to two or three significant digits, also.) Axes labels, and other text must also be easily read. Any font smaller than 24 pt will challenge easy reading.

Choose a *sans serif* font (Ariel, Lucida, or Garamond). *Sans serif* fonts, without "feet" are easier to read in PowerPoints. *San serif* characters, without extra lines, are clearer in slides. (The opposite is true for reports, where the *serif* enhances reading ease.) If you have any doubts about readability, test your slides in a room similar in size and shape to the presentation location.

Choose Complementary Colors and Limit the Number

In cases where the slides will be presented in a darkened room, the background should be darker than the title and key words. Choose a medium or darker background, with complementary, contrasting, lighter text color. PowerPoints in this setting are more like television, movies, and internet media, and less like books or reports, and should feature darker backgrounds like those you see in movie credits.

When presentations are in well-lit rooms, backgrounds can be lighter than title and key words. In a light setting, PowerPoints resemble text pages, with lighter backgrounds and darker text colors.

If we see more than five colors on a slide (including text), our brains overload and we have difficulty processing the message and remembering it. Limit the number of distinct colors in each slide.

8.2 Write Memos That Encourage Your Audience to Read and Use Results

Memos are the standard for communication in business. They are short and concise, which encourages the intended audience to read them right away. Memos which present statistical analysis to decision makers

- feature the bottom line in the subject line,
- quantify how the bottom line result influences decisions,
- are ideally confined to one single spaced page,
- include an attractive, embedded graphic which illustrates the key result.

Many novice analysts copy and paste pages of output. The output is for consumption by analysts, whose job it is to condense and translate output into general business language for decision makers. Decision makers need to be able to easily find the bottom line results without referring to a statistics textbook to interpret results. It is our job to explain in easily understood language how the bottom line result influences decisions. For the quantitative members of the audience, key statistics are included.

On the following page is an example of a memo which might have been written by the quantitative analysis team at Procter & Gamble to present a key result of a concept test of Pampers Preemies to brand management.

Notice that

- the subject line contains the bottom line result,
- results are illustrated,
- results are described in general business English.

Description of the concept test and results are condensed and translated. Brand management learns from reading the memo what was done, who was involved, what results were, and what implications are for decision making.

MEMO

Re: Worldwide Exports Forecast to Grow Modestly Through 2016
To: Concha y Toro Management
From: Concha y Toro Quantitative Analysis Team
Date: July 2011

Summary

Consolidation of naïve models of trend in exports to the U.S., Latin American, European and Asian global regions through Monte Carlo simulation suggest model growth in export volumes through 2016.

Sample and method

The Consolidated Simulated Samples. From 2016 naïve model forecasts of export volumes to each of the four global regions, a simulated sample of likely export volumes was drawn. Those four samples were consolidated to identify likely Worldwide export volumes in 2016.

Results

Worldwide exports in 2016: 26.5 to 28.2ML
Given the assumption that exports in each of the four major global export markets will continue to exhibit stable, linear growth, 2016 Worldwide export volume is forecast to fall between 26.5ML and 28.2ML. This forecasts suggests annual growth in Worldwide export volume between 7 and 8 percent. The forecast has a margin of error of .85ML.

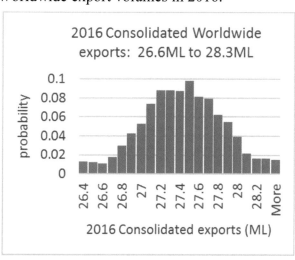

Europe and Asia will contribute slightly larger percentages to total exports, with Europe dominating 2016 export volumes (shown in Exhibit 1). U.S. exports will continue to be an important region, though the U.S. percentage of total worldwide exports will decline over the next six years. Global region shares of worldwide export volumes are shown in Exhibit 2.

Conclusions **Modest, stable growth forecast**

Growth worldwide exports over the next six years is forecast to slow to 7 to 8 percent, down from annual growth of 11 percent the past six years. Europe and Asian markets are increasingly more important, and exports to the U.S. are forecast to grow less.

Additional considerations **Latin American exports increasing, but at a declining rate**

In the Latin American market, exports have slowed in recent years. There, exports are growing at a decreasing rate, and a nonlinear naïve trend model would be more appropriate. Consequently, the forecast Latin American export contribution to consolidated Worldwide exports may overestimate the 2016 contribution and, consequently, the 2016 consolidated total.

Exhibit 1. Forecast 2016 Exports by Global Region

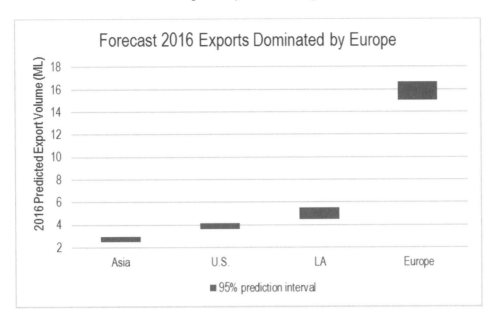

Exhibit 2. Worldwide Export Volume Shares by Global Region

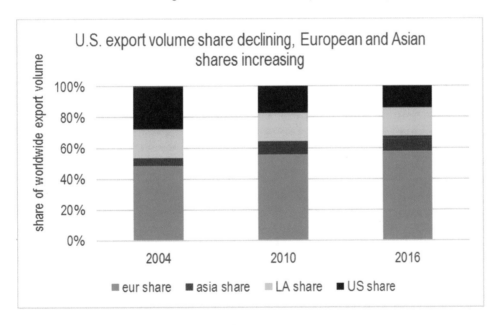

Chapter 9
Nonlinear Regression Models

In this chapter, nonlinear transformations are introduced that expand linear regression options to include situations in which marginal responses are either increasing or decreasing, rather than constant. We will explore Tukey's Ladder of Powers to identify particular ways to efficiently rescale variables to produce valid models with superior fit. An example will be offered in the context of trend models built for forecasting, and in Chapter 11, examples with explanatory multiple regression models will be added.

9.1 Consider a Nonlinear Model When Response Is Not Constant

To decide whether or not to use a nonlinear model, first rely on your logic:

- Do you expect the response, or change in the dependent, performance variable, to be constant, regardless of whether a change in an independent variable is at minimum values or at maximum values? Linear models assume constant response.
- Is the dependent variable limited or unlimited?

Linear models are unlimited. If your dependent variable couldn't be negative, because it is measured in purchases, people, or uses, a nonlinear model is logically more appropriate. After consulting your logic, plot your data.

9.2 Skewness Signals Nonlinear Response

When a dependent, performance variable y is skewed, performance response to differences or changes in drivers is nonlinear. Rescaling a skewed variable to roots or logarithms will linearize response, allowing use of multiple linear regression which will link the rescaled variables.

Increasing marginal response, in which differences or changes in x produce larger and larger responses in y, occurs if the dependent variable y is positively skewed, as in the upper plot in Figure 9.1.

Decreasing marginal response, in which differences or changes in x produce smaller and smaller responses in y, produces negative skewness in the dependent variable y. This possibility is shown in the lower plot in Figure 9.1.

Increasing marginal response, in which differences or changes in x produce larger and larger responses in y, yields positive skewness in the dependent variable y, shown in the upper plot in Figure 9.1.

© Springer Nature Switzerland AG 2019

C. Fraser, *Business Statistics for Competitive Advantage with Excel 2019 and JMP*,
https://doi.org/10.1007/978-3-030-20374-0_9

Marginal response of y to differences or changes in x is not constant

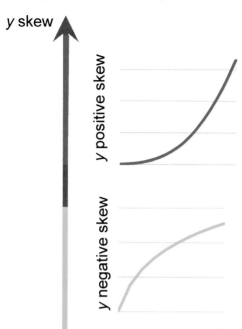

Figure 9.1 Nonconstant marginal response

To linearize response so that linear regression can be used, the goal is to rescale toward the center of Figure 9.1. Tukey offered a simple heuristic to quickly suggest ways to rescale variables when residuals from linear regression would be either skewed or heteroskedastic. A scale is chosen which reduces skewness of the dependent variable. A model built with a dependent variable which has been rescaled to reduce skewness will be nonlinear.

If a variable is positively skewed, as is the variable on the left in Figure 9.2, shrinking it by rescaling to roots, or natural logarithms will *Normalize*. Square roots are lower power, .5, than cube roots, .33, and are less radical. Natural logarithms make a bigger difference than square roots.

When a variable is negatively skewed, as is the variable on the left in Figure 9.3, expanding it by rescaling to squares or cubes will *Normalize*. A higher power, such as cubes, will make a bigger difference.

Moving from the center up or down the *Ladder of Powers,* Figure 9.4, changing the power more, changes the data and its skewness more. More skewness calls for adjusting more.

A Positively Skewed variable, y, becomes Normal with Square Roots, Cube Roots or Logarithms

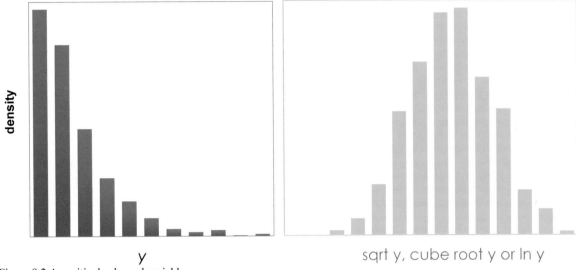

Figure 9.2 A positively skewed variable

A Negatively Skewed variable, y, becomes Normal with Squares or Cubes

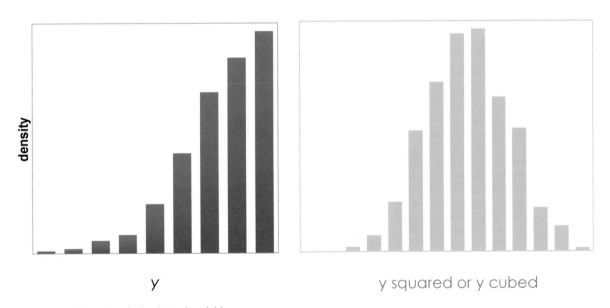

Figure 9.3 A negatively skewed variable

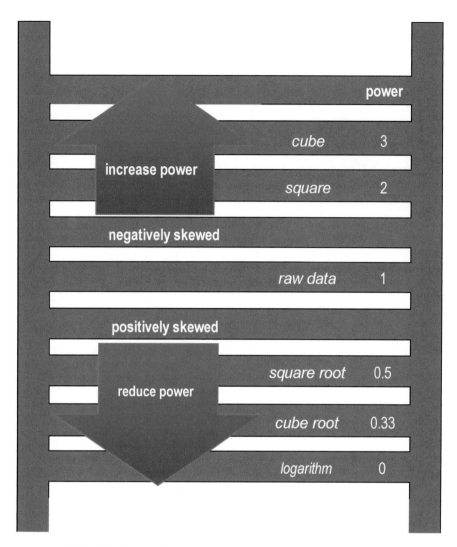

Figure 9.4 Tukey's Ladder of Powers

The upper, blue plot in Figure 9.5 reflects a positively skewed dependent variable. Rescaling values of that dependent variable to their natural logarithms or roots will linearize the relationship, moving the plot down to Normal skewness in Figure 9.5.

The lower, gold plot in Figure 9.5 features a negatively skewed dependent variable. Rescaling dependent variable values to their squares or cubes will linearize the plot, moving it up to Normal skewness in Figure 9.5.

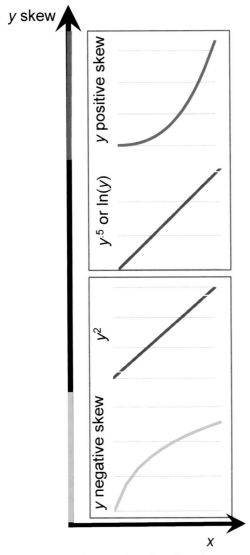

Figure 9.5 Rescaling to reduce skew linearizes.

9.3 Rescaling *y* Builds in Interactions

Jointly, two drivers may make a larger difference than the sum of their individual influences. For example, advertising levels may be more effective when sales forces are larger. The impact of population growth in a country may influence imports more if growth in GDP has been relatively high. When the dependent variable is rescaled, the model becomes multiplicative, with interactions between predictors. With this potential benefit of improved fit and validity, comes the cost of transforming predictions in rescaled units back to the original units.

9.4 When to Rescale

In the examples below, trend models to achieve long range forecasts are featured. When a long range forecast is desired, rescaling even modestly skewed dependent variables will produce a more accurate forecast. For cross sectional models to identify drivers, rescaling is only necessary if skewness of a dependent or an independent variable is outside the approximately Normal range, -1 to +1. Similarly, for time series models designed to identify drivers and produce a short term forecast, rescaling is important only for variables with skewness outside the approximately Normal range.

Example 9.1 The Market for Preemie Diapers. Deb Henretta, President of P&G's global baby care division, was about to commit substantial resources to launch *Pampers Swaddlers,* diapers for fragile, very preterm babies. Those babies weight between one and three pounds and have sensitive skin. *Swaddlers* have no adhesives and are made of breathable fabric, instead of plastic.

Due to advances in medicine and infertility treatments, this is an increasing market, Mothers of these babies are increasingly older or wealthier.

P&G managers believe that *Swaddlers* are a natural extension of their Pampers Stages line of diapers. If very preterm parents adopt *Swaddlers*, the hope is that they would remain loyal Pampers customers as their children grow.

Before resources are dedicated, Deb needs a forecast the number of very preterm babies that will be born through 2020 within the three largest ethnic segments. Her team assumes that revenue potential depends on the number of very preterm babies born in each of the three largest ethnic segments. The number of very preterm births in a year is the product of number of births and the chance that a newborn will be very preterm, the very preterm birthrate.

The number of very preterm babies is thought to vary by *ethnicity*. Advances in infertility treatments have led to more births by *older, predominantly white*, high risk mothers. Immigration has led to more births by the *youngest, predominantly Hispanic* mothers, many with little information about prenatal care and lack of access to adequate healthcare.

The global recession is thought to have affected birthrates. Following the recession, managers believe that some women have opted to bear fewer children. This impact is thought to vary by ethnicity.

Forecast of Very Preterm Babies (VPB) in the White Ethnic Segment

Using Census data, broken down by ethnicity the Team began with the largest White segment. To assess skewness, only years before the global recession were used, years 2001-2008, since any impact of the recession could affect skewness. VPBs in the White segment were declining and mildly positively skewed at .076. A plot of the data confirms that VPBs were decreasing at a decreasing rate before recession years. In Figure 9.6, births in years 2001 through 2004 and 2008 through 2010 are above the trendline, while births in years 2005-2007 are below the trendline.

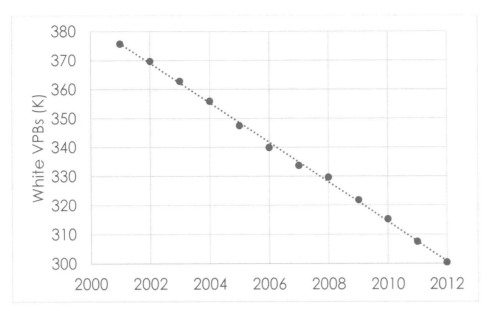

Figure 9.6 VPBs in the White ethnicity.

Rescaling to square roots, cube roots and natural logarithms (lns) reduced skewness to .050, .042 and .025. The team focused on the lns to build the model. A plot of the lns is shown in Figure 9.7.

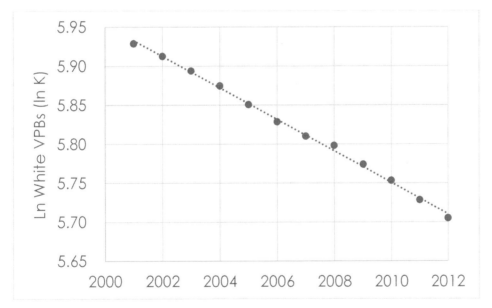

Figure 9.7 Natural logarithms of VPBs in the White ethnicity.

The one driver trend model was significant with RSquare of .998. (Census data is very accurate, and annual births reveal a very consistent trend.) However, Durbin Watson of 1.15 falls just short of the upper critical value, 1.33. The residual plot does indeed show potential impact of recession in 2011 and 2012, as shown in Figure 9.8.

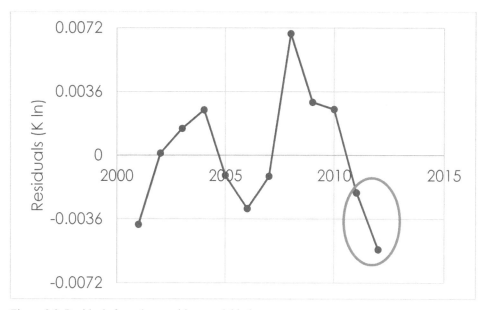

Figure 9.8 Residuals from the one driver model in lns

A recession indicator, set to one in 2011 and 2012, zero elsewhere, was added to the model. Results are shown in Table 9.1.

Recession did reduce births in 2011 and 2012. Durbin Watson of 1.82 exceeded the upper critical value of 1.58. The model correctly predicted births in the two most recent years, with recession set to one in 2013 and zero in 2014. The recalibrated model using all observations is shown in Table 9.2

Table 9.1 Two driver model of the lns of White VPBs.

Regression Statistics					
R Square	0.999				
Standard Error	0.0029				
Observations	12				

ANOVA	df	SS	MS	F	Signif F
Regression	2	.058	.029	3530.1	9.37E-14
Residual	9	7.5E-05	8.3E-06		
Total	11	.059			

	Coefficients	Standard Error	t Stat	P-value	Lower 95%	Upper 95%	one tail p value
Intercept	45.3	.634	71.5	1.0E-13	43.9	46.8	
year	-0.020	0.00032	-62.3	3.6E-13	-0.020	-0.019	
recession	-0.0077	0.0025	-2.6	0.028	-0.0143	0.0011	0.014

Table 9.2 Recalibrated model of the lns of White VPBs.

Regression Statistics							
R Square	0.999						
Standard Error	0.0027						
Observations	12						
ANOVA	df	SS	MS	F	Signif F		
Regression	2	.0924	.0462	6402.9	1.4E-17		
Residual	9	7.9E-05	7.2E-06				
Total	11	.0925					
	Coefficients	Standard Error	t Stat	P-value	Lower 95%	Upper 95%	one tail p value
Intercept	45.2	.44	102.7	9.3E-18	44.2	46.1	
year	-0.020	0.00022	-89.5	4.3E-17	-0.020	-0.019	
recession	-0.0090	0.0022	-4.2	0.0016	-0.014	-0.0042	0.008

The model in lns fit the data well.

$$\ln Whi\hat{t}e\ VPBs(K)_t = 45(\ln K) - .0090(\ln K) \times recession_t - .020(\frac{\ln K}{year}) \times t$$

From the model in lns, the model in the original scale of K births can be created with exponential functions of both sides:

$$\exp[\ln Whi\hat{t}e\ VPBs(K)_t] = \exp[45(\ln K) - .0090(\ln K) \times recession_t - .020(\frac{\ln K}{year}) \times t]$$

This is simplified with knowledge that the exponential function of a sum of part worths is the product of exponential functions of the part worths:

$$W hi\hat{t}e\ VPBs(K)_t = \exp(45(\ln K)) \times \exp(-.0090(\ln K) \times recession_t)$$

$$\times \exp(-.020(\frac{\ln K}{year}) \times t)$$

This further simplifies by finding the values of the multiplicative coefficients:

$$W hi\hat{t}e\ VPBs(K)_t = 4.1\,E + 19(K).99^{recession_t} \times .98^t$$

The equation informs managers that recession reduced White VPBs to 99% of nonrecessionary years, and each year, White VPBs are 98% of what they were the previous year. The model fit and forecast is shown in Figure 9.9.

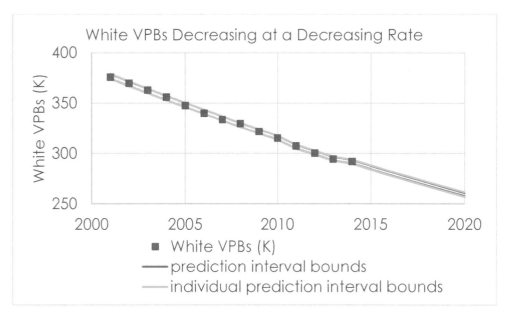

Figure 9.9 Fit and forecast of White VPBs.

The analysis team turned focus to the forecast of Black VPBs. Skewness in prerecession years was -.13 and the plot, shown in Figure 9.10, reveals a positive trend. Comparing skewness of the squares and cubes, at -.12 and -.11, led to the decision to model the cubes, which were more symmetric. The plot of the cubes is shown in Figure 9.11.

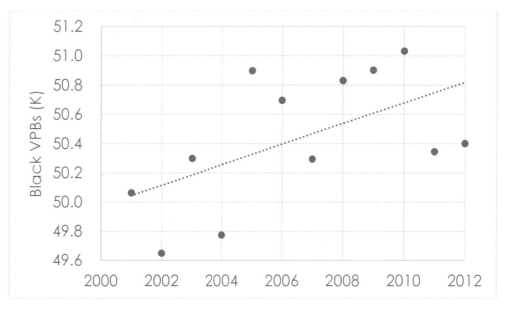

Figure 9.10 Black VPBs trend

The one driver model of trend with the cubes was just short of significance, with the p value of F equal to .06 and RSquare at .31. Durbin Watson was 2.01, suggesting pattern free residuals. However, the residual plot did reveal the likely impact of recession in 2011 and 2012, shown in Figure 9.12. To improve the model, a recession indicator was added, set to one in 2011 and 2012, zero elsewhere. Results are shown in Table 9.3

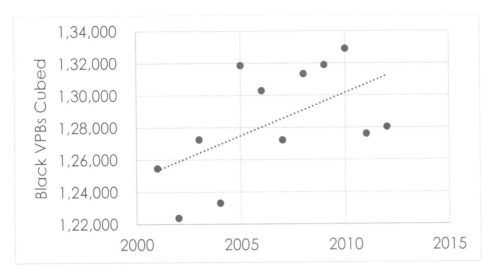

Figure 9.11 Black VPBs cubes trend

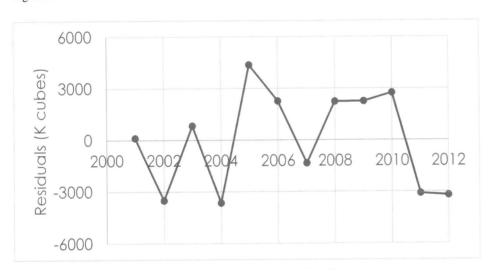

Figure 9.12 Residuals from the one driver model of Black VPBs cubes

Table 9.3 Regression of Black VPB cubes

Regression Statistics							
R Square	0.628						
Standard Error	2324						
Observations	12						

ANOVA	df	SS	MS	F	Significance F		
Regression	2	82046545	41023272	7.6	0.012		
Residual	9	48616539	5401838				
Total	11	130663083					

	Coefficients	Standard Error	t Stat	P-value	Lower 95%	Upper 95%	one tail p value
Intercept	-1858908	511629	-3.6	0.0055	-3016292.7	-701524	
Year	991	255	3.9	0.0037	414	1568	
Recession	-6518	2363	-2.8	0.0222	-11864	-1172	0.011

With the recession accounted for, the model and the trend were significant, and RSquare rose to .63. Durbin Watson was 3.01 and the model was valid with recession continuing. The recalibrated model is shown in Table 9.4. The model made sense, though a fairly large portion of variation remained unexplained.

The equation in cubes is:

$$Bl\hat{a}ck\ VPBs(K)_t^3 = -1{,}870{,}000(K^3) - 6{,}700(K^3) \times recession_t + 990(\frac{K^3}{t}) \times t$$

To rescale back to K VPBs, the cube roots of both sides was used:

$$[Bl\hat{a}ck\ VPBs(K)_t^3]^{\frac{1}{3}} = [-1{,}870{,}000(K^3) - 6{,}700(K^3) \times recession_t + 990(\frac{K^3}{t}) \times t]^{1/3}$$

$$Bl\hat{a}ck\ VPBs(K)_t = [-1{,}870{,}000(K^3) - 6{,}700(K^3) \times recession_t + 990(\frac{K^3}{t}) \times t]^{1/3}$$

The fit and forecast are shown in Figure 9.13

Table 9.4 Recalibrated regression of Black VPB cubes

Regression Statistics							
R Square	0.631						
Standard Error	2149						
Observations	12						

ANOVA	df	SS	MS	F	Significance F		
Regression	2	86692204	43346102	9.4	0.0042		
Residual	9	50800090	4618190				
Total	11	1.37E+08					

	Coefficients	Standard Error	t Stat	P-value	Lower 95%	Upper 95%	one tail p value
Intercept	-1865910	460739	-4.0	0.0019	-2879990	-851830	
Year	994	230	4.3	0.0012	489	1500	
Recession	-6720	2050	-3.3	0.0074	-11232	-2208	0.0037

Considering the White and Black VPB forecasts, Deb realized that the White segment was considerably larger, though declining; however, the Black segment was increasing. The recession had a larger and continuing impact in the Black segment, which may correspond to higher price sensitivity. The Hispanic segment forecast would be next.

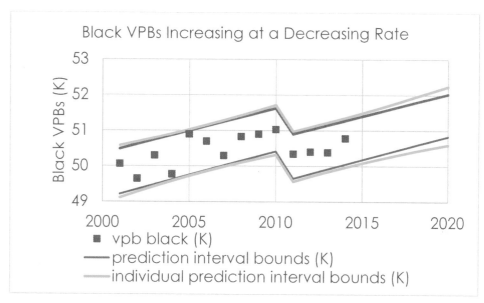

Figure 9.13 Fit and forecast of Black VPBs

9.5 Gains from Nonlinear Rescaling Are Significant

To see the gain from building nonlinear models, compare results with those from simpler linear models. The linear model of White VPBs, using the same sample, excluding the two most recent observations, is below in Figure 9.14.

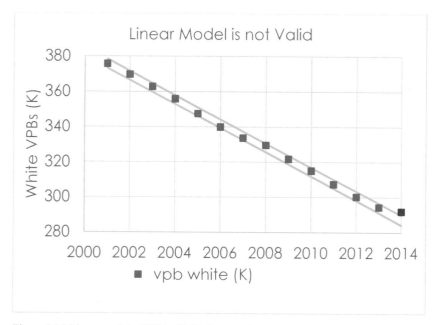

Figure 9.14 Linear model of White VPBs is not valid.

The linear model of White VPBs is not valid. White VPBs are overestimated, since the linear model assumes a constant annual decline, while actual VPBs are decreasing at a decreasing rate. The recession indicator was not significant and was removed.

9.6 Nonlinear Models Offer the Promise of Better Fit and Better Behavior

It is a challenge to think of an example of truly linear (constant) response. Responses tend to be nonconstant and nonlinear. The fifth dip of ice cream is less appetizing than the first. Consumers become satiated at some point, and beyond that point, additional consumption is less valuable. Adding the twentieth stock to a portfolio makes less difference to diversification than adding the third. A second ad insertion in a magazine enhances recall more than a tenth ad insertion. As a consequence of nonconstant marginal response, nonlinear models promise superior fit and better behaved models, with valid forecasts. Nonlinear models which feature a rescaled dependent variable incorporate interactions between drivers, adding another realistic and useful aspect. Nonlinear models do carry the cost of transformation to and back from logarithms, roots, or squares. In some cases, a linear model fits data quite well and is a reasonable approximation. Thinking logically about the response that you've set to explain and predict, and then looking at the distribution and skewness of your data and your residuals, will often lead you toward the choice of a nonlinear alternative.

Skewness signals nonlinear response. Tukey's Ladder of Powers can help quickly determine the particular nonlinear model which will fit a dataset best. When a variable is positively skewed, rescaling to roots or natural logarithms reduces the positive skew. Negatively skewed variables are Normalized by squaring or cubing. The amount of difference corresponds to the power---square roots with power .5 are less radical than logarithms with power 0 and squares with power 2 are less extreme than cubes with power 3.

Excel 9.1 Rescale to Build and Fit Nonlinear Regression Models with Linear Regression

Forecast of Very Preterm Births by Ethnicity for P&G. The Director of Baby Worldwide division at Procter & Gamble desires a forecast of very preterm births (VPBs) which would be targets for Pampers Swadlers. Build models to quantify trends and the potential impact on VPBs of the global recession.

Historical annual data in **9 VPBs** contains annual observations on VPBs for the three largest ethnic segments. Models for the White and Black segments are built below.

In order to validate the models for forecasting, hide the two most recent observations.

Assess skewness and choose scales.

Assess *skewness* of White and Black VPBs | =**SKEW**(*array*).
using data from prerecession years only.

DEVSQ	▾	⋮	×	✓	*fx*	=SKEW(C2:C9)

	A	B	C	D
1	year	vpb white	vpb black (K)	
3	2012	300.4	50.4	
4	2013	294.5	50.4	
5	2014	292.1	50.8	
6				
7		0.076	=SKEW(C2:C9)	

Create five columns for the square roots, cube roots and natural logarithms of White VPBs and the squares and cubes of Black VPBs.
Make the square roots.
Make the cube roots.
Make the natural logarithms (lns).
Make the squares.
Make the cubes.
Downfill through row 15,
Right fill skewness in row 17 from B17.

=*cell*^**.5**
=*cell*^**(1/3)**
=**LN**(*cell*)
=*cell*^2
=*cell*^3

Shift+right
Cntl+R

1	year	white VPBs (K)	Black VPBs (K)	sqrt White VPBs	cube root White VPBs	ln White VPBs	Black VPBs squares	Black VPB cubes
10	2009	321.8	50.9	17.9	6.9	5.77	2,591	131,889
11	2010	315.3	51.0	17.8	6.8	5.75	2,604	132,912
12	2011	307.5	50.3	17.5	6.7	5.73	2,535	127,608
13	2012	300.4	50.4	17.3	6.7	5.71	2,540	128,037
14	2013	294.5	50.4	17.2	6.7	5.69	2,539	127,939
15	2014	292.1	50.8	17.1	6.6	5.68	2,579	130,960
16								
17		0.076	-0.127	0.050	0.042	0.025	-0.754	-0.742

Use the scales that produce skewness closest to zero, *ln White VPBs*, and *Black VPBs cubes* and run regression with year *t*.

Excel 9.2 Forecast White VPBs with Natural Logarithms

	A	B	C	D	E	F	G
1	SUMMARY OUTPUT						
2							
3	*Regression Statistics*						
4	Multiple F	0.998876					
5	R Square	0.997753					
6	Adjusted I	0.997528					
7	Standard I	0.003629					
8	Observati	12					
9							
10	ANOVA						
11		*df*	*SS*	*MS*	*F*	*gnificance F*	
12	Regressio	1	0.058479	0.058479	4440.294	1.41E-14	
13	Residual	10	0.000132	1.32E-05			
14	Total	11	0.058611				
15							
16		*Coefficients*	*andard Err*	*t Stat*	*P-value*	*Lower 95%*	*Upper 95%*	*ov*
17	Intercept	46.39771	0.608928	76.19576	3.7E-15	45.04093	47.75448
18	year	-0.02022	0.000303	-66.6355	1.41E-14	-0.0209	-0.01955

Assess Durbin Watson, plot residuals, and set the major vertical units to the standard error.

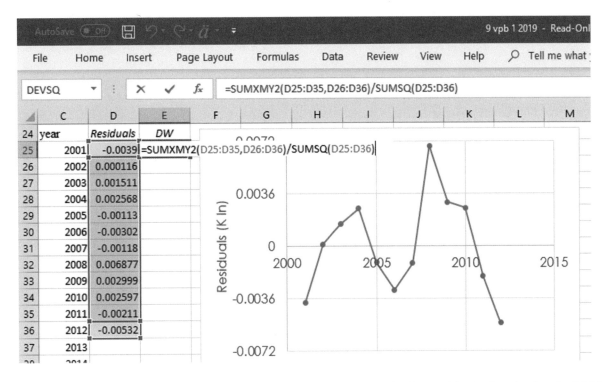

A shift, presumably due to the global recession, is apparent in the residuals, beginning in 2011.

Return to the data sheet and add a new column A, next to the year *t* for a *recession* indicator, equal to 1 in years 2011 onward.

	A	B	
			w
			V
1	*recession*	*year*	*(l*
11	0	2010	
12	1	2011	
13	1	2012	
14	1	2013	
15	1	2014	

225   Run regression including the *recession* indicator, assess Durbin Watson, and plot residuals.

	A	B	C	D	E	F	G
1	SUMMARY OUTPUT						
2							
3	*Regression Statistics*						
4	Multiple R	0.999363					
5	R Square	0.998727					
6	Adjusted R	0.998444					
7	Standard E	0.002879					
8	Observatio	12					
9							
10	ANOVA						
11		*df*	*SS*	*MS*	*F*	*ignificance F*	
12	Regression	2	0.058536	0.029268	3530.066	9.37E-14	
13	Residual	9	7.46E-05	8.29E-06			
14	Total	11	0.058611				
15							
16		*Coefficients*	*andard Err*	*t Stat*	*P-value*	*Lower 95%*	*Upper 95% c*
17	Intercept	45.32115	0.633854	71.50092	1.04E-13	43.88727	46.75503
18	recession	-0.00768	0.002928	-2.62386	0.027635	-0.0143	-0.00106
19	year	-0.01969	0.000316	-62.2835	3.58E-13	-0.0204	-0.01897

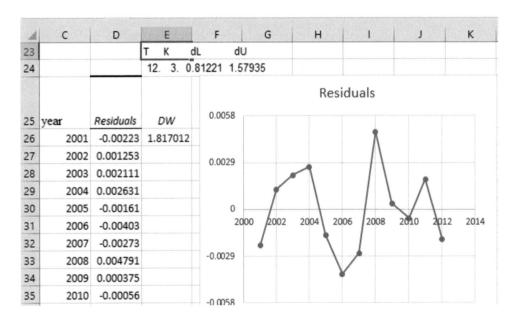

	C	D	E	F	G	H	I	J	K
23			T K dL dU						
24			12. 3. 0.81221 1.57935						
25	year	*Residuals*	*DW*						
26	2001	-0.00223	1.817012						
27	2002	0.001253							
28	2003	0.002111							
29	2004	0.002631							
30	2005	-0.00161							
31	2006	-0.00403							
32	2007	-0.00273							
33	2008	0.004791							
34	2009	0.000375							
35	2010	-0.00056							

The model is significant and makes sense. The residuals are free from positive autocorrelation and very small in most recent years.

Assess the predictive validity of the model. Copy the data used in the regression and paste next to the residuals. Find the three multiplicative part worths, beginning with the multiplicative constant (=exp($B$17). Use Fn 4 to lock the cell reference.

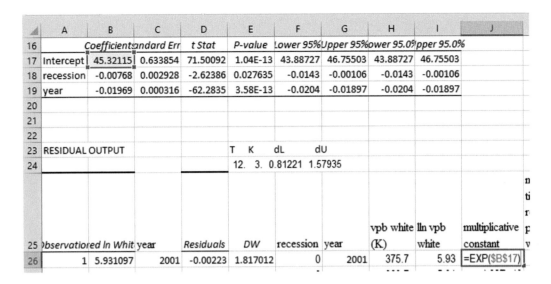

	A	B	C	D	E	F	G	H	I	J
16		Coefficient	andard Err	t Stat	P-value	Lower 95%	Upper 95%	ower 95.0%	pper 95.0%	
17	Intercept	45.32115	0.633854	71.50092	1.04E-13	43.88727	46.75503	43.88727	46.75503	
18	recession	-0.00768	0.002928	-2.62386	0.027635	-0.0143	-0.00106	-0.0143	-0.00106	
19	year	-0.01969	0.000316	-62.2835	3.58E-13	-0.0204	-0.01897	-0.0204	-0.01897	
20										
21										
22										
23	RESIDUAL OUTPUT				T	K	dL	dU		
24					12.	3.	0.81221	1.57935		
25	Observation	ed ln Whit	year	Residuals	DW	recession	year	vpb white (K)	lln vpb white	multiplicative constant
26	1	5.931097	2001	-0.00223	1.817012	0	2001	375.7	5.93	=EXP($B$17)

Find the multiplicative recession part worth (=exp($B$18)^recession).

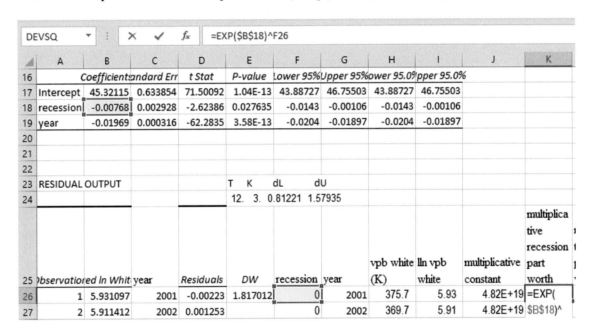

| DEVSQ | ▼ | ⋮ | × | ✓ | fx | =EXP($B$18)^F26 | | | | | |

	A	B	C	D	E	F	G	H	I	J	K
16		Coefficient	andard Err	t Stat	P-value	Lower 95%	Upper 95%	ower 95.0%	pper 95.0%		
17	Intercept	45.32115	0.633854	71.50092	1.04E-13	43.88727	46.75503	43.88727	46.75503		
18	recession	-0.00768	0.002928	-2.62386	0.027635	-0.0143	-0.00106	-0.0143	-0.00106		
19	year	-0.01969	0.000316	-62.2835	3.58E-13	-0.0204	-0.01897	-0.0204	-0.01897		
20											
21											
22											
23	RESIDUAL OUTPUT				T	K	dL	dU			
24					12.	3.	0.81221	1.57935			
25	Observation	ed ln Whit	year	Residuals	DW	recession	year	vpb white (K)	lln vpb white	multiplicative constant	multiplicative recession part worth
26	1	5.931097	2001	-0.00223	1.817012	0	2001	375.7	5.93	4.82E+19	=EXP(
27	2	5.911412	2002	0.001253		0	2002	369.7	5.91	4.82E+19	$B$18^

Find the multiplicative trend part worth (=exp($B$19)^year.

DEVSQ	▼	:	×	✓	fx	=EXP($B$19)^G26						

◢	A	B	C	D	E	F	G	H	I	J	K	L
16		Coefficient	andard Err	t Stat	P-value	Lower 95%	Upper 95%	ower 95.0%	pper 95.0%			
17	Intercept	45.32115	0.633854	71.50092	1.04E-13	43.88727	46.75503	43.88727	46.75503			
18	recession	-0.00768	0.002928	-2.62386	0.027635	-0.0143	-0.00106	-0.0143	-0.00106			
19	year	-0.01969	0.000316	-62.2835	3.58E-13	-0.0204	-0.01897	-0.0204	-0.01897			
20												
21												
22												
23	RESIDUAL OUTPUT				T	K	dL	dU				
24					12.	3.	0.81221	1.57935				
25	Observation	red ln Whit	year	Residuals	DW	recession	year	vpb white (K)	lln vpb white	multiplicative constant	multiplicative recession part worth	multiplicative trend part worth
26	1	5.931097	2001	-0.00223	1.817012	0	2001	375.7	5.93	4.82E+19	1.00	=EXP(
27	2	5.911412	2002	0.001253		0	2002	369.7	5.91	4.82E+19	1.0	$B$19)^

Find predicted White VPBs from the product of the three multiplicative part worths.

=PRODUCT(J26:L26)

AutoSave ⬤ Off	🖫	↻ · ↺ · ä · ⬒				

File	Home	Insert	Page Layout	Formulas	Data

DEVSQ	▼	:	×	✓	fx	=PRODUCT(J26:L26)

◢	H	I	J	K	L	M
25	vpb white (K)	lln vpb white	multiplicative constant	multiplicative recession part worth	multiplicative trend part worth	predicted White VPBs (K)
26	375.7	5.9	4.82E+19	1.0	7.82E-18	=PRODU
27	369.7	5.9				CT(J26:
28	362.8	5.9				L26)
29	355.9	5.9				

Find critical t in C7 and the margin of error in lns in D7.

=T.INV.2T(.05,B13)
=B7*C7

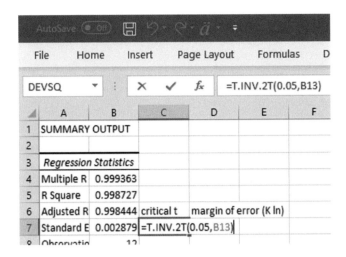

Divide and multiply the predicted values by the multiplicative margin of error (=exp($D$7).

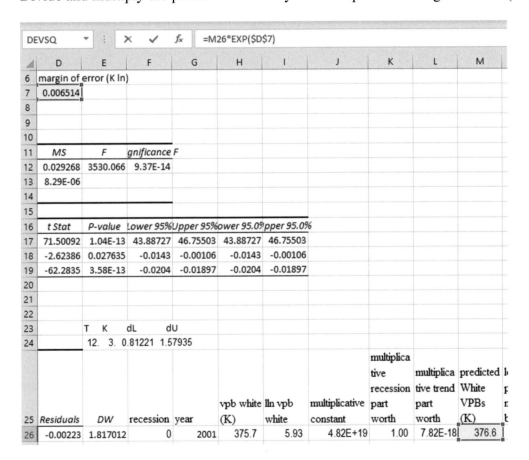

Downfill the multiplicative part worths, predicted values, lower and upper prediction interval bounds to assess validity.

	recession	year	vpb white (K)	lln vpb white	multiplicative constant	multiplicative recession part worth	multiplicative trend part worth	predicted White VPBs (K)	lower prediction interval bound	upper prediction interval bound
25										
26	0	2001	375.7	5.93	4.82E+19	1.00	7.82E-18	376.6	374.1	379.0
27	0	2002	369.7	5.91	4.82E+19	1.0	7.67E-18	369.2	366.8	371.6
28	0	2003	362.8	5.89	4.82E+19	1.0	7.52E-18	362.0	359.7	364.4
29	0	2004	355.9	5.87	4.82E+19	1.0	7.37E-18	355.0	352.7	357.3
30	0	2005	347.5	5.85	4.82E+19	1.0	7.23E-18	348.1	345.8	350.3
31	0	2006	339.9	5.83	4.82E+19	1.0	7.09E-18	341.3	339.1	343.5
32	0	2007	333.7	5.81	4.82E+19	1.0	6.95E-18	334.6	332.4	336.8
33	0	2008	329.7	5.80	4.82E+19	1.0	6.81E-18	328.1	326.0	330.2
34	0	2009	321.8	5.77	4.82E+19	1.0	6.68E-18	321.7	319.6	323.8
35	0	2010	315.3	5.75	4.82E+19	1.0	6.55E-18	315.4	313.4	317.5
36	1	2011	307.5	5.73	4.82E+19	1.0	6.42E-18	306.9	304.9	308.9
37	1	2012	300.4	5.71	4.82E+19	1.0	6.30E-18	300.9	299.0	302.9
38	1	2013	294.5	5.69	4.82E+19	1.0	6.17E-18	295.1	293.1	297.0
39	1	2014	292.1	5.68	4.82E+19	1.0	6.05E-18	289.3	287.4	291.2

The model underestimates VPBs in 2014 with the recession indicator set to one. Set the recession indicator to 0 in 2014 and reassess.

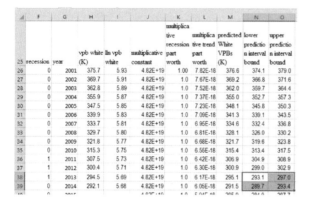

The model correctly predicts VPBs in 2013 and 2014, using the prediction intervals for the mean. (Had those prediction intervals not contained 2013 or 2014 actual values, the individual prediction interval bounds from JMP would be necessary to correctly assess validity.)

Recalibrate the model using all observations.

	A	B	C	D	E	F	G
1	SUMMARY OUTPUT						
2							
3	*Regression Statistics*						
4	Multiple R	0.999571					
5	R Square	0.999142					
6	Adjusted R	0.998986					
7	Standard E	0.002686					
8	Observatic	14					
9							
10	ANOVA						
11		*df*	*SS*	*MS*	*F*	*ignificance F*	
12	Regressior	2	0.092398	0.046199	6402.971	1.36E-17	
13	Residual	11	7.94E-05	7.22E-06			
14	Total	13	0.092477				
15							
16		*Coefficients*	*andard Err*	*t Stat*	*P-value*	*Lower 95%*	*Upper 95%*
17	Intercept	45.16448	0.439752	102.7045	9.32E-18	44.19659	46.13236
18	year	-0.01961	0.000219	-89.4529	4.25E-17	-0.02009	-0.01912
19	recession	-0.00897	0.002153	-4.16628	0.001573	-0.01371	-0.00423

Copy and paste formulas from the validation model.

JMP 9.1 Find Individual Prediction Interval Bounds with JMP

Copy and paste the recession, year, both through 2020, and ln White VPB columns and paste into JMP. Choose File, New, Data Table, and then Edit, Paste with Column Labels.

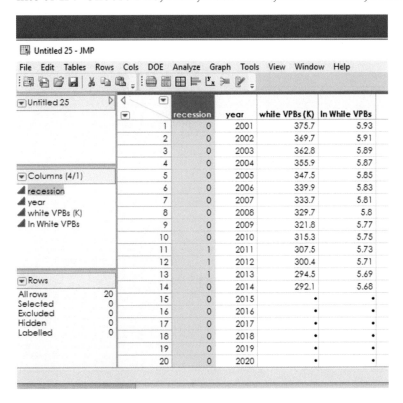

From the JMP Starter, choose Fit Model, Fit Model.

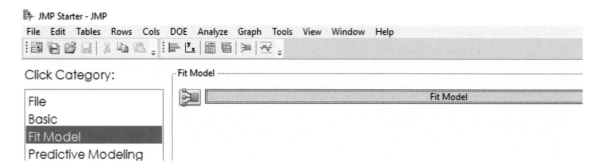

Drag ln White VPBs to the Y box and drag recession and year to the Construct Model Effects box, choose Emphasis: Minimal Report, and click Run.

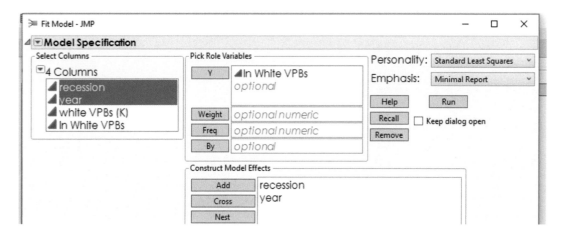

Click the red triangle next to Response ln White VPBs, Save Columns, Indiv Confidence Limit Formula, which will add the individual prediction interval bounds to the data.

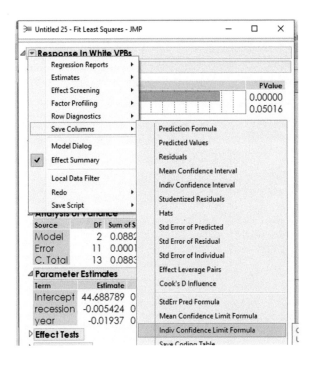

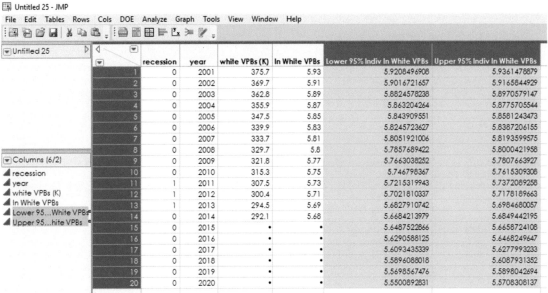

Select and copy the individual confidence interval bounds and paste into the recalibrated model in excel.

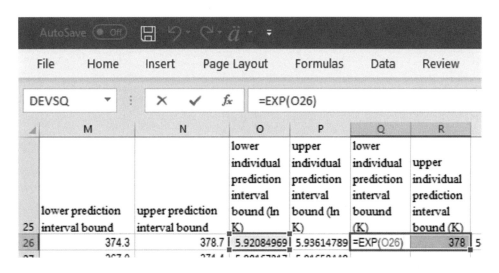

	M	N	O	P
25	lower prediction interval bound	upper prediction interval bound	lower individual prediction interval bound (ln K)	upper individual prediction interval bound (ln K)
26	374.3	378.7	5.92084969	5.93614789
27	367.0	371.4	5.90167217	5.91658449
28	359.9	364.1	5.88245782	5.89705791
29	352.9	357.1	5.86320426	5.87757055
30	346.0	350.1	5.84390955	5.85812435
31	339.3	343.3	5.82457236	5.83872062
32	332.7	336.7	5.8051921	5.81935996
33	326.3	330.1	5.78576894	5.8000422
34	319.9	323.7	5.76630383	5.78076639

The individual prediction interval bounds are in lns. Create individual prediction interval bounds in K VPBs with the exponential function and downfill the two new columns.

	M	N	O	P	Q	R
25	lower prediction interval bound	upper prediction interval bound	lower individual prediction interval bound (ln K)	upper individual prediction interval bound (ln K)	lower individual prediction interval bouund (K)	upper individual prediction interval bound (K)
26	374.3	378.7	5.92084969	5.93614789	=EXP(O26)	378

`=EXP(O26)`

Excel 9.3 Illustrate the Model Fit and Forecast

From F25, select the years and *ln White VPBs*.
Hold Cntl down and with your mouse, select the individual prediction interval bounds.
Create a scatterplot.

Cntl+Shift+Down
Alt ND

(Note that if you do not have access to JMP, plot the prediction interval bounds from excel as approximations. Both will be shown in the plot, below.)

year	White VPBs (K)	ln vpb white	multiplic ative constant	multiplicative recession part worth	multiplic ative trend part worth	predicted White VPBs (K)	lower prediction interval bound	upper prediction interval bound	lower individual prediction interval bound (ln K)	upper individual prediction interval bound (ln K)	lower individual prediction interval bouund (K)	upper individual prediction interval bound (K)
2001	375.7	5.9	4.12E+19	1.00	9.14E-18	376.5	374.3	378.7	5.92084969	5.93614789	373	37
2002	369.7	5.9	4.12E+19	1.00	8.96E-18	369.2	367.0	371.4	5.90167217	5.91658449	366	37
2003	362.8	5.9	4.12E+19	1.00	8.79E-18	362.0	359.9	364.1	5.88245782	5.89705791	359	36
2004	355.9	5.9	4.12E+19	1.00	8.62E-18	355.0	352.9	357.1	5.86320426	5.87757055	352	35
2005	347.5	5.9	4.12E+19	1.00	8.45E-18	348.1	346.0	350.1	5.84390955	5.85812435	345	35
2006	339.9	5.8	4.12E+19	1.00	8.29E-18	341.3	339.3	343.3	5.82457236	5.83872062	339	34
2007	333.7	5.8	4.12E+19	1.00	8.13E-18	334.7	332.7	336.7	5.8051921	5.81935996	332	33
2008	329.7	5.8	4.12E+19	1.00	7.97E-18	328.2	326.3	330.1	5.78576894	5.8000422	326	33
2009	321.8	5.8	4.12E+19	1.00	7.82E-18	321.8	319.9	323.7	5.76630383	5.78076639	319	32
2010	315.3	5.8	4.12E+19	1.00	7.66E-18	315.6	313.7	317.4	5.74679837	5.76153093	313	31
2011	307.5	5.7	4.12E+19	0.99	7.51E-18	306.7	304.9	308.5	5.72153199	5.73720893	305	31
2012	300.4	5.7	4.12E+19	0.99	7.37E-18	300.7	299.0	302.5	5.70218103	5.71781897	300	30
2013	294.5	5.685	4.12E+19	0.99	7.23E-18	294.9	293.1	296.6	5.68279107	5.69846801	294	29
2014	292.1	5.677	4.12E+19	1.00	7.09E-18	291.8	290.0	293.5	5.6684214	5.68494422	290	29
2015			4.12E+19	1.00	6.95E-18	286.1	284.4	287.8	5.64875229	5.66587241	284	28
2016			4.12E+19	1.00	6.81E-18	280.5	278.9	282.2	5.62905881	5.64682496	278	28
2017			4.12E+19	1.00	6.68E-18	275.1	273.5	276.7	5.60934353	5.62779932	273	27

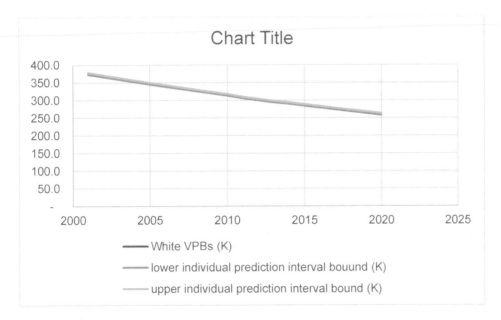

Chart Title

—— White VPBs (K)

—— lower individual prediction interval bouund (K)

—— upper individual prediction interval bound (K)

Add a vertical axis label.   Alt JCAAV
Adjust the axes to make good use of space   Cntl+1
by clicking an axis then opening the axis
menu.

Reduce decimals in the vertical axis.
Recolor one prediction interval bound to match the other.
Change actual VPBs from a line to markers.
Add a standalone chart title.

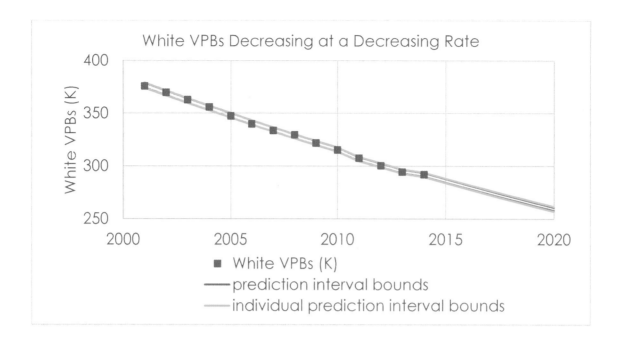

Excel 9.4 Forecast Black VPBs with Cubes

The one driver trend model of Black VPBs cubes is shown below:

	A	B	C	D	E	F	G
1	SUMMARY OUTPUT						
2							
3	*Regression Statistics*						
4	Multiple F	0.559824					
5	R Square	0.313402					
6	Adjusted I	0.244743					
7	Standard E	2995.212					
8	Observati	12					
9							
10	ANOVA						
11		*df*	*SS*	*MS*	*F*	*gnificance F*	
12	Regressio	1	40950121	40950121	4.564571	0.05838	
13	Residual	10	89712962	8971296			
14	Total	11	1.31E+08				
15							
16		*Coefficients*	*andard Err*	*t Stat*	*P-value*	*Lower 95%*	*Upper 95%*
17	Intercept	-945440	502573.3	-1.8812	0.089347	-2065243	174363.2
18	year	535.1303	250.4722	2.136486	0.05838	-22.9566	1093.217

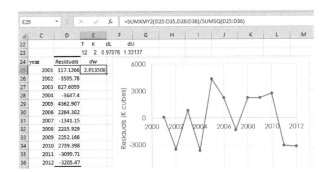

The model is just short of significance, and residuals suggest a recession impact in 2011 and 2012.

A recession indicator was added, set to one in 2011 onwards. Results are shown below:

	A	B	C	D	E	F	G	H
1	SUMMARY OUTPUT							
2								
3	*Regression Statistics*							
4	R Square	0.628						
5	Standard Error	2324						
6	Observatic	12						
7	ANOVA	*df*	*SS*	*MS*	*F*	*Significance F*		
8	Regressior	2	82046544.91	41023272.45	7.6	0.012		
9	Residual	9	48616538.52	5401837.613				
10	Total	11	130663083.4					
11								
12		*Coefficients*	*Standard Error*	*t Stat*	*P-value*	*Lower 95%*	*Upper 95%*	one tail pvalue
13	Intercept	-1858908	511629	-3.6	0.0055	-3016292.7	-701524	
14	recession	-6518	2363	-2.8	0.0222	-11864	-1172	0.011
15	year	991	255	3.9	0.0037	414	1568	

=J35-$J$5

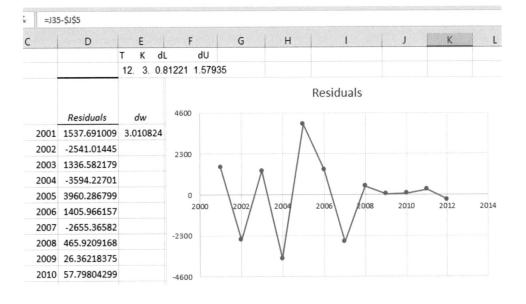

	T	K	dL	dU
	12.	3.	0.81221	1.57935

	Residuals	dw
2001	1537.691009	3.010824
2002	-2541.01445	
2003	1336.582179	
2004	-3594.22701	
2005	3960.286799	
2006	1405.966157	
2007	-2655.36582	
2008	465.9209168	
2009	26.36218375	
2010	57.79804299	

The model is significant, both the recession and trend are significant, and residuals are free from positive autocorrelation.

To assess validity, create the predicted VPBs cubes from the three additive part worths for the intercept, recession and trend. Copy the recession, year, Black VPBs and Black VPB cubes and paste next to residuals in E25.

Add the intercept part worth in I26 locking | =$B$17
the cell reference with Fn 4.

DEVSQ	▾	:	× ✓	f_x	=$B$17			

◢	A	B	C	D	E	F	G	H	I
			Standard				Upper	one tail	
16		Coefficients	Error	t Stat	P-value	Lower 95%	95%	pvalue	
17	Intercept	-1858908	511629	-3.6	0.0055	-3016292.7	-701524		
18	recession	-6518	2363	-2.8	0.0222	-11864	-1172	0.011	
19	year	991	255	3.9	0.0037	414	1568		
20									
21									
22									
23	RESIDUAL OUTPUT			T K dL	dU				
24				12. 3. 0.81221	1.57935				
					recessio		vpb black	cube vpb	intercept part
25	Observation	ted cube vpb	Residuals	dw	n	year	(K)	Black	worth (K cubes)
26	1	123935.426	1537.691009	3.010823573	0	2001	50.1	125,473	=$B$17

Create the recession part worth in J26, | =$B$18*E26
locking the coefficient cell reference with
Fn 4.

DEVSQ	▾	:	× ✓	f_x	=$B$18*E26				

◢	A	B	C	D	E	F	G	H	I	J
			Standard				Upper	one tail		
16		Coefficients	Error	t Stat	P-value	Lower 95%	95%	pvalue		
17	Intercept	-1858908	511629	-3.6	0.0055	-3016292.7	-701524			
18	recession	-6518	2363	-2.8	0.0222	-11864	-1172	0.011		
19	year	991	255	3.9	0.0037	414	1568			
20										
21										
22										
23	RESIDUAL OUTPUT			T K dL	dU					Plot A
24				12. 3. 0.81221	1.57935					
										recession
					recessio		vpb black	cube vpb	intercept part	part worth
25	Observation	ted cube vpb	Residuals	dw	n	year	(K)	Black	worth (K cubes)	(K cubes)
26	1	123935.426	1537.691009	3.010823573	0	2001	50.1	125,473	-1858908	=$B$18*E26

Create the trend part worth locking the | =$B$19*F26
coefficient cell reference with Fn 4.

DEVSQ ▾ : × ✓ *fx* =$B$19*F26

	A	B	C	D	E	F	G	H	I	J	K
16		Coefficients	Standard Error	t Stat	P-value	Lower 95%	Upper 95%	one tail pvalue			
17	Intercept	-1858908	511629	-3.6	0.0055	-3016292.7	-701524				
18	recession	-6518	2363	-2.8	0.0222	-11864	-1172	0.011			
19	year	991	255	3.9	0.0037	414	1568				
20											
21											
22											
23	RESIDUAL OUTPUT			T	K	dL	dU				
24				12.	3.	0.81221	1.57935				

					recessi		vpb black	cube intercept vpb	intercept part worth	recession part worth	trend part worth (K	p
25	Observation	ted cube vpb	Residuals	dw	on	year	(K)	Black	(K cubes)	(K cubes)	cubes)	d
26	1	123935.426	1537.691	3.01082	0	2001	50.1	#####	-1858908	0.00	=$B$19*F26	

Find the predicted VPBs cubes by adding | =SUM(I26:K26)
the three part worths in L26.

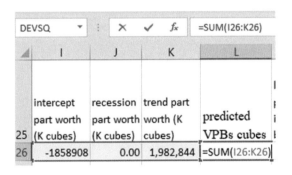

DEVSQ ▾ : × ✓ *fx* =SUM(I26:K26)

	I	J	K	L
25	intercept part worth (K cubes)	recession part worth (K cubes)	trend part worth (K cubes)	predicted VPBs cubes
26	-1858908	0.00	1,982,844	=SUM(I26:K26)

Find the critical t in C7 and margin of error (in cubes) in D7, and then subtract and add to the predicted cubes to create the prediction interval bounds.

Downfill the part worths, predictions and prediction interval bounds to assess validity.

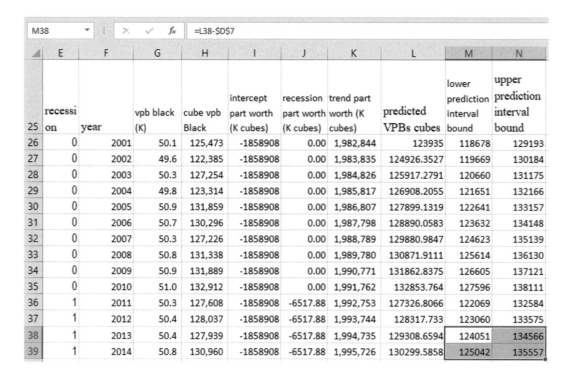

The model accurately forecasts 2013 and 2014 VPBs.

The recalibrated model using all the data is below:

| M8 | ▾ | : | × | ✓ | fx | =T.INV.2T(0.05,B13) |

⊿	A	B	C	D	E	F	G
1	SUMMARY OUTPUT						
2							
3	*Regression Statistics*						
4	Multiple R	0.79406					
5	R Square	0.63052					
6	Adjusted F	0.56335					
7	Standard E	2149					
8	Observati	14					
9							
10	ANOVA						
11		*df*	*SS*	*MS*	*F*	*gnificance F*	
12	Regressio	2	8.7E+07	4.3E+07	9.38595	0.00419	
13	Residual	11	5.1E+07	4618190			
14	Total	13	1.4E+08				
15							
16		*Coefficient*	*andard Err*	*t Stat*	*P-value*	*lower 95%*	*Upper 95%* ow
17	Intercept	-1865910	460739	-4.0	0.0019	-2879990	-851830 -;
18	recession	-6720	2050	-3.3	0.0074	-11232	-2208 -
19	year	994	230	4.3	0.0012	489	1500

Copy the data and formulas from the validation model and paste into the recalibrated model to update forecasts.

To rescale predictions back to VPBs from cubes, create three new columns in O26, P26 and Q26.
From O26, right fill.

=L25^(1/3)
Shift+right right
Cntl+R

Downfill the three new columns in VPBs (K).

O26			f_x	=L26^(1/3)		
	L	M	N	O	P	Q
25	predicted VPBs cubes	lower prediction interval bound (cubes)	upper prediction interval bound (cubes)	predicted VPBs (K)	lower prediction interval bound (K)	upper prediction interval bound (K) i
26	123920	119190	128650	49.9	49.2	50.5

If you have access to JMP, find the individual prediction interval bounds and paste into the recalibrated sheet in excel. Rescale those back to VPBs by raising to the (1/3) power.

DEVSQ			f_x	=R26^(1/3)	
	R	S	T	U
25	lower individual prediction interval bound (cubes)	upper individual prediction interval bound (cubes)	lower individual prediction interval bound (K)	upper individual prediction interval bound (K)
26	119638.42	133114	=R26^(1/3)	
27	120436.41	133357	49.38396	51.0903

Select and plot year, Black VPBS (K), and lower and upper prediction interval bounds. (Both the prediction interval bounds and the individual prediction interval bounds are shown below.) Add a vertical axis label, adjust axes to make good use of white space, remove unwanted decimals, recolor one of the prediction interval bounds to match the other, and show actual data with markers instead of a line.

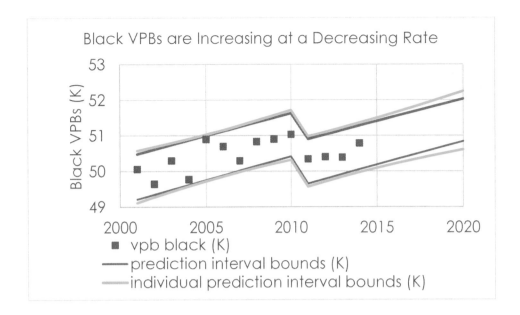

Lab 9-1 World Wine Consumption by Global Region

Concha y Toro executives had forecast CyT exports to the U.S., Asia and Europe, the three largest global regions, from chapter 5. In order to gauge export performance in those regions, forecasts of wine consumption in those regions were also needed. Worldwide wine consumption had been stable, but increasing in the U.S. and Asia, while decreasing in Europe.

Wine was thought to be a luxury. In some regions, consumption had only temporarily been depressed by the global recession; in other regions, the recession appeared to continue to depress consumption.

To compare trends in exports with trends in consumption, 2020 forecasts of wine consumption in the three global regions are needed.

I. U.S.

1. Assess skewness of wine consumption in the U.S. and rescale to move skewness closer to zero:

	MLs	MLs sqr	MLs cube
skewness			

2. Wine consumption in the U.S. is increasing at ____ an increasing rate ____ a decreasing rate.

3. Is your model valid for forecasting?
    The global recession of 2009 very likely reduced wine consumption. To account for this recent shock, it will not be possible to validate your model until one or two years have passed. Nonetheless, an unvalidated model which fits will provide the best available information to decision makers. Improve the one driver model of trend by accounting for the recession, using all available years.

Rescale predictions back to MLs.
If you have access to JMP, find the individual prediction interval bounds, and then rescale back to MLs.

4. Present your scatterplot of fit and forecast:

5. How much did recession reduce consumption in 2009? _____ MLs

6. Present your model equation in the original units of MLs:

$$U.S.\ cons\hat{u}mption\ (MLs)_t = [b_0(MLs\ ) + b_1(MLs\ ) \times rec_t + b_2(\frac{MLs}{year}) \times t\}$$

II. Asia

1. Assess skewness of wine consumption in Asia and rescale to move skewness closer to zero:

	MLs	Sqrt MLs	Cubrt MLs	Ln MLs
skewness				

2. Is your model valid for forecasting?

The recession very likely influenced wine consumption in Asia, as well. To provide the best possible information for decision makers, use all of the data and improve the model by accounting for the recession.
If you have access to JMP, find the individual prediction interval bounds and rescale back to MLs with the exponential function.

3. Present your scatterplot of your model fit and forecast:

4. What is the margin of error in your 2020 forecast? _____%

5. Annual consumption in 2020 is forecast to be ____% of consumption in 2019.

6. In 2020, recession would reduce consumption to ___ % of consumption would be without recession.

7. Present your model equation in the original units of MLs:

Case 9-1 Forecasting Wine Consumption in Europe

Concha y Toro vineyards, a Chilean global multinational, is the largest producer of wines in Latin America. The firm produces and exports wine to Europe, the U.S., and Asia. Concha y Toro has been successful in developing wine varieties that appeal to the unique tastes of the various global segments.

   In 2010, the Board of Directors was reviewing performance. While the firm's wines had earned multiple distinctions, export volume had grown only 6% in 2010, relative to 2009, which was a startling slow down, relative to annual export volume growth as high 27% in recent years. Eduardo Guilisasti, the CEO of CyT, is asking whether worldwide wine consumption had also slowed. Was consumption slowing? Or is CyT losing ground to competitors? In which regions is CyT performing well, and in which regions is CyT performing poorly?

Exports slowing. Heads of exports to the three major wine consuming regions, Europe, the U.S, and Asia, agreed to produce forecasts. Jorge Del Norte, Head of U.S. exports and Gunter Schmidt, Head of the European export business, agreed that wine consumption in both Europe and the U.S. appeared to be slowing.

Global Recession. The Heads of export businesses noted that the global recession might be responsible for slowing wine consumption, particularly in developed markets in the U.S. and Europe. Was wine consumption in the three major wine consuming regions sensitive to the global economy? (Note that, to account for the impact of global recession, you will not be able to validate a model, since the recession potentially affected exports and consumption in the two most recent years.) Where you find evidence of a continuing impact of the global recession, compare 2020 forecasts with and without continuing recession.

1. Assess skewness of wine consumption in Europe and rescale to move skewness closer to zero. Fill in skewness *for only the scales you considered*:

	MLs	Sqrt MLs	Cube root MLs	Ln MLs	MLs sqr	MLs cube
skewness						

If the one driver residuals suggest an shock or shift due to the recession, improve the model by accounting for the recession.

If you have access to JMP, find the individual prediction interval bounds and rescale back to MLs.

2. After recalibrating your model, present your scatterplot of fit and forecast, in the original units of MLs, pasting in here:
3. Present your model equation in the original units of MLs, editing the template to show coefficients and appropriate powers:

$$European\ cons\hat{u}mption\ (MLs)_t = [b_0(MLs\ ) + b_1(MLs\ ) \times rec_t + b_2(\frac{MLs}{year}) \times t\}$$

4. How much would ongoing recession reduce consumption in 2020? _____ MLs

Trends in Global region shares

Below are global region shares of 2010 consumption and CyT exports.

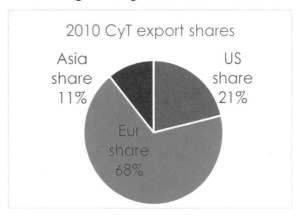

1. Add 2020 predicted consumption shares with a pie chart:

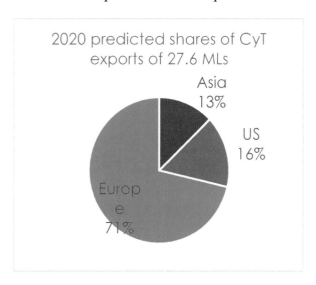

Case 9-2 Markets for Vastly Better Roots Soil Additive

Tranlin, a Chinese multinational firm, produces Vastly brand paper products from wheat straw, the stalks left, following wheat harvest. A byproduct from their process is then used to produce an enriching soil additive which encourages formation of deeper roots, enhancing produce quality, particularly in times of drought. Management is looking at California agriculture as a possible expansion opportunity. California is a major state in the U.S. for agricultural products. To prioritize the particular produce markets in California, your team is charged with crafting a 2020 forecast of the value of California production for two fruits or crops, and determining what shocks impact those markets.

Weather shocks. You can assume that, in some cases, California weather events impact agricultural production, which you can build into your forecasts with indicator variables. Tranlin's soil additive could promise a competitive advantage against California weather events, and the potential value of such a competitive advantage is desired. State-wide, California agricultural production was affected by drought in 2006-2009 and in 2014-2016. These droughts may or may not have affected particular types of produce. For some products, drought may have affected production in some years, such as 2007 and 2008, but not in other years, such as 2006 and 2009.

Drought generally reduces production, creating scarcity, which may result in higher prices. Drought may also reduce the quality of produce, which may result in lower prices. The impact of a weather event on prices and value of production could be either positive or negative, and so you should use a two tail test.

If weather event(s) impact the value of California production, forecast 2020 production value, with and without such (a) weather event(s). Note that, if the 2014-2016 drought impacted production value, you will not be able to validate your model for forecasting. (If a weather event did not impact production value in the two most recent years, your model should be validated for forecasting.)

Recession shock. In some cases, the global economy impacts the value of California agricultural production. Production of some fruits and crops was impacted by the recession. Since the recession began late in 2008, impact on agricultural production would not be felt until 2009 or 2010. The impact of recession would be negative, and so you should use a one tail test.

Other shocks. For some agricultural products, other events may have affected production value. If you find a shock in years other than 2006-2010, 2009-2011, 2014-2016, do research to learn what that shock was. Cite your source(s) if you add another shock.

The markets. From the largest California fruit and crop markets, your team will analyze two markets in one market segment. There are three promising market segments: (i) grapes (wine and table), (ii) berries (strawberries and raspberries), and (iii) field crops (rice and alfalfa).

Linear or nonlinear growth. The trend in value of most agricultural products is nonlinear. However, in exceptional cases, the trend in value of production may be nearly linear. If skewness cannot be improved by rescaling, build a linear model.

Production, prices and market value. The value of a California agricultural crop depends upon pounds produced and price per pound. Looking at pounds produced and prices per pound may help you decide which shocks to include in your forecast model, as well as likely influence. You can find California agricultural crop value, pounds produced, and price per pound by fruits and vegetables from https://quickstats.nass.usda.gov/ in **CA fruits vegs 2017.xlsx**. Note that in some cases, data is missing for a few years in which no data was collected. This will not affect your models.

Deliverables

Your PowerPoints. Present your results to Tranlin management with PowerPoints.
Your PowerPoints should explain the assumptions that you made to build your forecasts, and any competitive advantage that Tranlin's soil additive might have in either of the two markets you analyzed. If a market was affected by one or more shock(s) that could reoccur in the future,

illustrate your 2020 forecast under the default scenario (no shock) as well as the alternate scenario(s) (recurring shock(s)). If you were unable to validate your model(s), explain that a recent shock, the 2014-2016 drought, affected production value(s), and your forecast ought to be updated in a year or two. In addition to forecast 2020 market values, report forecast annual market growth rates, the average annual percent growth percentage.

Your PowerPoints ought to follow best practices (including 24 pt font *on everything*, including axes numbers), and a single point per slide). Add explanations and interpretations in Notes view that you will deliver verbally.

Assignment 9-3 Billionaires in 2020

Rolls-Royce believes that a major target market for supersonic business jets is the growing segment of billionaires. Forecast the trend in billionaires from data in **billionaires**.

1. Plot billionaires by year and identify patterns: ____ positive trend ____ shift ____ cycle

2. Find the skewness of billionaires.

3. The number of billionaires is increasing at: ____ an increasing ____ decreasing rate

4. Rescale to square roots and assess skewness:

	Square roots
Skew	

Build a model of trend in billionaires, including an indicator of the global recession from 2009 through 2015.

5. Is your model free from unaccounted for trend, shifts, shocks and cycles?

6. Plot the residuals and identify patterns: ____ positive trend ____ shift ____ cycle

7. Is your model valid?

8. If you have access to JMP, find the individual prediction interval bounds and rescale back to the original units.

9. Recalibrate and present your fit and forecast for 2020.

10. Present your equation for billionaires:

11. The global recession reduced the number of billionaires expected in 2020 by:

Chapter 10
Logit Regression for Bounded Dependent Variables

In this chapter we introduce *logit* regression, a particular type of nonlinear regression which accommodates responses which are *limited,* or bounded above and below. For example, the likelihood of trying a new product can neither be negative nor greater than one hundred percent. Market share is similarly limited to the range between zero and one hundred percent. In each of these cases, dependent response must be rescaled, acknowledging these boundaries. The odds ratio rescales probabilities or shares to a corresponding unbounded measure. The *logit,* or natural logarithm of an odds ratio, rescales responses, producing an S-shaped pattern, which reflects greater response among "fence sitters" with probabilities or shares that are mid-range.

10.1 Rescaling Probabilities or Shares to Odds Improves Model Validity

With each response probability, π, there is an *odds ratio*, the chance that the response occurs relative to the chance that it does not occur.

$$odds = \pi/(1 - \pi)$$

Response shares, such as market share, also have odds ratios, which reflect percent of the market owned, relative to the percent of the market owned by competitors:

$$odds = MarketShare/(100 - MarketShare)$$

While probabilities and shares are bounded by zero, below, and one or one hundred percent, above, the corresponding odds ratio and its natural logarithm, the logit, are not bounded:

$$Logit = \ln(odds)$$

Rescaling to logits produces an S-shaped curve, which, for a probability at .5, or a share at 50%, has a logit of zero. Figure 10.1 illustrates this S-shaped scale.

© Springer Nature Switzerland AG 2019
C. Fraser, *Business Statistics for Competitive Advantage with Excel 2019 and JMP,*
https://doi.org/10.1007/978-3-030-20374-0_10

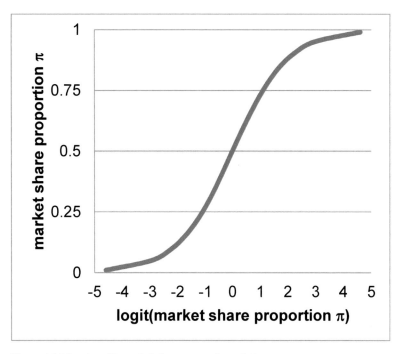

Figure 10.1 Logits of bounded shares are unbounded

Example 10.1 Airline Passenger Load Factor. Stamina Group required a long range forecast of international airline passenger load, the proportion of seats on international flights which are filled, to project passenger demand for a new international airline service.

Bureau of Transportation Statistics data on the international load factor were available for 2002-2017. Since load factors are bounded between zero and one, the logits were used to enable linear regression. The series of international load factor and their logits are shown in Figure 10.2. International load was increasing, and shocks from the terrorist incident of 2001 and the global recession were apparent.

The one driver model of trend was significant with RSquare of .74. Durbin Watson was 1.69, above the upper critical value of 1.35 for T=14 and K-2. The residual plot confirmed that trend had been accounted for, though shocks from the 2001 terrorist incident and recession in 2008 and 2009 were apparent. Residuals in those years were negative, though they were within two standard errors of zero. Accounting for the two shocks promised to improve the model and increase explanatory power.

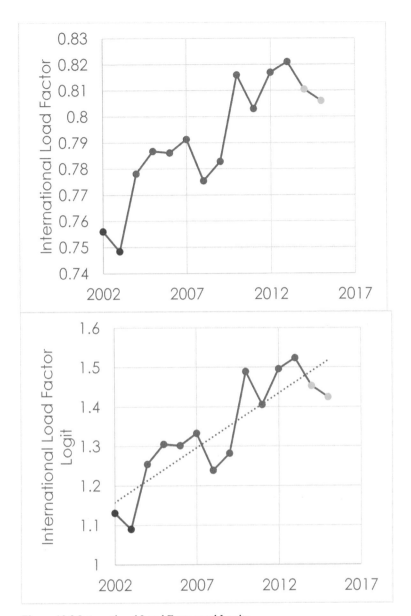

Figure 10.2 International Load Factor and Logits

Including indicators for terrorism and recession produced a significant model, with RSquare improved to .89. All coefficients were significant and with the correct signs. Durbin Watson was 1.51, between the lower and upper critical values of .77 and 1.78. Residuals, shown in Figure 10.3, show no overall trend and are all within two standard errors of zero. The model produced valid forecasts for the two hidden years, 2016 and 2017, and was recalibrated. The final model results are shown in Table 10.1.

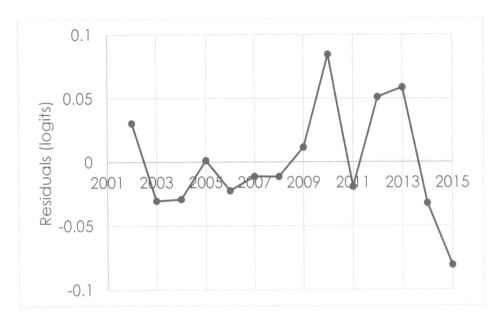

Figure 10.3 Residuals from the model with terrorism and recession indicators.

Table 10.1 International load logit regression

Regression Statistics					
R Square	0.862				
Standard Error	0.054				
Observations	16				
ANOVA	df	SS	MS	F	Significance F
Regression	3	0.218	.072	25.0	1.91E-05
Residual	12	0.035	.0029		
Total	15	0.252			
	Coefficients	Standard Error	t Stat	P-value	Exp(coefficients)
Intercept	-29.1	7.32	-4.0	.002	2.3E-13
terrorism t	-.17	0.051	-3.3	0.006	.85
Recession t	-.11	0.042	-2.6	0.023	.90
year	.015	0.0036	4.4	0.0013	1.015

The predicted load odds, from the exponential function of the predicted logits, is the product of the four multiplicative part worths:

$$International\ L\hat{o}ad\ Odds_t = 2.3E - 13 \times .85^{terrorism_t} \times .90^{recession_t} \times 1.015^t$$

Predicted load factor is then

$$International\ L\^{o}ad\ Factor_t = \frac{International\ L\^{o}ad\ Odds_t}{1 + International\ L\^{o}ad\ Odds_t}$$

$$= \frac{2.3E - 13 \times .85^{terrorism_t} \times .90^{recession_t} \times 1.015^t}{1 + 2.3E - 13 \times .85^{terrorism_t} \times .90^{recession_t} \times 1.015^t}$$

The multiplicative margin of error is

$$margin\ of\ error = \exp(critical\ t \times standard\ error)$$
$$= \exp(2.2 \times .054)$$
$$= 1.12$$

Multiplying the predicted load factor by the margin of error provides the upper 95% prediction interval bound. Dividing the predicted load factor by the margin of error provides the lower 95% prediction interval bound.

The fit and forecast are shown in Figure 10.4.

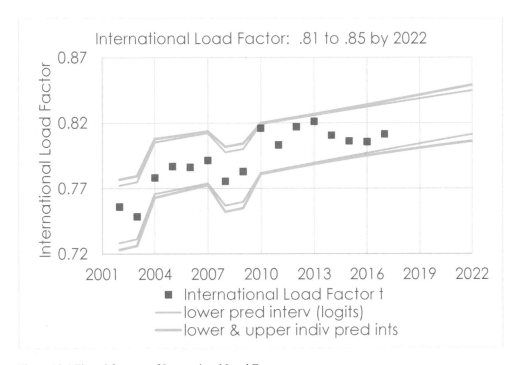

Figure 10.4 Fit and forecast of International Load Factor

Stamina Group could conclude that *International Load Factor* is increasing at a decreasing rate.

10.2 Logit Models Provide the Means to Build Valid Models of Shares and Proportions

When responses are bounded below and above, these limits must be built into models to get accurate pictures of drivers and valid forecasts. Rescaling shares or proportions to odds, and then to their natural logarithms, the logits, provides more valid models. Though both odds and logits are unbounded, the corresponding predicted proportions or shares are bounded below and above, providing believable forecasts.

Excel 10.1 Regression of a Limited Dependent Variable Using Logits

International Load Factor Forecast. Build a model of *international load factor* to produce a long range forecast through 2022.

Rescale bounded dependent variables to unbounded logits. In **Excel 10 International Load Factor.xls**, find *international load factors* for 2002 through 2017. Hide the two most recent datapoints.

From *international load factor*, which is bounded between zero and one, make

      load odds, the percent of seats filled to the percent unfilled

and

      load logit, the natural logarithms of the *load odds*:

DEVSQ	▾	:	×	✓	*fx*	=LN(B2/(1-B2))

◢	B	C	D
1	International Load Factor t	International Load Odds t	International Load Factor logit t
2	0.756	3.098	=LN(B2/(1-B2))

Plot the logits and add a trendline.

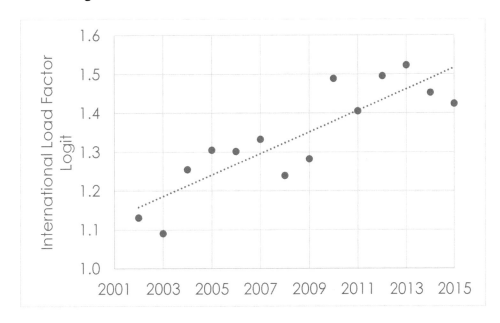

Run a one driver regression with year:

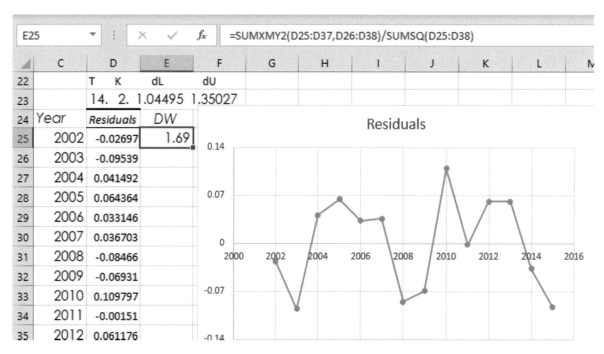

	A	B	C	D	E	F	G
1	SUMMARY OUTPUT						
2							
3	*Regression Statistics*						
4	Multiple F	0.862844					
5	R Square	0.7445					
6	Adjusted I	0.723209					
7	Standard E	0.070518					
8	Observati	14					
9							
10	ANOVA						
11		*df*	*SS*	*MS*	*F*	*gnificance F*	
12	Regressio	1	0.173885	0.173885	34.96682	7.11E-05	
13	Residual	12	0.059674	0.004973			
14	Total	13	0.233559				
15							
16		*Coefficient*	*andard Err*	*t Stat*	*P-value*	*Lower 95%*	*Upper 95%o*
17	Intercept	-54.1904	9.390415	-5.77083	8.87E-05	-74.6504	-33.7305
18	Year	0.027646	0.004675	5.913275	7.11E-05	0.01746	0.037833

Plot residuals and assess Durbin Watson.

| E25 | | ✗ ✓ *fx* | =SUMXMY2(D25:D37,D26:D38)/SUMSQ(D25:D38) |

	C	D	E	F
22		T K	dL	dU
23		14. 2.	1.04495	1.35027
24	*Year*	*Residuals*	*DW*	
25	2002	-0.02697	1.69	
26	2003	-0.09539		
27	2004	0.041492		
28	2005	0.064364		
29	2006	0.033146		
30	2007	0.036703		
31	2008	-0.08466		
32	2009	-0.06931		
33	2010	0.109797		
34	2011	-0.00151		
35	2012	0.061176		

In the data sheet, add a terrorism indicator next to year, set to one in 2002 and 2003, zero thereafter. Run a two driver model with year and terrorism and add the one tail p value for the terrorism indicator.

H19	▼	:	×	✓	f_x	=E19/2		

◢	A	B	C	D	E	F	G	H
1	SUMMARY OUTPUT							
2								
3	*Regression Statistics*							
4	Multiple F	0.896541						
5	R Square	0.803786						
6	Adjusted I	0.768111						
7	Standard I	0.064546						
8	Observati	14						
9								
10	ANOVA							
11		*df*	*SS*	*MS*	*F*	*gnificance F*		
12	Regressio	2	0.187732	0.093866	22.53066	0.000129		
13	Residual	11	0.045827	0.004166				
14	Total	13	0.233559					
15								
16		*Coefficient*	*andard Err*	*t Stat*	*P-value*	*Lower 95%*	*Upper 95%*	*e tail pvalue*
17	Intercept	-42.1857	10.82753	-3.89615	0.002493	-66.0169	-18.3544	
18	Year	0.021678	0.005388	4.023183	0.002005	0.009818	0.033537	
19	terrorism	-0.11316	0.062071	-1.82309	0.095557	-0.24978	0.023457	0.047778

Plot residuals and assess Durbin Watson.

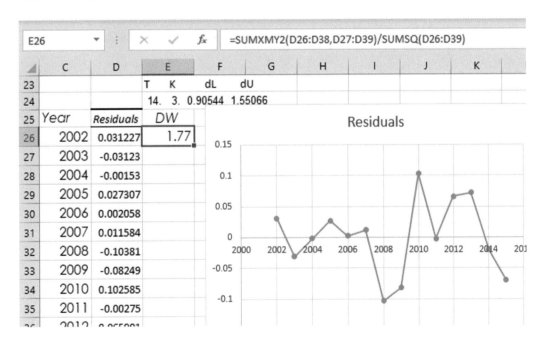

E26	▼	:	×	✓	f_x	=SUMXMY2(D26:D38,D27:D39)/SUMSQ(D26:D39)		

◢	C	D	E	F	G	H	I	J	K
23			T	K	dL	dU			
24			14.	3.	0.90544	1.55066			
25	Year	Residuals	DW						
26	2002	0.031227	1.77						
27	2003	-0.03123							
28	2004	-0.00153							
29	2005	0.027307							
30	2006	0.002058							
31	2007	0.011584							
32	2008	-0.10381							
33	2009	-0.08249							
34	2010	0.102585							
35	2011	-0.00275							

Add a recession indicator next to the terrorism indicator in the data sheet, set to one in 2008 and 2009, zero elsewhere. Run a three driver regression with year and the two indicators, adding one tail p values for the two indicators.

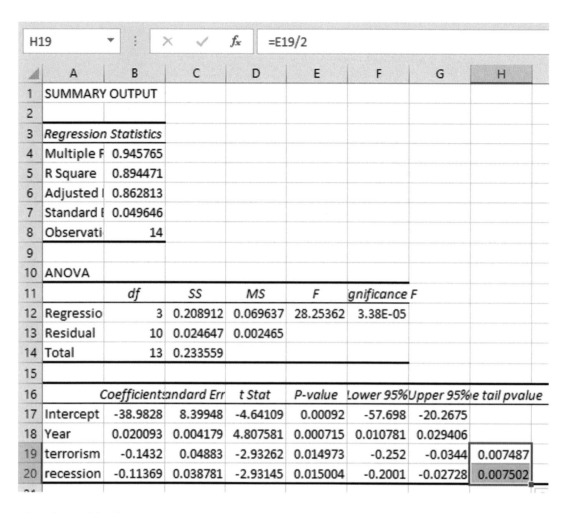

Plot the residuals and assess Durbin Watson.

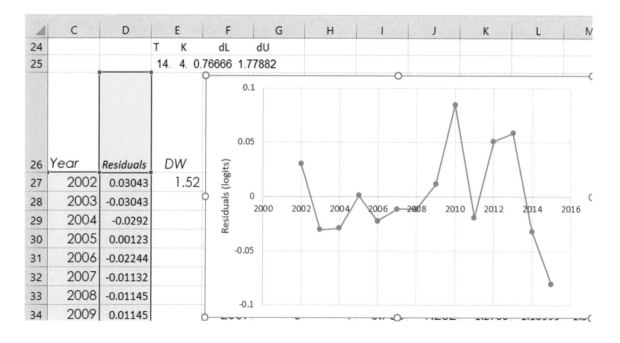

To test the validity of the model, copy the year, terrorism and recession indicators, International Load factor, odds and logits and paste next to residuals. Then find the multiplicative part worths for the multiplicative constant, terrorism, recession and year.

The multiplicative constant is the exponential function of the intercept. The three driver part worths are each the exponential function of the corresponding coefficient raised to the power of the driver. Predicted odds are the product of the four multiplicative part worths.

DEVSQ	▾	:	×	✓	f_x	=PRODUCT(L27:O27)

	K	L	M	N	O	P	Q
26	Interna tiona l Load Factor logit t	multipli cative consta nt	trend pw	terroris m pw	recessi on pw	predic ted odds	
27	1.131	1.17E-17	2.95E+17	0.867	1.000	=PRODUCT(L27:O27)	
28	1.090	1.17E-17	3.01E+17	0.867	1.000	3.066	
29	1.255	1.17E-17	3.07E+17	1.000	1.000	3.610	

If you have access to JMP, find the individual prediction interval bounds, which will be in logits. From those, find the lower and upper individual prediction interval bounds in odds with the exponential function. Otherwise, use the tougher test by finding the mean prediction intervals. The lower prediction interval bound is the predicted odds divided by the exponential function of the margin of error in logits, while the upper bound is predicted odds multiplied by the exponential function of the margin of error.

V42	▾	:	×	✓	f_x	=EXP(T42)

	J	K	L	M	N	O	P	Q	R	S	T	U	V
26	Interna tiona l load odds t	Interna tiona l Load Factor logit t	multipli cative consta nt	trend pw	terro rism pw	rece ssion pw	pred icte d odds	lower pred interv (odds)	upper pred interv (odds)	lower indiv pred interv (logit)	upper indiv pred interv (logit)	lower indiv pred interv (odds)	upper indiv pred interv (odds)
40	4.155	1.424	1.17E-17	3.83E+17	1.000	1.000	4.503	4.032	5.030	1.3788	1.6307	3.9699	5.1073
41	4.136	1.420	1.17E-17	3.91E+17	1.000	1.000	4.595	4.114	5.132	1.3949	1.6546	4.0345	5.2312
42	4.299	1.458	1.17E-17	3.99E+17	1.000	1.000	4.688	4.197	5.236	1.4105	1.6792	4.098	5.361
43	0.000		1.17E-17	4.07E+17	1.000	1.000	4.783	4.282	5.343	1.4256	1.7042	4.1604	5.4967

With a valid model, recalibrate, adding the two most recent datapoints. Copy the data and the formulas from the validation model to update forecasts.

E7		▼	⋮	×	✓	f_x	=EXP(D7)		

⊿	A	B	C	D	E	F	G	H
1	SUMMARY OUTPUT							
2								
3	*Regression Statistics*							
4	Multiple F	0.928425						
5	R Square	0.861973						
6	Adjusted I	0.827467	critical t	me (logits	me (odds)			
7	Standard I	0.053877	2.178813	0.117388	1.124556			
8	Observati	16						
9								
10	ANOVA							
11		*df*	*SS*	*MS*	*F*	*gnificance F*		
12	Regressio	3	0.21753	0.07251	24.97994	1.9E-05		
13	Residual	12	0.034833	0.002903				
14	Total	15	0.252363					
15								
16		*Coefficient*	*andard Err*	*t Stat*	*P-value*	*Lower 95%*	*Upper 95%*	*exp(coef)*
17	Intercept	-29.0927	7.32638	-3.97095	0.001856	-45.0555	-13.1299	2.32E-13
18	Year	0.015167	0.003643	4.162755	0.001316	0.007228	0.023105	1.015282
19	terrorism	-0.16827	0.051138	-3.29057	0.006452	-0.27969	-0.05685	0.845122
20	recession	-0.1092	0.042018	-2.5989	0.023273	-0.20075	-0.01765	0.89655

Plot the fit and forecast in the original units.

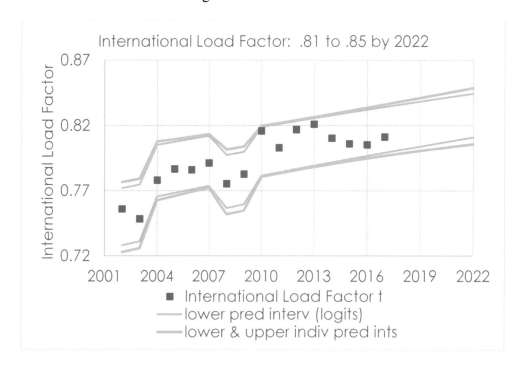

Lab 10-1 Explaining and Forecasting International Air Travel Load Factor

To enable a forecast of aircraft needed to accommodate international travelers, a 2022 forecast of the *international air travel load factor* is needed. The load factor is the proportion of seats available which are booked by passengers.

Build a model of *international load factor* to find the 2022 forecast.

International load factor is a proportion, bounded by zero and one. Rescale to logits.

1. Hide the two most recent observations, and then plot the load factor logits.

2. Run a one driver trend regression.

3. Assess residuals and plot to see unaccounted for pattern(s).

4. Create a terrorism indicator, equal to one in 2002 and 2003, zero elsewhere, and run a two driver regression.

5. Assess residuals and plot to see unaccounted for pattern(s).

6. Create a recession indicator, equal to one in 2008 and 2009, zero elsewhere, and run a three driver regression.

7. Assess residuals and plot to see unaccounted for pattern(s).

8. Test to validity of the model for forecasting. If you have access to JMP, use individual prediction interval bounds. (Those will be in logits.) Otherwise, use mean prediction intervals from excel.

9. recalibrate, and present your model equation, fit and forecast, in the original load factor units. (From forecasts in logits, use the exponential function to convert to odds, and then move from odds to prediction load factors with
International Load Factor = Odds/(1+Odds)

10. Compare predicted 2022 load factors, with and without terrorism in 2021. How much would terrorism reduce the load factor?

11. Compare predicted 2022 load factors, with and without recession in 2022. How much would a global recession reduce the load factor?

Assignment 10-1 Big Drug Co Scripts

The leading manufacturer of a popular anti-allergy drug would like to know how reformulations affect their share of prescriptions dispensed. Big Drug's major competition comes from generic copycat brands. When the generic competition begins to gain share, Big Drug introduces a reformulation, which sends the generics back to the lab to reformulate their copies. Reformulation is expensive, since it includes research and development, as well as repackaging and reformulating promotional materials.

Semi-annual data in **Assignment 13-1 Big Drug Co.xls** include time series of a semi-annual counter of time periods, the share of prescriptions dispensed of Big Drug Co's anti-allergy drug, and indicators for a major and a minor reformulation.

Build a logit trend model to estimate the impact of reformulations on Big Drug Co's share and to forecast Big Drug Co's share in the next five years.

1. Hide the two most recent datapoints and plot dispensed shares.

2. Rescale to dispensed logits.

3. Run regression with the semi-annual counter and the two indicators.

4. Assess and plot residuals.

5. Validate, recalibrate and rescale back to dispensed shares.

6. Present your model equation, fit and forecast:

7. How much did the first, major reformulation increase dispensed share in the semiannual period introduced?

8. How much did the second, minor reformulation increase dispensed share in the semiannual period introduced?

Assignment 10-2 Forecasting Hotel Occupancy Rates

Hilton is planning to introduce a new brand of hotels targeting gig economy workers. A large mid-east city, which is a major airline hub, seems promising. Occupancy rates have been increasing, suggesting that demand is increasing faster than the supply of rooms.

Occupancy.xlsx contains percents of rooms occupied from 2009 through 2016. Build a model of occupancy trend to forecast occupancy in 2017 through 2022.

1. Hide the two most recent observations and plot occupancy.

2. Rescale occupancy to logits.

3. Build a one driver model of trend in occupancy logits.

4. Assess and plot residuals.

5. Validate, recalibrate and rescale back to occupancy percents.

6. Present your model equation, fit and forecast:

Chapter 11
Building Multiple Regression Models

Explanatory multiple regression models are used to accomplish *two* complementary goals: *identification of key drivers of performance* and *prediction of performance under alternative scenarios*. The variables selected affect both the explanatory accuracy and power of models, as well as forecasting precision. In this chapter, the focus is on variable selection, the first step in the process used to build powerful and accurate multiple regression models.

Multiple regression offers a major advantage over simple regression. Multiple regression enables us to account for the joint impact of multiple drivers. Accounting for the influence of multiple drivers provides a truer estimate of the impact of each one individually. In real world situations, multiple drivers together influence performance. Looking at just one driver, as we do with simple regression, we are very likely to conclude that its impact is much greater than it actually is. A single driver takes the credit for the joint influence of multiple drivers working together. For this reason, multiple regression provides a clearer picture of influence.

Use logic to choose variables initially. Some of the variables which logically belong in a model may be insignificant, either because they truly have no impact, or because their influence is part of the joint influence of a correlated set of predictors which together drive performance. *Multicollinear* predictors create the illusion that important variables are insignificant.

If an insignificant predictor adds little explanatory power, it is removed from the model. It is either not a performance driver, or it is a driver, but it is a redundant driver, because other variables reflect the same driving dimension. Simple regression of the potential driver in question helps to distinguish whether or not it is multicollinearity that is producing insignificance for a variable.

11.1 Explanatory Multiple Regression Models Identify Drivers and Forecast

Explanatory multiple regression models are used to achieve two complementary goals: identification of key *drivers* of performance and prediction of performance under alternative scenarios. With time series models, this prediction can be either what would have happened had an alternate course of action been taken, or what can be expected to happen under alternative scenarios in the future.

Decision makers want to know, given uncontrollable external influences, which controllable variables make a difference in performance. We also want to know the nature and extent of each of the influences when considered together with the full set of important influences. A multiple regression model will provide this information.

Once key drivers of performance have been identified, a model can be used to compare performance predictions under alternative scenarios. This *sensitivity analysis* allows managers to compare expected performance levels and to make better decisions.

In earlier chapters, regression has been used with *time series* data, in which the variation to be explained is across time periods, such as years. In this chapter, multiple regression with *cross sectional* data is illustrated. Differences across people, firms, countries, comprise the variation to be explained. Cross sectional models differ from time series models in several ways. All

© Springer Nature Switzerland AG 2019

C. Fraser, *Business Statistics for Competitive Advantage with Excel 2019 and JMP*,

https://doi.org/10.1007/978-3-030-20374-0_11

potential drivers are used in the initial *full* model, then removed, one at a time. All data is used, since forecasting validity is not an issue. There can be no autocorrelation with cross sectional data, since all datapoints were collected at a single point in time, and so, Durbin Watson is not relevant.

11.2 Use Your Logic to Choose Model Components

The first step in model building happens before looking at data or using software. Using logic, personal experience, and others' experiences, first decide which of the potential influences ought to be included in a model. From the set of variables with available data, which could reasonably be expected to influence performance? In most cases, a reason is needed for including each independent variable in a model. Independent variables tend to be related to each other in our correlated world, and models are unnecessarily complicated if variables are included which don't logically affect the dependent performance variable. This complication from correlated predictors, *multicollinearity,* is explored later in the chapter.

Example 11.1 Fast Food Nations. Fast food restaurants have been sprouting in diverse global regions. Whataburger, a Texas based chain, is planning to expand globally. Whataburger is known for "bigger, better burgers." Tasting the burgers is rumored to prompt consumers to say, "What a burger!" Some managers are eyeing China as the most promising global location. However, others suspect that other global regions may be more fruitful. They have agreed to identify drivers of fast food establishments in a country to inform the decision.

Executives believe that countries with larger urban populations, and more populations under 15 years are likely the most promising locations for potential fast food establishments. Education may reduce popularity of fast food, and more establishments are expected in countries where fewer years of school are expected. Personal wealth, such as GDP per capita, is a suspected driver of the number of fast food establishments in a country. While fast food popularity may increase with GDP per capita in poorer countries where families become able to afford to dine out, the opposite is expected in richer countries, where increasing wealth enables families to dine is full service restaurants.

The multiple linear regression model of fast food establishments in a country will include all four potential drivers, initially. When more than one independent variable is included in a linear regression, the coefficient estimates are *marginal*. They estimate the marginal impact of each predictor on performance, given average levels of each of the other predictors.

Fast Food Nations contains data on number of fast food establishments, demographics, and the GDP per capita of 47 countries. Several variables are highly positively skewed, outside the approximate Normal range, -1 to +1. Unlike time series models designed to produce a long range forecast, it is not necessary to rescale skewness that indicates approximate Normality. However, variables not approximately Normal are rescaled, to satisfy the assumptions of linear regression. *Fast food establishments, urban population,* and *population under 15,* shown in Table 11.1 and Figure 11.1, are each positively skewed, and outside the approximately Normal range -1 to +1. Logarithms of those three will be used in the model.

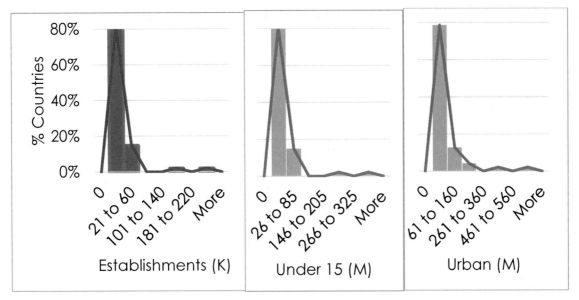

Figure 11.1 Positively skewed country characteristics in the Fast Food Nations sample

Table 11.1 Skewness in the Fast Food Nations sample

	Establishments (K)	Under 15 (M)	Urban (M)
Skewness	4.4	4.4	4.0

11.3 Multicollinear Variables Are Likely When Few Variable Combinations Are Popular in a Sample

Since these data come directly from actual countries, many characteristic combinations do not exist. For example, there is no country with GDP per capita over $40K and expected years of school less than 16. The four country characteristics tend to be related to each other and come in particular combinations in existing countries. We are knowingly introducing correlated independent variables, also called *multicollinear* independent variables, into the model, because the characteristic combinations which are not represented do not exist.

Results from Excel are shown in Table 11.2.

Table 11.2 Multiple linear regression of establishments with four country characteristics

SUMMARY OUTPUT					
Regression Statistics					
R Square		.980			
Standard Error		.205			
Observations		47			
ANOVA	*df*	*SS*	*MS*	*F*	*Significance F*
Regression	4	86.4	21.6	516	<.0001
Residual	42	1.8	.042		
Total	46	88.2			

RSquare is .980, or 98%, indicating that, *together*, variation in the four country characteristics accounts for 98% of the variation in fast food establishments.

11.4 *F* Tests the Joint Significance of the Set of Independent Variables

F tests the null hypothesis that *RSquare* is 0%, or, equivalently, that all of the coefficients are zero:

$$\textbf{H}_0\text{: } Rsquare = 0$$

Versus

$$\textbf{H}_1\text{: } Rsquare > 0$$

OR

$$\textbf{H}_0\text{: All of the coefficients are equal to zero, } \beta_i = 0$$

Versus

$$\textbf{H}_1\text{: At least one of the coefficients is not equal to zero.}$$

The F test compares explained to unexplained variation, which would be zero, under the null hypothesis. Sample evidence, shown in Figure 11.2, will enable rejection of the null hypothesis if the explained slice is large enough.

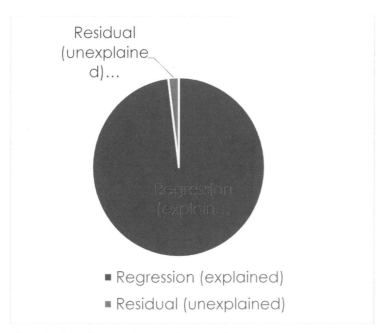

Figure 11.2 Explained and unexplained variation.

More drivers increase potential variation explained. The *F* test accounts for the number of drivers, as well as the sample size, with the comparison of explained variation per predictor (the *regression degrees of freedom*) with unexplained variation for a given sample and model size, the residual degrees of freedom. The ratio of these produces an F statistic with the regression and residual degrees of freedom:

$$F_{regression\ df, residual\ df} = \frac{RSquare/regression\ df}{(1 - RSquare)/residual\ df}$$

For **Fast Food Nations**, the *F* statistic is 516, with 4 and 42 degrees of freedom:

$$F_{4,42} = \frac{.980/4}{(1 - .980)/42} = \frac{.245}{.00048} = 516$$

The *F* statistic is compared to the *F* distribution with the same degrees of freedom. Figure 11.3 illustrates *F* distributions for 1, 2, 4, and 7 predictors with a sample of 30.

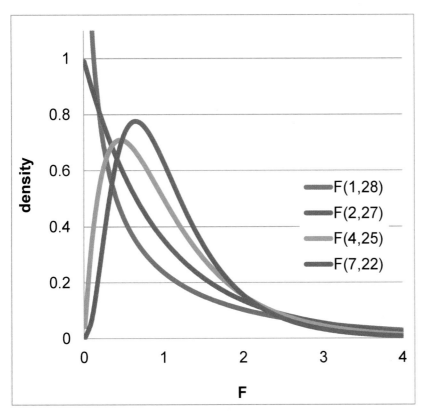

Figure 11.3 A family of F distributions for a regression with sample of 30

The **Fast Food Nations** model *F* is 516, which lies to the extreme right of the $F_{4,42}$ distribution. The *p value,* labeled *Significance F* in Excel, is less than .0001, indicating that it is unlikely that we would observe these data patterns, were none of the four car characteristics driving establishments. It may be that just one of the four characteristics drives establishments, or it may be that all four are significant influences. With this set of four predictors, some of the variation in establishments has been explained.

11.5 Insignificant Parameter Estimates Signal Multicollinearity

To determine which of the four country characteristics are significant drivers of fast food establishments, we initially look at the significance of t *tests* of the individual regression parameter estimates. A t statistic in multiple regression is used to test the hypothesis that a marginal coefficient is zero.

When we have no information about the direction of influence, a two tail test of each marginal slope is use4

$$\mathbf{H_0:}\ \beta_i = 0$$

Versus

$$\mathbf{H_1:}\ \beta_i \neq 0$$

In the more likely case that, when, from theory or experience, we know the likely direction of influence, a one tail test is used. When the suspected direction of influence is positive, the null and alternate hypotheses are:

$$\mathbf{H_0:}\ \beta_i \leq 0$$

Versus

$$\mathbf{H_1:}\ \beta_i > 0.$$

Conversely, when the expected direction of influence is negative the hypotheses are:

$$\mathbf{H_0:}\ \beta_i \geq 0,$$

Versus

$$\mathbf{H_1:}\ \beta_i < 0.$$

Excel provides a two tail t statistic for each marginal slope by calculating the number of standard errors each marginal slope is from zero:

$$t_{residual\ df,i} = b_i / s_{b_i}$$

Notice that a t statistic of a marginal slope in multiple regression is compared with the t distribution for the residual degrees of freedom. For each predictor in the model, we lose one degree of freedom. Excel provides the corresponding p *value* for the two tail t test of each marginal slope. In the case that we want to use a one tail test, the p *value* is divided by two.

In the establishments model, managers were confident that the influences of population *under 15* and *urban* population ought to be positive, and *GDP per capita* and *school years* ought to be negative. For all four potential drivers, one tail t tests could be used. Those are shown in Table 11.3.

Table 11.3 Marginal slopes and their t tests

	Coefficients	Standard Error	t Stat	P-value	one tail p value
Intercept	-.64	.31	-2.0	.05	
Ln Under 15	.45	.12	3.7	.0006	.0003
Ln Urban	.54	.12	4.5	<.0001	<.0001
GDPPC	.0038	.0038	1.0	.31	.16
School years	-.017	.024	-.7	.47	.23

[a]p *values* corresponding to one tail tests are not provided by Excel and have been added here.

Excel t tests of the marginal slopes, shown in Table 11.3, suggest that only population *under 15* and *urban* population drive differences in *establishments*. *GDP per capita* and *school years* appear not to influence *establishments*. Further, the coefficient estimate for *GDP per capita* has the "wrong sign," or the sign opposite of expected. Wealthier families are expected to trade up from fast food to full service restaurants. These are surprising and nonintuitive results.

When predictors which ought to be significant drivers appear to be insignificant, or when parameter estimates are of the wrong sign, we suspect *multicollinearity*. Multicollinearity, the correlation between predictors, thwarts driver identification. When the independent variables are themselves related, they jointly influence performance. It is difficult to tell which individual variables are more important drivers, since they vary together. Because of their correlation, the standard errors s_{b_i} of the marginal slope coefficient estimates, b_i, are inflated. We are not very certain of each true influence in the population is since their influence is joint. The confidence intervals of the true partial slopes are large, since these are multiples of the standard errors of the partial slope estimates. Individual predictors seem to be insignificant though they may be truly significant. In some cases, coefficient signs may be "wrong."

11.6 Combine or Eliminate Collinear Predictors

We have two remedies for multicollinearity cloudiness:

- We can combine correlated variables, with ratios or in additive indices, or
- we can eliminate variables that are contributing redundant information.

Correlations between the predictors are shown in Table 11.4.

Table 11.4 Pairwise correlations between predictors

	Ln under 15	Ln urban	School years	GDP per capita ($K)
Ln under 15	1			
Ln urban	0.96	1		
School years	-0.70	-0.54	1	
GDP per capita ($K)	-0.67	-0.51	0.78	1

Some of correlated predictors can be eliminated, assuming that several reflect a common dimension. If *GDP per capita,* and *school years* each reflect socioeconomic status, one is possibly redundant and may be represented by the other. The alternative is to combine correlated predictors, either by constructing an index from a weighted average of the correlated predictors, or by forming ratios of pairs of correlated predictors.

An index of socioeconomic status could be made from a weighted average of *GDP per capita* and *school years*. *Factor analysis* is a statistical procedure that would provide the weights to form such an index. The challenge associated with use of an index is in its interpretation. Whataburger managers need to know how much difference particular country characteristics make, and they may not be satisfied knowing that a *socioeconomic status index* influences *establishments*. Factor analysis is beyond the scope of this text, but does enable construction of indices from correlated predictors.

Ratios of correlated predictors are used when they make intuitive sense. For example, economic models sometimes use the ratio of *GDP* and *population* to make *GDP per capita,* an intuitively appealing measure of personal wealth.

We will eliminate the seemingly redundant predictors to build a model for Whataburger though combining correlated predictors would be an acceptable alternative. This will not eliminate multicollinearity, but it will reduce multicollinearity by removing correlated predictors.

We will remove one driver at a time, since the removal of any one reduces multicollinearity and changes coefficient estimates and significance levels. We'll choose the driver with the coefficient estimate that is furthest from significance, the one with the largest p value, which is *school years*. *School years* is highly correlated with each of the other three potential drivers. Its removal may increase significance of the coefficients for those drivers.

Regression statistics for the first, full model with *school years,* and the second model without *school years,* are shown in Table 11.5. Removing *school years* improved the model. The standard error, our measure of precision, is smaller. The reduction in RSquare is negligible, .0016%. *School years* is either redundant, since *GDP per capita* continues to represent the impact of socioeconomic status, or it may simply not be a driver of *establishments.*

Table 11.5. Regression statistics of the original, full model and the model without school years.

Regression Statistics			
	full model	*School years out*	*Change*
R Square	0.9800	0.9798	0.0003
Standard Error	0.205	0.204	-0.001

Coefficient estimates and significance levels are shown in Table 11.6. Though coefficient standard errors are slightly smaller, t statistics are slightly larger, and p values are slightly smaller, *GDP per capita* remain insignificant and has an incorrect sign. *GDP per capita* is correlated with both population *under 15* and *urban* population. *Ln Population under 15* and *ln urban* population will represent *GDP per capita,*

Table 11.6 Coefficients after school years has been removed.

	Coefficients	Standard Error	t Stat	P-value	one tail p value
Intercept	-.84	.15	-5.5	<.0001	
Ln under 15	.49	.10	4.8	<.0001	<.0001
Ln urban	.50	.11	4.6	<.0001	<.0001
GDPPC ($K)	.0030	.0036	.8	.40	.20

Regression statistics for the third model, without *school years* and *GDP per capita,* are shown in Table 11.7. The standard error has improved slightly, and the loss of explanatory power, measured with RSquare, is minimal, .03%. \With just two of the four country characteristics, we can account for 98% of the variation in *establishments.*

Table 11.7 Regression without horsepower and diesel.

Regression Statistics			
	School years out	School years and GDP per capita out	Change
R Square	.9798	.9795	.0003
Standard Error	.279	.278	-.0016

Table 11.8 presents coefficient estimates and p values for the third, two driver regression. Standard errors are generally slightly smaller, t statistics are larger, and p values are smaller.

Table 11.8 Coefficients after school years and GDP per capita have been removed.

	Coefficients	Standard Error	t Stat	P-value	one tail p value
Intercept	-.82	.15	-5.5	<.0001	
Ln under 15	.43	.07	6.1	<.0001	<.0001
Ln urban	.56	.08	6.6	<.0001	<.0001

Both of the predictors are significant drivers. Both coefficient estimates have correct signs. As was the case in the full model, *establishments* are higher for populations under 15 and for higher urban populations.

To determine whether or not our model satisfies the assumptions of linear regression, the distribution of residuals is examined, just as with a simple regression model. The residuals, with skewness of .46, are approximately *Normal.*

The final multiple linear regression model of e*stablishments,* in logarithms, is:

$$Ln(est\hat{a}b(K))_i = -.82(\ln K \; estab) + .43(\frac{\ln K \; estab}{\ln M \; under \; 15}) \times \ln(under \; 15(M))_i$$

$$+ .56(\frac{\ln K \; establ}{\ln M \; urban}) \times \ln(urban(M))_i$$

To rescale back to the original *establishments (K),* exponential functions of both sides provide the final equation:

$$\exp[Ln(est\hat{a}b(K))_i] = \exp[-.82(\ln K \ estab)$$

$$+.43(\frac{\ln K \ estab}{\ln M \ under \ 15}) \times \ln(under \ 15(M))_i$$

$$+.56(\frac{\ln K \ establ}{\ln M \ urban}) \times \ln(urban(M))_i]$$

Which simplifies to:

$$est\hat{a}b(K)_i = .44 \ estab(K) \quad under \ 15(M)_i^{.43} \times \ urban(M)_i^{.56}$$

RSquare: .980

11.7 Sensitivity Analysis Quantifies the Marginal Impact of Drivers

We want to compare influences of the significant drivers to identify those which make the greatest difference. In this case, the coefficient estimates, indicating the impacts of unit differences in the drivers, are directly comparable, since the drivers are measured in the units of population. However, this is often not the case. If, for example, either GDP per capita or school years had been significant, those driver units are not comparable to populations. The *part worths*, which with this logarithmic model are multiplicative, are directly comparable multipliers. We will forecast *establishments*. Predicted establishments are equal to the product of the multiplicative part worths, which in the case of Fast Food Nations, is the product of the multiplicative constant from the intercept and the impacts of *under 15* and *urban.*

In a multiplicative model, a measure of the importance of each driver comes from the ratio of the maximum multiplicative part worth to the minimum multiplicative part worth. These are shown below in Table 11.9 and Figure 11.4 for the two drivers.

Table 11.9 Driver importances from multiplicative part worths

	Maximum multiplicative part worth (1)	Minimum multiplicative part worth (2)	Importance ratio (1)/(2)
Under 15	12.4	.9	14.0
Urban	37.5	1.8	20.5

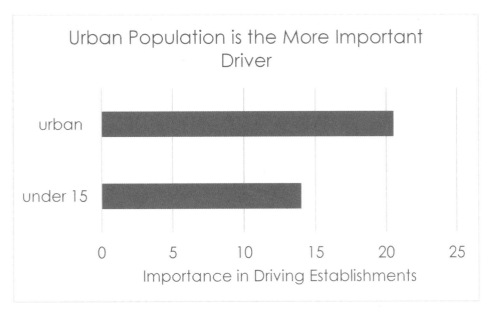

Figure 11.4 Driver importances

The country with the largest population under 15 is expected to host 14 times as many fast food establishments as the country with the smallest population under 15. The country with the largest urban population is expected to host 20.5 times as many fast food establishments as the country with the smallest urban population. Thus, urban population is the more important driver of establishments.

In additive models predicted values are the sum of the part worths. Driver importance is then assessed with differences between the maximum and the minimum.

A measure of potential for more fast food establishments can be made by subtracting existing establishments from predicted establishments. Results suggest that both China and India offer lowest potential, since both currently host many more establishments that predicted. Brazil promises the most potential, followed by the U.S. Whataburger could consider expanding to Brazil, or simply expanding within the U.S.

11.8 Decide Whether Insignificant Drivers Matter

It is typical to find that potential drivers, which logically ought to matter, are insignificant and fail to improve a model. The model is improved by removing those insignificant drivers. However, those apparently insignificant drivers should not be forgotten. They may be performance drivers that do matter, but their correlation with other drivers makes them redundant additions to the model. Management will want to know whether potential drivers that were removed from a model are drivers that do matter, or whether they simply do not matter.

Potential drivers which do matter, but are insignificant and appear not to matter, can be identified with simple regression. If multicollinearity has diminished the significance of a driver, that driver will be significant in a simple regression. Using simple regression to assess significance of a variable that appears not to matter gives that variable an "unfair" chance to claim credit for the joint impact of the set of correlated drivers. Simple regression will overstate a driver's importance, and we would not use the simple regression model in sensitivity analysis or forecasts. However, simple regression can provide important evidence that a potential driver matters, but is redundant.

In **Fast Food Nations,** *GDP per capita* and *school years* were removed from the multiple regression model. Both were correlated with the two drivers that remained in the model, as well as with each other. It seemed likely that those two were drivers of establishments that mattered, but simply could not be included in the multiple regression model, because of redundancy. The modeling team ran simple regressions to decide whether or not this was the case for *GDP per capita* and *school years*.

Results of the two simple regressions, shown in Tables 11.11-11.12 provide evidence that both of the country characteristics drive *establishments*. Management intuition was correct. In countries with higher GDP per capita, fewer fast food establishments are expected, and in countries with higher school years, fewer fast food establishments are expected.

Table 11.10 Simple regression with GDP per capita alone.

Regression Statistics					
R Square	.33				
Standard Error	1.14				
ANOVA	Df	SS	MS	F	Significance F
Regression	1	29	29	22	<.0001
Residual	45	59	1.3		
Total	46	88			
	Coefficients	Standard Error	t Stat	P-value	one tail p value
Intercept	.35	1.105	9.4	<.0001	
GDPPC	-.055	.012	-4.7	<.0001	<.0001

Table 11.11 Regression with school years alone.

Regression Statistics					
R Square	.39				
Standard Error	1.1				
ANOVA	Df	SS	MS	F	Significance F
Regression	1	34	34	29	<.0001
Residual	45	54	1.2		
Total	46	88			
	Coefficients	Standard Error	t Stat	P-value	One tail p value
Intercept	7.1	1.0	7.1	<.0001	
diesel	-.36	.066	-5.4	<.0001	<.0001

11.9 Model Building Begins with Logic and Considers Multicollinearity

Novice model builders sometimes mistakenly think that the computer can choose those variables which belong in a model. Computers have no experience making decisions and can never replace decision makers' logic. (Have you ever tried holding a conversation with a computer?)

The first step in superior model building is to use your head. Use logic and experience to identify independent variables which ought to influence the performance variable which you are interested in explaining and forecasting. Both your height and GDP increased over the past ten years. Given data on your annual height and annual GDP, the computer could churn out a significant parameter estimate relating variation in your height to variation in GDP (or variation in GDP to variation in your height). Decision makers must use their logic and experience to select model variables. Software will quantify and calibrate the influences that we know, from theory or experience, ought to exist.

It is a multicollinear world. Sets of variables together jointly influence performance. Using ratios of collinear predictors reduces multicollinearity. Removing redundant predictors allows us to more accurately explain performance and forecast. Simple regressions are used to determine whether insignificant variables matter, but simply look as though they don't because of multicollinearity---or whether they simply do not matter.

From the logically sound set of variables, pruned to eliminate redundancies and reduce multicollinearity, we have a solid base for superior model building.

Excel 11.1 Build and Fit a Multiple Linear Regression Model

Identifying High Potential Global Markets for Fast Food.

Open Fast Food Nations.xls and assess skewness of the dependent variable, *establishments,* and the four potential drivers:

DEVSQ	▾ :	×	✓	fx	=SKEW(B2:B48)

◢	A	B	C	D	E	F
1	Country	Establish ments (K)	under 15 (M)	urban (M)	GDP per capita ($K)	school years
46	UK	10.5	10.7	50.4	36.5	16
47	US	51.0	62.8	257.4	48.3	16
48	Venezuela	4.9	8.1	26.1	12.6	14
49		=SKEW(B2:B48)		3.98		0.13	-0.70

Create lns of *establishments, under 15* and *urban* and move *under 15* and *urban* to columns H and I so that the potential drivers to be used in the model are in adjacent columns.

Right fill skewness in row 49 to check skewness of the lns.

◢	A	B	C	D	E	F	G	H	I
1	Country	Establish ments (K)	ln estab	ln under 15	ln urban	GDP per capita ($K)	school years	under 15 (M)	urban (M)
44	Thailand	14.6	2.7	2.6	3.1	9.4	12	13.4	22.8
45	Turkey	11.4	2.4	3.0	4.0	14.4	12	20.7	55.8
46	UK	10.5	2.3	2.4	3.9	36.5	16	10.7	50.4
47	US	51.0	3.9	4.1	5.6	48.3	16	62.8	257.4
48	Venezuela	4.9	1.6	2.1	3.3	12.6	14	8.1	26.1
49		4.37	0.531	0.448	0.362	0.13	-0.70	4.43	3.98

Run multiple regression with the dependent variable *establishments* and the independent variables, *ln under 15, ln urban, GDP per capita,* and *school years.*

Alt AY*n*R down down
C1:C48 tab D1:G48 tab LR

	A	B	C	D	E	F	G
5	*Regression Statistics*						
6	R Square	0.980					
7	Standard Err	0.205					
8	Observation	47					
10	ANOVA						
11		*df*	*SS*	*MS*	*F*	*Significance F*	
12	Regression	4	86.4	21.6	515.7	4.32E-35	
13	Residual	42	1.8	0.042			
14	Total	46	88.2				
16		*Coefficients*	*andard Err*	*t Stat*	*P-value*	*Lower 95%*	*Upper 95%*	*ov*
17	Intercept	-0.64	0.31	-2.0	0.047959	-1.27	-0.01
18	ln under 15	0.45	0.12	3.7	0.000615	0.20	0.69
19	ln urban	0.54	0.12	4.5	6.1E-05	0.30	0.79
20	school years	-0.017	0.024	-0.7	0.467147	-0.065	0.030
21	GDP per capita ($K)	0.0038	0.0037	1.0	0.311688	-0.0037	0.0114

Delete the duplicate lower and upper columns.
In H

Shift+right
Alt HDC

Add one tail *t* test p values of the drivers.
In H16
In H18 find the one tail *p values* by dividing Excel's two tail *p values* by 2.
In H18

One tail p value

=e17/2
Shift+down to H21
Cntl+D

| DEVSQ | ▾ | : | × | ✓ | *fx* | =E18/2 |

	E	F	G	H
16	*P-value*	*Lower 95%*	*Upper 95%*	one tail pvalue
17	0.047959	-1.27	-0.01	
18	0.000615	0.20	0.69	=E18/2
19	6.1E-05	0.30	0.79	0.00003
20	0.467147	-0.065	0.030	0.23357
21	0.311688	-0.0037	0.0114	0.15584

Multicollinearity symptoms. While the model is significant (*Significance F* <.0001), *only two of the country characteristics are significant (p value <.05).* We are not certain that either *GDP per capita* or *school years* are influential, since their *p values* >.05. Both have "incorrect" positive signs. Wealthier, more educated countries ought to host fewer fast food establishments.

Together, the lack of significance of seemingly important predictors and the sign reversals signal multicollinearity.

Look at correlations to confirm suspicions that potential driver correlations are high.

Move back to the data sheet and run correlations between the country characteristics.	**Alt AY*n*C** **D1:G48 tab L**

▲	A	B	C	D	E
1		ln under 15	ln urban	GDP per capita ($K)	school years
2	ln under 15	1			
3	ln urban	0.961	1		
4	GDP per capita ($K)	-0.668	-0.513	1	
5	school years	-0.699	-0.545	0.776	1

School years is furthest from significance, with the highest p value in the regression, its coefficient has an incorrect positive sign, and it is highly correlated with the other three potential drivers.

Move back to the data sheet and run regression without *school years*.	**Alt AY*n*R down down OK** **Tab D1:F48**

Add one tail *p values.* Move to the first regression sheet, select and copy the one tail p values in column H. In H16 Move back to the second regression sheet, and then paste into column H. In H16,	**Cntl+Shift+down** **Cntl+C** **Cntl+V**

	A	B	C	D	E	F	G	H
5	*Regression Statistics*							
6	R Square	0.980						
7	Standard Error	0.204						
8	Observations	47						
10	ANOVA							
11		*df*	*SS*	*MS*	*F*	*Significance F*		
12	Regression	3	86.4	28.8	694.8	1.96E-36		
13	Residual	43	1.8	0.041				
14	Total	46	88.2					
16		Coefficients	andard Err	t Stat	P-value	Lower 95%	Upper 95%	one tail pvalue
17	Intercept	-0.839	0.151	-5.5	1.69E-06	-1.14	-0.53	
18	ln under 15	0.495	0.104	4.8	2.27E-05	0.28	0.70	1.13E-05
19	ln urban	0.504	0.109	4.6	3.43E-05	0.28	0.72	1.72E-05
20	GDP per capita ($K)	0.00302	0.00356	0.8	0.401155	-0.0042	0.0102	0.20

GDP per capita is insignificant, and has an incorrect sign.

Return to the data page and run multiple regression without *GDP per capita*.

**Alt AYnR down down OK Tab
Shift+left
OK**

From the third regression, move to the second regression, select and copy one tail p values in column H, and then paste into the third regression in column H.

	A	B	C	D	E	F	G	H
5	*Regression Statistics*							
6	R Square	0.979						
7	Standard Error	0.203						
8	Observations	47						
9								
10	ANOVA							
11		*df*	*SS*	*MS*	*F*	*Significance F*		
12	Regression	2	86.3	43.2	1048.6	7.6E-38		
13	Residual	44	1.8	0.041				
14	Total	46	88.2					
16		Coefficients	andard Err	t Stat	P-value	Lower 95%	Upper 95%	one tail pvalue
17	Intercept	-0.820	0.149	-5.5	1.9E-06	-1.121	-0.519	
18	ln under 15	0.429	0.070	6.1	2.2E-07	0.288	0.571	1.09E-07
19	ln urban	0.562	0.085	6.6	3.9E-08	0.392	0.733	1.95E-08

Look at residuals to check model assumptions. Find the skewness of the residuals to assess their symmetry, evidence of a Normal distribution.

▲	A	B	C	D
				fx =SKEW(C26:C72)
70	45	2.40322	-0.05471	UK
71	46	4.07867	-0.14674	US
72	47	1.91398	-0.32434	Venezu
73		skewness	=SKEW(C26:C72)	

Excel 11.2 Use Sensitivity Analysis to Compare the Marginal Impacts of Drivers

For sensitivity analysis, to determine the impacts of populations under 15 and urban, create the multiplicative part worths.

Move to the data sheet and move *under 15* and *urban* columns to columns C and D so that the data needed to find *predicted establishments*, *under 15* and *urban* are in adjacent columns, next to *country* and *establishments.*

Select the two columns to be moved, cut and paste into column C.	**Cntl+spacebar** **Shift+left**
In C1	**Cntl+X**
Select and copy data in columns A through D.	**Alt HIE**
In A1	**Cntl+Shift+Down** **Shift+right right right** **Cntl+C**
Move back to the third regression sheet data and paste next to residuals.	**Enter**
In D25	

▲	C	D	E	F	G
25	Residuals	Country	Establishments (K)	under 15 (M)	urban (M)
26	-0.19252	Argentina	6.4	10.5	27.0
27	-0.09128	Australia	3.9	4.0	19.6
28	0.18477	Austria	1.5	1.2	5.6

To assess driver importances and to predict *establishments,* make the three part worths. (These will be multiplicative since the dependent variable is in lns.)

In H, make the multiplicative constant, locking the cell reference with Fn 4.
In H26 | **=exp($B$17)**

	A	B	C	D	E	F	G	H
	DEVSQ	▾	:	×	✓	*fx*	=EXP($B$17)	
16		Coefficients	andard Err	t Stat	P-value	Lower 95%	Upper 95%	one tail pvalue
17	Intercept	-0.820	0.149	-5.5	1.9E-06	-1.121	-0.519	
18	In under 15	0.429	0.070	6.1	2.2E-07	0.288	0.571	1.09E-07
19	In urban	0.562	0.085	6.6	3.9E-08	0.392	0.733	1.95E-08
23	RESIDUAL OUTPUT							
25	Observation	licted ln es	Residuals	Country	Establish ments (K)	under 15 (M)	urban (M)	multiplicative constant
26	1	2.04506	-0.19252	Argentina	6.4	10.5	27.0	=EXP($B$17)

In I, make the *under 15* multiplicative part worth, locking the cell reference with Fn 4.
In I26 | **=F26^$B$18**

	A	B	C	D	E	F	G	H	I
	DEVSQ	▾	:	×	✓	*fx*	=F26^$B$18		
16		Coefficients	andard Err	t Stat	P-value	Lower 95%	Upper 95%	one tail pvalue	
17	Intercept	-0.820	0.149	-5.5	1.9E-06	-1.121	-0.519		
18	In under 15	0.429	0.070	6.1	2.2E-07	0.288	0.571	1.09E-07	
19	In urban	0.562	0.085	6.6	3.9E-08	0.392	0.733	1.95E-08	
23	RESIDUAL OUTPUT								
25	Observation	licted ln es	Residuals	Country	Establish ments (K)	under 15 (M)	urban (M)	multiplicative constant	under 15 multiplicative part worth
26	1	2.04506	-0.19252	Argentina	6.4	10.5	27.0	0.4	=F26^$B$18

In J, make the *urban* multiplicative part worth, locking the cell reference with Fn 4.
In J26 | **=G26^$B$19**

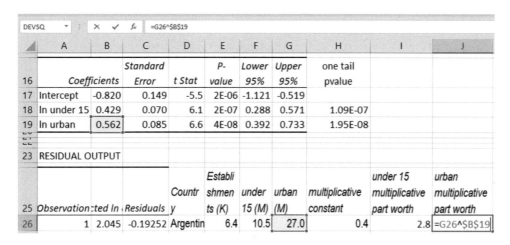

In K, find the predicted *establishments.* | **=PRODUCT(H26:J26)**
In K26

	H	I	J	K
	multiplicative	under 15 multiplicative	urban multiplicative	predicted
25	constant	part worth	part worth	establishments (K)
26	0.4	2.8	6.4	=PRODUCT(H26:J26)

Downfill the four new columns.

To assess driver importances, find the ratio of maximum to minimum part worths for *under 15* and *urban.*

In I73 | **=max(I26:I72)**
In I74 | **=min(I26:I72)**
In I75 | **=I73/I74**
Rightfill to find max, min and ratio for *urban.*
In I73 | **Shift+down down**
                                                                      | **Shift+right**
                                                                      | **Cntl+R**

I73 | | ✕ ✓ *fx* | =MAX(I26:I72)

◢	H	I	J
71	0.4	5.9	22.7
72	0.4	2.5	6.3
73	maximum	12.4	37.5
74	minimum	0.9	1.8
75	max to min	13.9995636	20.5197978

Plot the driver importances with a bar chart.   **| Alt C1**
Add driver labels above the two driver importances, select the four cells,

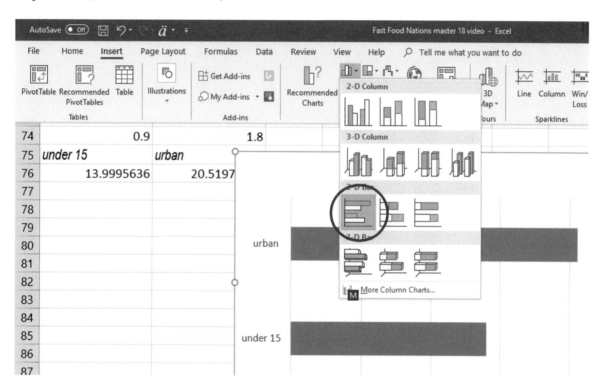

To see *establishment* potential, find the difference between predicted and actual *establishments* in column L:

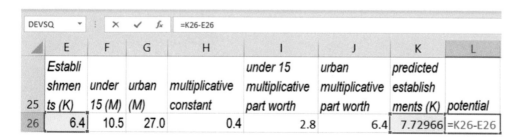

DEVSQ | | ✕ ✓ *fx* | =K26-E26

◢	E	F	G	H	I	J	K	L
25	Establi shmen ts (K)	under 15 (M)	urban (M)	multiplicative constant	under 15 multiplicative part worth	urban multiplicative part worth	predicted establish ments (K)	potential
26	6.4	10.5	27.0	0.4	2.8	6.4	7.72966	=K26-E26

Sort countries by potential.   **CNTL+Shift+down**
From A25   **CNTL+Shift+right**
                                                     Alt ASS
                                                     OK

Tab to columns and select potential.

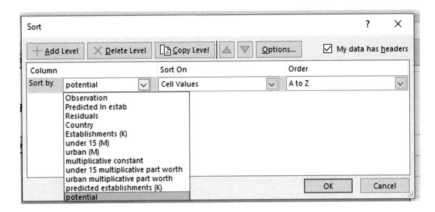

Lab 11-1 Fast Food Establishments Around the Globe

Find skewness and rescale variables that are outside the approximately Normal range of -1 to +1.

1. Is the model *RSquare* significantly greater than 0?

2. Mark potential drivers that have slopes significantly different from 0.

School life expectancy	GDPPC	Population < 15	Urban Population
not sig	not sig	sig <.001	.734

Confirm suspected multicollinearity.

3. Run correlations and mark characteristic pairs that are highly correlated ($|r_{x1,x2}|>.4$).

	School life expectancy	GDPPC	Population < 15	Urban Population
School life expectancy	not sig	not sig	<.001	.436
GDPPC	sig	sig	>.001	.014
Population <15	not sig	sig	.009	.235
Urban population	not sig	not sig	<.001	.007

Remove one seemingly redundant characteristic and re-run the regression.

4. How much did RSquare decline?

     .866

5. Did much did the standard error decline?

     16.07

6. Is the model *RSquare* significantly greater than 0?

     ~~te~~ NO

7. Mark potential drivers that have slopes significantly different from 0. (Leave the one that you removed blank.)

School life expectancy	GDPPC	Population < 15	Urban Population
sig	sig	sig	sig

Remove one seemingly redundant characteristic and re-run the regression.

8. How much did RSquare decline?

     .932

9. Did much did the standard error decline?

     11.473

10. Is the model *RSquare* significantly greater than 0?

     NO

11. Mark potential drivers that have slopes significantly different from 0. (Leave the ones that you removed blank.)

School life expectancy	GDPPC	Population < 15	Urban Population
no sig	no sig	no sig	no sig

Assess residuals.

12. Are residuals approximately *Normal*? .459 yes

13. Present your equation linking country characteristics to establishments in the original scale of establishments.

Do variables removed from the model matter?

Run simple regressions with each of the variables removed to decide whether each is a driver of stores in a country.

14. Mark country characteristics that drive establishments. (Mark both those in your model and not in your model.)

School life expectancy	GDPPC	Population < 15	Urban Population
Sig	Sig	Sig	Sig

Sensitivity analysis.

Find the ratio of largest to smallest part worth for all of the continuous drivers in your final model. The higher ratio indicates the most important driver.

1. Which driver is most influential?

    Driver 1

2. Compare predicted and actual establishments, and then, suggest three countries which offer the highest potential locations for future establishments.

Lab 11-2 Where the Starbucks Stores Are Around the Globe

McDonalds has an eye on Starbucks' successes, globally. If countries with high potential for McCafes could be identified, it is thought that those ought to be the next locations for McCafes. Starbucks has stores in 22 countries outside the U.S. Build a model to find the factors that favor more stores.

Starbucks is thought to be a luxury. Does Starbucks target countries with higher GDP per capita?

More people ought to be linked to higher business potential. Are countries with higher populations favored? Or, are countries with higher population density favored?

It may be more difficult to compete in countries that export coffee, where consumers are "coffee snobs," preferring locally grown coffee.

Starbucks treats their global business as three broad segments: the Americas, Europe and the Middle East (EURME), and China and Asia Pacific (CAP). Are countries in the New World, CAP and Americas, favored, because Old World coffee drinkers in EURME are harder to please?

SBUX stores.xlsx contains data for 22 countries on Starbucks stores, GDP per capita, population, population density, and coffee exports, as well as data for seven additional countries. Use the 22 countries to build your model. To account for possible differences between CAP, Americas and EURME countries, create two indicator variables, CAP and EURME, with Americas countries set as the baseline (=0 for both indicators).

Some variables are skewed. If skewness is outside "approximately Normal," rescale to square roots, cube roots, lns, squares or cubes. (For coffee exports, which are zero in some countries, lns are not a viable option.)

Regression results.

1. Is the model *RSquare* significantly greater than 0?

   NO

2. Mark potential drivers that have slopes significantly different from 0:

EURME	CAP	Coffee exports	Population	GDPPC	Population density
	✓		✓		✓

Confirm suspected multicollinearity.

3. Run correlations and mark characteristic pairs that are highly correlated ($|r_{x1,x2}|>.4$).

	EURME	CAP	Coffee exports	Population	GDPPC	Population density
EURME					✓	
CAP			✓			
Coffee exports						
Population					✓	
GDPPC		✓				
Population density				✓		

Remove one seemingly redundant characteristic and re-run the regression.

4. How much did RSquare decline?

.72

5. How much did the standard error decline?

266.83

6. Mark potential drivers that have slopes significantly different from 0:

EURME	CAP	Coffee exports	Population	GDPPC	Population density
				✓	

Remove one seemingly redundant characteristic and re-run the regression.

7. How much did RSquare decline?

.0281

8. How much did the standard error decline?

428.91

9. Mark potential drivers that have slopes significantly different from 0:

EURME	CAP	Coffee exports	Population	GDPPC	Population density
	✓			✓	

Remove one seemingly redundant characteristic and re-run the regression.

10. How much did RSquare decline?

.72

11. How much did the standard error decline?

287.75

12. Mark potential drivers that have slopes significantly different from 0:

EURME	CAP	Coffee exports	Population	GDPPC	Population density
✓				✓	

Assess residuals.

13. Are residuals approximately *Normal*?

NO

14. Present your equation linking country characteristics to Starbucks stores.

15. Everything else equal (coffee exports and population), countries in EURME can be expected

be home to __3__ % of stores in Americas or CAP (the new baseline).

Do variables removed from the model matter?

Run simple regressions with each of the variables removed to decide whether each is a driver of stores in a country.

16. Mark country characteristics that drive stores in a country.

GDPPC	Population density
✓	

Sensitivity analysis.

Use your regression equation to find predicted stores. The product of the multiplicative constant and the multiplicative driver part worths will reveal predicted stores in each country.

Find the ratio of largest to smallest part worth for each of the drivers. The higher ratio indicates the more important driver.

17. Which driver is more influential?

 Coffce exports

Rumors suggest that Starbucks may be entering two new markets. The short list includes Denmark, India, Indonesia, Israel, Italy, Sweden and Viet Nam. Find predicted stores in each of these potential new markets.

18. In which two of these countries do you expect Starbucks to add more stores?

India, Sweden

19. What distinguishes those two countries from others? $.001$

Case 11-1 What Is Driving Prices in the Laptop Backpack Market?

Under Armour has capitalized on brand recognition in the college market to enter the laptop backpack business. They believe that The North Face and Swiss Gear are major competitors.

Competitive offerings differ with respect to number of colors offered, weight, size and price. The North Face offers laptop backpacks designed especially for women. UA offers a more limited number of women's designs. (Does this drive price?) UA prides itself in offering the lightest weight laptop backpacks. (Is this an advantage?) TNF offers many color options. Is this an advantage? Or do multiple colors create the perception that other features are lacking? UA managers wonder whether more colors ought to be offered or whether more women's models ought to be offered to command higher prices.

Laptop backpacks.xlsx contains data on price, ratings, weight, colors offered, for women, and laptop size for laptop backpacks sold on Amazon for $50 or more. Three companies' laptops are included. Make indicators of TNF and UA brands to distinguish from SG.

Several variables are skewed. Find skewness and rescale those that are outside the approximately Normal range of -1 to +1.

1. Is the model *RSquare* significantly greater than 0?

2. Mark potential drivers that have slopes significantly different from 0.

UA	TNF	Women's	colors	weight	size	Rating

Confirm suspected multicollinearity.

3. Run correlations and mark characteristic pairs that are highly correlated ($|r_{x1,x2}|>.4$).

	UA	TNF	Women's	Colors	weight	size	Rating
UA							
TNF							
Women's							
Colors							
weight							
Size							
Rating							

Remove one seemingly redundant characteristic and re-run the regression.

4. How much did RSquare decline?

5. Did much did the standard error decline?

6. Is the model *RSquare* significantly greater than 0?

7. Mark potential drivers that have slopes significantly different from 0. (Leave the one that you removed blank.)

UA	TNF	Women's	colors	weight	size	Rating

Remove one seemingly redundant characteristic and re-run the regression.

8. How much did RSquare decline?

9. Did much did the standard error decline?

10. Is the model *RSquare* significantly greater than 0?

11. Mark potential drivers that have slopes significantly different from 0. (Leave the ones that you removed blank.)

UA	TNF	Women's	colors	weight	size	Rating

Assess residuals.

12. Are residuals approximately *Normal*?

13. Present your equation linking laptop backback characteristics to price.

14. Everything else equal (brand, size, weight, rating, colors), women's designs can be expected to be priced at ___% of unisex designs.

15. Everything else equal (size, women/unisex design, weight, rating, colors), The North Face laptop backpacks can be expected to be price at _____% of UA laptop backpacks.

Do variables removed from the model matter?

Run simple regressions with each of the variables removed to decide whether each is a driver of laptop prices.

16. Mark laptop backpack characteristics that drive prices. (Mark both those in your model and not in your model.)

UA	TNF	Women's	colors	weight	size	Rating

Sensitivity analysis.

Use your regression equation to find predicted prices. The product of the multiplicative constant and the multiplicative driver part worths will reveal predicted prices.

Find the ratio of largest to smallest part worth for all of the continuous drivers in your final model. The higher ratio indicates the most important driver.

17. Which driver is most influential?

18. Suggest changes that UA could make to justify raising prices, in order of potential impact, based on your analysis.

Case 11-2 Costco's Warehouse Location Scheme

Wal-Mart executives have been tracking Costco's success. They would like to identify the drivers of Costco's location choices. Will Costco enter China? Will Costco enter the other BRICs (Brazil, Russia and India)?
    From Costco press releases, they have learned that Costco targets locations

- which are surrounded by affluent households,
- where there are a lot of college educated consumers.

A Costco spokesperson has also noted that Costco likes to have a gas station at every warehouse, since gas stations drive business. From Costco's press releases, Wal-Mart executives believe that Costco locations may be in countries with (i) high GDP per capita, (ii) high percentage of urban population, (iii) a large percentage of college educated consumers, (v) a high percentage of cars per person, (vi) located in the Americas.

Warehouse locations contains GDP per capita, urban population, percent 25-34 with college degrees, and vehicles per K population for each of 14 countries. Add indicators of location in the Americas or Europe, with Asia, India and Russia as the baseline location.

    Several variables are skewed. Find skewness and rescale those that are outside the approximately Normal range of -1 to +1. (Note that warehouses is zero in some countries. If skewness of warehouses is not approximately Normal, limit your choices for rescaling to square roots, cube roots, squares and cubes to avoid logarithms of zero.)

1. Is the model *RSquare* significantly greater than 0?

2. Mark potential drivers that have slopes significantly different from 0.

Americas	urban	GDPPC	vehicles	25-34 population w college

Confirm suspected multicollinearity.

3. Run correlations and mark characteristic pairs that are highly correlated ($|r_{x1,x2}| > .4$).

	Americas	urban	GDPPC	vehicles	25-34 population w college
Americas					
Urban					
GDPPC					
vehicles					
25-45 pop w college					

Remove one seemingly redundant characteristic and re-run the regression.

4. How much did RSquare decline?

5. Did much did the standard error decline?

6. Is the model *RSquare* significantly greater than 0?

7. Mark potential drivers that have slopes significantly different from 0. (Leave the one that you removed blank.)

Americas	urban	GDPPC	vehicles	25-34 population w college

Remove one seemingly redundant characteristic and re-run the regression.

8. How much did RSquare decline?

9. Did much did the standard error decline?

10. Is the model *RSquare* significantly greater than 0?

11. Mark potential drivers that have slopes significantly different from 0. (Leave the ones that you removed blank.)

Americas	urban	GDPPC	vehicles	25-34 population w college

Remove one seemingly redundant characteristic and re-run the regression.

12. How much did RSquare decline?

13. Did much did the standard error decline?

14. Is the model *RSquare* significantly greater than 0?

15. Mark potential drivers that have slopes significantly different from 0. (Leave the ones that you removed blank.)

Americas	urban	GDPPC	vehicles	25-34 population w college

Assess residuals.

16. Are residuals approximately *Normal*?

17. Present your equation linking country characteristics to warehouses in the original scale of establishments.

Sensitivity analysis.

Find predicted warehouses in countries in cube roots.
Find the range (maximum-minimum) in part worths for all of the drivers in your final model. The higher range indicates the more important driver.

18. Which driver is more influential?

Rescale predicted values in roots to find predicted values in the original warehouse units.

19. Compare predicted and actual warehouses, and then, suggest two countries which offer the highest potential locations for future establishments.

20. Wal-Mart executives expect Costco to enter China, soon, though Costco press releases suggest that France or Spain will be the next Costco destination. Why might Costco locate in France next, instead of China? (List a possible reason.)

Do variables removed from the model matter?

Run simple regressions with each of the variables removed to decide whether each is a driver of warehouses in a country.

21. Mark country characteristics that drive warehouses. (Mark both those in your model and not in your model.)

Urban	GDPPC	vehicles	25-34 population w college

Case 11-3 Store24 (A): Managing Employee Retention* and Store24 (B): Service Quality and Employee Skills**

Download and read the HBS cases before you begin your analysis.

Problem. Management needs to know what controllable "people" factors are driving store sales. If management or crew tenure or service quality are driving performance, programs to increase tenure or quality will be created.

A number of uncontrollable factors probably influence store sales, in addition to "people" influences. While these cannot be changed by management, at least in the short term, managers are aware that those influences cannot be ignored.

There has been some grumbling from managers of stores located in residential neighborhoods, as well as from managers of stores not open 24 hours, since sales potential may be limited in those stores. While location and hours open cannot be changed, at least in the short term, management compensation could be adjusted if some stores are found to have lower performance potential.

The case hints that some store performance responses to drivers may be nonlinear, and some potential drivers are skewed. Rescale those to move skewness closer to Normal. (Note, if *management tenure* or *crew tenure* are skewed, rescale with cube roots, square roots, squares or cubes, to avoid logarithms of zero.)

Build a model of Store24 sales, removing insignificant variables, one at a time, until all remaining are significant. Use one tail t tests for any potential driver for which the direction of influence is known.

Data are in **Store24.**

1. Is the model *RSquare* significantly greater than 0?

2. Mark potential drivers that have slopes significantly different from 0.

Residential	Open 24 hrs	Competition	Ped count	Pop	Visibility	Management tenure	Crew tenure	Service quality

Confirm suspected multicollinearity.

3. Run correlations and mark characteristic pairs that are highly correlated ($|r_{x1,x2}|>.4$).

	Resid	Open 24	comp	Ped count	pop	Visib	Mgmt. ten	Crew ten	Serv qual
residential									
Open 24									
competition									
Ped count									
population									
Visibility									
Mgmt. tenure									
Crew tenure									
Serv qual									

Remove one seemingly redundant characteristic and re-run the regression.

4. How much did RSquare decline?

5. Did much did the standard error decline?

6. Is the model *RSquare* significantly greater than 0?

7. Mark potential drivers that have slopes significantly different from 0. (Leave the one that you removed blank.

Residential	Open 24 hrs	Competition	Ped count	Pop	Visibility	Management tenure	Crew tenure	Service quality

Remove one seemingly redundant characteristic and re-run the regression.

8. How much did RSquare decline?

9. Did much did the standard error decline?

10. Is the model *RSquare* significantly greater than 0?

11. Mark potential drivers that have slopes significantly different from 0. (Leave the ones that you removed blank.

Residential	Open 24 hrs	Competition	Ped count	Pop	Visibility	Management tenure	Crew tenure	Service quality

12. Present your regression model equation.

13. How much does residential location reduce sales, on average? $_____

14. How much does not being open 24 hours reduce sales, on average? $_____

Sensitivity analysis.

Use your regression equation to find predicted sales in stores.

15. From the part worths, find the expected improvement in sales from improvements that could be accomplished in two years:

- encouraging new managers to stay 24 months (the median): _____

- encouraging managers with 24 months tenure to stay 24 months more: ____

- encouraging new crew to stay 24 months: _____

- encouraging crew with 7 months (the median) tenure to stay 24 months more: _____

- improve service quality from the minimum to the median: _____

- improve service quality from median to maximum: _____

16. Should the focus be on improving the "worst" to the median? Or improving the median to the "best?"

Do variables removed from the model matter?

Run simple regressions with each of the variables removed to decide whether each is a driver of sales.

17. Mark store characteristics that drive sales. (Mark both those in your model and not in your model.)

Residential	Open 24 hrs	Competition	Ped count	Pop	Visibility	Management tenure	Crew tenure	Service quality

*Harvard Business School case 9602096
**Harvard Business School case 9602097

Assignment 11-1 Identifying Promising Global Markets

Harley-Davidson would like to identify the most promising global markets for motorcycle sales.

Some managers believe that motorcycle sales potential is greater in developed countries with higher GDP. Others believe that per capita GDP may a better driver, with wealthier drivers choosing cars instead of motorcycles.

Management believes that motorcycle sales potential will necessarily be greater in more populated countries. Some believe that population density may matter more, since motorcycles may be preferred to cars for parking and commuting in larger cities.

Build a model to identify the drivers of motorcycle market potential. **11 Global Moto** contains measures of *motorcycle sales, GDP, per capita GDP, population,* and *population density* for 20 countries with the highest motorcycle sales. A number of these variables are skewed and ought to be rescaled. Remove variables that aren't significant, one at a time. One tail tests should be used for drivers for which the direction of expected influence is known.

1. Present your regression equation in the original scale of motorcycles sold:

2. Which economic and population variables drive motorcycle sales? (Test drivers not in your final model separately.)

   ___GDP   ___ per capita GDP   ___ population   ___ population density

3. From the ranges in part worths, the most important driver is:

   ___ GDP   ___ per capita GDP   ___ population   ___ population density

4. Illustrate importances of the drivers in your final model with a bar chart:

5. Compare predicted sales with actual sales in all countries in the sample to identify two markets with the greatest unrealized potential that Harley-Davidson should target:

Assignment 11-2 Promising Global Markets for EVs.

Shiso Motors has designed an inexpensive Electric Vehicle (EV) which targets global segments where air pollution is severe. Shiso executives believe that the level of carbon emissions is a good surrogate for potential demand.

It is generally believed that economic productivity, population, and carbon based fuels drive emissions, and Shiso managers would like quantify these impacts, in order to prioritize targeted global segments.

There is disagreement whether GDP or GDP per capita is the stronger driver of emissions. Some believe that population is a key driver, while others argue that GDP per capita matters more.

It is thought that emissions are highest in the BRIC countries, though rapidly emerging markets that have not yet reached the level of economic development of the BRICs may be attractive.

A. Build a Model to Explain Emissions Differences across Countries

Shiso has asked you to build a model to explain differences in emissions across countries. **Shiso** contains data on *emissions, GDP, population, urban population, GDP per capita, oil production*, and fuel sources used to generate electricity in 32 countries. The 32 include developed nations, the *BRIC* and "*fast emerging*" nations.

Use natural logarithms when rescaling variables would improve skewness.

1. Which potential continuous drivers influence emissions?

   ___ GDP   ___ GDP per capita   ___ Population   ___ Urban population

   ___ Oil Production   ___ Electricity generated from oil

   ___ Electricity generated from coal

2. Write your model of emissions (in the original scale of *kt*) in a form which shows the separate impacts of the intercept (first), country development indicators, and each continuous driver.

3. One of the Shiso managers is convinced that emissions (and potential demand for an EV) are higher in countries where more electricity is produced from oil. Is this manager correct? ___ Y ___ N

4. Another Shiso manager is convinced that emissions (and potential demand for an EV) are higher in countries with a larger urban population. Is this manager correct?

   ___ Y ___ N

B. Sensitivity Analysis of Driver Impacts

1. Illustrate the impacts of two continuous drivers on expected emissions in three global segments. Produce a bar chart of part worth ranges for the model drivers.

2. Emissions in South Africa are noticeably higher than emissions in Thailand. Explain why this is the case:

3. If GDP grows by 10% in both China and Columbia, how much will expected emissions increase in each of the two countries?

   _____% increase in China   _____% increase in Columbia

Case 11-1 Promising Global Markets for Water Purification

Alcoa has developed a process to remove pollutants from water contaminated by coal mining. Alcoa executives would like to know if the coal intensities (for electricity generation and for export sales) of countries drive water pollutants.

Data are available for 37 coal producing countries on annual water pollutants by country, as well as use of coal to generate electricity, and coal rents from export sales. In addition to coal intensity, it is thought that level of development, reflected in a country's GDP, and mineral rents, the value of exported minerals, may also drive the level of annual water pollution.

It is thought that water pollution is greater among the rapidly industrializing BRIC and emerging countries.

I. Build a Model to Explain Water Pollution Differences Across Countries

Alcoa has asked you to build a model to explain differences in annual water pollution across countries. **Water pollution segmentation** contains data on *water pollution, coal use to generate electricity, coal rents from export, mineral rents from export,* and *GDP* in 37 countries. The 37 include developed nations, the *BRIC*s, emerging countries, and underdeveloped countries.

For variables which are zero for some countries, limit your choices of scales to square roots, cube roots, squares, or cubes. (One cannot rescale zero values with logarithms.)

1. Which potential continuous drivers do influence emissions?

     ___ GDP   ___ coal to generate electricity   ___ coal rents   ___ mineral rents

2. Write your model of water pollution (in the original scale of K BODs:

3. One of the Alcoa managers is convinced that water pollution (and potential demand for the Alcoa process) is higher in countries where mineral rents are higher. Is this manager correct?

4. In order to use linear regression, the residuals must be approximately Normally distributed.

    Are your model residuals approximately Normal? ___Y or ___N

    Cite the statistic (and its value) that you used to reach your conclusion: _____

I.   Sensitivity Analysis of Driver Impacts

1. Water pollution levels in BRIC countries are ___% higher than those in developed countries.

2. Water pollution in Ukraine is nearly four times that in Hungary. Provide one reason based on your results to explain this difference.

Chapter 12
Model Building and Forecasting with Multicollinear Time Series

An explanatory regression model from time series data allows us to identify performance drivers and forecast performance given specific driver values, just as regression models from cross sectional data do. When decision makers want to forecast *future* performance in the shorter term, a time series of past performance is used to identify drivers and fit a model. A time series model can be used to identify drivers whose variation over time is associated with later variation in performance over time.

In time series models with dual goals of forecasting in the shorter term and explaining performance over time, we seek links between past variation in drivers with later variation in performance. These links between drivers and performance require that changes in the drivers precede change in performance. Therefore, lagged predictor variables are used. Patterns of change in drivers that also occur in the dependent variable in later time periods are identified to choose driver lags. Time series models are built using predictor values from past periods to explain and forecast later performance. Figure 12.1 illustrates the differences in model building processes between time series models based on trend, for longer term forecasts, and explanatory time series models for shorter term forecasts.

Four differences in the model building process distinguish explanatory cross sectional and time series models:

- the use of lagged predictors,
- start with a single predictor and add additional predictors, one at a time to explain unaccounted for variation (instead of all potential predictors in first, then removed one at a time)
- assessment of autocorrelation with Durbin Watson to identify additional drivers, and
- the model validation process.

Figure 12.2 illustrates the differences in model building processes between explanatory cross sectional and time series models.

Most business performance variables and economic indicators are cyclical. Economies cycle through expansion and recession, and performance in most businesses fluctuates following economic fluctuation. Business and economic variables are also often seasonal. Cyclicality and seasonality can accounted for by adding cyclical and seasonal predictors or by adding seasonal indicators.

© Springer Nature Switzerland AG 2019
C. Fraser, *Business Statistics for Competitive Advantage with Excel 2019 and JMP*,
https://doi.org/10.1007/978-3-030-20374-0_12

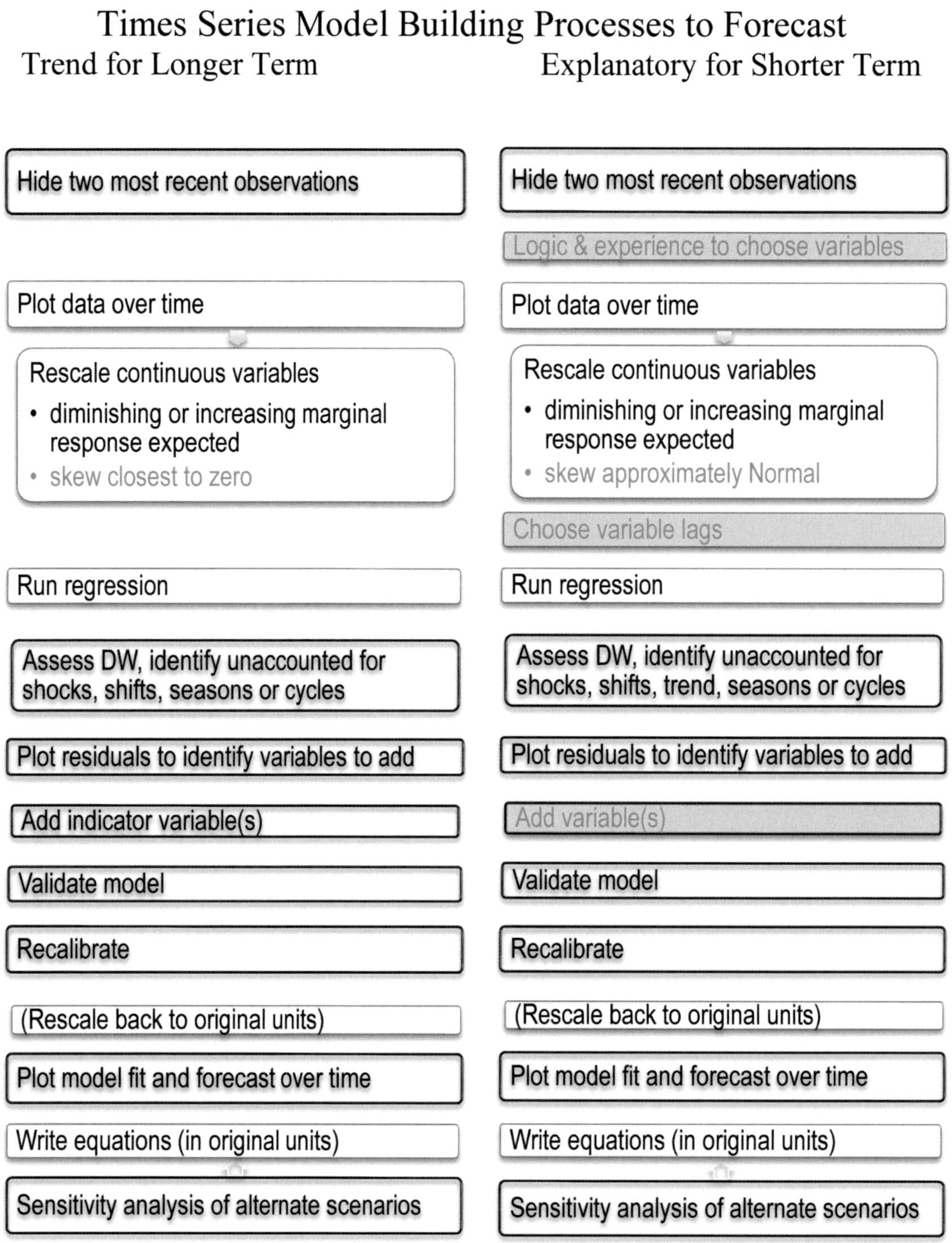

Times Series Model Building Processes to Forecast

Trend for Longer Term	Explanatory for Shorter Term
Hide two most recent observations	Hide two most recent observations
	Logic & experience to choose variables
Plot data over time	Plot data over time
Rescale continuous variables • diminishing or increasing marginal response expected • skew closest to zero	Rescale continuous variables • diminishing or increasing marginal response expected • skew approximately Normal
	Choose variable lags
Run regression	Run regression
Assess DW, identify unaccounted for shocks, shifts, seasons or cycles	Assess DW, identify unaccounted for shocks, shifts, trend, seasons or cycles
Plot residuals to identify variables to add	Plot residuals to identify variables to add
Add indicator variable(s)	Add variable(s)
Validate model	Validate model
Recalibrate	Recalibrate
(Rescale back to original units)	(Rescale back to original units)
Plot model fit and forecast over time	Plot model fit and forecast over time
Write equations (in original units)	Write equations (in original units)
Sensitivity analysis of alternate scenarios	Sensitivity analysis of alternate scenarios

Figure 12.1 Model building processes with time series data

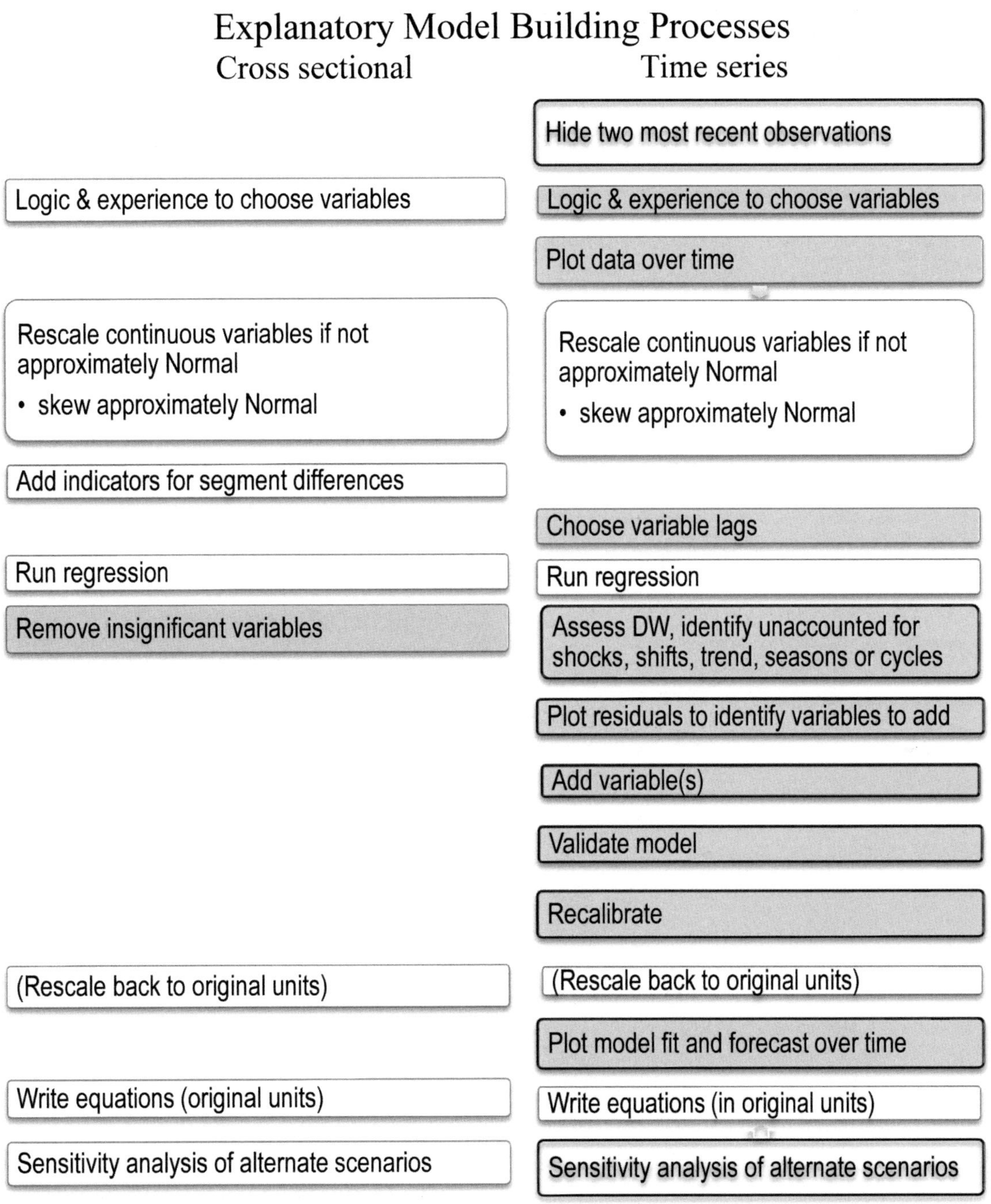

Explanatory Model Building Processes

Cross sectional	Time series

	Hide two most recent observations
Logic & experience to choose variables	Logic & experience to choose variables
	Plot data over time
Rescale continuous variables if not approximately Normal • skew approximately Normal	Rescale continuous variables if not approximately Normal • skew approximately Normal
Add indicators for segment differences	
	Choose variable lags
Run regression	Run regression
Remove insignificant variables	Assess DW, identify unaccounted for shocks, shifts, trend, seasons or cycles
	Plot residuals to identify variables to add
	Add variable(s)
	Validate model
	Recalibrate
(Rescale back to original units)	(Rescale back to original units)
	Plot model fit and forecast over time
Write equations (original units)	Write equations (in original units)
Sensitivity analysis of alternate scenarios	Sensitivity analysis of alternate scenarios

Figure 12.2 Explanatory model building processes

Before a time series model is used to forecast future performance, whether for short term or longer term forecasts, it is validated:

- the two most recent observations are hidden while the model is built,
- the model equation is used to forecast performance in those two most recent periods,
- model prediction intervals are compared with actual performance values in those two most recent periods, and if the prediction intervals contain actual performance values, this is evidence that the model has *predictive validity* and can be reliably used to forecast unknown performance in future periods.

12.1 Time Series Models Include Decision Variables, External Forces, and Leading Indicators

Most successful forecasting models logically assume that performance in a period, y_t, depends upon

- decision variables under the management control,
- external forces, including
    - shocks such as 9/11, Hurricane Katrina, change in Presidential Party
    - market variables,
    - competitive variables,
- Leading indicators of the economy, industry or the market
- Seasonality
- Cyclicality

Ultimately, the multiple regression explanatory forecasting models contain several of these components, which together account for variation in performance. This chapter introduces leading indicator components of regression models built from time series.

Performance across time depends on decision variables and the economy. Decision variables, such as spending on advertising, sales effort and research and development tend to move together. In periods of prosperity, spending in all three areas may increase; in periods where performance is sluggish, spending in all three areas may be cut. Firm strategy guides resource allocation to the various firm functions. As a result, it is common for spending and investment variables to be correlated in time series data.

Many economic indicators also move together across time. In times of economic prosperity, GDP is growing faster, consumer expectations increase, and investments increase. Increasing wealth filters down from the economy to consumers and stock holders, where some proportion of gains are channeled back into consumption or investments.

It is common for decision variables, past performance, and leading indicators to be correlated in time series data. This inherent correlation of performance drivers in time series data makes logical choice of drivers a critical component of good model building.

It is also often more promising to build models by adding variables, one at a time, looking at residuals for indications of the most promising variables to add next.

Example 12.1 Marriott Quarterly Revenues. Marriott executives desire a quarterly revenue forecast. A four quarter forecast is needed for quarterly reports, and an eight quarter forecast is desired.

Marriott acquired Starwood in the third quarter of 2016, which substantially enhanced revenues.

What is driving revenue growth? Executives suspect that the hotel business is driven by economic productivity. When GDP, for example, is improving, businesses spend more on travel. Some time between growth in GDP and consequent Marriott revenues is expected, since travel requires planning.

The hotel industry is thriving, and competition is fierce. A major competitor, Wyndham, is third largest, following Marriott, in first place, in the industry. Are Wyndham revenues a leading indicator of industry growth? Or do they represent competition? If the industry is growing, both may be growing, together, and profiting from promotions of both. (Note that, Marriott markets to Spring Break travelers and sees highest revenues in the second quarter, while Wyndham markets to summer travelers and sees highest revenues in the third quarter.)

Population growth probably drives revenues. More people lead to more travel.

Executives would like to learn which particular age groups drive revenues. Do Baby Boomers (50 to 65) and Seniors, 65+, who have presumably more resources, drive revenues more than younger consumers? There is also expected to be a delay between retirement and increased travel, since travel requires planning.

12.2 Indicators of Economic Prosperity Lead Business Performance

A *leading indicator* model links changes in a leading indicator, such as *GDP,* and later performance:

$$
re\hat{v}enue(\$B)_q = b_0(\$B) + b_1 \left(\frac{\$B}{\$T} \right) \times GDP(\$B)_{q-l}
$$

where *l* denotes the length of lag, or delay from change in GDP to change in revenues.

Andrew Snyder, a recent business school graduate with modeling expertise, was asked to build a model of Marriott quarterly revenues, which would both explain revenue fluctuations and forecast revenues in the next four to eight quarters.

After being briefed by the executives, Andrew created a model reflecting their logic. The following potential drivers would be considered:

- $GDP(K)_{q-l}$
- *Wyndham revenues$_{q-l}$*
- *World Millennial population$_{q-l}$*
- *World XGen population$_{q-l}$*
- *World Baby Boomer population$_{q-l}$*
- *World population 65+$_{q-l}$*
- *World population 20+$_{q-l}$*

12.3 Hide the Two Most Recent Datapoints to Validate a Time Series Model

Andrew used datapoints for quarterly revenue in 2013 through 2017. Before Andrew proceeded further, he excluded the two most recent observations from second and quarter 2017. These *hold out* observations would allow him to compare forecasts for the two most recent periods with actual revenues to *validate* his model. If the 95% prediction intervals from the model contained the actual revenues for both quarters, he would be able to conclude that his model is valid. He could then use the model to forecast with confidence.

12.4 Compare Scatterplots to Choose Driver Lags: Visual Inspection

The potential drivers reflect economic conditions and demographics and move together over time. Consequently, they are highly correlated. Including all of the drivers in a multiple regression model at once would introduce a high degree of multicollinearity and make it difficult to identify each of their marginal impacts. To most effectively build a time series model, start with one driver, and then add additional drivers, one at a time.

Andrew began by plotting *Marriott revenues* by quarter. Since skewness would be affected by the shift from the acquisition, it was assessed using quarters before the Starwood shift. Revenues were mildly, positively skewed at .11, indicating approximate Normality. He focused more heavily on pattern in recent quarters, since his goal was to build a model which produced valid forecasts. He added a trend line for reference. (The trend is the average linear growth over the series.) He noted that revenues had grown consistently over the 2013-2017 period, with a noticeable upward shift late in 2016, presumably due to the acquisition. Revenues were also seasonal. His scatterplot is shown in Figure 12.3. It was obvious that the Starwood acquisition was a significant shift that ought to be accounted for first. Regression results are shown in Table 12.1.

The acquisition was a driver of revenue. However, Durbin Watson suggested that other drivers were unaccounted for. The plot of residuals, the variation not yet accounted for, is shown in Figure 12.4.

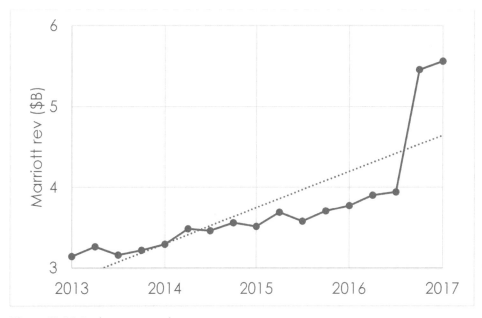

Figure 12.3 Marriott revenues by quarter.

Table 12.1 One driver model with Starwood acquisition

Regression Statistics					
R Square	0.881				
Standard Error	0.251				
Observations	17				

ANOVA	df	SS	MS	F	Significance F
Regression	1	7.03	7.03	111.6	2.4E-08
Residual	15	0.946	0.063		
Total	16	7.98			

	Coefficients	Standard Error	t Stat	P-value	one tail p value
Intercept	3.51	0.065	54.1	1.3E-18	
Starwood	2.00	0.189	10.6	2.4E-08	1.2E-08

DW		dL	dU		
0.43		1.13	1.38		

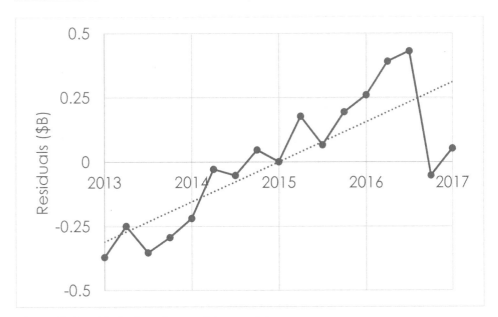

Figure 12.4 Residuals from the one driver model.

To choose lags for the seven potential drivers, Andrew plotted past *GDP, Wyndham revenues, Millennial, XGen, Baby Boomer, 65+* and *20+ populations.* An eight quarter lag was used for *GDP,* to enable an eight quarter forecast, and account for the delay between *GDP* gains and later increased spending. This is shown in Figure 12.5. The positive trend in past *GDP* could explain the positive trend in revenues, not yet accounted for, though past *GDP* did not explain the drop in revenues in late 2016.

Wyndham revenues were seasonal and consistently highest in the third quarters. For an eight quarter forecast, an eleven quarter lag was used to line up *Wyndham* seasonality with seasonality in *Marriott revenues* where second quarters were consistently highest. The *Wyndham revenue* and the residuals, shown in Figure 12.6, reveal similarities. Both show increasing trend, as well as seasonality. *Wyndham revenues,* lagged eleven quarters, did show declines in 2016, but the declines began one quarter earlier than the decline in residuals.

World population data, from The World Bank, was available through 2016, and so twelve quarter lags were needed to produce an eight quarter forecast. This correspondence is shown in Figure 12.7. Like *GDP*, the generations of World population were also consistently increasing.

To choose between the seven potential drivers, all of which had patterns which matched residuals in three of the four most recent quarters, Andrew compared correlations, shown in Table 12.2. World Millennials, XGen, Boomers and World population 20+ had stronger correlations, shown in Table 12.2. The population of World Millennials was greatest, and so Andrew selected that to add to the model. Results are shown in Table 12.3.

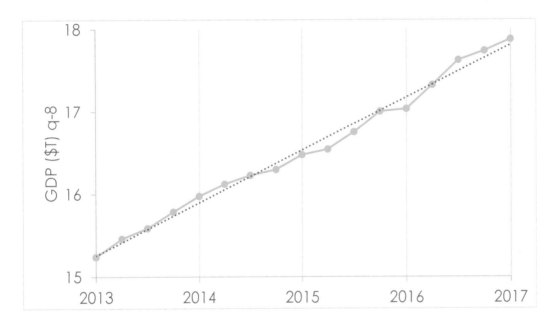

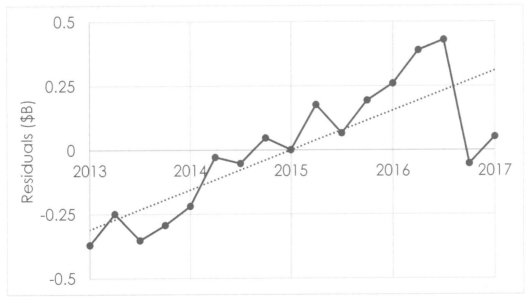

Figure 12.5 Past GDP with residuals from one driver model

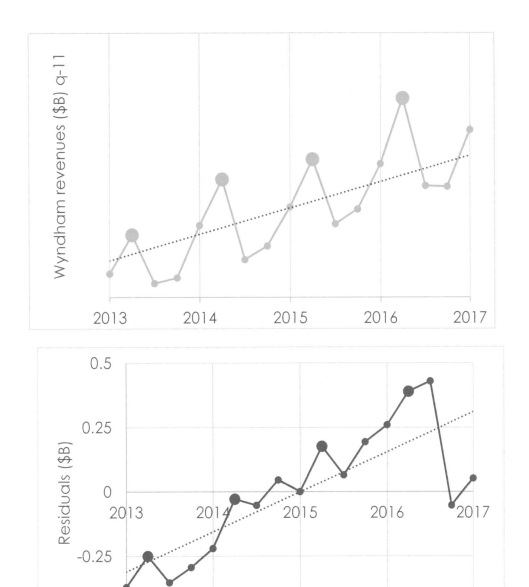

Figure 12.6 Past Wyndham revenues with residuals from the one driver model.

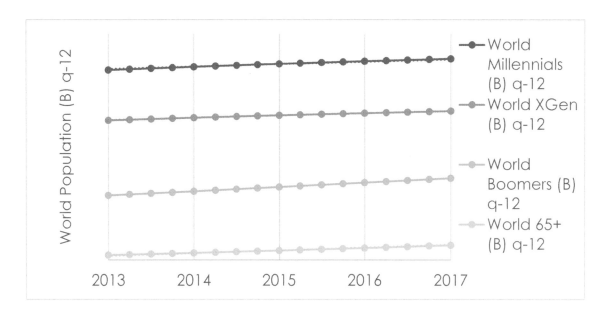

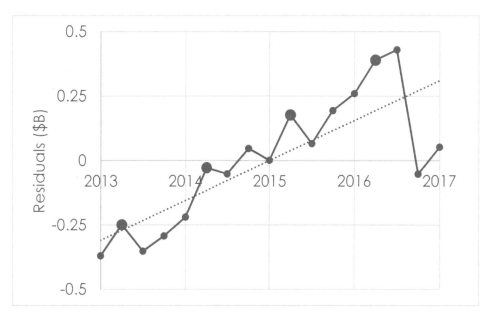

Figure 12.7 World populations with residuals from the one driver model.

Table 12.2 Correlations between potential drivers and one driver residuals

	GDP ($T) q-8	Wyndham revenue ($B) q-11	World Millennials (B) q-12	World XGen (B) q-12	World Boomers (B) q-12	World 65+ (B) q-12	World 20+ (B) q-12
Residuals	0.780	0.761	0.819	0.814	0.802	0.789	0.806

Table 12.3 Regression of Marriott revenues with Starwood and past World Millennial population.

Regression Statistics					
R Square	0.993				
Standard Error	0.065				
Observations	17				

ANOVA	df	SS	MS	F	Significance F
Regression	2	7.92	3.96	930.3	1.3E-15
Residual	14	0.060	0.004		
Total	16	7.98			

	Coefficients	Standard Error	t Stat	P-value	one tail p value
Intercept	-17.6	1.46	-12.0	9.1E-09	
Starwood	1.55	0.058	26.7	2E-13	1E-12
World Millennials (B) q-12	12.3	0.86	14.4	8.5E-10	4E-10
DW	2.22				

The addition of past World Millennial population improved the model, increasing RSquare, and reducing the standard error. However, Durbin Watson was now larger than two, suggesting unaccounted for, negative autocorrelation due to unaccounted for seasonality. The residuals, shown in Figure 12.8, also reveal seasonality. Adding the seasonal past *Wyndman revenue* driver promised to improve the model. Correlations with the residuals from the two driver model, in Table 12.4, confirm this. Results from the three driver model are shown in Table 12.5.

Adding past *Wyndham revenues* improved the model, and also produced Durbin Watson closer to two. Seasonality had been accounted for. Residuals, shown in Figure 12.9 are random, and display no pattern, and all are within one standard error of zero.

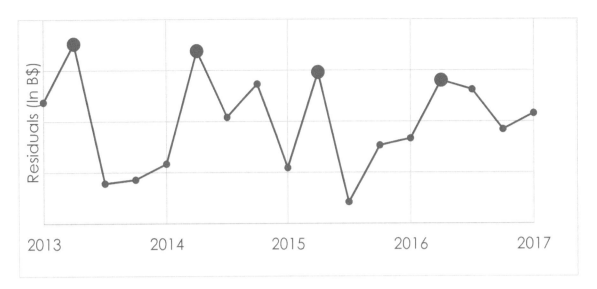

Figure 12.8 Residuals from the two driver model.

Table 12.4 Correlations between the two driver model residuals and potential drivers.

	Wyndham rev ($B) q-11	GDP ($T) q-8
residuals	0.388	0.028

Table 12.5 Regression with Starwood, past World Millennial population, and past Wyndham revenues.

Regression Statistics					
R Square	.995				
Standard Error	.053				
Observations	17				
ANOVA	df	SS	MS	F	Significance F
Regression	3	7.94	2.65	924.1	2.1E-15
Residual	13	.037	.0029		
Total	16	7.98			
	Coefficients	Standard Error	t Stat	P-value	one tail p value
Intercept	-14.4	1.65	-8.8	8.1E-07	
Starwood	1.56	.048	32.7	7.2E-14	3.6E-14
Wyndham rev ($B) q-11	.42	.15	2.8	.015	
World Millennials (B) q-12	10.2	1.03	9.9	2.0E-07	1.0E-07
DW	2.06				

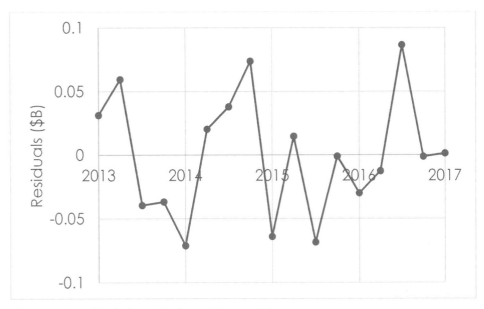

Figure 12.9 Residuals from the three driver model

12.5 Forecast the Recent, Hidden Points to Assess Predictive Validity

The model is significant, all coefficient estimates are significant and of correct, expected sign. Andrew moved on to validate the model for forecasting.

Comparing actual *revenues* in the two most recent, hidden quarters, with model mean prediction intervals suggested that the model underestimated revenue in the second quarter, 2017.26. However, comparisons with the individual prediction interval bounds from JMP confirmed model validity. Both quarters' revenues fell within the 95% individual prediction interval bounds, shown in Table 12.6.

Table 12.6 Evidence of predictive validity of the model

quarter	Marriott revenues	Lower 95% prediction interval bound	Upper 95% prediction interval bound	Upper 95% Individual Prediction Interval Bound (JMP)	Lower 95% Individual Prediction Interval Bound (JMP)
2017.25	5.80	5.55	5.78	5.51	5.83
2017.5	5.66	5.46	5.69	5.44	5.73

12.6 Add the Most Recent Datapoints to Recalibrate

With evidence of predictive validity, Andrew used the model to forecast revenues in the next eight quarters. Before making the forecast, he added the two most recent observations that were hidden. The recalibrated model equation is:

$$Marriott\ quarterly\ revenues(\$B)_q = -14.0(\$B) + 1.61(\$B) \times Starwood_q$$
$$+.505\left(\frac{\$B}{\$B}\right) \times Wyndham\ revenues(\$B)_{q-11}$$
$$+9.93\left(\frac{\$B}{B\ population}\right) \times Millennials(B)_{q-12}$$

RSquare: .996

Variation in past *Wyndham revenue* and the *World Millennial population*, with the *Starwood acquisition*, together account for 99.6% of the quarterly variation in *Marriott revenues*. Because the two continuous drivers are lagged eleven and twelve quarters, a ten quarter forecast is possible, shown in Figure 12.10. (Were *World Millennial population* values for the second quarter of 2017 available, an eleven quarter forecast would be possible.)

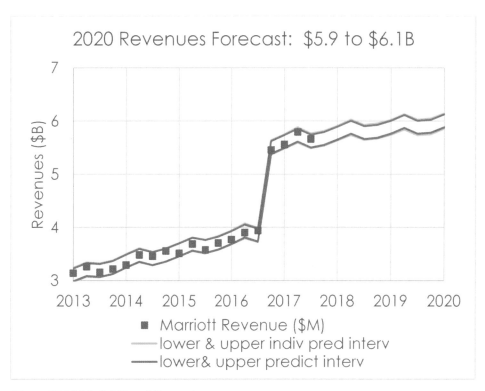

Figure 12.10 Model fit and forecast

12.7 Driver Part Worths Reveal Importances

The model equation sums four part worths. Those part worths are each in billion dollars and are directly comparable. The ranges of the part worths reflect the influence that each of the three drivers has in influencing revenues. Table 12.7 contains those ranges.

The Starwood acquisition is most influential, followed by the Millennial population. The importances are displayed graphically in Figure 12.11.

Table 12.7 Driver importances from ranges in part worths

Part Worth Range		
Starwood Acquisition	Millennial Population	Wyndham Revenues
1.61	1.02	0.32

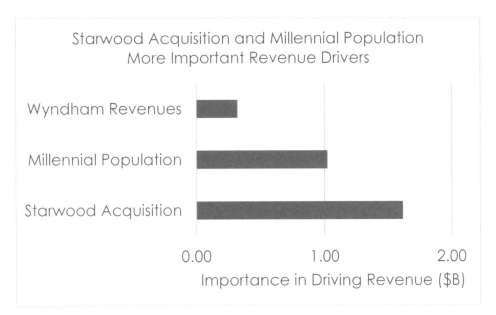

Figure 12.11 Driver importances

12.8 Do Potential Drivers Not in the Model Matter?

The model could suggest that Marriott should target Millennials and worry less about the economy. Or, it could be that other generations also drive revenues and leading indicators of economic growth further drive revenues. To investigate, Andrew replaced past *World Millennial population* with each of the other generations of *World population*, leaving *Starwood* and *Wyndham revenues* in each model Regressions using any one of the population drivers produced significant models with significant driver coefficients. All were nearly as powerful as the final model with *World Millennial population*. Marriott should not focus on Millennials, to the exclusion of other generations. All are important drivers. To emphasize the broader the target market, Andrew presented the model using World population 20+, instead of World Millennial population, shown in the memo, below.

Andrew repeated that process, replacing population with *GDP*. *GDP* also produced a significant model with significant driver coefficients. The *GDP* model was nearly as powerful as the final model with *World population 20+*. Past economic growth is also an important driver.

Andrew summarized his model results for Management:

MEMO

Re: Slow, Stable Growth Forecast in Next Ten Quarters
To: Marriott Management
From: Andrew Snyder

Following past growth in World population and Wyndham revenues, quarterly revenues are expected to increase an average of $190 million quarterly over the next ten quarters.

A regression model of quarterly revenues was built from past World population and Wyndham revenues, accounting for the Starwood acquisition. This model predicts Marriott revenue from a weighted average of Starwood acquisition, past World population aged 20+ and past Wyndham revenue, and accounts for 99.7% of the variation in revenues. The model fit and forecast are shown in the attached Exhibit.

$$Marriott\ qua\hat{r}terly\ revenues(\$B)_q = -8.3(\$B) + 1.58(\$B) \times Starwood_q$$
$$+.491\left(\frac{\$B}{\$B}\right) \times Wyndham\ revenues(\$B)_{q-11}$$
$$+2.46\left(\frac{\$B}{B\ population}\right) \times World\ Population(B)_{q-12}$$

Revenues are driven by growth in the World population. Revenues have benefitted from growth in the World population, and from hotel industry growth, represented by Wyndham revenues, to a smaller degree. The driver importances are shown to the right.

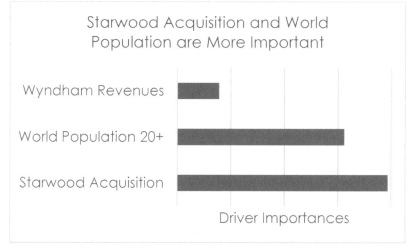

Modest growth is forecast. Revenues in the next ten quarters are expected to increase about $190 million quarterly. This is slower growth than in quarters before the acquisition, where quarterly growth averaged $230 million. World population growth has slowed, driving lower growth in Marriott revenues.

Another driver of revenue. Economic growth also drives revenues. Past GDP is a powerful driver. It is not a part of the model shown here, since it is highly correlated with both population and Wyndham revenues.

Exhibit. 2020 Revenue Forecast

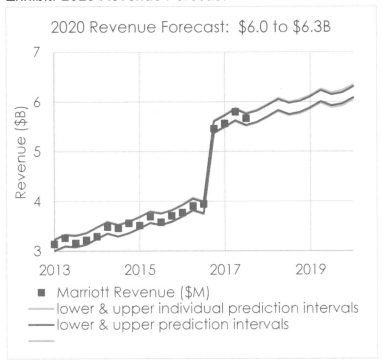

12.9 Leading Indicator Components Are Powerful Drivers and Often Multicollinear

Like cross sectional models, explanatory time series models allow identification of performance drivers. However, time series models differ from cross sectional models, with forecasts as a dual goal, and the model building process with time series contains additional steps.

- Lagged predictors are used to make driver identification more certain and to enable forecasts.
- Lagged predictors tend to move together across time and are often highly correlated. Consequently, to minimize multicollinearity issues, model building begins with one predictor, and then others are added, considering their joint influence and incremental model improvement.

Predictors in time series models tend to be highly correlated, since most move with economic variables and most exhibit predictable growth (*trend*). Model building with time series begins with the strongest among logical predictors, and additional predictors are added which improve the model.

Like time series models based on trend, where the singular focus is on forecasting, explanatory time series models are also validated. Forecasting accuracy of time series models is tested, or validated, before they are used for prediction of future performance.

Time series typically contain trend, business cycles, or seasonality. Unaccounted for trend, cycles, or seasonality are detected through inspection of the residual plot and the Durbin Watson statistic. Leading indicators are often stable and predictable performance drivers. Competitive variables may account for trend, seasonality or cycles common to a market.

Useful forecasting models must be valid. Holding out the two most recent performance observations allows a test of the model's forecasting capability. With successful prediction of the most recent performance, the model is validated and the recalibrated model can be used with confidence to forecast performance in future periods.

Excel 12.1 Build and Fit a Multiple Regression Model with Multicollinear Time Series

Marriott Revenues. Build a model of Marriott quarterly revenues which potentially includes past growth in World population, the hotel industry, represented by a major competitor, Wyndham, and the economy, represented by GDP. The data are in **Marriott quarterly revenues**.

Plot *Marriott revenues* by quarter to see the pattern of movement over time. (Hide or ignore the two most recent datapoints, 2017.25 and 2017.5.)

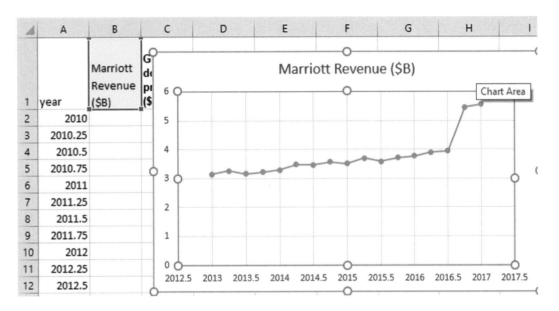

	A	B	C
1	year	Marriott Revenue ($B)	G do pr ($
2	2010		
3	2010.25		
4	2010.5		
5	2010.75		
6	2011		
7	2011.25		
8	2011.5		
9	2011.75		
10	2012		
11	2012.25		
12	2012.5		

Add a trendline. | **Alt JCATL**

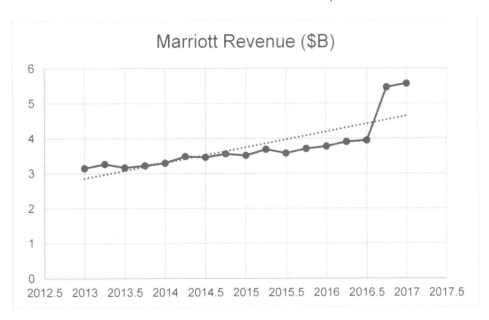

The shock due to the Starwood acquisition is obvious and ought to be accounted for first in the one driver model. Before running regression, assess skewness of the revenues using only quarters before the acquisition. (The acquisition would create a misleading skewness value.) Having confirmed that revenues are approximately Normal, run the one driver model.

	A	B	C	D	E	F	G
3	*Regression Statistics*						
4	Multiple R	0.93887					
5	R Square	0.88147					
6	Adjusted F	0.87357					
7	Standard E	0.2511					
8	Observatic	17					
9							
10	ANOVA						
11		*df*	*SS*	*MS*	*F*	*gnificance F*	
12	Regressior	1	7.0332	7.0332	111.55	2.4E-08	
13	Residual	15	0.94575	0.06305			
14	Total	16	7.97895				
15							
16		*Coefficient*	*andard Err*	*t Stat*	*P-value*	*Lower 95%*	*Upper 95%*
17	Intercept	3.51213	0.06483	54.172	1.3E-18	3.37395	3.65032
18	starwood	1.99637	0.18902	10.5617	2.4E-08	1.59348	2.39925

Excel 12.2 Plot Residuals to Identify Unaccounted for Trend, Cycles, or Seasonality and Assess Autocorrelation

Plot residuals, setting the vertical axis units to the standard error, .25, and add a trendline.

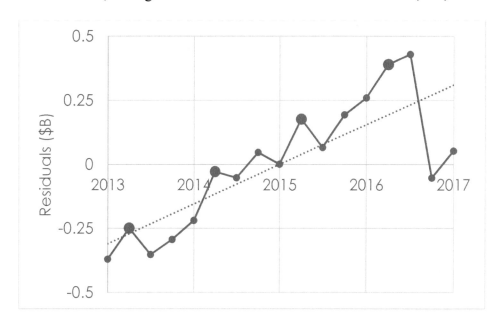

The residual plot shows trend and seasonality. Adding a lagged driver with trend and/or seasonality will likely improve the regression.

Assess Durbin Watson to confirm that trend, cycles, shifts or shocks remain.

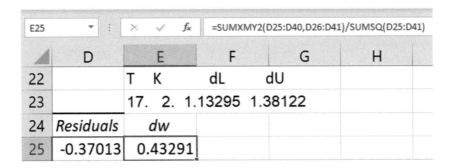

DW is below the lower critical value, 1.13, confirming that positive autocorrelation from unaccounted for trend, cycles, shifts or shocks is present.

Excel 12.3 Create Potential Driver Lags

Create working columns that will contain the lagged drivers by copying columns A through I and then pasting into column K:

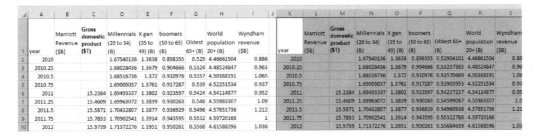

GDP is seasonal, and so lags that are multiples of four are preferred, to align with the seasonality in Marriott revenues. To achieve an eight quarter forecast, GDP must be lagged at least eight quarters.

Make the eight quarter lags in column M by inserting eight blank cells in rows 2 through 9.	In M2, **Shift+down to M9** **Alt HIID**

Change the label to GDP q-8.

	M
	Gross domestic product ($T) q-8
1	
2	
3	
4	
5	
6	
7	
8	
9	
10	
11	
12	
13	
14	15.2384
15	15.4609

In order to make an eight quarter forecast using the World population drivers, lags of at least ten quarters are needed, since the most recent population data is in 2017.0, two quarters earlier than the Marriott data through 2017.5. A multiple of four will translate to a year of age. Lag the population columns by twelve quarters.

In N2   **Shift+right right right right**
                                                 Shift + down to row 13
                                                 Alt HIID

Change the labels by adding q-12

	N	O	P	Q	R
1	Millennials (20 to 34) (B) q-12	X gen (35 to 49) (B) q-12'	boomers (50 to 65) (B) q-12	Oldest 65+ (B) q-12	World population 20+ (B) q-12
2					
3					
4					
5					
6					
7					
8					
9					
10					
11					
12					
13					
14	1.67540136	1.3638	0.898355	0.52904101	4.46661504
15	1.68028436	1.3679	0.904666	0.53237385	4.48524847

Wyndham revenues are seasonal. To account for seasonality in Marriott revenues, Wyndham's high summer seasons need align with Marriott's high spring seasons. Lagging by three lines up the high seasons. To achieve an eight quarter forecast, an eleven quarter lag (three+eight) is needed.

In S2   **Shift+down** to S12
                                                               Alt HIID

Change the label by adding q-11.

	S
1	Wyndham revenue ($B) q-11
2	
3	
4	
5	
6	
7	
8	
9	
10	
11	
12	
13	0.886
14	0.963

Finish creating the potential driver lags by selecting cells in rows of columns K through S that contain blanks (K2:S13) and delete those cells.

In K2,   **Shift+down** to K13
                                                              Shift+right to S
                                                              Alt HDDU

◢ J	K	L	M	N	O	P	Q	R	S
1	year	Marriott Revenue ($B)	Gross domestic product ($T) q-8	Millennials (20 to 34) (B) q-12	X gen (35 to 49) (B) q-12'	boomers (50 to 65) (B) q-12	Oldest 65+ (B) q-12	World population 20+ (B) q-12	Wyndham revenue ($B) q-11
2	2013	3.142	15.2384	1.67540136	1.3638	0.898355	0.52904101	4.46661504	0.963
3	2013.25	3.263	15.4609	1.68028436	1.3679	0.904666	0.53237385	4.48524847	1.065
4	2013.5	3.16	15.5871	1.68516736	1.372	0.910976	0.53570669	4.50388191	0.937
5	2013.75	3.219	15.7853	1.69005037	1.3761	0.917287	0.53903953	4.52251534	0.952
6	2014	3.293	15.9739	1.69493337	1.3802	0.923597	0.54237237	4.54114877	1.09
7	2014.25	3.484	16.1219	1.69963072	1.3839	0.930263	0.54599087	4.55983307	1.212
8	2014.5	3.46	16.2279	1.70432807	1.3877	0.936929	0.54960938	4.57851736	1
9	2014.75	3.559	16.2973	1.70902541	1.3914	0.943595	0.55322788	4.59720166	1.036
10	2015	3.513	16.4754	1.71372276	1.3951	0.950261	0.55684639	4.61588596	1.139
11	2015.25	3.689	16.5414	1.71804593	1.3984	0.957098	0.56076837	4.63434116	1.265
12	2015.5	3.578	16.7493	1.7223691	1.4018	0.963936	0.56469036	4.65279635	1.094
13	2015.75	3.706	16.9999	1.72669228	1.4052	0.970773	0.56861235	4.67125155	1.133
14	2016	3.772	17.0313	1.73101545	1.4085	0.97761	0.57253434	4.68970675	1.253
15	2016.25	3.902	17.3209	1.73483464	1.4119	0.984464	0.57686366	4.70803263	1.427

Plot the potential drivers, looking for trend or seasonality to explain the trend and seasonality in the Marriott revenues data.

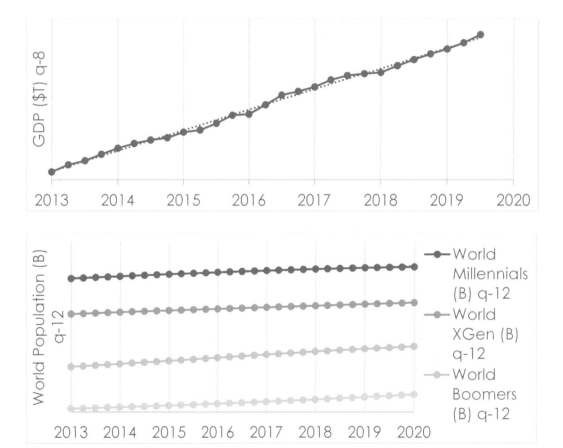

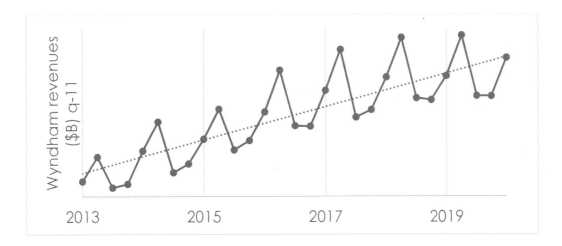

All potential drivers show positive trends. Wyndham revenues also shows seasonality.

Excel 12.4 Select the Most Promising Driver

To increase the chances that the model will be valid, identify the potential driver(s) that show a matching pattern in the recent quarters (excluding the two most recent quarters). Copy and residuals from the one driver model and paste in column T. Highlight cells in which the residuals declined from the prior quarter. Similarly, highlight cells in the potential driver columns which declined from the prior quarter.

	M	N	O	P	Q	R	S	T
1	Gross domestic product ($T) q-8	Millennials (20 to 34) (B) q-12	X gen (35 to 49) (B) q-12'	boomers (50 to 65) (B) q-12	Oldest 65+ (B) q-12	World population 20+ (B) q-12	Wyndham revenue ($B) q-11	Residuals
14	17.0313	1.73101545	1.4085	0.97761	0.57253434	4.68970675	1.253	0.259867
15	17.3209	1.73483464	1.4119	0.984464	0.57686366	4.70803263	1.427	0.389867
16	17.6223	1.73865382	1.4152	0.991318	0.58119298	4.72635851	1.195	0.429867
17	17.7359	1.74247301	1.4185	0.998172	0.58552229	4.7446844	1.193	-0.0525
18	17.8747	1.7462922	1.4218	1.005025	0.58985161	4.76301028	1.343	0.0525
19	18.0932	1.74950596	1.4253	1.011775	0.59465227	4.78122509	1.514	
20	18.2277	1.75271973	1.4287	1.018525	0.59945293	4.7994399	1.231	

Past GDP and population drivers are increasing in each of the recent quarters. Wyndham revenues show declines in two recent quarters. The residuals show a single decline in recent quarters. All seven potential drivers match residuals in three out of four recent quarters.

To identify the strongest potential driver, run correlations between the potential drivers and the residuals.

	A	B	C	D	E	F	G	H	I
1		Gross domestic product ($T) q-8	Millennia ls (20 to 34) (B) q-12	X gen (35 to 49) (B) q-12'	boomers (50 to 65) (B) q-12	Oldest 65+ (B) q-12	World populati on 20+ (B) q-12	Wyndha m revenue ($B) q-11	Residuals
2	Gross domestic product ($T) q-8	1							
3	Millennials (20 to 34) (B) q-12	0.991218	1						
4	X gen (35 to 49) (B) q-12'	0.992236	0.99989	1					
5	boomers (50 to 65) (B) q-12	0.995273	0.998346	0.998396	1				
6	Oldest 65+ (B) q-12	0.996441	0.99597	0.996198	0.999467	1			
7	World population 20+ (B) q-12	0.994594	0.999207	0.999266	0.999832	0.998749	1		
8	Wyndham revenue ($B) q-11	0.760842	0.770888	0.770177	0.771407	0.770262	0.77131	1	
9	Residuals	0.780067	0.819376	0.814692	0.801505	0.788759	0.806278	0.760648	1
10									

World Millennial population is most highly correlated with the unaccounted for variation in the residuals. Add Millennial population to the regression.

	A	B	C	D	E	F	G
3	*Regression Statistics*						
4	Multiple R	0.99626					
5	R Square	0.99253					
6	Adjusted R Square	0.99146					
7	Standard Error	0.06524					
8	Observations	17					
9							
10	ANOVA						
11		df	SS	MS	F	gnificance F	
12	Regression	2	7.91936	3.95968	930.277	1.3E-15	
13	Residual	14	0.05959	0.00426			
14	Total	16	7.97895				
15							
16		Coefficients	andard Err	t Stat	P-value	Lower 95%	Upper 95%
17	Intercept	-17.5764	1.46165	-12.025	9.1E-09	-20.7113	-14.4414
18	starwood	1.55065	0.05802	26.7264	2E-13	1.42621	1.67509
19	World Millennials (B) q-12	12.3449	0.85557	14.4288	8.5E-10	10.5099	14.1799

Plot the residuals and assess Durbin Watson. (Reuse the Durbin Watson formula from the simple regression. Copy and paste into the same cells in your new regression.)

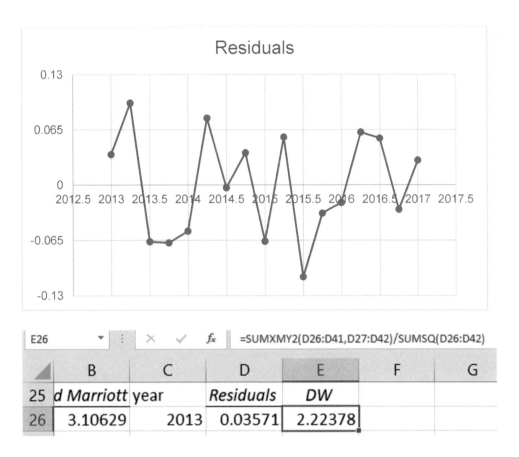

| E26 | ▼ | : | × | ✓ | *fx* | =SUMXMY2(D26:D41,D27:D42)/SUMSQ(D26:D42) |

	B	C	D	E	F	G
25	d Marriott	year	Residuals	DW		
26	3.10629	2013	0.03571	2.22378		

Durbin Watson above two suggests unaccounted for seasonality, which is observed in the residuals. Wyndham revenues, which are seasonal is likely to improve the model. To confirm that that is a better choice than GDP, compare correlations with residuals from the two driver model.

	A	B	C	D
1		Wyndham rev ($B) q-11	Gross domestic product ($T) q-8	Residuals 2
2	Wyndham rev ($B) q-11	1		
3	Gross domestic product ($T) q-8	0.760842	1	
4	Residuals 2	0.388275	0.028305	1

Add Wyndham revenues and run the three driver model.

⊿	A	B	C	D	E	F	G
4	Multiple F	0.997663					
5	R Square	0.995332					
6	Adjusted I	0.994255					
7	Standard E	0.053524					
8	Observati	17					
9							
10	ANOVA						
11		df	SS	MS	F	gnificance F	
12	Regressio	3	7.941704	2.647235	924.0629	2.14E-15	
13	Residual	13	0.037242	0.002865			
14	Total	16	7.978946				
15							
16		Coefficients	andard Err	t Stat	P-value	Lower 95%	Upper 95%o
17	Intercept	-14.4298	1.64532	-8.7702	8.06E-07	-17.9843	-10.8753
18	starwood	1.563478	0.04782	32.69523	7.2E-14	1.46017	1.666787
19	World Mil	10.22646	1.033415	9.895789	2.03E-07	7.993899	12.45901
20	Wyndham	0.422682	0.151335	2.793032	0.015231	0.095744	0.749621

Plot residuals and assess Durbin Watson. (Reuse the Durbin Watson formula from the two driver regression. Copy and paste into the same cells in your new regression.)

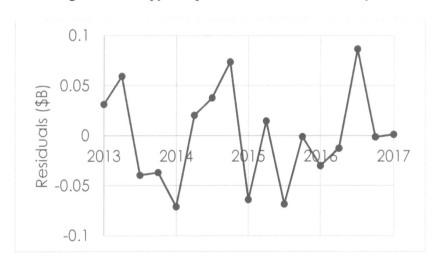

E27	▼	:	×	✓	fx	=SUMXMY2(D27:D42,D28:D43)/SUMSQ(D27:D43)		
⊿	A	B	C	D	E	F	G	H
26	Observation	Marriott	year	Residuals	DW			
27	1	3.11067	2013	0.03133	2.062435			

Excel 12.5 Test the Model's Forecasting Validity.

Given a significant model with high RSquare, significant drivers with correct signs, and DW just above two, test the model's validity.

Copy Year, Marriott revenues, the Starwood indicator, Millennial population and Wyndham revenues from the data sheet and paste next to residuals.

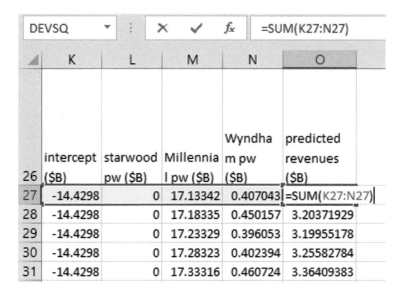

	D	E	F	G	H	I	J
26	Residuals	DW	year	Marriott Revenue ($B)	starwood	World Millennial populatio n (B) q-12	Wyndha m Revenue ($B) q-11
27	0.03133	2.062435	2013	3.142	0	1.675401	0.963
28	0.059281		2013.25	3.263	0	1.680284	1.065
29	-0.03955		2013.5	3.16	0	1.685167	0.937
30	-0.03683		2013.75	3.219	0	1.69005	0.952
31	-0.07109		2014	3.293	0	1.694933	1.09

Use the regression equation to make the four part worths in columns K through N, and then sum to find predicted *Marriott revenues* in column O.

DEVSQ	▼	:	✕	✓	f_x	=SUM(K27:N27)

	K	L	M	N	O
26	intercept ($B)	starwood pw ($B)	Millennia l pw ($B)	Wyndha m pw ($B)	predicted revenues ($B)
27	-14.4298	0	17.13342	0.407043	=SUM(K27:N27)
28	-14.4298	0	17.18335	0.450157	3.20371929
29	-14.4298	0	17.23329	0.396053	3.19955178
30	-14.4298	0	17.28323	0.402394	3.25582784
31	-14.4298	0	17.33316	0.460724	3.36409383

370   Find the *margin of error* from *critical t* and the *standard error*:

	A	B	C	D
3	Regression Statistics			
4	Multiple R	0.997663		
5	R Square	0.995332		
6	Adjusted F	0.994255	critical t	me ($B)
7	Standard E	0.053524	2.160369	0.115631

D7 ... fx =B7*C7

Add and subtract the *margin of error* from *predicted* values to find the *lower* and *upper 95%* *prediction interval bounds* in columns P and Q, locking the cell reference to D7:

	O	P	Q
26	predicted revenues ($B)	lower	upper
27	3.11066986	=O27-$D$7	3.226301
28	3.20371929	3.08808854	3.31935
29	3.19955178	3.08392104	3.315183
30	3.25582784	3.1401971	3.371459

Compare actual revenues with the 95% prediction interval in the two most recent quarters to assess the model's validity for forecasting:

	F	G	H	I	J	K	L	M	N	O	P	Q
44	2017.25	5.80	1	1.749506	1.514	-14.4298	1.563478	17.891246	0.63994104	5.6648737	5.55	5.78
45	2017.5	5.66	1	1.7527197	1.231	-14.4298	1.563478	17.924111	0.52032194	5.57812	5.46	5.69
46	2017.75		1	1.7559335	1.262	-14.4298	1.563478	17.956977	0.5334251	5.6240886	5.508	5.74

The model may have overestimated revenues in 2017.25, and may not be valid. Using the mean prediction interval bounds is a tougher test of validity than using the individual prediction interval bounds. Since validity is in question, if you have access to JMP, find the individual prediction interval bounds to more fairly test validity.

JMP 12.1 Find Individual Prediction Interval Bounds

Open JMP. Copy the columns used in the validation regression and paste into a new dataset:
File, New, Data Table
Edit, Paste with Column Names.

Untitled 5 - JMP

File Edit Tables Rows Cols DOE Analyze Graph Tools View Window Help

Untitled 5

Columns (5/1)
- year
- Marriott Revenue ($B)
- starwood
- Millennial...4) (B) q-12
- Wyndha...e ($B) q-11

	year	Marriott Revenue ($B)	starwood	Millennials (20 to 34) (B) q-12	Wyndham revenue ($B) q-11
1	2013	3.142	0	1.675401356	0.963
2	2013.25	3.263	0	1.68028436	1.065
3	2013.5	3.16	0	1.685167365	0.937
4	2013.75	3.219	0	1.690050369	0.952
5	2014	3.293	0	1.694933373	1.09
6	2014.25	3.484	0	1.699630719	1.212
7	2014.5	3.46	0	1.704328065	1
8	2014.75	3.559	0	1.709025411	1.036
9	2015	3.513	0	1.713722757	1.139
10	2015.25	3.689	0	1.71804593	1.265
11	2015.5	3.578	0	1.722369103	1.094
12	2015.75	3.706	0	1.726692275	1.133
13	2016	3.772	0	1.731015448	1.253
14	2016.25	3.902	0	1.734834635	1.427
15	2016.5	3.942	0	1.738653823	1.195
16	2016.75	5.456	1	1.74247301	1.193
17	2017	5.561	1	1.746292197	1.343
18	2017.25	5.795	1	1.749505962	1.514
19	2017.5	5.663	1	1.752719728	1.231
20	2017.75	•	1	1.755933493	1.262
21	2018	•	1	1.759147258	1.398
22	2018.25	•	1	1.761976656	1.564
23	2018.5	•	1	1.764806053	1.311
24	2018.75	•	1	1.767635451	1.303
25	2019	•	1	1.770464848	1.403
26	2019.25	•	1	1.772470211	1.573
27	2019.5	•	1	1.774475574	1.32
28	2019.75	•	1	1.776480937	1.319
29	2020	•	1	1.7784863	1.479

Rows
All rows   29
Selected   0
Excluded   0
Hidden   0

To exclude the two most recent quarters, select rows 18 and 19, right click, Hide and Exclude.

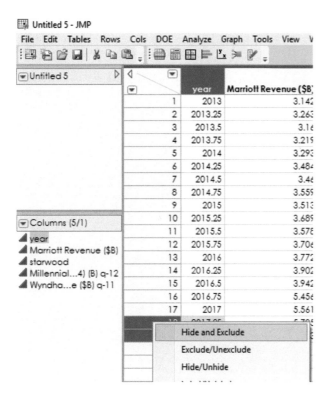

Open the JMP Starter.
Open Fit Model
View, JMP Starter
Fit Model, Fit Model

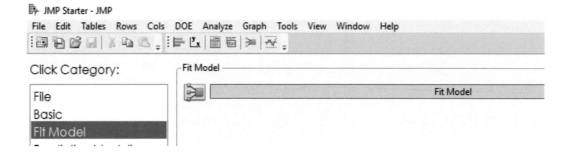

Run regression.   Drag Marriott revenues to Pick Role Variables, drag the three drivers to Construct Model Effects, change Emphasis to Minimal Report, Run.

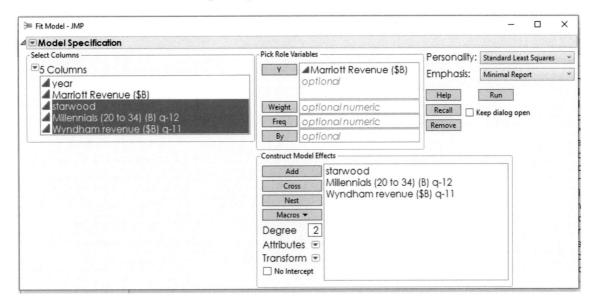

Save individual prediction interval bounds.   Click the red triangle, Save Columns, Indiv Confidence Limit Formula.

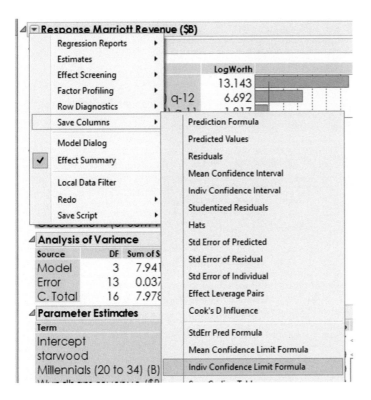

Copy the individual prediction interval bounds from the data sheet and paste into the excel validation page:

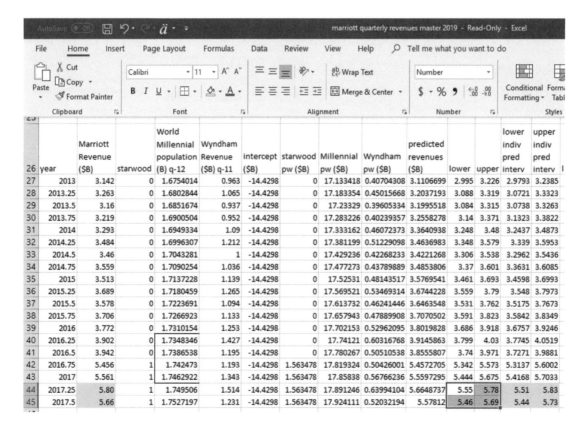

With the fair test of validity the model is validated.

Excel 12.6 Recalibrate to Forecast.

Recalibrate the model to update the coefficients by rerunning regression, this time with all rows of data.

	A	B	C	D	E	F	G
1	SUMMARY OUTPUT						
2							
3	*Regression Statistics*						
4	Multiple F	0.998382					
5	R Square	0.996766					
6	Adjusted I	0.996119					
7	Standard E	0.056903					
8	Observati	19					
9							
10	ANOVA						
11		*df*	*SS*	*MS*	*F*	*gnificance F*	
12	Regressio	3	14.96872	4.989574	1540.992	6.81E-19	
13	Residual	15	0.048568	0.003238			
14	Total	18	15.01729				
15							
16		*Coefficient*	*andard Err*	*t Stat*	*P-value*	*Lower 95%*	*Upper 95%*
17	Intercept	-14.0073	1.623947	-8.6255	3.37E-07	-17.4687	-10.546
18	starwood	1.612434	0.043426	37.1302	3.53E-16	1.519873	1.704996
19	World Mil	9.925381	1.008524	9.841488	6.16E-08	7.775762	12.075
20	Wyndham	0.504906	0.13609	3.710098	0.002095	0.214838	0.794975

Reuse your formulas for *critical t, margin of error, part worths, predicted revenues,* and *95% prediction interval bounds* to update your forecast.

If you have access to JMP, unhide the two most recent years: Select, right click, Hide and Exclude. Then rerun the regression, copy the individual prediction interval bounds and paste into Excel. (If you do not have access to JMP, use the mean prediction interval bounds.

	E	F	G	H	I	J	K	L	M	N	O	P	Q	R
26	year	Marriott Revenue ($M)	starwood	Wyndham Revenue ($B) q-11	world Millenni al populati on (B) q-12	intercept ($B)	starwood pw	Millennia l pw	Wyndha m pw	predicte d revenues ($B)	lower predict interv	upper predict interv	lower indiv pred interv	upper indiv pred interv
27	2013	3.142	0	0.963	1.675401	-14.0073	0	16.629	0.486225	3.107873	2.986588	3.2292	2.972	3.24
28	2013.25	3.263	0	1.065	1.680284	-14.0073	0	16.67746	0.537725	3.207839	3.086554	3.3291	3.072	3.3395
29	2013.5	3.16	0	0.937	1.685167	-14.0073	0	16.72593	0.473097	3.191676	3.070391	3.313	3.062	3.3224
30	2013.75	3.219	0	0.952	1.69005	-14.0073	0	16.77439	0.480671	3.247716	3.126431	3.369	3.121	3.378

Excel 12.7 Illustrate the Fit and Forecast.

To see the model fit and forecast, plot the prediction intervals with actual revenues through 2020. After selecting Year and Marriott Revenues through 2020, hold **CNTL** and then, with your mouse, select the prediction interval bounds. Then plot. **ALT ND**

(Note that both the mean an individual prediction interval bounds are plotted, below.)

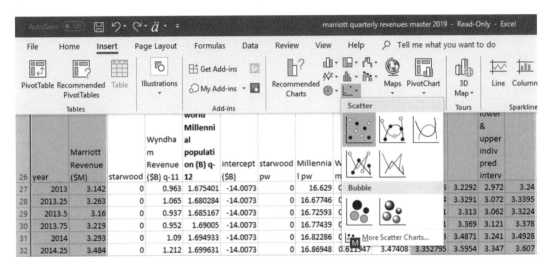

year	Marriott Revenue ($M)	starwood	Wyndham Revenue ($B) q-11	Millenni al populati on (B) q-12	intercept ($B)	starwood pw	Millennia l pw	W m		lower & upper indiv pred interv	
27	2013	3.142	0	0.963	1.675401	-14.0073	0	16.629	C	3.2292	2.972	3.24
28	2013.25	3.263	0	1.065	1.680284	-14.0073	0	16.67746	C	3.3291	3.072	3.3395
29	2013.5	3.16	0	0.937	1.685167	-14.0073	0	16.72593	C	3.313	3.062	3.3224
30	2013.75	3.219	0	0.952	1.69005	-14.0073	0	16.77439	C	3.369	3.121	3.378
31	2014	3.293	0	1.09	1.694933	-14.0073	0	16.82286	C	3.4871	3.241	3.4928
32	2014.25	3.484	0	1.212	1.699631	-14.0073	0	16.86948	0.611947	3.47408	3.352795	3.5954	3.347	3.607

Recolor one of the 95% prediction intervals so that both are the same color.

Change the *Marriott revenue ($B)* series from a line to markers.

Format axes to reduce white space, add a vertical axis label and a chart title that summarizes your conclusion, and set font size to 12:

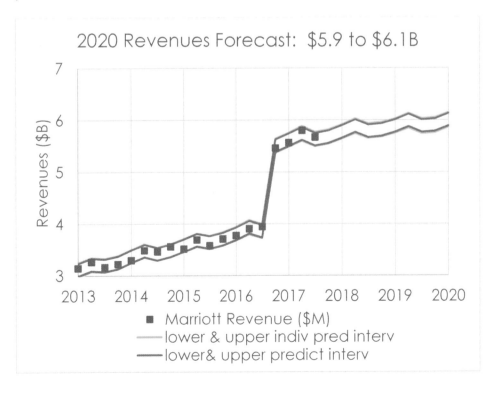

Excel 12.8 Assess the Impact of Drivers.

Use the part worths to compare the impacts of each of the drivers on model forecasts. The ranges (maximum-minimum) in the part worths is an measure of driver importances.

Copy driver labels and paste above the part worth ranges, and then graph with a 2D bar chart. **Alt NC1**

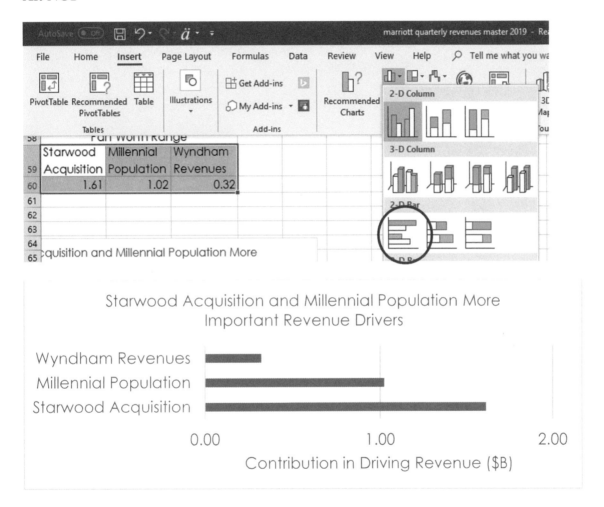

The acquisition has made the greatest difference in revenues. Between the two external influences, the Millennial population is the more influential.

Lab 12-1 Identifying Drivers and Forecasting Marriott Revenues

Marriott executives desire a quarterly revenue forecast. A four quarter forecast is needed for quarterly reports, and an eight quarter forecast is desired.

Marriott acquired Starwood in the third quarter of 2016, which substantially enhanced revenues.

What is driving revenue growth? Executives suspect that the hotel business is driven by economic productivity. When GDP, for example, is improving, businesses spend more on travel. Some time between growth in GDP and consequent Marriott revenues is expected, since travel requires planning.

The hotel industry is thriving, and competition is fierce. A major competitor, Wyndham, is third largest, following Marriott, in first place, in the industry. Are Wyndham revenues a leading indicator of industry growth? Or do they represent competition? If the industry is growing, both may be growing, together, and profiting from promotions of both. (Note that, Marriott markets to Spring Break travelers and sees highest revenues in the second quarter, while Wyndham markets to summer travelers and sees highest revenues in the third quarter.)

Population growth probably drives revenues. More people lead to more travel. Executives would like to learn which particular age groups drive revenues. Do Baby Boomers (50 to 65) and Seniors, 65+, who have presumably more resources, drive revenues more than younger consumers? There is also expected to be a delay between retirement and increased travel, since travel requires planning.

Marriott quarterly revenues.xlsx contains data on quarterly revenues, quarterly GDP, Wyndham quarterly revenues, and population. Build a model of Marriott quarterly revenues.

1. **Hide the two most recent quarterly revenues**, so that your model can be tested for forecasting validity.

2. **Plot performance** and identify patterns to be explained:

3. **Assess skewness** of quarterly revenues, using quarters before the Starwood acquisition. Rescale if skewness is outside the -1 to +1 range considered approximately Normal.

4. **Account for the shift** with a one driver model

5. **Assess and plot residuals** to identify patterns not yet accounted for.

6. **Set up potential driver lags** which will enable an 8 quarter forecast.

7. **Assess skewness** of potential driver lags. Rescale if skewness is outside the -1 to +1 range considered approximately Normal.

8. **Identify potential drivers which show pattern matches in recent quarters**. Choosing one of those with most pattern matches will increase chances that your model is valid.

9. **Compare correlations with residuals** and potential drivers with best pattern matches. Consider those within .02 of the highest, positive correlation to add to your model. Choose one to add to your model.

10. **Build a two driver model to account for some of the unexplained variation** in residuals and assess.

11. **Assess and plot residuals** to identify patterns not yet accounted for.

12. **Compare correlations with residuals** and potential drivers. Consider those within .02 of the highest, positive correlation to add to your model. Choose one to add to your model.

13. **Build a three driver model to account for some of the unexplained variation in residuals**.

14. **Assess and plot residuals** to identify patterns not yet accounted for.

15. **Test the validity** of your three driver model, using individual prediction intervals if you have access to JMP.

16. **Recalibrate your model, then present and explain your model.**

    Present your fit and forecast

    Present your model equation.

17. **Find driver importances** with the ranges in part worths. Which is the more important driver, Wyndham revenues or the Millennial population?

18. Do other potential drivers also drive quarterly revenues?

19. **What are the implications of your model?**

    Should Marriott focus on promoting to Millennials? Or to all consumers?

    Should Marriott advertise comparisons with Wyndham? Or offer to cosponsor promotions?

Lab 12-2 Identifying Drivers and Forecasting EAP Air Traffic

Rolls-Royce is exploring the market for a new class of aircraft and would like to identify drivers of air traffic in the East Asia and Pacific (EAP) region.

Managers believe that both GDP and GDP per capita drive air traffic, since air travel is considered a luxury. They are not sure which is the more powerful driver.

Managers also believe that population drives air traffic. As population grows, they expect air traffic to grow.

The price of oil influences flight costs to airlines. Corresponding fare prices, following higher oil prices may reduce air traffic.

R-R would like a forecast of EAP air traffic, ideally for the next five years, 2016-2020, but at least through 2019.

EAP traffic.xlsx contains EAP air traffic from 2000 through 2015, EAP GDP and per capita GDP, and population, as well as World oil prices from 1995 to 2015.

1. **Hide the two most recent observations** for air traffic

2. **Assess skewness** of EAP traffic and rescale if not approximately Normal.

3. **Plot** EAP traffic to identify patterns to be explained.

4. **Identify potential drivers and set up lags** for EAP GDP, EAP GDP per capita, EAP population and World oil prices, which would allow a four to five year forecast.

5. **Assess skewness.** One or more potential drivers is skewed (skewness outside -1 to +1). Rescale to improve skewness.

6. **Plot potential driver lags** to identify patterns seen in EAP traffic.

7. **Identify the potential drivers with most pattern matches** to EAP traffic in the four most recent years. Choosing one of those with most pattern matches will increase chances that your model is valid. GDP, GDPPC and population ought to show same pattern to match; oil price ought to have opposite pattern to match. Specify best matches with their lag(s):

	t-___		t-___
GDP		Population	
GDPPC		Oil price	

8. **Find stronger potential drivers.** Among potential drivers with most matches in the four most recent years, which are more highly correlated with traffic? (Consider "more highly correlated" those within .02 of the highest correlation.) Specify higher correlations with their lag(s).

	t-___		t-___		t-___		t-___
GDP		GDPPC		Population		Oil price	

9. **Build a one driver model**, favoring a highly correlated driver with longer lag, and assess.

10. **Assess and plot residuals** to look for patterns, such as trend, cycles, shifts or shocks, which serve as clues to identify potential drivers.

11. **Identify next strongest potential driver.** Which remaining potential driver lag exhibits pattern similar to residuals and is most highly correlated (in the correct direction) with residuals? (Consider only those which were not chosen for the one driver model.)

	t-___		t-___		t-___		t-___
GDP		GDPPC		Population		Oil price	

12. **Build a two driver model**, adding one of the more highly correlated drivers, preferably with a longer lag.

13. Assess and plot residuals to identify unaccounted for variation.

14. **Add an indicator** to account for the recession shock and build a three driver model.

15. **Assess and plot residuals** to identify unaccounted for variation.

16. **Adjust the indicator and rerun.**

17. Which model has higher RSquare?

    Which model has lower standard error?

18. **Assess and plot residuals** to identify unaccounted for variation.

19. **Validate, recalibrate and present your final model.**

    Plot your fit and forecast.

    Present your final model equation.

20. Illustrate driver importance with a bar chart of part worth ranges to identify the more important driver.

21. **Sensitivity analysis.** Which of the remaining potential drivers NOT in your model actually drive(s) air traffic?

    ___ GDP   ___ World oil price

Assignment 12-1 Identifying Drivers and Forecasting Aluminum Production in China and North America

Alcoa (and other U.S. aluminum producers) face increasing competition from Chinese aluminum production. China has designated aluminum as a strategic resource, and now produces more than demanded in China. Overproduction has produced a glut in World markets, lowering prices and profits of producers. To bolster aluminum production and sales in the U.S., the Whitehouse placed tariffs on aluminum imports from China in March 2018.

Alcoa managers are interested in forecasting production of aluminum in China and in North America, as well as identifying drivers of production in both global regions

Managers believe that population, GDP and GDP per capita drive aluminum production. Increasing population and increasing wealth drive demand for aluminum intensive products, such as soft drinks, beer, cars, and construction. They are not sure which is the more powerful driver.

The price of aluminum probably influences production. Higher prices motivate increased production, while falling prices lead to reduced production.

Finally, aluminum supply may drive aluminum production. Production in North America may influence production in China, and production in China may influence production in North America.

Have tariffs significantly driven production in China and in North America? (Address this question after you've built valid models by then adding a tariff indicator to your recalibrated models.)

Alcoa would like forecasts of aluminum production in China and North America, ideally for the next five years, 2019-2023, but at least through 2022.

Production in China

CHN aluminum.xlsx contains Chinese aluminum production for 2007 through 2018, North American aluminum production, World population, World GDP and per capita GDP, as well as World aluminum prices from 2002 to 2018.

Hide the two most recent observations for aluminum production (until you are ready to recalibrate).

Plot Chinese aluminum production to identify patterns to be explained.

Identify potential drivers and set up lags which will allow a four to five year forecast.

Assess skewness and rescale if skewness is outside the approximately Normal -1 to +1 range.

1. **Plot the potential drivers and identify those with most pattern matches** to aluminum production in China in the four most recent years (among those not hidden). Choosing one of those with most pattern matches will increase chances that your model is valid. Specify best matches with their lag(s). (Note: matches with NA production need to be moving in the opposite direction.)

	t-___		t-___	
NA prod		GDPPC		Population
GDP		Aluminum price		

2. Among potential driver lags with most matches in the four most recent years, **identify those that have higher correlations** (of correct sign) with aluminum production. (Consider "higher" correlations those within .02 of the highest correlation.) Specify higher correlations with their lag(s). (If a potential driver does not have the most matches in the four most recent years, leave that cell blank.)

	t-_		t-_		t-_		t-_	
NA prod		GDP		GDPPC		Aluminum price		Population

3. **Build a one driver model**, favoring a highly correlated driver with a longer lag to enable a longer forecast. Driver you chose: _____

   Assess and plot residuals to identify patterns to be explained.

4. **Add an indicator** to account for the apparent shock to improve the model. (Compare results with the indicator turned on alternate years to find the best years to turn on.)

   Your indicator is turned on in years: _____ to _____

   Assess and plot residuals to look for patterns to be explained.

5. **Compare correlations with residuals**, identifying potential lagged drivers with higher (.02 of highest) correlations. (Consider only those which were not chosen for the one driver model.)

	t-_		t-_		t-_		t-_		t-_
NA prod		GDP		GDPPC		Population		Aluminum price	

   Build a three driver model, adding one of the more highly correlated drivers, preferably with a longer lag.

   Validate and recalibrate your best model, either two or three driver. (Note: if the third driver is not significant, go with your two driver model.) Then, add a tariff indicator to assess significance on production.

6. How much have the 2018 tariffs on Chinese imports significantly reduced production? _____ to _____ K mt.

7. Present your fit and forecast of your best model (with the tariff, is significant; without the tariff is not significant), removing unwanted decimals, adding axes and chart titles, and using 12 pt font:

8. Present your final model equation:

9. **Illustrate driver importances** with a bar chart of part worth ranges.

10. Which driver is most important? _____

11. **Identify all continuous lagged drivers** of Chinese aluminum production. Run regressions with each continuous driver not in your model, including the indicator(s). (Choose one lag for each.) Which potential drivers, including those not in your model and those in your model, drive China aluminum production? (Note: to be a driver, the coefficient must be of correct sign.)

____ NA production ____ GDP ____ GDPPC ____ aluminum price ____ Population

Production in North America

NA aluminum.xlsx contains North American aluminum production for 2007 through 2018, Chinese aluminum production, World GDP, per capita GDP, and population, as well as World aluminum prices from 2002 to 2018.

Hide the two most recent observations for aluminum production (until you are ready to recalibrate).
Plot North American aluminum production to identify patterns to be explained.
Identify potential drivers and set up lags which will allow a four to five year forecast.
Assess skewness and rescale if skewness is outside the approximately Normal -1 to +1 range.

1. **Plot the potential drivers and identify those with most pattern matches** to aluminum production in North America in the four most recent years (among those not hidden). Choosing one of those with most pattern matches will increase chances that your model is valid. Specify best matches with their lag(s). (Note: to match, Chinese production needs to move in the opposite direction.)

	t-___		t-___	
Chinese prod		GDPPC		Population
GDP		Aluminum price		

2. Among potential driver lags with most matches in the four most recent years, **identify those that have higher correlations** (of correct sign) with aluminum production. (Consider "higher" correlations those within .02 of the highest correlation.) Specify higher correlations with their lag(s). (If a potential driver does not have the most matches in the four most recent years, leave that cell blank.)

	t-_		t-_		t-_		t-_	
Chinese prod		GDP		GDPPC		Aluminum price		Population

3. **Build a one driver model**, favoring a highly correlated driver with longer lag.

   Driver you chose: _____

Assess and plot residuals to identify patterns to be explained.

4. **Add an indicator** to account for the apparent shock to improve the model. (Compare results with the indicator turned on alternate years to find the best years to turn on.)

Your indicator is turned on in years: _____

Assess and plot residuals to look for patterns to be explained.

5. **Compare correlations with residuals**, identifying potential lagged drivers with higher (.02 of highest) correlations. (Consider only those which were not chosen for the one driver model.)

	t-_		t-_		t-_		t-_	
Chinese prod		GDP		GDPPC		Aluminum price		Population

   Build a three driver model, adding one of the more highly correlated drivers, preferably with a longer lag.
   Validate and recalibrate your best model. (Note: if the third driver is not significant, go with your two driver model.) Then, add a tariff indicator to assess significance on production.

6. How much have the 2018 tariffs on Chinese imports significantly increased North American

   production? _____ to _____ mt.

7. Present your fit and forecast. (Note: if the tariff is not significant, go with your recalibrated model without tariff.) Remove unwanted decimals, add axis and chart titles, and using 12 pt font:

8. Present your final model equation:

9. **Illustrate driver importances** with a bar chart of part worth ranges.

10. Which driver is most important? _____

11. **Identify all continuous lagged drivers** of North American aluminum production. Run regressions with each continuous driver not in your model, including the indicator(s). (Choose one lag for each continuous driver.) Which potential drivers, including those not in your model and those in your model, drive North American aluminum production? (Note: to be a driver, the coefficient sign must be correct.)

   ___ Chinese production ___ GDP   ___ GDPPC   ___aluminum price   ___Population

The Tariff: Good for Alco or Not?

Alco wants to know: Based on your models, are the tariffs on Chinese aluminum

___ effective OR ___ ineffective?

Assignment 12-2 Identifying Drivers and Forecasting the Market for Fertilizer in the U.S.

As a byproduct of sustainable tissue production, Tranlin has developed a soil additive, "Better Roots," which acts like a fertilizer, with particular advantages of stronger roots and water retention during droughts. While popular in China, "Better Roots" has only been sold in a few select test markets in the U.S. Management would like to see a four or five (five, preferred) year forecast of the U.S. fertilizer market. Tranlin's soil amendment would compete in this market. Consumption was lower in 2015 than 2014, and there is concern that the market might shrink in the near future.

The market for fertilizer may depend upon the U.S. population, the number for which food is grown and the amount of arable (farmable) land in the U.S..

Fertilizer is probably a luxury item, and consumption probably increases with higher levels of personal income (GDP per capita). It is also thought that higher levels of economic wealth in a country (GDP) will be reflected in the amount of fertilizer consumed, since agriculture is government subsidized.

Build a valid model to identify drivers and to forecast the market for fertilizer in the U.S. in 2019 or 2020 (2020, preferred). Data are in 12 fertilizer.xlsx.

Set up potential driver lags that will enable a four or five year forecast.

Plot fertilizer consumed in the U.S. by year and add a trendline. You will notice that the recession impact is the most apparent source of variation. (Every data set is unique. In this case, acknowledging and accounting for the global recession, first, is the best course of action.)
Account for the recession, and then improve that one driver model.

1. What years did you decide to turn the recession indicator on? ___

2. Which potential driver lags best match pattern in the *residuals* in the four most recent years?

    ___ GDP with lag(s) ___   ___ GDP per capita with lag(s) ___   ___population with lag(s) ___

    ___ arable land with lag(s) ___

3. Among potential driver lags that best match pattern in the residuals, which have higher (with .02 of the highest) correlations of "correct" sign?

    ___ GDP with lag(s) ___   ___ GDP per capita with lag(s) ___   ___population with lag(s)

    ___

    ___ arable land with lag(s) ___

    Continue to improve your model and confirm validity. Then recalibrate.

4. Present your model equation. Be sure to indicate length(s) of lag(s) and units.

5. Present a plot of your fit and forecast. Be sure to adjust and label axes and include a standalone title.

6. With 95% certainty, in which years will fertilizer consumption exceed consumption in 2015?

7. Which is the more influential driver among those in your model?

    ___ GDP   ___ GDP per capita   ___ Population   ___ Arable land

8. Which are drivers of fertilizer consumed?

    ___ GDP   ___ GDP per capita   ___ Population   ___ Arable land

Chapter 13
Association Between Two Categorical Variables: Contingency Analysis with Chi Square

Categorical variables, including nominal (where numbers are simply labels) and ordinal, rank order variables, are described by tabulating their frequencies or probability. If two categorical variables are associated, the frequencies of values of one will depend on the frequencies of values of the other. Chi square tests the hypothesized association between two categorical variables and contingency analysis quantifies their association.

13.1 When Conditional Probabilities Differ from Joint Probabilities, There Is Evidence of Association

Contingency analysis begins with the crosstabulation of frequencies of two categorical variables. Figure 13.1 shows a crosstabulation of sandwich spreads and topping combinations chosen by forty students:

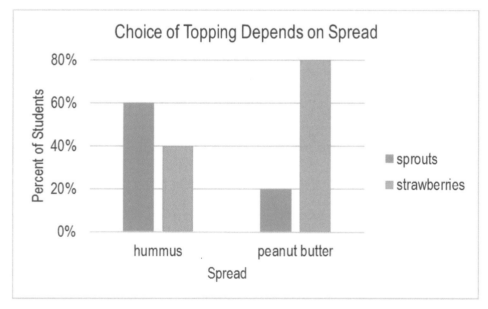

Counts	sprouts	strawberries	total
hummus	12	8	20
peanut butter	4	16	20
total	20	20	40

%Row	sprouts	strawberries	total
Hummus	60	40	100
peanut butter	20	80	100
Total	50	50	100

Figure 13.1 Crosstabulation: Sandwich topping depends on spread

If the unconditional probabilities of category levels, such as sprouts versus strawberries topping, differ from the probabilities, conditional on levels of another category, such as hummus or peanut

© Springer Nature Switzerland AG 2019
C. Fraser, *Business Statistics for Competitive Advantage with Excel 2019 and JMP*,
https://doi.org/10.1007/978-3-030-20374-0_13

butter spread, we have evidence of association. In this sandwich example, sprouts were chosen by half the students, making its unconditional probability .5. If a student chose hummus spread, the conditional probability of sprouts topping was higher (.60). If a student chose peanut butter spread, sprouts was the less likely topping choice (.40).

Example 13.1 Recruiting Stars. Human Resource managers are hoping to improve the odds of hiring outstanding performers and to reduce the odds of hiring poor performers by targeting recruiting efforts. Management believes that recruiting at the schools closer to firm headquarters may improve the odds of hiring stars. Students familiar with local customs may feel more confident at the firm. Removing schools far from headquarters may reduce the odds of hiring poor performers. Management's hypotheses are:

H_0: Job performance is not associated with undergraduate program location.
H_1: Job performance is associated with undergraduate program location.

To test these hypotheses, department supervisors throughout the firm sorted a sample of forty recent hires into three categories based on job performance: poor, average, and outstanding. The sample employees were also categorized by the proximity to headquarters: Home State, Same Region, and Outside Region. These cross-tabulations are shown in the PivotChart and PivotTable in Figure 13.2.

The crosstabs indicate that a quarter of the firm's new employees are *Poor* performers, about forty percent are *Average* performers, and about forty percent are *Outstanding* performers. From the PivotChart we see that more than a quarter of employees from programs *Outside Region* are *Poor* performers. Were program location and performance *not* associated, a quarter of the recruits from each location would be *Poor* performers. We would, for example, expect a quarter of ten employees recruited from *Outside Region* to be Poor performers, or 2.5 (=.25(10)). Instead, there are actually five (*Outside Region, Poor*) employees. There is a greater chance, 50%, of *Poor* performance, given *Outside Region*, relative to *Same Region* or *Home State*. Ignoring program location, the probability of poor performance is .25; acknowledging program location, this probability of poor performance varies from .13 (*Same Region*) to .50 (*Outside Region*). These differences in row percentages suggest an association between program rank and performance.

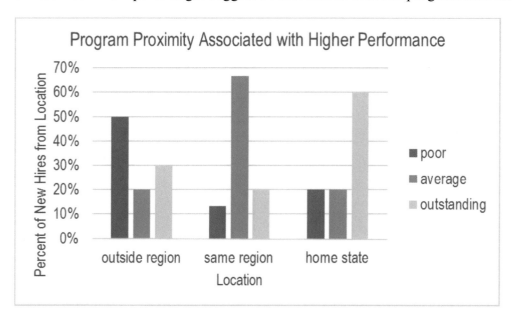

Count	Performance			
Location	Poor	Average	Outstanding	Total
Outside Region	5	2	3	10
Same Region	2	10	3	15
Home State	3	3	9	15
Total	10	15	15	40

% of Row	Performance			
Location	Poor	Average	Outstanding	Total
Outside Region	50%	20%	30%	100%
Same Region	13%	67%	20%	100%
Home State	20%	20%	60%	100%
Total	25%	38%	38%	100%

χ^2_4 12.5   *p value*   .02

Figure 13.2 Job Performance Depends on Program Location

13.2 Chi Square Tests Association Between Two Categorical Variables

The chi square (χ^2) statistic tests the significance of the association between performance and program location, by comparing expected cell counts with actual cell counts, squaring the differences, and weighting each cell by the inverse of expected cell frequency.

$$\chi^2_{(R-1),(C-1)} = \sum_{ij}^{RC} (e_{ij} - n_{ij})^2 / e_{ij} ,$$

Where R is the number of row categories,
$\quad$ C is the number of column categories,
$\quad$ n is the number in the i'th row and j'th column,
$\quad$ e is the number expected in the i'th row and j'th column.

The expected cell counts,

$$e_{ij,} = N_i \times \frac{N_j}{N}$$

where N_i are the number in row i,
$\quad$ N_j are the number in column j,
$\quad$ N is the total number in the sample,

are needed to find χ^2, and are shown in Table 13.1.

Table 13.1 Expected cell counts from joint probabilities.

Expected Count			
Location	Poor	Average	Outstanding
Outside Region	2.5	3.8	3.8
Same Region	3.8	5.6	5.6
Home State	3.8	5.6	5.6

13.3 Chi Square Is Unreliable If Cell Counts Are Sparse

Since the chi square components include expected cell counts in the denominator, *sparse* (with expected counts less than five) cells inflate chi square. When sparse cells exist, we must either combine categories or collect more data.

In the **Recruiting Stars** example, management was most interested in increasing the chances of hiring *Outstanding* performers. Since some believed that *Outstanding* performers were recruited from programs in the *Home State*, these categories were preserved. *Same Region* and *Outside Region* program locations were combined. *Poor* and *Average* performance categories were combined. We are left with a 2 x 2 contingency analysis, shown in Table 13.2:

Table 13.2 Crosstabulation after combining categories.

Location	Poor or Average	Outstanding	Total
Outside or Sam Region	19	6	25
Home State	6	9	15
Total	10	15	40

With fewer categories, all expected cell counts, shown in Table 13.3, are now greater than five,

Table 13.3 Expected cell counts after combining categories.

	Poor or Average	Outstanding
Outside or Same Region	15.7	9.4
Home State	9.4	5.6

In the **Recruiting Stars** example, chi square, χ_1^2, is 5.2, which can be verified using the formula:

$$\chi^2 = (15.7 - 19)^2/15.7 + (9.4 - 6)^2/9.4$$
$$+ (9.4 - 6)^2/9.4 + (5.6 - 9)^2/5.6$$
$$= \qquad .7 + 1.2$$
$$+ \qquad 1.2 + 2.0 \qquad\qquad = 5.2$$

Table 13.4 Contributions to chi square.

	Contribution to Chi Square		
	Poor or Average	Outstanding	Row totals
Outside or Same Region	.7	1.2	1.9
Home State	1.2	**2.0**	3.2
column totals	1.9	3.2	5.2 Chi Square
			0.0228 p value

   Those cells which contribute more to chi square indicate the nature of association. In this example, we see in Table 13.4 that the *Home State, Outstanding*) cell reveals the greatest surprise and contributes most to chi square.

   χ^2 distributions are skewed and with means equal to the number of degrees of freedom. Several χ^2 distributions with a range of degrees of freedom are shown in Figure 13.3.

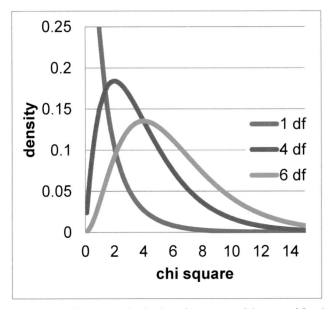

Figure 13.3 Chi square distributions for a range of degrees of freedom

   From a table of χ_1^2 distributions, we find that for a crosstabulation of this size, with two rows and two columns, (df=(Rows-1) x (Columns – 1)=1 x 1 = 1), χ_1^2 =5.2 indicates that the p-value is .02. Two percent of the distribution lies right of 5.2. There is little chance that of observing the sample data were performance and program location not associated. The null hypothesis of lack of association is rejected.

   The row percents, which reveal the association between location and performance, are shown in Figure 13.4. The PivotChart continues to suggest that the incidence of *Outstanding* performance is greater among employees recruited from *Home State* programs. The impact of program location on *Poor* performance is unknown, since *Poor* and *Average* categories were combined. Also unknown is the difference between employees from *Same* and *Outside Regions* programs, since these categories were likewise combined.

Recruiters would conclude:

"Job performance of newly hired employees is associated with undergraduate program location. Twenty-four percent of our new employees recruited from Same or Outside Region undergraduate programs have been identified as Outstanding performers. Within the group recruited from Home State undergraduate programs, more than twice this percentage, 60%, are Outstanding performers, a significant difference. Results suggest that in order to achieve a larger percent of Outstanding performers, recruiting should be focused on Home State programs."

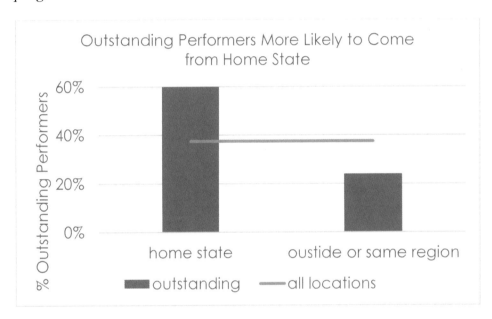

Figure 13.4 Association between location and performance.

13.4 Simpson's Paradox Can Mislead

Using contingency analysis to study the association between two variables can be potentially misleading, since all other related variables are ignored. If a third variable is related to the two being analyzed, contingency analysis may indicate that they are associated, when they may not actually be. Two variables may appear to be associated because they are both related to a third, ignored variable.

Example 13.2 American Cars. The CEO of American Car Company was concerned that the oldest segments of car buyers were avoiding cars that his firm assembles in Mexico. Production and labor costs are much cheaper in Mexico, and his long term plan is to shift production of all models to Mexico. If older, more educated and more experienced buyers avoid cars produced in Mexico, American Car could lose a major market segment unless production remained in The States.

The CEO's hypotheses were:

H_0: Choice between cars assembled in the U.S. and cars assembled in Mexico is not associated with generation.

H_1: Choice between cars assembled in the U.S. and cars assembled in Mexico is associated with generation.

He asked Travis Henderson, Director of Quantitative Analysis, to analyze the association between age category and choice of U.S. made versus Mexican made cars. The research staff drew a random sample of 263 recent car buyers, identified by age category. After preliminary analysis, age categories were combined into generations (with Millennials, 35 or younger, XGen, 36 to 49, and Boomers, 50+) to insure that all expected cell counts in an [Generation Category x Origin Choice] crosstabulation were each at least five. Contingency analysis is shown in the PivotChart and Pivot Table in Figure 13.5.

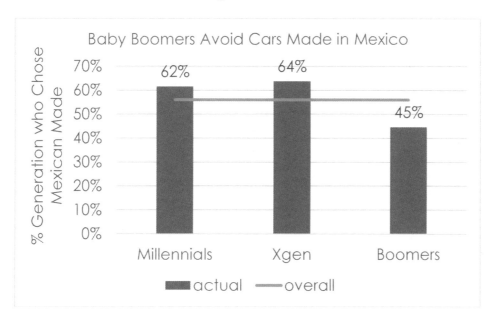

Count	Assembled in			Expected count	
Generation	Mexico	U.S.	Total	Mexico	U.S.
Millennials	56	35	91	51	40
XGen	51	29	80	45	35
Boomers	41	51	92	52	40
Total	148	115	263	148	115

Chi Square	8.0
df	2
p value	.02

Figure 13.5 Contingency analysis of U.S. vs. Mexican made car choices by generation

A glimpse of the PivotChart confirmed suspicions that older buyers did seem to be rejecting cars assembled in Mexico.   The *p value* for chi square was .02, indicating that the null hypothesis, lack of association, ought to be rejected. Choice between U.S. and Mexican made cars seemed to be associated with generation. Fifty six percent of the entire sample across all ages chose cars assembled in Mexico. Within the older, Boomer segment, however, the Mexican assembled car share was lower: 45%. While nearly two thirds of the younger segments chose cars assembled in Mexico, less than half of the oldest Boomer buyers chose Mexican made cars.

The CEO was alarmed with these results. His company could lose the business of older, more experienced Boomers if production were shifted South of the Border. Brand managers were about to begin planning "Made in the U.S.A." promotional campaigns targeted at Boomers. Emily Ernst, the Director of Strategy and Planning, suggested that generation was probably not the correct basis for segmentation. She explained that Boomers shop for a particular *type* of car---a family sedan or station wagon---and few family sedans or wagons were being assembled in Mexico. Models assembled at home in the U.S. tended to be large sedans and station wagons--- styles sought by Boomers. She proposed that it was *style* that influenced the U.S. versus Mexican assembled choice, and not generation, and that it was *style* that was dependent on generation. Her hypotheses were:

H_0 : Choice of car style is not associated with generation.
H_1 : Choice of car style is associated with generation.

To explore this alternate hypothesis, the research team ran contingency analysis of style choice (SUV, Sedan/Wagon and Coupe) by generation, Figure 13.6. Contingency analysis of this sample indicates that choice of style is associated with generation. More than half (53%) of the car buyers chose a sedan or wagon, though only about a third (36%) of Millennials chose a sedan or wagon, and nearly twice as many (65%) Boomers chose a sedan or wagon. Thirty percent of the sample bought a coupe, and just nearly half (49%) of Millennials chose a coupe. Only 17% of Boomers bought a coupe. These are significant differences supporting the conclusion that style of car chosen is associated with generation.

This is the news that the CEO was looking for. If older car buyers are choosing U.S.-made cars because they desire sedans or wagons, which tend to be assembled in the U.S., then perhaps these older buyers aren't shunning Mexican-made cars. His hypotheses were:

H_0: Given choice of a sedan or wagon, choice of U.S. versus Mexican
      assembled is not associated with generation.

H_1: Given choice of a sedan or wagon, choice of U.S. versus Mexican
      assembled is associated with generation.

To test these hypotheses, the analysis team conducted three contingency analyses of origin choice (U.S. versus Mexican assembled) by generation, looking at each style separately. Expected coupe buyers of coupes made in the U.S. who were Boomers was sparse. Since important information would be lost if Boomers were combined with XGen buyers, coupes were combined with SUVs to eliminate sparseness. Results are shown in Figure 13.7.

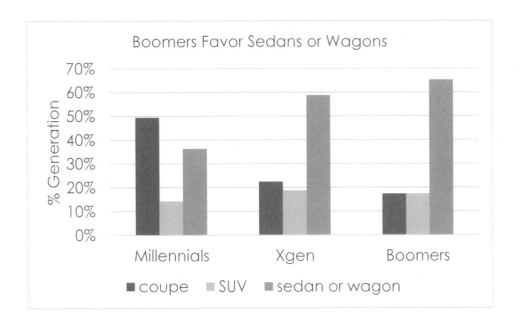

	Style					Row%			
χ^2_4		26.2	*p value*			.0000			
Count						Row%			
			sedan/						sedan/
Generation	coupe	SUV	wagon	Total		Generation	coupe	SUV	wagon
Millennials	45	13	33	91		Boomers	49%	14%	36%
XGen	18	15	47	80		XGen	23%	19%	59%
Boomers	16	16	60	92		Boomers	17%	17%	65%
Total	79	44	140	263		Total	30%	17%	53%

Figure 13.6 Contingency analysis of car style choice by age category

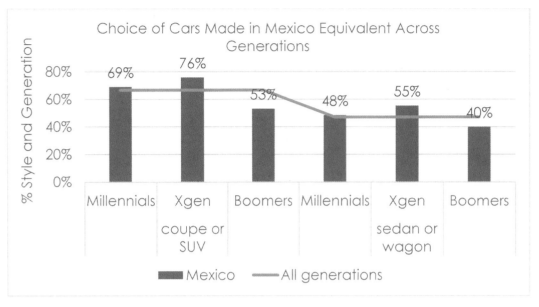

Generation by Style		Assembled In		Expected		χ^2	p value
Style	Generation	Mexico	U.S.	Mexico	U.S.		
sedan	Millennials	16	17	16	17		
or	XGen	26	21	22	25		
wagon	Boomers	24	36	28	32	2.5	.28
Coupe	Millennials	40	18	39	19		
or SUV	XGen	25	8	22	11		
	Boomers	17	15	21	11	4.0	.13

Figure 13.7 Contingency analysis: Origin choice given generation by style

Controlling for style of car by looking at each style separately reveals lack of association between origin preference for U.S. versus Mexican made cars and generation. Across styles, *p values* are greater than .05. There is not sufficient evidence in this sample to reject the null hypothesis. We conclude from this sample that the U.S. versus Mexican assembled choice is not associated with generation. The domestic automobile manufacturer should therefore not alter plans to move production South.

Simpson's Paradox describes the situation where two variables appear to be associated only because of their mutual association with a third variable. If the third variable is ignored, results are misleading. Because contingency analysis focuses upon just two variables at a time, analysts should be aware that apparent associations may come from confounding variables, as the **American Cars** example illustrates.

The Research Team summarized these results in this memo:

MEMO

Re.:   Country of Assembly Does Not Affect Older Buyers' Choices
To: CEO, American Car Company
         Emily Ernst, Director of Planning and Strategy
         Brand Management
From: Travis Hendershott, Director of Quantitative Analysis

Analysis of a sample of new car buyers reveals that styles of car drive the choices of distinct generations. Choices of all generations are independent of country of manufacture.

Contingency Analysis. Choices of 263 new car buyers were analyzed to assess the dependence of choice on country of manufacture, U.S. or Mexico, and generation.

Choice between Mexican and U.S. cars does not depend on buyer age.

Car choices between Mexican and U.S. cars do not depend on buyer age, though choices between *styles* are age dependent.

Younger buyers are more likely to choose a sporty
coupe. Older buyers are more likely to buy a sedan or wagon.

Production in Mexico will not influence car choices

Production in Mexico is not expected to affect car
buyer choices, providing the opportunity to shift assembly South to take advantage of cheaper labor.

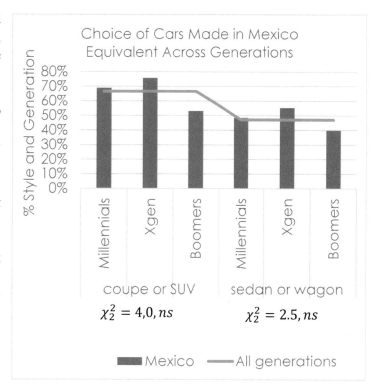

Choice of Cars Made in Mexico Equivalent Across Generations

coupe or SUV   sedan or wagon
$\chi_2^2 = 4,0, ns$ $\chi_2^2 = 2.5, ns$

13.5 Contingency Analysis Is Demanding

Contingency analysis requires a large and balanced dataset to insure a stable chi square. Even large samples may contain small proportions of particular categories, forcing combinations that aren't ideal. In the **American Cars** example, the sample, though large, was not balanced and contained a sparse combination for Boomers who bought coupes made in Mexico. Coupes were combined with SUVs to allow expected cell counts greater than five. With smaller samples, just two categories for a variable may remain, which may limit hypothesis testing. In the **Recruiting Stars** example, final results could not be used to assess the association between recruiting and poor employee performance after Poor and Average performing employees were combined.

13.6 Contingency Analysis Is Quick, Easy, and Readily Understood

Despite the fairly demanding data requirements, contingency analysis is appealing because it is simple, and results are easily understood. For very large samples, sparse cells are not a problem and many categories may be used, increasing the specificity of results and allowing a range of hypothesis tests.

For smaller samples, other alternatives, such as logit analysis, discussed in detail in Chapter 15, exist for analyzing categorical variable associations. These carry fewer data demands and allow incorporation of multiple variables. Multivariate analysis helps us avoid drawing incorrect conclusions in cases where Simpson's Paradox might mislead.

Excel 13.1 Construct Crosstabulations and Assess Association Between Categorical Variables with PivotTables and PivotCharts

American Cars. In order to explore the possible association between choice of U.S.-assembled and Mexican-assembled cars by age, begin by making a PivotTable to see the crosstabulation.

Open **Excel 13.1 American Cars.**

Select filled cells in the *Age* and *Made In* columns and then insert a PivotTable.

Drag *Age* to **ROW,** *Made In* to **COLUMN,** and *Made In* to ∑ **Values.**

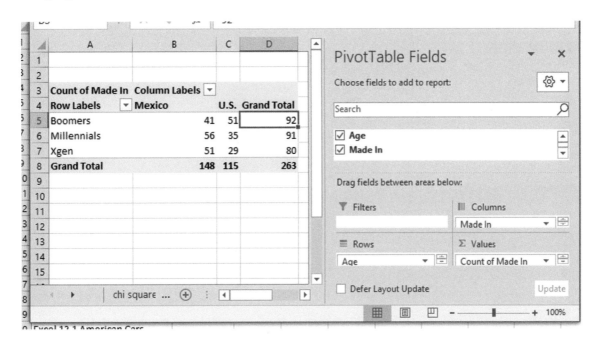

To see the conditional probabilities of choice of cars *Made In* the U.S. and Mexico given *age* category, convert cell counts to **% of row**.
From a data cell in the table:

Alt JTG Tab > Tab down to **% of Row Total, Enter**

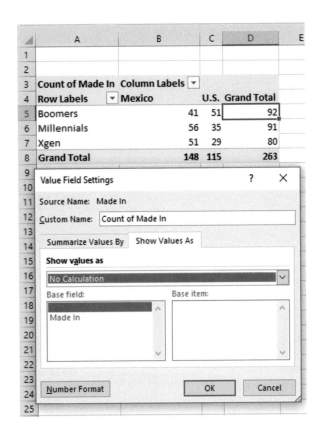

To put the generation categories in order, select drag the *>32* cell to the end.

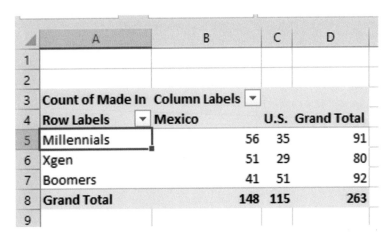

Make a PivotChart of *Made In* by *Age:* | **Alt JT C**

Choose a design and style, and add a chart title that reflects your conclusion.

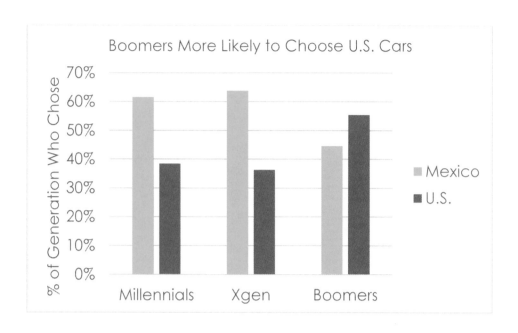

Excel 13.2 Use Chi Square to Test Association

To find the chi square statistic, change the PivotTable cells back to counts.
From a cell in the PivotTable,

Alt JT G Tab > Tab up to **No Calculation, Enter**

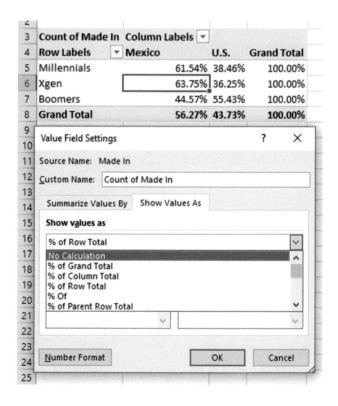

For chi square, make a table of *expected* cell counts and a table of cell contributions to chi square.

Select B3:C7, copy, and paste right of the PivotTable with values and formats, but not formulas,

Repeat to paste in a second copy.

	A	B	C	D	E	F	G	H
1								
2								
3	Count of Made In	Column Labels ▾			Column Labels		Column Labels	
4	Row Labels ▾	Mexico	U.S.	Grand Total	Mexico	U.S.	Mexico	U.S.
5	Millennials		56	35	91	56	35	56	35
6	Xgen		51	29	80	51	29	51	29
7	Boomers		41	51	92	41	51	41	51
8	Grand Total		148	115	263				
9								

Find expected counts from the row, column and grand totals.

In E5, enter the formula for the expected count, multiplying cells containing the Grand Total of buyers < 28, D5, and the Grand Total of cars assembled in Mexico, B8, and then dividing by the Grand Total, D8:

=D5 fn4 fn4 fn4*B8 fn4 fn4/D8 fn4.

Pressing **fn 4** three times locks the column, pressing **fn 4** twice locks the row, and pressing **fn 4** once locks both, so that we can fill in the remaining cells in the table with this formula.

Fill in the column, and then fill in the adjacent row.

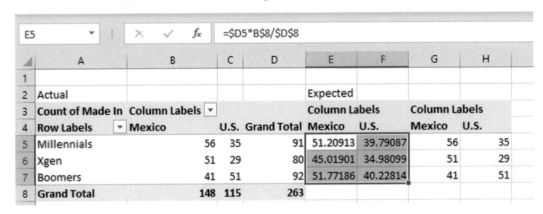

E5		▾	:	×	✓	f_x	=$D5*B$8/$D$8		

	A	B	C	D	E	F	G	H
1								
2	Actual				Expected			
3	Count of Made In	Column Labels ▾			Column Labels		Column Labels	
4	Row Labels ▾	Mexico	U.S.	Grand Total	Mexico	U.S.	Mexico	U.S.
5	Millennials		56	35	91	51.20913	39.79087	56	35
6	Xgen		51	29	80	45.01901	34.98099	51	29
7	Boomers		41	51	92	51.77186	40.22814	41	51
8	Grand Total		148	115	263				

In the third table, find each cell's contribution to chi square, the squared difference between expected counts, in the second table, and actual counts, in the first table, divided by expected counts in the second table.

| =(E5-B5)^2/E5.

In the first cell, G5, of the third contributions to chi square table, enter:

Fill in the column and the rows:

	A	B	C	D	E	F	G	H	I
1									
2	Actual				Expected		Contribution to chi square		
3	Count of Made In	Column Labels ▾			Column Labels		Column Labels		
4	Row Labels ▾	Mexico		U.S. Grand Total	Mexico	U.S.	Mexico	U.S.	
5	Millennials		56	35	91 51.20913	39.79087	0.448211	0.576828	
6	Xgen		51	29	80 45.01901	34.98099	0.794603	1.022619	
7	Boomers		41	51	92 51.77186	40.22814	2.241237	2.884375	
8	Grand Total		148 115	263					
9									

Use the Excel function **SUM**(*array1,array2*) to find contributions to chi square from each of the age categories.
In I5,

| =sum(G5:H5)

Add the cell contributions in the Mexico column, I:

In the Grand Total row, find the Mexico sum. In G8,

| **Alt MUS**

Right fill to add contributions to chi square from U.S. cars and chi square:

G8 ▾ : ✕ ✓ *fx* =SUM(G5:G7)

	A	B	C	D	E	F	G	H	I
1									
2	Actual				Expected		Contribution to chi square		
3	Count of Made In	Column Labels ▾			Column Labels		Column Labels		
4	Row Labels ▾	Mexico		U.S. Grand Total	Mexico	U.S.	Mexico	U.S.	
5	Millennials		56	35	91 51.20913	39.79087	0.448211	0.576828	1.025038
6	Xgen		51	29	80 45.01901	34.98099	0.794603	1.022619	1.817222
7	Boomers		41	51	92 51.77186	40.22814	2.241237	2.884375	5.125612
8	Grand Total		148 115	263			3.484051	4.483822	7.967873
9									

Find the *p value* for this chi square using the Excel function

CHISQ.DIST.RT(*chisquare,df*) with degrees of freedom *df* of 2

I9	▼	⋮	✕	✓	*fx*	=CHISQ.DIST.RT(I8,2)	

◢	E	F	G	H	I	J
1						
2	Expected		Contribution to chi square			
3	Column Labels		Column Labels			
4	Mexico	U.S.	Mexico	U.S.		
5	51.2091	39.7909	0.44821	0.57683	1.02504	
6	45.019	34.981	0.7946	1.02262	1.81722	
7	51.7719	40.2281	2.24124	2.88438	5.12561	
8			3.48405	4.48382	7.96787	chisquare
9					0.01861	pvalue
10						

Excel 13.3 Conduct Contingency Analysis with Three Categories

To control for type of car, make a new pivot table with all three variables, *Age, Made In* and *Style*. Drag *Style* then *Age* to the rows. Drag *Made In* to the columns and ∑ values. Again, drag Boomers to the third generation.

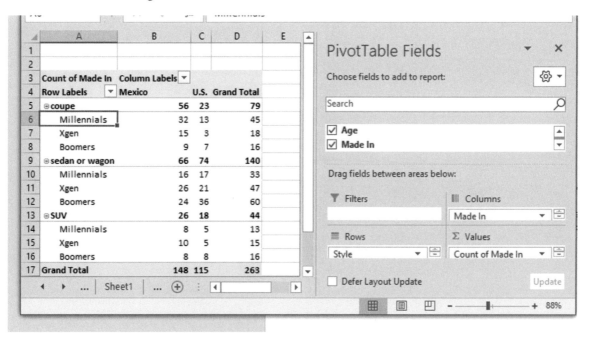

Copy B4:C16 and paste twice to the right of the table of actual counts.

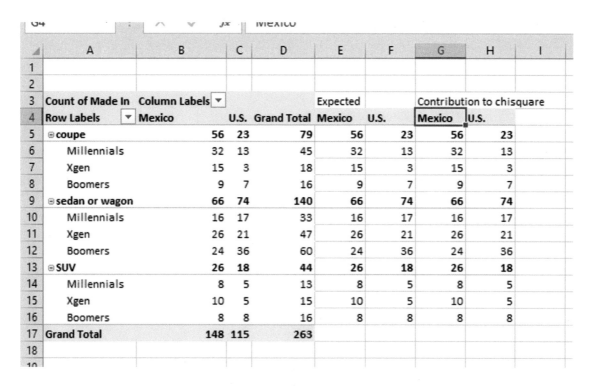

Find expected counts for each of the styles. Use style subtotals instead of the grand total.

| DEVSQ | | | f_x | =$D6*B$5/$D$5 | | | | |

One of the cells (coupe, Boomers, U.S.) has fewer than five expected. To eliminate the sparse cell, combine coupes and SUVs.

Drag *Age* out of the Pivot Table.

Drag SUVs up so that SUVs and coupes are in adjacent rows.

Select A5:A6, then combine. | **Alt JTK**

Change the Group 1 label to SUV coupes.

	A	B	C	D	E	F	G	H	I
1									
2									
3	Count of Made In	Column Labels ▼			Expected		Contribution to chisquare		
4	Row Labels ▼	Mexico		U.S.	Grand Total	Mexico	U.S.	Mexico	U.S.
5	⊟sedan or wagon							56	23
6	sedan or wagon		66	74	140	#DIV/0!	#DIV/0!	32	13
7	⊟Coupe or SUV					#DIV/0!	#DIV/0!	15	3
8	coupe		56	23	79	#DIV/0!	#DIV/0!	9	7
9	SUV		26	18	44			66	74
10	Grand Total		148	115	263	155.409	107.591	16	17
11						0	0	26	21
12						0	0	24	36
13								26	18
14						#DIV/0!	#DIV/0!	8	5
15						#DIV/0!	#DIV/0!	10	5
16						#DIV/0!	#DIV/0!	8	8

To see the subtotals needed to update expected counts, right click *Sean or Wagon* and choose Subtotal "style2".

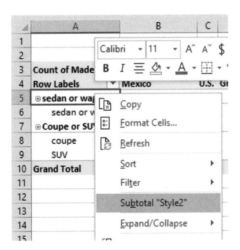

Drag *Style* out of the rows (leaving *Style2*) and drag *Age* back into the rows.

	A	B	C	D	E	F	G	H	I
1									
2									
3	Count of Made In	Column Labels ▼			Expected		Contribution to chisquare		
4	Row Labels ▼	Mexico		U.S.	Grand Total	Mexico	U.S.	Mexico	U.S.
5	⊟sedan or wagon		66	74	140			56	23
6	Millennials		16	17	33	15.5571	17.4429	32	13
7	Xgen		26	21	47	22.1571	24.8429	15	3
8	Boomers		24	36	60	28.2857	31.7143	9	7
9	⊟Coupe or SUV		82	41	123			66	74
10	Millennials		40	18	58	38.6667	19.3333	16	17
11	Xgen		25	8	33	22	11	26	21
12	Boomers		17	15	32	21.3333	10.6667	24	36
13	Grand Total		148	115	263			26	18
14						0	0	8	5

Find contributions to chi square, then sum by rows and by columns to find separate chisquares and p values for both *style2.*

◢	G	H	I	J	K
1					
2					
3	Contribution to chisquare				
4	Mexico	U.S.			
5					
6	0.01261	0.01124	0.02385		
7	0.66649	0.59444	1.26093		
8	0.64935	0.57915	1.2285		pvalue
9	1.32845	1.18483	2.51328	chisquare	0.28461
10	0.04598	0.09195	0.13793		
11	0.40909	0.81818	1.22727		
12	0.88021	1.76042	2.64063		pvalue
13	1.33528	2.67055	4.00583	chisquare	0.13494
14					

To illustrate, plot the percent who chose cars made in Mexico by style and generation. Copy A6:B8 and paste below the Pivot Table in column B. Copy A10:B12 and paste below that, also in column B. Add a column A label *style* , labelling the first three rows sedan or wagon, and the next three rows SUV or coupe. Label column D *overall generations* and copy and paste the subtotals below. (This will allow the graph to include a reference line.)

◢	A	B	C	D
1				
2				
3	Count of Made In	Column Labels ▾		
4	Row Labels ▾	Mexico	U.S.	Grand Total
5	⊟sedan or wagon	47.14%	52.86%	100.00%
6	Boomers	40.00%	60.00%	100.00%
7	Millennials	48.48%	51.52%	100.00%
8	Xgen	55.32%	44.68%	100.00%
9	⊟SUV or coupe	66.67%	33.33%	100.00%
10	Boomers	53.13%	46.88%	100.00%
11	Millennials	68.97%	31.03%	100.00%
12	Xgen	75.76%	24.24%	100.00%
13	Grand Total	56.27%	43.73%	100.00%
14				
15	Style	Generation	Made in Mexico	Over all Generations
16	sedan or wagon	Boomers	40.00%	47.14%
17	sedan or wagon	Millennials	48.48%	47.14%
18	sedan or wagon	Xgen	55.32%	47.14%
19	SUV or coupe	Boomers	53.13%	66.67%
20	SUV or coupe	Millennials	68.97%	66.67%
21	SUV or coupe	Xgen	75.76%	66.67%

Select the cells in the reformatted table and insert a column chart **Alt NC1.**

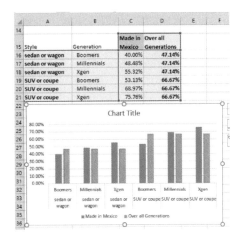

Next, change the chart type to Combo. | **Alt JCC**

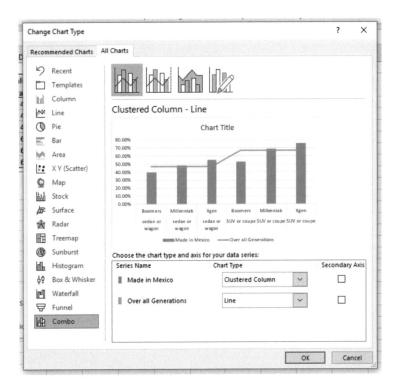

Add a vertical axis title, remove unwelcome zeros in the vertical axis, and add a chart title.

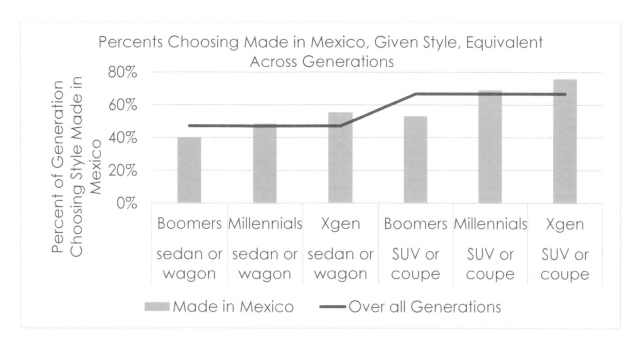

Note that with just two Made in columns, it is not necessary to plot both. Knowing the percent who chose Made in Mexico reveals the percent who chose Made in the U.S.

Lab 13-1 Skype Appeal

Microsoft acquired Skype in 2011, and faces competition from Apple's FaceTime. While the two share many similarities, Skype users pay for long distance calls, which can be made to any phone, land line, Android or Apple. FaceTime allows free video conferencing and doesn't charge for long distance calls; however, FaceTime callers can reach only other Apple device owners.

Microsoft managers would like to know who chooses Skype, instead of FaceTime. Some suspect that Skype may appeal more to older, Baby Boomers, who may be more likely to call friends or family who don't have an Apple device.

Microsoft conducted a survey of 133 randomly chosen smartphone owners, from ages 14 through 65. Consumers were asked which they relied on more: (i) FaceTime, or (ii) Skype.

Responses are in **Lab 13 Skype Appeal.**

    a. What are Microsoft manager's hypotheses regarding Skype preference and generation?

    b. Make a PivotTable of the cross tabs of callers by generation and preference.

    c. Make a table with the ***expected*** number of callers by generation and preference:

$$expected \text{ count in row } i \text{ column } j = number \text{ in row } i \text{ x percent in column } j$$

$$e_{ij} = n_i p_j$$

OR   *expected users in generation i with preference j = number in generation i x percent*
With preference j

    d. Make a table of cell contributions to chi square: $(e_{ij} - n_{ij})^2/e_{ij}$

    e. Sum the cell contributions to chi square to find chi square: _____

    f. Find the p value for your chi square with __ (=(rows-1)x(columns-1)) df: _____

    g. Illustrate your results using a column chart of percents of row by generation, adding a reference line for all generations. (Since there are only two columns, show only Skype column row percentages.)

The apparent dependence of Skype preference on generation could possibly be due to differences in preference for an Android device instead of an Apple device. Test this hypothesis.

    h. Make a PivotTable of the cross tabs of callers by generation and type of device.

    i. Make a table with the expected number of callers by generation and device type.

    j. Make a table of cell contributions to chi square.

    k. Sum the cell contributions to chi square to find chi square:

    l. Find the p value for your chi square with __ df.

    m. Illustrate your results with a column chart of device type by generation, including a reference line of overall percent who own an Apple device. (Since there are only two columns, show only Android device column row percentages.)

Since FaceTime can only be used to call owners of Apple electronics, management believes that Skype choice may differ between consumers with and without an Apple iPhone or iPad. Repeat your analysis, using only consumers who own an Apple device.

    n. Make a PivotTable of the cross tabs of callers by generation and preference, using only Apple device owners.

    o. Make a table with the expected number of callers by generation and preference.

    p. Which cells are sparse?

    q. Combine categories to eliminate sparseness, and then revise your table of expected cell counts.

    r. Make a table of cell contributions to chi square.

    s. Sum the cell contributions to chi square to find chi square.

    t. Find the p value for your chi square with __ df.

    u. Make a PivotChart of percents of row, adding a reference line for all generations to illustrate your results. (Since there are only two columns, show only Skype column row percentages.)

    v. What are the implications of your analysis? Should Microsoft target Baby Boomers? Or all generations?

Lab 13-2 Identifying the Target Market for Vastly Sustainable Paper

Tranlin, a Chinese company with a proprietary process, is building a plant in Virginia to produce sustainable paper products from wheat straw. Managers seek to identify the target market(s) to whom their sustainable paper concepts appeal.

    A concept test was conducted with 1,522 consumers who reacted to a verbal description of Tranlin's Vastly sustainable toilet tissue. Consumers were asked to rate their interest in purchasing Vastly toilet tissue, on a 1 to 5 point scale. Data in Tranlin.xlsx contain consumer household size, employment status, interest in Vastly tissue, tissue purchase frequency and monthly expenditure for paper products.

A consultant has advised that Tranlin's toilet tissue appeals most to households with children (larger households).

A manager would like to know whether interest or spend on paper products is associated with employment status, which wasn't assessed by the consultant.

Interest by Employment Status

1. What are the hypotheses linking interest to employment status?

Test the *hypothetical association between interest and employment status with contingency analysis.*
Exclude "Prefer not to say."
Combine the "top two" interest categories, Very and Extremely, to make a new "Likely Trier" category; combine the bottom three interest categories, Not, Not Very and Somewhat, to make a new "Unlikely Trier" category.

2. *Use the joint probabilities of particular employment status and likely trial to find the expected number for each combination. PPT*

3. *Compare the expected number with the actual number for each combination of employment status and trial likelihood to find contribution to chi square. PPT*

4. *Sum the contributions to chi square and find the p value.*

   Is interest associated with employment status?

5. *Interest differs most from expected for:*

   ___*Retired* ___ *Employed full time* ___ *Unemployed* ___ *Self-employed at home*

   ___*Employed part time* ___ *Self-employed, away from home* ___ *Students*

   ___*Household managers*

6. *Illustrate your results with a column chart of likely trial by employment status, including a reference line for all employment types. (Since there are just two columns, show only the likely trial percents.)*

Spend by Employment Status

7. What are the hypotheses linking spend to employment status?

Test the hypothetical association between spend and employment status with contingency analysis.
Exclude "Prefer not to say."

8. Use the joint probabilities of particular employment status and spend category to find the expected number for each combination.

9. Identify sparse cells among the expected numbers.

10. Combine employment categories with similar spend patterns to eliminate sparse cells.

11. Compare the expected number with the actual number for each combination of employment status and spend to find contribution to chi square.

12. Sum the contributions to chi square and find the p value.

13. Spend differs most from expected for:

___Retired ___ Employed full time ___ Unemployed ___ Self-employed at home

___Employed part time ___ Self-employed, away from home ___ Students
___Household managers

14. Produce a stacked column chart of spend probabilities given employment status.

Interest by Household Size

Test the consultant's conclusion that larger households are more interested in Vastly tissue.

15. What are the hypotheses linking interest to household size?

16. Use the joint probabilities of particular household size and likely trial to find the expected number for each combination.

17. Compare the expected number with the actual number for each combination of household size and trial likelihood to find contribution to chi square.

18. Sum the contributions to chi square to find the p value.

19. Is interest associated with household size?

Interest differs most from expected for households of size:

___ 1 ___ 2 ___ 3 ___ 4 ___ 5+

Alternate explanation

Are students, full time workers and household managers possibly more interested, because they possibly live in larger households? Are retirees possibly less interested, because retirees live in smaller households?

20. What is the hypothesis regarding employment status and household size?

Test the hypothesis that household size is associated with employment status.

21. Use the joint probabilities of particular employment status and household size to find the expected number for each combination.

22. Compare the expected number with the actual number for each combination of household size and trial likelihood to find contribution to chi square.

23. Sum the contributions to chi square to find the p value.

24. Household size differs most from expected for:

    ___Retired ___ Employed full time ___ Unemployed ___ Self-employed at home

    ___Employed part time ___ Self-employed, away from home ___ Students

    ___Household managers

Test the hypothesis that employment status is associated with interest, given particular household sizes.

25. Use the joint probabilities of employment status and likely trial, given household size, to find the expected number for each combination.

Sort employment status by proportion likely to try.
Combine similarly interested categories to remove sparse cells.

26. Compare the expected number with the actual number for each combination to find contribution to chi square, given household size.

27. Sum the contributions to chi square to find the p value, given household size.

28. Produce column charts of % likely triers by employment status, and display 1-2, 3 and 4+ side by side. Include reference lines for each household size.

The bottom line:

What segment(s) ought Tranlin target?

Case 13-1 Paper Expenditure and Interest in Vastly Sustainable Paper Products

Tranlin managers seek to identify the target market(s) to whom their sustainable paper concepts appeal, and those that spend more on paper products.

A concept test was conducted with 1,522 consumers who reacted to a verbal description of Vastly paper products. Data in Vastly 1.xlsx contain consumer interest, household size, and monthly expenditure for paper products. Monthly expenditure has been recoded into categories:: (i) $5 to $24, (ii) $25 to $49, (iii) $50 to $100. Outliers were recoded as either less than $5 or more than $100.

Interest and spend. Is interest in Vastly toilet tissue associated with spend on paper products? Tranlin would like to claim, in conversations with retailers, that Vastly customers spend more on paper products than other customers. Is interest in Vastly toilet tissue associated with paper product expenditure level?

Interest by Expenditure

Test the hypothesis that interest in Vastly toilet tissue is associated with expenditure.

Combine "Not," "Not very," and "Somewhat" interest categories into a new "Unlikely" trier category; combine "Very" and "Extremely" interest categories into a new "Likely" trier category. Exclude those who spend less than $5 or more than $100 per month on paper products.

Is interest in Vastly toilet tissue associated with expenditure?

Produce a chart of interest in Vastly toilet tissue by expenditure, including a reference line for all expenditures. (Since there are only two interest categories, show only Likely percents.) Order expenditure categories from least to most.

Interest by household size

Test the hypothesis that interest is associated with household size.

Produce a column chart of % likely to try by household size. (Since there are just two interest categories, show only Likely Trier percents.) Order household size categories from smallest to largest.

Alternate explanation

Are higher spenders possibly more interested, because higher spenders possibly live in larger households? Or do higher spenders simply prefer more expensive paper products?

First, test the hypothesis that household size is associated with spend in this sample.

Is household size associated with spend?

Produce a stacked column chart of % of household sizes by spend. Order household size categories from smallest to largest and order spend categories from least to most.

Interest by spend, controlling for household size

Controlling for household size, is interest associated with spend?

Show the likely trier %, conditional on spend, given household size, including reference lines of overall likely trier percents, given household size. (Order spend categories by increasing expenditure, and order household size categories by increasing size.)

Deliverables

Present your results to Tranlin executives with approximately five PowerPoints, one with your bottom line and your names, three illustrating your results, and an fifth with your conclusions. Enter your interpretation of each graph in Notes view in your PowerPoints. PowerPoints will be graded for solid analysis and effectiveness in conveying results (which includes readable text).

Case 13-2 Purchase Frequency and Interest in Vastly Sustainable Paper Products

Tranlin managers would like to know whether households that are likely to try tend to buy less frequently (in bulk). Which will be more important, to gain distribution in the Big Boxes (e.g., Costco, Sam's Club) or to focus on grocery stores (e.g., Harris Teeter, Whole Foods, Kroger, Trader Joes, Wegmans)?

A concept test was conducted with 1,522 consumers who reacted to a verbal description of Vastly paper products. Data in Vastly 2.xlsx contain consumer interest, household size, and frequency of toilet tissue purchases.

Interest by Purchase Frequency

Test the hypothesis that interest in Vastly toilet tissue is associated with purchase frequency.

Remove those who "Never" purchase toilet tissue. Combine "Not," "Not very," and "Somewhat" interest categories into a new "Unlikely" trier category; combine "Very" and "Extremely" interest categories into a new "Likely" trier category.

Is interest in Vastly toilet tissue associated with purchase frequency?

Produce a chart of interest in Vastly toilet tissue by purchase frequency, including a reference line for overall interest. (Since there are only two interest categories, show only Likely percents.) Order purchase frequency categories from least to most.

Interest by household size

Test the hypothesis that interest is associated with household size.

Produce a column chart of % likely to try by household size. (Since there are just two interest categories, show only Likely Trier percents.) Order household size categories from smallest to largest.

Alternate explanation

Are more frequent purchases possibly more interested, because more frequent purchasers possibly live in larger households?

First, test the hypothesis that household size is associated with purchase frequency in this sample.

Is household size associated with purchase frequency?

Produce a stacked column chart of % of household sizes by purchase frequency. Order household size categories from smallest to largest and order purchase frequency categories from least to most.

Interest by purchase frequency, controlling for household size

Controlling for household size, is interest associated with purchase frequency?

Show the likely trier %, conditional on purchase frequency, given household size, including reference lines of overall likely trier percents, given household size. (Order purchase frequency categories by increasing frequency, and order household size categories by increasing size.)

Deliverables

Present your results to Tranlin executives with approximately five PowerPoints, one with your bottom line and your names, three illustrating your results, and an fifth with your conclusions. Enter your interpretation of each graph in Notes view in your PowerPoints. PowerPoints will be graded for solid analysis and effectiveness in conveying results (which includes readable text).

Case 13-3 Sustainable Toilet Tissue Appeal

Tranlin managers seek to identify the target market(s) to whom their sustainable paper concepts appeal.

A concept test was conducted with 1,522 consumers who reacted to a verbal description of Tranlin's paper products. Consumers were asked to rate their interest in purchasing Vastly sustainable toilet tissue. Data in Vastly 3.xlsx contain consumer interest, gender, and household size.

A consultant has advised that their products appeal most to women with children (larger households). Some managers are skeptical.

Interest by gender

Test the hypothesis that interest is associated with gender.

Combine interest categories "Very" and "Extremely" to make a Likely Trier category; combine interest categories "Not," "Not very," and "Somewhat" to make an Unlikely Trier category.

Is interest associated with gender?

Show the probabilities of likely trial conditional on gender in a column chart, including a reference line of overall likely trial probability. (Since there are just two trial likelihood columns, show only the percents likely to try.)

Interest by household size

Show the probabilities of likely trial conditional on household size in a column chart, including a reference line showing overall percent likely to try. (Since there are just two trial likelihood columns, show only the percents likely to try.)

Alternate explanation

Are women possibly more interested, because women possibly live in larger households? First, test the hypothesis that women in the sample live in larger households.

Test the hypothesis that household size is associated with gender in this sample.

Is household size associated with gender?

Show the probabilities of household size conditional on gender in a stacked column chart.

Interest by gender, controlling for household size

Controlling for household size, is interest associated with gender?

Show the probabilities of likely trial conditional on gender given household size. Include a reference line showing overall likely trial, given household size. (Since there are only two trial categories, show only likely trial.)

Deliverables

Present your results to Tranlin executives with approximately six PowerPoints, one with your bottom line and your names, four illustrating your results (interest by gender, interest by household size, household size by gender and interest by gender conditional on household size), and an sixth with your conclusions. Enter your interpretation of each graph in Notes under each PowerPoint slide. PowerPoints will be graded for solid analysis and effectiveness in conveying results (which includes readable text).

Case 13-4 Generation, Household Size and Interest in Vastly Sustainable Toilet Tissue

Tranlin managers seek to identify the target market(s) to whom their sustainable paper concepts appeal.

A concept test was conducted with 1,522 consumers who reacted to a verbal description of Tranlin's sustainable toilet tissue. Consumers were asked to rate their interest in purchasing Vastly toilet tissue. Data in Vastly 4.xlsx contain consumer interest, generation, and household size.

A consultant has advised that their products appeal most to Millennials with children (larger households). Some managers are skeptical.

Interest by generation

Test the hypothesis that interest is associated with generation.

  Combine interest categories "Not," "Not very," and "Somewhat," to make an Unlikely Trier category; combine interest categories "Very" and "Extremely" to make a Likely Trier category.

Is interest associated with generation?

Produce a column chart of % likely to try by generation, including a reference line of the percent interested overall. (Since there are just two interest categories, show only Likely Trier percents.) Order generation categories by increasing age.

Interest by household size

Test the hypothesis that interest is associated with household size.

Produce a column chart of % likely to try by household size. (Since there are just two interest categories, show only Likely Trier percents.) Order household size categories from smallest to largest.

Alternate explanation

Are Millennials possibly more interested, because Millennials possibly live in larger households?

First, test the hypothesis that household size is associated with generation in this sample.

Is household size associated with generation?

Produce a stacked column chart of % of household sizes by generation. Order household size categories from smallest to largest and order generation categories from youngest to oldest.

Interest by generation, controlling for household size

Controlling for household size, is interest associated with generation? You will need to combine categories to remove sparse cells.

Show the likely trier %, conditional on generation, given household size, including a reference lines of overall likely trier percents, given household size. (Order generation categories by increasing age, and order household size categories by increasing size.)

Deliverables

Present your results to Tranlin executives with approximately six PowerPoints, one with your bottom line and your names, four illustrating your results, and an sixth with your conclusions. Enter your interpretation in Notes under each graph. PowerPoints will be graded for solid analysis and effectiveness in conveying results (which includes readable text).

Case 13-5 Tony's GREAT Advertising

Kellogg spends a hefty proportion of its advertising budget to expose children to ads for sweetened cereal on Saturday mornings. Kellogg brand ads feature cartoon hero characters similar to the cartoon hero characters that children watch on Saturday morning shows. This following press release is an example:

Advertising Age
Kellogg pounces on toddlers; Tiger Power to wrest tot monopoly away from General Mills' $500M Cheerios brand. (News) *Stephanie Thompson.*

Byline: STEPHANIE THOMPSON

In the first serious challenge to General Mills' $500 million Cheerios juggernaut, Kellogg is launching a toddler cereal dubbed Tiger Power.

The cereal, to arrive on shelves in January, will be endorsed by none other than Frosted Flakes icon Tony the Tiger and will be "one of our biggest launches next year," according to Kellogg spokeswoman Jenny Enochson. Kellogg will position the cereal-high in calcium, fiber and protein-as "food to grow" for the 2-to-5 set in a mom-targeted roughly $20 million TV and print campaign that begins in March from Publicis Groupe's Leo Burnett, Chicago.

Cereal category leader Kellogg is banking on Tiger Power's nutritional profile as well as the friendly face of its tiger icon, a new shape and a supposed "great taste with or without milk" to make a big showing in take-along treats for tots.

Tony Grate, the brand manager for Frosted Flakes would like to know whether or not there is an association between Saturday morning cartoon viewing and consumption of his brand.

The Saturday morning TV viewing behaviors, *Saturday Morning Cartoons*, and consumption of Frosted Flakes, *Frosted Flake Eater*, are contained in **Case 13-2 Frosted Flakes.** A random sample of 300 children ages 2 through 5 were sorted into four groups based on whether or not each watches at least three hours of television on Saturday morning at least twice a month and whether or not each consumes Frosted Flakes at least two times a week. The number of *Children* indicates popularity of each *Saturday Morning Cartoons, Frosted Flake Eater* combination.[1]

1. Is there an association between watching *Saturday morning cartoons* and consumption of Frosted Flakes?

2. Illustrate your results with a properly labeled column chart, including a reference line for percent of all children who eat Frosted Flakes. Include a bottom-line title.

3. What are the implications of results for Tony Grate?

---

[1] These data are fictitious, though designed to reflect a realistic scenario.

Case 13-6 Hybrid Motivations

American car executives have asked you to analyze data collected from a stratified sample of 301 car owners. The goal is to develop a profile of hybrid owners, which distinguishes them from conventional car owners. If differences are identified, those differences will be used to promote American's hybrid models.

One third of the owners surveyed own Priuses, one third own other hybrids, and one third own a conventional car. Car owners were asked to indicate the primary motivation which led to the last car choice. Possible responses included three *functional* benefits (fuel economy, lower emissions, tax incentives), *aesthetics/style* and *vanity* ("makes a statement about me"). Data are in **13 hybrid motivations.**

It is thought that choice of a hybrid is associated with vanity. . . the desire to make a statement.

1. Is choice of car type associated with motivation? Y or N

2. Statistic and p value you used to reach your conclusion in 5:

3. Embed a column chart which illustrates the association between motivation and car choice. Include axes labels with units and a title which describes what the conclusions which the audience should see.

Some American executives believe that Prius owners are unique.

4. Excluding Prius owners, is choice of car type associated with motivation? Y or N

5. Statistic and p value you used to reach your conclusion in 8:

Chapter 14
Conjoint Analysis and Experimental Data

This chapter introduces the use of indicators to analyze data from conjoint analysis experiments. Conjoint analysis is used in experiments to quantify customer preferences for better design of new products and services.

Analysis of variance is used when potential drivers are categorical, as they are in experiments. In this case, the categorical drivers could be represented with indicators in regression, or analyzed directly with analysis of variance with software such as JMP or SPSS.

14.1 Indicators Estimate the Value of Product Attributes

New product development managers sometimes use *conjoint analysis* to identify potential customers' most preferred new product design and to estimate the relative importance of product attributes. The conjoint analysis concept assumes that customers' preferences for a product are the sum of the values of each of the product's attributes, and that customers *trade off* features. A customer will give up a desired feature if another, more desired feature is offered. The offer of a more desired feature compensates for the lack of a second, less desired feature.

Example 14.1 New Smartphone Design. As an example, consider preferences for smartphones. Management believes that customers choose smartphones based on desired size, brand/operating system, and price. For a new smartphone design, they are considering

- three sizes: bigger than shirt-pocket, shirt-pocket, and ultrathin shirt-pocket
- three brand/platforms: Apple/ios, LG/Android, or Samsung/Android
- three prices: $299, $799 and $1000

Management believes that price may be a quality signal, and that customers may suspect the quality of less expensive smartphones. Consumers might expect the least expensive smartphone to lack quality, while also believing $1000 exorbitant, therefore preferring the mid-range priced choice. Alternatively, consumers may simply prefer the least expensive option. Or, consumers may desire the most expensive phone, to be consumed conspicuously.

The conjoint analysis process assumes that it is easier for customers to rank or rate products or brands, rather than estimating the value of each feature.

The three smartphone attributes could be combined in 27 ($=3^3$) unique ways. 27 hypothetical smartphones would be too many for customers to accurately evaluate. From the 27, a set of nine are carefully chosen so that the chance of each feature is equally likely (33%), and each feature is uncorrelated with other features. Ultra slim size, for example, is equally likely to be paired with each of the three brand/platforms, and each of the three prices. This will eliminate multicollinearity among the indicators used in the regression of the conjoint model. Such a subset of hypothetical combinations is an *orthogonal array* and is shown in Table 14.1.

© Springer Nature Switzerland AG 2019

C. Fraser, *Business Statistics for Competitive Advantage with Excel 2019 and JMP*, https://doi.org/10.1007/978-3-030-20374-0_14

Table 14.1 Orthogonal subset of smartphone attribute combinations.

Brand/os	bigger than shirt pocket	shirt pocket	ultra slim shirt pocket
Apple/ios	$ 299	$ 1,000	$ 799
LG/Android	$ 799	$ 299	$ 1,000
Samsung/Android	$ 1,000	$ 799	$ 299

Notice that for any smartphone attribute, attribute levels are equally likely to be paired with both of other attribute levels. For example, one third of the hypotheticals are *Apple/ios*, and one third of the three *Apple ios* hypotheticals are *bigger than shirt pocket*, one third are *shirt pocket*, and one third are *ultra slim*. One third of the three *Apple ios* hypotheticals are *$299*, one third are *$799*, and one third are *$1000*. Similarly, one third of the three *bigger than shirt pocket* hypotheticals are *$299*, one third are *$799*, and one third are *$1000*. Because attribute combination pairs are equally like, the subset is *orthogonal*, and free of multicollinearity.

To find the *part worth preferences,* the value of each cell phone feature with regression, indicators are used to represent features that differ from an arbitrary baseline. (The baseline can be any combination of size, brand/platform and price.) Here, we will choose *shirt-pocket* size, *LG/Android* priced at *$799* as the baseline. We will need two indicators for sizes other than the baseline shirt-pocket: *bigger* and *ultra slim*. We will need two indicators brand/platform other than the baseline of LG/Android: *Apple/ios* and *Samsung/Android*. And the we will need two indicators of price other than the $799 baseline: *$299* and *$1000*. The indicators for those nine hypothetical smartphones are shown in Table 14.2, below.

The conjoint analysis regression model is:

$$Smartphone\ pr\hat{e}ference_i = b_0 + b_1 \times bigger\ than\ shirt\ pocket\ size_i$$
$$+ b_2 \times ultrathin\ shirt\ size_i$$
$$+ b_3 \times Apple/ios_i + b_4 \times Samsung/Android_i$$
$$+ b_5 \times \$299_i + b_6 \times \$1000_i$$

for the *i'th* smartphone configuration, where

b_0 is the intercept, which reflects preference for the baseline configuration,
b_1, b_2, b_3, b_4, b_5, and b_6 are estimates of the *part worth preferences* of features.

Three customers rated the nine hypothetical smartphones after viewing concept descriptions with sketches. The configurations judged extremely attractive were rated 9 and those judged not at all attractive were rated 1. The regression with eight indicators is shown in Table 14.2.

Although several coefficient estimates are not significant, there is no need to remove those indicators and rerun. The indicators are free from multicollinearity, and so there is no advantage from removing insignificant indicators.

Table 14.2 Indicators distinguishing the nine hypothetical smartphones.

hypothetical smartphone	bigger than shirt pocket	ultrathin shirt pocket	Apple /ios	Samsung /Android	$299	$1,000
1	1	0	1	0	1	0
2	1	0	0	0	0	0
3	1	0	0	1	0	1
4	0	0	1	0	0	1
5	0	0	0	0	1	0
6	0	0	0	1	0	0
7	0	1	1	0	0	0
8	0	1	0	0	0	1
9	0	1	0	1	1	0

Table 14.3 Regression of conjoint analysis smartphone data.

Regression Statistics						
R Square	0.64					
Standard Error	1.64					
Observations	27					
ANOVA	df	SS	MS	F	Significance F	
Regression	6	98	16.4	6.1	0.0009	
Residual	20	54	2.7			
Total	26	152				

	Coefficients	Standard Error	t Stat	P-value	Lower 95%	Upper 95%
Intercept	4.9	0.84	5.9	9E-05	3.2	6.7
bigger than shirt pocket	2.1	0.78	2.7	0.01	0.5	3.7
ultrathin shirt pocket	1.0	0.78	1.3	0.21	-0.6	2.6
Apple/ios	2.1	0.78	2.7	0.01	0.4	3.7
Samsung/Android	1.0	0.78	1.3	0.21	-0.6	2.6
$299	-3.6	0.78	-4.6	0.0001	-5.2	-1.9
$1,000	-1.3	0.78	-1.7	0.10	-3.0	0.3

Significant coefficient estimates indicate significant difference from the baseline level. *Bigger than shirt pocket* size is significantly preferred to *shirt pocket* size, the baseline, while *ultra slim shirt pocket* size is not significantly preferred to *shirt pocket* size. If a smartphone is *bigger than shirt pocket,* it is rated 2.1 rating scale points higher, on average, than a *shirt pocket* size smartphone.

Apple/ios is preferred to *LG/Android*, the baseline; however, *Samsung/Android* is not significantly more preferred to *LG Android.* Offering *Apple/ios* produces ratings higher by 2.1 rating scale points than a comparable *LG/Android* smartphone.

Consumers in the sample prefer a *$799* smartphone to a *$299* option. The more expensive phone at *$1000* does not differ from the *$799* baseline smartphone. Consumers rate the cheapest smartphones lower than the more expensive *$799* option.

The most preferred combination is *bigger than shirt pocket, Apple/ios,* priced at *$799 or $1000.*

The part worth preferences from coefficient estimates are shown in Figure 14.1.

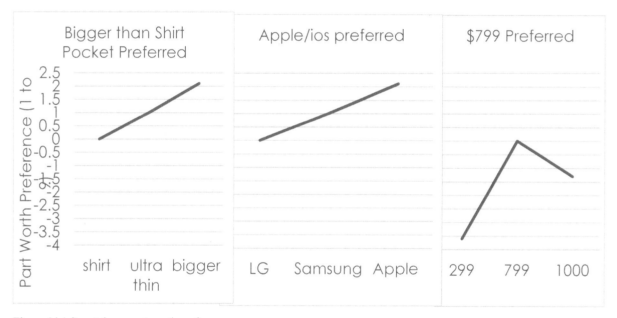

Figure 14.1 Smartphone part worth preferences

From the part worth preference ranges, we can gauge the importance of the three smartphone attributes. Comparing the most to least preferred size, the range in part worth preferences is 2.1 scale points (= 2.1, for *bigger than shirt pocket,* - 0 for *shirt pocket,* the baseline). Comparing most to least preferred brand/os, the range in part worth preferences is 2.1 scale points (= 2.1 for *Apple/ios* – 0 for *LG/Android*). The preferred price, *$799,* adds 3.6 scale points, relative to the least preferred price, *$299.* Thus, price is most. The attribute importances are shown in Table 14.4.

Table 14.4 Attribute importances from ranges in part worth preferences

Attribute	Level	Part worth	Importance
Size	bigger than shirt pocket	2.1	
	ultrathin	1.0	
	shirt pocket	0	2.1
Brand/os	Apple/ios	2.1	
	Samsung Android	1	
	LG Android	0	2.1
Price	$799	0	
	$1,000	-1.3	
	$299	-3.6	3.6

What is not known, is the significance of differences between the attribute levels which are not the baseline levels.

The coefficient estimates suggest that *bigger than shirt size* is preferred to *ultra slim,* since *bigger than shirt size* adds 2.1 to expected ratings, while *ultra slim* adds just 1 scale point. But whether or not that difference of 1.1 scale points is significant has not been tested. There are two possibilities:

$$b_{shirt\ size} < b_{ultraslim} = b_{bigger\ than\ shirt\ size} \quad \text{or} \quad b_{shirt\ size} < b_{ultra\ slim} < b_{bigger\ than\ shirt\ size}$$

Similarly, coefficient estimates suggest that *Apple/ios* is preferred to *Samsung/Android,* since *Apple/ios* contributes 1.1 (= 2.1 - 1.0) more scale points to expected ratings, but significance of the difference has not been tested. There are two possibilities:

$$b_{LG\ Android} < b_{Samsung\ Android} = b_{Apple\ ios} \quad \text{or} \quad b_{LG\ Android} < b_{Samsung\ Android} < b_{Apple\ ios}$$

$1000 appears to be preferred to *$299,* contributing 2.1 (= -1.3 – (-3.6))scale points more to expected ratings, though this comparison has not been tested, leaving two possibilities:

$$b_{\$299} < b_{\$1000} = b_{\$799} \quad \text{or} \quad b_{\$299} < b_{\$1000} < b_{\$799}$$

A second regression, with a different baseline, will provide tests of the significance of these differences. Changing the baseline to *ultra slim* or *bigger than shirt size, Samsung/Android* or *Apple ios,* and *$1000* or *$299,* will produce regression results with the same RSquare and the same attribute importances, but this will test the three attribute level comparisons that are lacking from the first regression. These results are shown in Table 14.5, with *ultra slim, Samsung Android* and *$1000* as the baseline.

Table 14.5 Regression with an alternate baseline.

	Coefficients	Standard Error	t Stat	P-value	Lower 95%	Upper 95%
Intercept	5.6	0.84	6.7	2E-06	3.8	734
bigger than shirt pocket	1.0	0.78	1.4	0.17	-0.5	2.7
shirt pocket	-1.0	0.78	-1.3	0.21	-2.6	0.6
Apple/ios	1.1	0.78	1.4	0.17	-0.5	2.7
LG/Android	-1.0	0.78	-1.3	0.21	-2.6	0.6
$299	-2.2	0.78	-2.9	0.01	-3.8	-0.6
$799	1.3	0.78	1.7	0.10	-0.3	3.0

Now it is clear that *bigger than shirt pocket* is not significantly preferred to *ultra slim:*

$$b_{shirt\ size} < b_{ultra\ slim} = b_{bigger\ than\ shirt\ size}$$

Samsung/Android is not significantly preferred to *Apple/ios:*

$$b_{LG\ Android} < b_{Samsung\ Android} = b_{Apple\ ios}$$

$1000 is significantly preferred to *$299:*

$$b_{\$299} < b_{\$1000} = b_{\$799}$$

Thus, the ideal smartphone would be *bigger than shirt pocket* or *ultra slim, Apple/ios* or *Samsung Android,* priced at *$799* or *$1000*.

Using coefficient estimates from the first regression, the expected rating for one of the ideal smartphones (*bigger than shirt pocket, Apple ios,$799*) is 9.1, shown below in Table 14.6. Equivalently, using coefficient estimates from the second regression, shown in Table 14.7, the expected rating is 9.1:

Table 14.6 Predicted rating from sum of part worth utilities.

intercept	Bigger than shirt pocket pw	Ultrathin pw	Apple ios pw	Samsung Android pw	$299 pw	$1000 pw	$\hat{rating}$
4.9	+ 2.1 × *bigger than shirt pocket$_i$*	+ 1.0 × *ultrathin$_i$*	+2.1 × *Apple ios$_i$*	+1.0 × *Samsung Android$_i$*	−3.6 × *299_i$*	−1.3 × *1000_i$*	
4.9	+ 2.1 × 1	+ 1.0 ×0	+2.1 × 1	+ 1.0 × 0	− 3.6 × 0	−1.3 × 0	
4.9	+ 2.1	+ 0	+ 2.1	+ 0	+ 0	+ 0	= 9.1

Table 14.7 Predicted rating from the sum of part worth preferences of the second regression.

intercept	Bigger than shirt pocket pw	Shirt pocket pw	Apple ios pw	LG Android pw	$299 pw	$799 pw	rating
5.6	+ 1.1 $\times$ bigger than shirt pocket$_i$	$- 1.0$ $\times$ ultrathin$_i$	$+1.1$ $\times$ Apple ios$_i$	-1.0 $\times$ LG Android$_i$	-2.2 $\times$ 299_i$	$+1.3$ $\times$ 799_i$	
5.6	+ 1.1 $\times$ 1	- 1.0 $\times$ 0	+1.1 $\times$ 1	$- 1.0$ $\times$ 0	$- 2.2$ $\times$ 0	+1.3 $\times$ 1	
5.6	+ 1.1	- 0	+ 1.1	- 0	+ 0	+ 1.3	= 9.1

This particular combination did not appear in the nine hypotheticals evaluated, and so it is not surprising that the expected rating of this ideal combination exceeds the average ratings of the nine hypotheticals, which is 8.0.

Conjoint analysis been used to improve the designs of a wide range of products and services, including:

- seating, food service, scheduling and prices of airline flights
- offer of outpatient services and prices for a hospital
- container design, fragrance and design of an aerosol rug cleaner,
- digital camera pixels, features and prices

Conjoint analysis is versatile and the attributes studied can include characteristics that are difficult to describe, such as fragrance, sound, feel, or taste. It is difficult for customers to tell us how important color, package design, or brand name is in shaping preferences, and conjoint analysis often provides believable, valid estimates.

14.2 Analysis of Variance Offers an Alternative to Regression with Indicators

ANalysis Of VAriance is an alternative to regression with indicators for situations in which all of the drivers are categorical, including conjoint analysis. ANOVA also tests hypotheses regarding factor level means and provides an F statistic for each factor by comparing the average variation explained between factors, MSB (MSR in regression), to average unexplained variation within factors, MSW (MSE in regression). .

With ANOVA, hypotheses concern the impact of each attribute, or factor. In the smartphone example, the hypotheses linking factors to preference are:

$H_{size\ 0}$: mean preferences for *bigger than shirt pocket, shirt pocket* and *ultraslim* are equivalent

$H_{size\ 1}$: mean preference for one or more of the *size* options differs from others

$H_{brand\ os\ 0}$: mean preferences for *Apple ios, LG Android* and *Samsung Android* are equivalent

$H_{brand\ os\ 1}$: mean preference for one or more of the *brand operating system* options differs from others

$H_{price\ 0}$: mean preferences for *$299, $799* and *$1000* prices are equivalent

$H_{price\ 1}$: mean preference for one or more of the *price* options differs from others

OR

$H_{size\ 0}$: $\mu_{bigger\ than\ shirt\ pocket} = \mu_{shirt\ pocket} = \mu_{ultraslim}$

$H_{size\ 1}$: mean preference for one or more of the *size* options differs from others

$H_{brand\ os\ 0}$: $\mu_{Apple\ ios} = \mu_{LG\ Android} = \mu_{Samsung\ Android}$

$H_{brand\ os\ 1}$: preference for one or more of the *brand operating system* options differs from others

$H_{price\ 0}$: $\mu_{\$299} = \mu_{\$799} = \mu_{\$1000}$

$H_{price\ 1}$: preference for one or more of the *price* options differs from others

To explore what ANOVA does, in the focus on average variation explained by each factor, the ratings by hypothetical smartphone and factor levels are shown in Table 14.8, first focusing on the size factor level averages:

Table 14.8 Hypothetical smartphone ratings between size levels.

hyp	size	Brand os	price	rating	average
1	bigger	Apple	$299	7,7,2	
2	bigger	LG	$799	6,8,8	
3	bigger	Samsung	$1000	4,9,7	6.4
4	pocket	Apple	$1000	7,5,6	
5	pocket	LG	$299	2,1,1	
6	pocket	Samsung	$799	5,5,7	4.3
7	ultraslim	Apple	$799	9,6,9	
8	ultraslim	LG	$1000	3,4,6	
9	ultraslim	Samsung	$299	4,5,2	5.3
average					5.4

Variation in ratings between the three size levels, ignoring variation due to *brand/operating system* and *price*, is:

$$SSB_{size} = n_{bigger\ than\ shirt\ pocket} \times (\bar{X}_{bigger\ than\ shirt\ pocket} - \bar{\bar{X}})^2$$

$$+ n_{shirt\ pocket} \times (\bar{X}_{shirt\ pocket} - \bar{\bar{X}})^2$$

$$+ n_{ultraslim} \times (\bar{X}_{ultraslim} - \bar{\bar{X}})^2$$

$$= 9 \times (6.4 - 5.4)^2 + 9 \times (4.3 - 5.4)^2 + 9 \times (5.3 - 5.4)^2$$

$$= 20.1$$

There are three *size* levels, or options. The degrees of freedom for variation between *size* levels is two, comparing two of the levels to the third baseline. Mean variation explained by size is:

$$MSB_{size} = SSB_{size} / df_{size}$$

$$= 20.1 / 2$$

$$= 10.0$$

Table 14.9 focuses on variation between brand/operating system levels, ignoring size and price.

Tables 14.9 Variation in ratings between brand/operating system levels.

hyp	size	Brand os	price	rating	average
1	bigger	Apple	$299	7,7,2	
2	bigger	LG	$799	6,8,8	
3	bigger	Samsung	$1000	4,9,7	
4	pocket	Apple	$1000	7,5,6	
5	pocket	LG	$299	2,1,1	
6	pocket	Samsung	$799	5,5,7	
7	ultraslim	Apple	$799	9,6,9	6.4
8	ultraslim	LG	$1000	3,4,6	4.3
9	ultraslim	Samsung	$299	4,5,2	5.3
Average					5.4

$$SSB_{brand\ os} = n_{Apple\ ios} \times (\bar{X}_{Apple\ ios} - \bar{\bar{X}})^2$$

$$+ n_{LG\ Android} \times (\bar{X}_{LG\ Android} - \bar{\bar{X}})^2$$

$$+ n_{Samsung\ Android} \times (\bar{X}_{Samsung\ Android} - \bar{\bar{X}})^2$$

$$= 9 \times (6.4 - 5.4)^2 + 9 \times (4.3 - 5.4)^2 + 9 \times (5.3 - 5.4)^2$$

$$= 20.1$$

Mean variation between the three *brand operating system* levels is:

$$MSB_{brand\ os} = SSB_{brand\ os} / df_{brand\ os}$$

$$= 20.1 / 2$$

$$= 10.0$$

Table 14.10 highlights variation between levels of the third factor levels, *price:*

Table 14.10 Variation in ratings between price levels.

hyp	size	Brand os	price	rating	average
1	bigger	Apple	$299	7,7,2	
2	bigger	LG	$799	6,8,8	
3	bigger	Samsung	$1000	4,9,7	
4	pocket	Apple	$1000	7,5,6	
5	pocket	LG	$299	2,1,1	
6	pocket	Samsung	$799	5,5,7	
7	ultraslim	Apple	$799	9,6,9	7.0
8	ultraslim	LG	$1000	3,4,6	5.7
9	ultraslim	Samsung	$299	4,5,2	3.4
average					5.4

$$SSB_{price} = n_{\$299} \times (\bar{X}_{\$299} - \bar{\bar{X}})^2$$

$$+ n_{\$799} \times (\bar{X}_{\$799} - \bar{\bar{X}})^2$$

$$+ n_{\$1000} \times (\bar{X}_{\$1000} - \bar{\bar{X}})^2$$

$$= 9 \times (3.4 - 5.4)^2 + 9 \times (7.0 - 5.4)^2 + 9 \times (5.7 - 5.4)^2$$

$$= 58.1$$

Mean variation between the three *price* levels is:

$$MSB_{price} = SSB_{price} / df_{price}$$

$$= 58.1 / 2$$

$$= 29.0$$

To compare mean variation across *size* levels, *brand operating system* levels, and *price* levels with mean residual variation within *size, brand operating system* and *price* levels, the residual variation within levels is calculated by subtracting SSB_{size}, $SSB_{brand\ os}$ and SSB_{price} from total variation, *SST*:

$$SST = (7 - 5.4)^2 + (6 - 5.4)^2 + (4 - 5.4)^2$$

$$+ (7 - 5.4)^2 + (2 - 5.4)^2 + (5 - 5.4)^2$$

$$+ (9 - 5.4)^2 + (3 - 5.4)^2 + (4 - 5.4)^2$$

$$+ (7 - 5.4)^2 + (8 - 5.4)^2 + (9 - 5.4)^2$$

$$+ (5 - 5.4)^2 + (1 - 5.4)^2 + (5 - 5.4)^2$$

$$+ (6 - 5.4)^2 + (4 - 5.4)^2 + (5 - 5.4)^2$$

$$+ (2 - 5.4)^2 + (8 - 5.4)^2 + (7 - 5.4)^2$$

$$+ (6 - 5.4)^2 + (1 - 5.4)^2 + (7 - 5.4)^2$$

$$+ (9 - 5.4)^2 + (6 - 5.4)^2 + (2 - 5.4)^2$$

$$= 152$$

Of the total variation of 152, 20.1 has been explained by differences across *size* levels, 20.1 has been explained by differences across *brand operating system* levels, and 58.1 has been explained by differences across *price* levels, leaving 54.1 unexplained from variation within levels:

$$SSW = SST - SSB_{size} - SSB_{brand\ os} - SSB_{price}$$

$$= 152 - 20.1 \quad - 20.1 \quad - 58.1$$

$$= 54.1$$

Notice that the sum of variation explained by the three factors is equivalent to *Regression Sum of Squares* in regression cell C12 (from Table 14.3), 87, total variation, *SST,* 144, is the same as *Total Sum of Squares* in the regression in cell C14, and *SSW* is equivalent to the *Residual Sum of Squares* in regression cell C13, 57. ANOVA provides the variation explained by each of the three, orthogonal factors, while regression provides only total variation explained by all three. Figure 14.2 illustrates the contributions to RSquare by the three orthogonal factors.

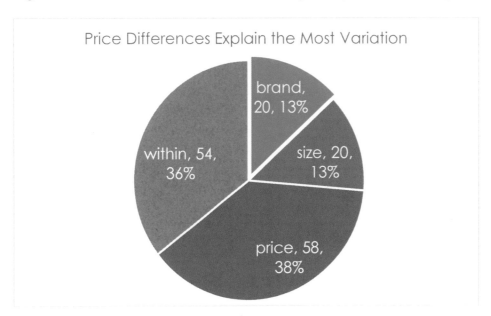

Figure 14.2 Variation explained by the three smartphone factors.

Mean unexplained variation, *MSW* (which is equivalent to *Residual Mean Square, or MSE,* in regression cell D13) is:

$$MSW = SSW\ /\ (N - df_{size} - df_{brand\ os} - df_{price} - 1)$$

$$= 54.1\ /\ 20$$

$$= 2.7$$

To test each of the three sets of hypotheses, the corresponding *F* statistics are calculated from the ratio of *mean squares between, MSB_{size}, MSB_{brand\ os}* or *MSB_{price},* and *mean square within, MSW:*

$$F_{size_{2,20}} = MSB_{size}\ /\ MSW$$

$$= 10.0\ /\ 2.7$$

$$= 3.7$$

$$F_{brand\ os_{2,20}} = MSB_{brand\ os} / MSW$$

$$= 10.0 / 2.7$$

$$= 3.7$$

$$F_{price_{2,20}} = MSB_{price} / MSW$$

$$= 29.0 / 2.7$$

$$= 10.7$$

With 2 and 20 degrees of freedom, F_{size} and F_{os}, both at 3.7 have pvalues of .045. F_{price} of 10.7 has a pvalue of .0007. Based on the sample data, there is evidence that *size*, the *brand operating system* and *price* alternatives are not equally preferred. Null hypotheses for *size, brand operating system* and *price* are rejected.

Rather than compute the *SSBs*, in cases in which the factors are orthogonal, as they are in conjoint analysis data, single factor regressions will provide *SSR* and *MSR* for each of the factors. There are shown below in Tables 14.11, 14.12 and 14.13.

Table 14.11 Regression of the size factor levels.

Regression Statistics					
R Square	0.132				
Standard Error	2.347				
Observations	27				

ANOVA	df	SS	MS	F	Significance F
Regression	2	20.1	10.0	1.8	0.18
Residual	24	132.2	5.5		
Total	26	152.3			

	Coefficients	Standard Error	t Stat	P-value	Lower 95%	Upper 95%
Intercept	5.33	0.78	6.8	4.74E-07	3.72	6.95
bigger than shirt pocket	1.11	1.11	1.0	0.33	-1.17	3.39
shirt pocket	-1.00	1.11	-0.9	0.38	-3.28	1.28

Table 14.12 Regression of the brand/operating system factor levels.

Regression Statistics	
R Square	0.132
Standard Error	2.347
Observations	27

ANOVA

	df	SS	MS	F	Significance F
Regression	2	20.1	10.0	1.82	0.18
Residual	24	132.2	5.5		
Total	26	152.3			

	Coefficients	Standard Error	t Stat	P-value	Lower 95%	Upper 95%
Intercept	4.33	0.78	5.54	0.00	2.72	5.95
Apple/ios	2.11	1.11	1.91	0.07	-0.17	4.39
Samsung/Android	1.00	1.11	0.90	0.38	-1.28	3.28

Table 14.13 Regression of the brand/operating system factor levels.

Regression Statistics	
R Square	0.381
Standard Error	1.981
Observations	27

ANOVA

	df	SS	MS	F	Significance F
Regression	2	58.07	29.04	7.40	0.003
Residual	24	94.22	3.93		
Total	26	152.30			

	Coefficients	Standard Error	t Stat	P-value	Lower 95%	Upper 95%
Intercept	3.44	0.66	5.22	2.4E-05	2.08	4.81
799	3.56	0.93	3.81	0.00	1.63	5.48
1000	2.22	0.93	2.38	0.03	0.29	4.15

The *MSBs* required to find corresponding factor *Fs* are highlighted. (Note that the *F* test of the model is not accurate, since the impact of the other factors is ignored.)

14.3 ANOVA in Excel

Excel offers ANOVA, but it is basic. It accommodates just two factors at a time. If an experiment includes more than two factors, results will produce misleading statistics. (Note that this is not a problem with other software packages that specialize in statistics for analyzing experimental data, such as JMP and SPSS.) It further requires an equal number of observations for each *treatment,* or combination of factor levels. It does not provide pairwise factor level comparisons.

14.4 ANOVA from JMP

As an alternative to ANOVA in Excel, JMP offers a *General Linear Model* with ANOVA which accommodates multiple factors and includes paired comparisons between factor levels JMP provides the model F, Fs for each factor, regression coefficients, and t tests of pairwise differences between factor levels. JMP recognizes category level labels, so there is no need to make indicator variables. JMP results are shown in Table 14.14 and 14.15. In Table 14.14, the factor F tests are shown under Effect Tests, and all three factors are significant. In Table 14.15, the pairwise comparisons of the factor levels are shown. Out of the three paired *size* comparisons, only *bigger than shirt* and *shirt size* are significantly different. In the pairwise comparisons of the three operating system levels, one out of three pairwise comparisons, *Apple/ios* with *LG/Android* is significant. In the comparisons of the three prices levels, both *$799* and *$1000* are significantly preferred to *$299.*

Results are consistent with regression results, above. 64.5% of the variation in preferences is explained. *Bigger than shirt pocket* is preferred to *shirt pocket, Apple ios* is preferred to *LG Android. $799* and *$1000* are preferred to *$299.*

If you have access to JMP, analysis of conjoint analysis data, and data from experiments more generally, is easier. In addition, JMP also accommodates continuous variables as covariates. If the unexplained variation is due to differences across the participants who provided ratings, demographics of the participants can be included. If, for example, Baby Boomers prefer *bigger than shirt pocket* size, but Millennials and XGen consumers prefer *ultrathin shirt pocket* size, *generation* could be added to the three factors, as well as interactions between the factors and *generation.*

Table 14.14 ANOVA of three factors driving cell phone preferences.

Summary of Fit

RSquare	0.644942
Root Mean Square Error	1.644294
Mean of Response	5.37037
Observations (or Sum Wgts)	27

Analysis of Variance/

Source	DF	Sum of Squares	Mean Square	F Ratio
Model	6	98.22222	16.3704	6.0548
Error	20	54.07407	2.7037	Prob > F
C. Total	26	152.29630		0.0010*

Parameter Estimates

Term	Estimate	Std Error	t Ratio	Prob>|t|
Intercept	5.3703704	0.316445	16.97	<.0001*
size[bigger than shirt pocket]	1.0740741	0.44752	2.40	0.0262*
size[shift pocket]	-1.037037	0.44752	-2.32	0.0312*
brand/os[Apple/ios]	1.0740741	0.44752	2.40	0.0262*
brand/os[LG/Android]	-1.037037	0.44752	-2.32	0.0312*
price[$299.00]	-1.925926	0.44752	-4.30	0.0003*
price[$799.00]	1.6296296	0.44752	3.64	0.0016*

Effect Tests

Source	Nparm	DF	Sum of Squares	F Ratio	Prob > F
size	2	2	20.074074	3.7123	0.0425*
brand/os	2	2	20.074074	3.7123	0.0425*
price	2	2	58.074074	10.7397	0.0007*

Table 14.15 Pairwise comparisons of facto levels

Student's t All Pairwise Comparisons
Quantile = 2.08596, DF = 20.0
All Pairwise Differences

size	-size	Difference	Std Error	t Ratio	Prob>|t|
bigger than shirt pocket	shift pocket	2.11111	0.7751278	2.72	0.0131*
bigger than shirt pocket	ultrathin shirt pocket	1.11111	0.7751278	1.43	0.1672
shift pocket	ultrathin shirt pocket	-1.00000	0.7751278	-1.29	0.2117

brand/os	-brand/os	Difference	Std Error	t Ratio	Prob>|t|
Apple/ios	LG/Android	2.11111	0.7751278	2.72	0.0131*
Apple/ios	Samsung/Android	1.11111	0.7751278	1.43	0.1672
LG/Android	Samsung/Android	-1.00000	0.7751278	-1.29	0.2117

price	-price	Difference	Std Error	t Ratio	Prob>|t|
$299.00	$799.00	-3.55556	0.7751278	-4.59	0.0002*
$299.00	$1,000.00	-2.22222	0.7751278	-2.87	0.0095*
$799.00	$1,000.00	1.33333	0.7751278	1.72	0.1008

14.5 ANOVA and Regression with Indicators Are Substitutes

The *F* statistics used to test hypotheses with analysis of variance and with regression are equivalent. Both compare average variation explained by model drivers or factors with average unexplained variation. Analysis of variance (or four regressions) enables us to determine whether each factor matters, and each factor's contribution to RSquare. ANOVA (or two regressions) also identifies particular levels which produce higher or lower expected performance relative to the baseline. Multiple regression with indicators and analysis of variance are substitutes, though ANOVA in a specialized statistical package is a one step process. With software such as JMP or SPSS, which use a *General Linear Model*, accepting both categorical and continuous variables, all of the desired statistics are available from a single model.

Excel 14.1 Use Indicators to Find Part Worths and Attribute Importances

Three consumers rated their preferences for nine hypothetical smartphones which differed in *size, brand/operating system* and *price,* using a nine point rating scale. The data are in **Excel 14 smartphone conjoint.**

In columns G and H, create two *size* indicators, in columns I and J, create two *brand operating system* indicators. And in columns K and L, create indicators for two *price* levels. For each of the three factors, the level not described by an indicator is the baseline. (Which level you choose for a factor baseline is arbitrary.)   Below, the baseline levels are *shirt pocket, LG/Android,* and *$299.* Coefficients for the indicators will indicate extent of difference from the baseline level.

	C	D	E	F	G	H	I	J	K	L
					bigger than shirt pocket	ultra thin shirt pocket	Apple/ios	Samsung/Andriud		
1	size	brand/os	price	rating					$799	$1,000
2	bigger than shirt pocket	Apple/ios	$299	7	1	0	1	0	0	0
3	bigger than shirt pocket	LG/Android	$799	6	1	0	0	0	1	0
4	bigger than shirt pocket	Samsung/Android	$1,000	4	1	0	0	1	0	1
5	shift pocket	Apple/ios	$1,000	7	0	0	1	0	0	1
6	shift pocket	LG/Android	$299	2	0	0	0	0	0	0
7	shift pocket	Samsung/Android	$799	5	0	0	0	1	1	0
8	ultra thin shirt pocket	Apple/ios	$799	9	0	1	1	0	1	0
9	ultra thin shirt pocket	LG/Android	$1,000	3	0	1	0	0	0	1
10	ultra thin shirt pocket	Samsung/Android	$299	4	0	1	0	1	0	0

Run a regression of *rating*, with the six indicators:

	A	B	C	D	E	F	G
1	SUMMARY OUTPUT						
2							
3	*Regression Statistics*						
4	Multiple F	0.803083					
5	R Square	0.644942					
6	Adjusted I	0.538424					
7	Standard E	1.644294					
8	Observati	27					
9							
10	ANOVA						
11		*df*	*SS*	*MS*	*F*	*gnificance F*	
12	Regressio	6	98.22222	16.37037	6.054795	0.000966	
13	Residual	20	54.07407	2.703704			
14	Total	26	152.2963				
15							
16		*Coefficient*	*andard Err*	*t Stat*	*P-value*	*Lower 95%*	*Upper 95%o*
17	Intercept	1.37037	0.837234	1.636784	0.117315	-0.37607	3.116809
18	bigger tha	2.111111	0.775128	2.723565	0.013085	0.494223	3.727999
19	ultra thin	1	0.775128	1.29011	0.21173	-0.61689	2.616888
20	Apple/ios	2.111111	0.775128	2.723565	0.013085	0.494223	3.727999
21	Samsung/	1	0.775128	1.29011	0.21173	-0.61689	2.616888
22	799	3.555556	0.775128	4.587057	0.000179	1.938667	5.172444
23	1000	2.222222	0.775128	2.866911	0.009532	0.605334	3.83911

Ultrathin does not influence *ratings* relative to *shirt pocket size*, though *bigger than shirt pocket* improves ratings, relative to the baseline. *Samsung/Android brand/operating system* generates ratings equivalent to *LG/Android,* the baseline *brand/operating system*, though *Apple/ios* improves ratings relative to the baseline. Both *$799* and *$1000* enhance ratings, relative to the baseline *$299.*

While this regression provides two pairwise tests for each of the three factors, not yet tested are *bigger than shirt pocket* versus *ultraslim shirt pocket, Apple/ios* versus *Samsung/Android,* and *$799* versus *$1000.* To see the additional pairwise comparisons, run a second regression, replacing each of the three baseline factor levels with another level.

Part worths. The *coefficients* are estimates of the part worths, the impact of each background feature on interest rating. Copy the data in columns A through G in the data sheet and paste below regression results. Then, add the intercept and part worths to find predicted ratings:

	size	brand/os	price	rating	bigger than shirt pocket	ultra thin shirt pocket	Apple/ios	Samsung/Andriud	$799	$1,000	intercept	bigger than shirt size pw	ultra thin shirt pocket pw	Apple/ios pw	Samsung/Android pw	$799 pw	$1000 pw	predicted rating
33	bigger tha	Apple/ios	$299	7	1	0	1	0	0	0	1.37037	2.111111	0	2.111111	0	0	0	5.592593
34	bigger tha	LG/Androi	$799	6	1	0	0	0	1	0	1.37037	2.111111	0	0	0	3.555556	0	7.037037
35	bigger tha	Samsung/	$1,000	4	1	0	0	1	0	1	1.37037	2.111111	0	0	1	0	2.222222	6.703704
36	shift pocke	Apple/ios	$1,000	7	0	0	1	0	0	1	1.37037	0	0	2.111111	0	0	2.222222	5.703704
37	shift pocke	LG/Androi	$299	2	0	0	0	0	0	0	1.37037	0	0	0	0	0	0	1.37037
38	shift pocke	Samsung/	$799	5	0	0	0	1	1	0	1.37037	0	0	0	1	3.555556	0	5.925926
39	ultra thin sl	Apple/ios	$799	9	0	1	1	0	1	0	1.37037	0	1	2.111111	0	3.555556	0	8.037037
40	ultra thin sl	LG/Androi	$1,000	3	0	1	0	0	0	1	1.37037	0	1	0	0	0	2.222222	4.592593
41	ultra thin sl	Samsung/	$299	4	0	1	0	1	0	0	1.37037	0	1	0	1	0	0	3.37037

To see the difference that each smartphone feature makes, plot the part worth utilities for each attribute.

Insert a row above the two *size* indicators in rows 18 and 19 for the *shirt pocket* baseline with part worth of zero, then select the six cells with *size* labels and part worths and request a line plot. In A18, In row 18, In B18, In A18,	**Alt HIR** Shirt pocket 0 **Shift+down down** **Shift+right** **Alt NN**

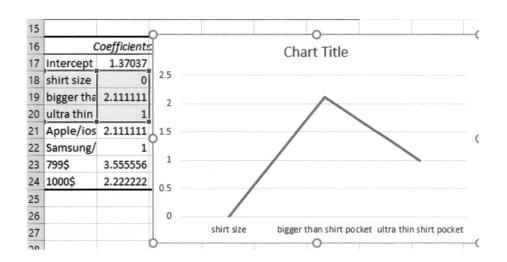

15		
16		Coefficients
17	Intercept	1.37037
18	shirt size	0
19	bigger tha	2.111111
20	ultra thin	1
21	Apple/ios	2.111111
22	Samsung/	1
23	799$	3.555556
24	1000$	2.222222
25		
26		
27		

Similarly, insert a new row 21 for *LG/Android* with baseline partworth of zero and plot the *brand/operating system* part worths. Insert a new row 24 for *$299* with baseline part worth of zero. Change the three price levels to text with **Alt H text,** and plot the *price* part worths. So that attributes can be compared, reformat the vertical axis range, from the most negative to the most positive part worth, 0 to 4, choosing a value for major unit, such as .5:

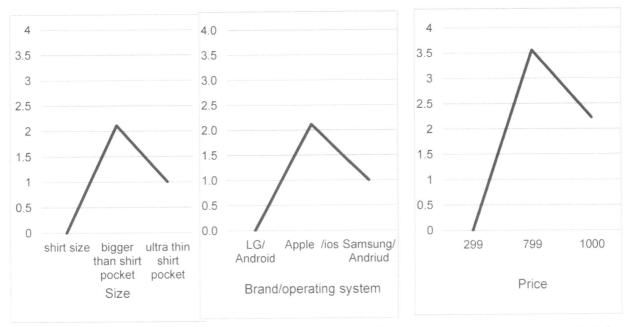

The range in part worths is a measure of importance. The range in *price* part worths, 3.6, is larger than the ranges of *size* and *brand* part worths, 2.1. *Price* is the most important smartphone attribute.

JMP 14.1 Run ANOVA and Pairwise Comparisons of Factor Levels

Fit Model in JMP is a General Linear Model. If potential drivers are categorical, output will be ANOVA with paired comparisons.

Copy and paste columns C, D, E and F into a new JMP data file. JMP reads the price levels as continuous. To see the *F* for *price,* change *price* to an ordinal variable.

Right click *price,* Column Info, Modelling Type, ordinal.

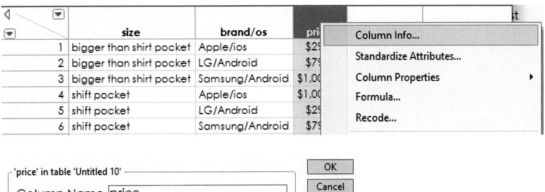

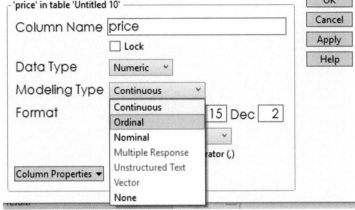

Access the General Linear Model   From the JMP Starter, Fit Model, Fit Model.
Drag *rating* to Pick Role Variables Y.
Drag the three factors, *size, brand/ios,* and *price* to Construct Model Effects.
Set Emphasis to Minimal Report.
Run.

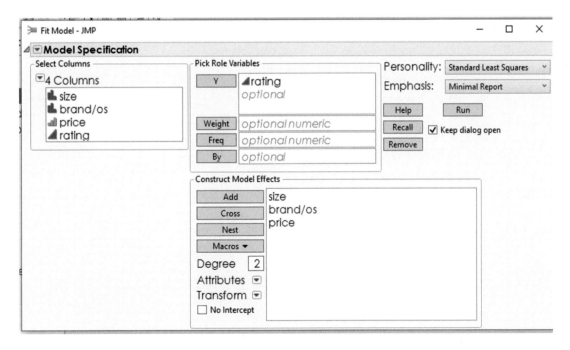

Summary of fit contains multiple regression results with indicators set up by JMP. (JMP will do this if drivers are recognized as ordinal or nominal and not continuous.)

Click on the triangle next to **Parameter Estimates** to see the coefficient estimates. **Effect Tests** presents the factor *F* tests and p values.

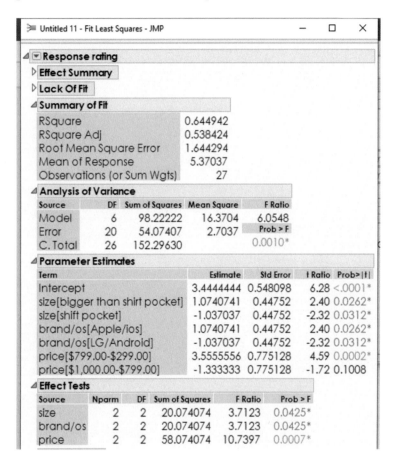

All three factors make a significant difference in ratings. The *Fs* are equivalent to those found from the ratios of *MSRs* from three single factor regressions to *MSE* from the three factor regression in Excel.

Click on the triangle next to **Effect Details** to see the factor level means.
For each factor, click on the red triangle next to the factor, such as *size*, and choose LSMeans Student's t to see pairwise comparisons with t tests and p values.

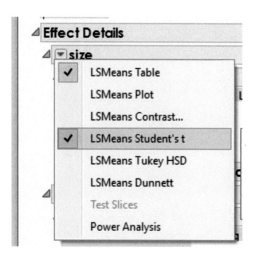

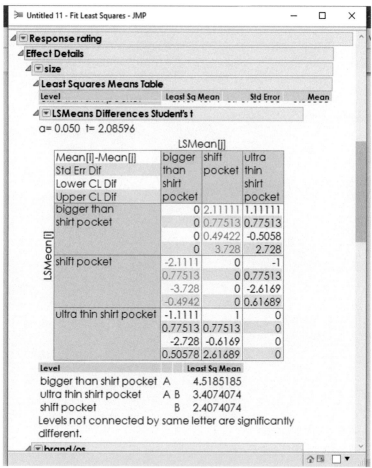

Significant differences are shown in red. *Bigger than shirt pocket* differs from *shirt pocket*. The other two pairs are not significantly different. Below the table, the part worths are sorted in descending order. Equivalent part worths share the same letter. *Bigger than shift pocket* and *ultrathin shirt pocket* share A and are equivalent. *Bigger than shirt pocket* is A and *shirt pocket* is B, so they are significantly different, and *Bigger than shirt pocket* is preferred. These results are the same as those provided by two regressions in Excel.

Lab 14-1 Smartphone Design Preferences

Help management identify preferred smartphone designs. Design options include *size* (bigger than shirt pocket, shirt pocket, and ultraslim shirt pocket), *brand/operating system* (Apple ios, LG Android, or Samsung Android), and *price* ($299, $799, $1000).

The conjoint analysis design is shown below:

Brand/os	bigger than shirt pocket	shirt pocket	ultra slim shirt pocket
Apple/ios	$ 299	$ 1,000	$ 799
LG/Android	$ 799	$ 299	$ 1,000
Samsung/Android	$ 1,000	$ 799	$ 299

Data from conjoint analysis from three consumers' ratings is in **Excel 14 smartphones conjoint.xlsx.**

Regression

Use regression with indicators to identify differences between factor levels and the baseline factor levels.

Assess pairwise differences between factor levels

1. What are hypotheses regarding smartphone features and preferences that can be tested with a three factor regression?

2. Which *size(s)* lead to higher preferences?

    ___ *bigger than shirt pocket*   ___ *ultra slim shirt pocket*   ___ *shirt pocket*

3. Which *brand/operating system(s)* lead to higher preferences?

    ___ *Apple/ios*   ___ *Samsung/Android*   ___ *LG/Android*

4. Which *price(s)* lead to higher preferences?

    ___ *$299*   ___ *$799*   ___ *$1000*

5. Which factor level pairs are not tested in this regression?

Predict ratings

6. What preference rating is expected from the most preferred design?

Find factor importances

7. Plot the part worth preference scores for *size, brand/operating system* and *price*, side by side.

8. How important are each of the three smartphone factors? (What are the part worth preference ranges?)

    Size: ___   Brand/operating system: ___   Price: ____

Run a second regression, changing the baselines.

Assess pairwise differences between factor levels

9. Which *size(s)* lead to higher preferences?

    ___ *bigger than shirt pocket*   ___ *ultra slim shirt pocket*   ___ *shirt pocket*

10. Which *brand/operating system(s)* lead to higher preferences?

    ___ *Apple/ios*   ___ *Samsung/Android*   ___ *LG/Android*

11. Which *price(s)* lead to higher preferences?

    ___ *$299*   ___ *$799*   ___ *$1000*

Run three single factor regressions.

Test hypotheses regarding factor effects on preference ratings

12. Find the *Fs* and p values for each factor with the ratio of *MSR* (=*MSB*) to *MSE* from the three factor regression:

	size	Brand/operating system	price
F			
p value			

13. Which null hypotheses can be rejected?

ANOVA with JMP

Test hypotheses regarding factor effects on preference ratings

Run ANOVA in JMP.

1. Which null hypotheses regarding factor effects on preference ratings can be rejected?

Assess pairwise differences between factor levels

2. Which *size(s)* lead to higher preferences?

    ___ *bigger than shirt pocket*   ___ *ultra slim shirt pocket*   ___ *shirt pocket*

3. Which *brand/operating system(s)* lead to higher preferences?

    ___ *Apple/ios*   ___ *Samsung/Android*   ___ *LG/Android*

4. Which *price(s)* lead to higher preferences?

    ___ *$299*   ___ *$799*   ___ *$1000*

Case 14-1 Background Music to Enhance Ad Message Recall

A brand manager suspects that the background music featured in a brand's advertising may affect consumers' recall of information presented in ads. Some music backgrounds are more distracting than others, and may compete with audience attention to the advertising message. Several background options are being considered, and those options differ along three categories, or *factors*.

Three *vocals* options are: backgrounds which feature vocals, backgrounds with brand related vocals substituted for original vocals, and backgrounds with vocals removed.

Three *orchestration* options are: saxophone, saxophone and percussion, and saxophone and piano.

Three *tempo* options are: slow tempo, moderate tempo, and fast tempo

It has been established that multiple timbres (from multiple instruments) distract more. It is also known that changes in the music background distract, and the rate of distraction is lower for slower tempos; yet, faster tempos allow *streaming*---music changes heard before become less surprising and distracting at faster tempos.

To determine whether vocals, orchestration and tempo of backgrounds affect brand message recall, the ad agency creative team designed nine backgrounds for a brand ad using conjoint analysis. Since the ad message, visuals, and length of ad could also influence message recall, the agency creatives were careful to make those ad features identical across the nine versions. By using ads that were identical, except for their musical backgrounds, any difference in resulting brand message recall could be attributed to the difference in backgrounds. The conjoint analysis design is shown below:

Orchestration	*None*	*Original*	*Brand specific*
Sax	Slow	Moderate	Fast
Sax & percussion	Moderate	Fast	Slow
Sax & piano	Fast	Slow	Moderate

Eighteen consumers were randomly selected and then randomly assigned to one of the nine background *treatments,* or combination of *vocals, orchestration* and *tempo.* Each viewed the brand advertisement with one of the nine backgrounds, and then message elements in the ad, which could be six, if all elements were recalled, or as low as zero, if no elements were recalled.

The data are in **music backgrounds.xlsx**.

Regression

Use regression with indicators to identify differences between factor levels and the baseline factor levels.

Assess pairwise differences between factor levels

1. What are hypotheses regarding background music features and message recall that can be tested with a three factor regression?

2. Which *vocal(s)* lead to higher recall?

   ___ *none*   ___ *original*   ___ *brand specific*

1. Which *orchestration(s)* lead to higher recall?

   ___ *sax*   ___ *sax and percussion*   ___ *sax and piano*

2. Which *tempo(s)* lead to higher recall?

   ___ *slow*   ___ *moderate*   ___ *fast*

3. Which factor level pairs are not tested in this regression?

Predict recall

4. What recall is expected from the most effective design?

Find factor importances

5. Plot the part worth preference scores for *vocals, orchestrations* and *tempos*, side by side.

6. How important are each of the three background music factors? (What are the part worth recall ranges?)

   vocals: ___   orchestrations: ___   tempos: ___

Run a second regression, changing the baselines.

Assess pairwise differences between factor levels

7. Which *vocal(s)* lead to higher recall?

   ___ *none*   ___ *original*   ___ *brand specific*

8. Which *orchestration(s)* lead to higher recall?

   ___ *sax*   ___ *sax and percussion*   ___ *sax and piano*

9. Which *tempo(s)* lead to higher recall?

   ___ *slow*   ___ *moderate*   ___ *fast*

Run three single factor regressions.

Test hypotheses regarding factor effects on recall

10. Find the *Fs* and p values for each factor with the ratio of *MSR* (in D12) to *MSE* (in D13) from the three factor regression:

	vocals	orchestrations	tempos
F			
p value			

11. Which null hypotheses can be rejected?

ANOVA with JMP

Test hypotheses regarding factor effects on message recall

1. Which null hypotheses regarding factor effects on recall can be rejected?

Assess pairwise differences between factor levels

2. Which *vocal(s)* lead to higher recall?

     ____ *none*   ____ *original*   ____ *brand specific*

3. Which *orchestration(s)* lead to higher recall?

     ____ *sax*   ____ *sax and percussion*   ____ *sax and piano*

4. Which *tempo(s)* lead to higher recall?

     ____ *slow*   ____ *moderate*   ____ *fast*

Case 14-2 Power PowerPoints

Corporate Relations management is considering alternate designs for the firm's PowerPoint presentation. Content will focus on performance in firm divisions and new ventures by the firm in several global markets. Ideally, audience members would remember twelve key points made in the presentation.

Graphics. Some managers believe that graphics illustrating performance and market potential are easier for audience members to digest and remember. Others argue that tables with precise numbers are more effective. A third group prefers to use photographs with visual images that support conclusions from the numbers stated directly in text.

Text. There is also difference of opinion regarding the amount of text to include in each slide. Some favor a single sentence. Others prefer to use bullet points to remind presenters what material should be covered. A third group prefers paragraphs with more detail.

Background. There were advocates of simple, dark backgrounds, thought to be easier to read. Others favored white simple, white backgrounds, similar to memos. A third group felt multicolor background designs, like those offered by Microsoft, added interest, engaging attention.

To identify the most effective design, Corporate Relations personnel created nine PowerPoint sets using an orthogonal conjoint analysis design:

Hypothetical	visuals	text	background
1	tables	bullets	gray
2	tables	sentence	multicolor
3	tables	paragraph	white
4	photos	bullets	multicolor
5	photos	sentence	white
6	photos	paragraph	gray
7	graphs	bullets	white
8	graphs	sentence	gray
9	graphs	paragraph	multicolor

A random sample of 18 shareholders not employed for the firm viewed one of the nine PowerPoint sets, then answered questions about the content. For each of the twelve key points mentioned, one point was added, making scores from zero to twelve possible.
14 Power PowerPoints.xlsx contains this data.

Regression

Use regression with indicators to identify differences between factor levels and the baseline factor levels.

Assess pairwise differences between factor levels
1. Which *visuals* levels lead to higher recall?
   ___ *tables* ___ *photos* ___ *graphs*
2. Which *text* levels lead to higher recall?
   ___ *sentence* ___ *bullets* ___ *paragraph*
3. Which *background* levels lead to higher recall?
   ___ *white* ___ *graph* ___ *multicolor*
4. Which factor level pairs are not tested in this regression?

Predict recall

5. What recall is expected from the most effective design?

Find factor importances

6. Plot the part worth recall scores for *visuals, text* and *background*, side by side.

7. How important are each of the three PowerPoint factors? (What are the part worth recall ranges?)

     visuals: ___   text: ___   background: ____

Run a second regression, changing the baselines.

Assess pairwise differences between factor levels

8. Which *visuals* levels lead to higher recall?

     ___ *tables* ___ *photos* ___ *graphs*

9. Which *text* levels lead to higher recall?

     ___ *sentence* ___ *bullets* ___ *paragraph*

10. Which *background* levels lead to higher recall?

     ___ *white* ___ *graph* ___ *multicolor*

Run three single factor regressions.

Test hypotheses regarding factor effects on recall

11. Find the *F*s and p values for each factor with the ratio of *MSR* (in D12) to *MSE* (in D13) from the three factor regression:

	vocals	*orchestrations*	*tempos*
F			
p value			

12. Which null hypotheses can be rejected?

ANOVA with JMP

Test hypotheses regarding factor effects on message recall

1. Which null hypotheses regarding factor effects on recall can be rejected?

Assess pairwise differences between factor levels

2. Which *visuals* levels lead to higher recall?

    ___ *tables*   ___ *photos*   ___ *graphs*

3. Which *text* levels lead to higher recall?

    ___ *sentence*   ___ *bullets*   ___ *paragraph*

4. Which *background* levels lead to higher recall?

    ___ *white*   ___ *graph*   ___ *multicolor*

Index

© Springer Nature Switzerland AG 2019
C. Fraser, *Business Statistics for Competitive Advantage with Excel 2019 and JMP*,
https://doi.org/10.1007/978-3-030-20374-0